AN ANATOMY OF LITERARY NONSENSE

COSTERUS NEW SERIES
VOL 67

Edited by

C.C. Barfoot, Hans Bertens and Theo D'haen

AMSTERDAM 1988

AN ANATOMY OF LITERARY NONSENSE

by

Wim Tigges

ISBN (CIP) 90-5183-019-X
ISSN 0165-9618
©Editions Rodopi B.V., Amsterdam 1988
Printed in The Netherlands

CONTENTS:

Contents		i
Introduction		1
Chapter 1	Towards a Definition	6
Chapter 2	Definition and Typology	47
	2.1 Genre, Mode and Device	47
	2.2 The Essence of Nonsense	51
	2.3 The Nonsense Repertoire	56
	2.3.1 Mirroring	56
	2.3.2 Imprecision	57
	2.3.3 Infinity	58
	2.3.4 Simultaneity	59
	2.3.4.1 The Pun	60
	2.3.4.2 The Portmanteau	65
	2.3.4.3 The Neologism	67
	2.3.5 Arbitrariness	69
	2.3.6 An Illustration	70
	2.3.7 Some Final Notes on the Use of Language	73
	2.4 The Themes and Motifs of Nonsense	77
	2.5 A Typology of Literary Nonsense	81
	2.6 Conclusion	86
Chapter 3	What Nonsense Is Not	90
	3.1 Nonsense and Humour	90
	3.2 The Nursery Rhyme	99
	3.3 The Curiosity	102
	3.4 Light Verse	104
	3.5 Fantasy	107
	3.6 The Grotesque	112
	3.7 Surrealism	116
	3.8 Dada	122
	3.9 Absurdity and Absurdism	125
	3.10 Metafiction	131
	3.11 Conclusion	134

Chapter 4	A Literary Appraisal		138
	4.1 Introduction. Early Samples and Nonsense as Device		138
	4.2 Lear and Carroll		140
		4.2.1 Edward Lear	140
		4.2.2 Lewis Carroll	150
	4.3 The Development of the Lear-type		165
		4.3.1 Survey	165
		4.3.2 Christian Morgenstern	173
		4.3.3 Edward Gorey	183
	4.4 The Development of the Carroll-type		196
		4.4.1 Survey	196
		4.4.2 Flann O'Brien	205
	4.5 Borderline Cases and Partial Nonsense		216
	4.6 Conclusion		226
Chapter 5	Some Remarks about the Historical, Cultural, and Psychological Backgrounds of Nonsense		229
	5.1 Social History		229
	5.2 Cultural History		234
	5.3 Psychology		242
Conclusions			255
Bibliography			261
	1 Primary Literature		261
	2 Secondary Literature		264
Index			277
	1 Index of Critics		277
	2 Index of Authors and Subjects		283

INTRODUCTION

> "What do you know about this business?"
> the King said to Alice.
> "Nothing," said Alice.
> "Nothing *whatever*?" persisted the King.
> "Nothing *whatever*," said Alice.
> "That's very important," the King said ...
> (Lewis Carroll, *Alice's Adventures in Wonderland*, chapter XII)

"In gewisser Weise befindet sich der Leser von Unsinn in einer Situation, die analog der eines Museumsbesuchers ist, der vor unbeschrifteten Schaukästen steht."[1] The aim of this study is to illuminate what is to be understood by the phenomenon of literary nonsense. In terms of Reichert's simile, it is to serve as a combined guide and catalogue to the museum of nonsense. The epithet "literary" has been appended here in the first place to make it clear that this book is not about nonsense in the colloquial senses of meaningless gibberish or messages of whose contents one is supposed to disapprove. Nor is it about the sociological concept of nonsense as the "Final Solution to the Problem of Meaning".[2] In the second place, the term "literary" is to indicate that nonsense can be and has been used for aesthetic purposes, and is by no means to be inherently equated with trivial writing or mere "kids' stuff".

The term "nonsense" will here be mainly used as a generic label. As such, it has never been properly defined, although some attempts have been made, as will be seen in the first chapter. That there is no clear theoretical consensus about a definition of nonsense is proven by the fact that all collections that are labelled Anthologies or Books of Nonsense verse and/or prose in fact contain items which are widely divergent in manner and time of composition, as well as in literary value. Sometimes such collections are advertised under a vague label like "comic and curious" (e.g. Cohen 1952 and 1956); at other times such books of nonsense are compiled on the

---

1. Reichert (1974: 21). References in the footnotes and main text of this thesis will be to author's surname, year of publication and page number(s) only. For full bibliographical data the reader is referred to the Bibliography at the back of this book.
2. See Hilbert (1977), who treats nonsense as a mental test category which people can use to "allow irreconcilable contradictions to count as evidence of a noncontradictory Reality" (25).

single ground of the "topsyturvydom" that is found to be prevalent in the items collected (e.g. Benayoun 1977).

One of the confusing aspects of the concept of "nonsense" is that, like that of "satire", it is used indiscriminately to indicate a stylistic device, a literary mode, or a genre. Thus, for instance, leaving a blank page in a book, as Sterne does in *Tristram Shandy*, is a nonsensical device, but it does not make the novel "a nonsense"—on the contrary, it continues to make good sense as a partly (self-)parodistic account of what happens if one applies Locke's theory of the association of ideas to one's own Life and Opinions. As characters, My Father, Uncle Toby, Corporal Trim, Dr Slop, the Widow Wadman and Tristram himself are as convincing as any characters in a realistic novel from any period of literary history. The narrative quandaries that the persona finds himself in are as clearly recognizable from "real life" as the ways in which dirty-mindedness or bigotry are shown to operate in this novel. But the relevant questions here are: why do we call leaving a blank page a nonsense device, and why for instance could the noses that feature so prominently in this book be called a nonsense motif? My answer would be that this is so because they can be shown to be important features in generic nonsense, and that it can be demonstrated to a large extent why this is so. It will prove, in fact, to be most convenient to take generic nonsense as a starting-point, and then to work one's way back to nonsense as a device and as a mode.[3] To limit my subject in this thesis I will primarily establish what I understand by generic nonsense.

In order to arrive at a viable genre definition of nonsense I will use a method which could, I think, be best described as "dialectic". It must be realized that nonsense is a relatively recent phenomenon in literature, originating in Britain in the Romantic and post-Romantic era. To some extent it is subject to the problems that Schnur-Wellpot has signalled in connection with avant-gardist art, namely that it is by its very nature elusive to a genre-theoretical approach, which implies an aesthetic of continuity and tradition.[4] At the same time, however, it is almost generally acknowledged that whatever nonsense is, specific works by Edward Lear and Lewis Carroll belong

---

3. I am here and in the following pages using the word "mode" in the sense in which it is applied by Fowler (1982). For a definition, see Ch. 2, pp. 49-50 below, and cf. Fowler, pp. 56, 106ff.

4. Schnur-Wellpot (1983: 229, 233).

to its canon. Working on the assumption that Lear's "Complete Nonsense" as well as Carroll's Alice books and *The Hunting of the Snark* are nonsense texts in their own right, it should be possible to discover what these works have in common, and thus to arrive at a set of characteristics of literary nonsense, which can then be traced in other works as well. By means of a more detailed analysis of such texts, it will then also be possible to discover other common aspects that may have been overlooked at first sight. Thus, a relatively clear picture of the features of literary nonsense can be obtained, without of course necessarily claiming the establishment of a traditional, institutionalized type of literature. The features that will be investigated can indeed very well be brought to the surface by a semiotic approach, as favoured by both Schnur-Wellpot and Hempfer (1973), and in some cases it will turn out that this is exactly what I have been doing. Basically, however, I will be on the look-out for a set of what Fowler has referred to as the "family resemblances" between a limited but not necessarily closed set of texts.[5]

This approach will save me the trouble of having to enter into a futile because regressive argument as to the way in which the term "genre" itself must or must not be defined. In fact, in what follows I will not take issue with the current commonsensical definitions of any critical terms used except that of "nonsense". My definition of the latter term will be chosen in such as way as to do justice to a kernel corpus of texts as well as to prevent overlapping with generally accepted labels that belong to related but essentially different types of literature. The definition itself will be arrived at by a constant interaction between texts and theory; it is this procedure which, following Hempfer (1973: 124-5) I refer to as "dialectic".

A new definition of generic literary nonsense, then, is not to preclude any texts as such *a priori* from the corpus. What it will lead to is in the first place a key to the literary-aesthetic interpretation of a number of texts which have so far been regarded as being generically related. Secondly, it will enable the literary critic who follows my tracks to distinguish such texts on theoretical grounds from other types of literature, which have often been confused with it. Thirdly, it will make possible a better understanding of the nature and workings of nonsense devices in texts which

---

5. See Fowler (1982: 41), and cf. e.g. Elliott (1962: 22, 23). This approach is ultimately derived from Ludwig Wittgenstein's theory of games (Fowler, *loc.cit.*).

are not generically nonsensical. Only when it has been made evident what elements belong to the "repertoire" of nonsense will it be possible to recognize these devices as nonsensical elements in other works of art.

To write about nonsense is like going to sea in a sieve. I have entitled this study "An Anatomy of Literary Nonsense". An anatomy is a dissection, and, as a recent critic puts it, "[e]very dissection ... is an analytic process that modifies the unity of the structure. In order to show a specific cohesion, often a number of other cohesions have to be demolished. Apart from the analytic process of dissecting, anatomy is primarily based on observation" (Elderhorst 1987: 98). In my anatomy of nonsense, I have chosen for a "dissecting" procedure that leaves as much as possible for the reader to be observed. I will survey concrete phenomena rather than offer an abstract anatomical lesson.

In the first chapter I give a critical survey of earlier scholarship on the subject, chronologically presented. Chapters 2, 3 and 5 are greatly extended versions of an earlier study (Tigges 1986a). These chapters attempt to provide satisfactory answers to the questions what literary nonsense is, how it works, what it is not, and when, where and why it originated and developed. Already in the second and third chapters, but especially in chapter 4, the theory is tested by the concrete phenomena. It is hoped that this fourth chapter in particular conveys the aesthetic quality of texts which have long been regarded as "mere" entertainment for children or childlike adults, lacking as they are in "moral seriousness", or as the utterances of frustrated and failed artists. The most important conclusions of my thesis are summarized in a final section.

A final word needs to be said here about the frequently assumed inanity of writing in all seriousness on such a supposedly non-serious subject as "nonsense", and, which is a more reasonable objection, of attempting to analyse and interpret texts which by their very nature are ultimately the embodiment of lack of meaning. My argument in this study is not that nonsense is or ought to be regarded as a very prominent type of literature, although I find it more interesting and more appealing than many other kinds. It is, however, a phenomenon that cannot and indeed has not been ignored. As such, it requires the honest attention of the literary critic. Its essence, as I will demonstrate in what follows, is that it maintains a perfect tension between meaning and absence of meaning. Such a balance cannot be successfully maintained if a text appears to be meaningless from the very start. In suggesting an initial meaning, the most successful nonsense texts set up a playful framework of themes and motifs which appeal to the reader's imagination, to his sense of language, as well as to his knowledge and appreciation of literary conventions of form and theme, plot and character. The success, and hence the intrinsic interest of nonsense depends on the creativity and intelligence with which these elements are presented. That it appeals to children does not automatically entitle us to relegate it to an inferior category of literature labelled "juvenile" or "trivial". Its assumed simplicity is often as deceptive as that of much modern abstract art. It is often easier to fill a space than to leave it empty.

Quotations in German and French have been left untranslated. Nonsense is often hard to translate without losing an essential element. Also, the quotations from secondary literature are mostly supported by statements in the main text. Abbreviations of titles are sparse, and in all cases they are indicated upon their first occurrence; because of the frequency of references to them, Carroll's *Alice's Adventures in Wonderland* and *Through the Looking-Glass* are abbreviated throughout as *AW* and *TLG* respectively.

Footnotes have been kept to a minimum; to this end, I have made use of the convenient referential system in general use among linguists. The bibliography has been divided into two parts: a list of primary sources and one containing all secondary literature. To promote representativity, I have only included those works from which actual quotations are given in the main text, or to which more extensive references are made. Primary sources as well as general reference books which I consider to belong to a common literary or scholarly heritage, and which are referred to only in passing, are therefore left out. On the other hand, for completeness' sake I include in the list of secondary literature some lesser items which are not explicitly referred to in the text, but which might be of interest to the reader who wishes to trace as much material which is relevant to the topic as possible. For the same reason, but only sparingly, I have included (and marked as such) works I have not been able to consult. Biographical works, which can be easily traced in relevant bibliographies, and which I have not made use of, are not included. For a purely nonsense-orientated bibliography, I refer the reader to my "Select Annotated Bibliography on Literary Nonsense" in *Explorations in the Field of Nonsense* (Tigges 1987: 245-55).

CHAPTER 1: TOWARDS A DEFINITION

"What is Sense? What is Nonsense?" It is exactly a century ago that Edmund Strachey opened his review of the works of the practically undisputed "Father" of literary nonsense, Edward Lear, with these questions (1888: 335). A hundred years after the death of Edward Lear and the appearance of Strachey's article many answers have been attempted. In this chapter I intend to present a survey of those definitions of nonsense that contribute to a better understanding of nonsense as a literary phenomenon. In order to avoid infinite regression I will not investigate into the question "What is Sense?", nor will I open a fruitless discussion on the nature of literature. May the dictionary meanings of those terms be sufficient unto both the writer and the reader of this study. The dictionary meaning of literature, according to the sixth edition of the *Concise Oxford Dictionary* is "writings whose value lies in beauty of form or emotional effect". To me, the nonsense works of Edward Lear, Lewis Carroll, and other authors to be discussed in these pages are valuable both for their beauty of form and their emotional effect. This evaluation of nonsense has not always been the norm, and it is one of the aims of this work to elucidate the term so as to contribute to a better insight.

Nonsense used within a literary context is often stated to be a typically Victorian phenomenon. Why this should be so is a matter I will touch upon in chapter 5. It is indeed true that the word "nonsense" in a favourable sense is only encountered for the first time in the Victorian era. According to the *Oxford English Dictionary*, the word is first recorded in writing by Ben Jonson in 1614, in the meaning of "spoken or written words which make no sense or convey absurd ideas". All the sample quotations given under the lemma, as under that of the derived adjective, show an unfavourable or depreciative attitude. Thus, "nonsense verses" are glossed as "verses consisting of words and phrases arranged solely with reference to the metre and without regard to the sense". This is apparently how Samuel Taylor Coleridge applied that phrase in 1830. This unfavourable attitude is also prominent in the definitions of the great eighteenth-century lexicographer and stylist, Dr Samuel Johnson, whose 1755 Dictionary gives: "unmeaning or ungrammatical language" and "trifles; things of no importance".[1]

---

1. For a somewhat more extensive etymology and history of the word "nonsense", see Hildebrandt (1962: 11-17).

This attitude made a turnabout in the course of the nineteenth century. In his *Formen und Funktionen der englischen Nonsense-Dichtung im 19. Jahrhundert*, Dieter Petzold records the reception of nonsense books during that era (1972: 144-75). Obviously, the authors that were most usually discussed in nineteenth-century reviews and critical articles were Lear and Carroll, and the term nonsense came to be associated with an endearing, imaginative type of children's literature.[2] As Petzold makes clear, in as far as these writings were appreciated by adults, they were mostly regarded as offering a way of escape, a way back into childhood (1972: 154-6)[3] or an escape from everyday reality (157-9). Some critics discerned a deeper meaning in them, mainly of an allegorical, a satirical or a parodistic nature (160-4).

I take Petzold's word for it that a precise definition of the concept of nonsense was not attempted in this period (173). Strachey's classical article in *The Quarterly Review* of 1888 is a case in point. He begins by stating that "Nonsense ... is the proper contrary of Sense". It "sets itself to discover and bring forward the incongruities of all things within and without us" (1888: 335). It is the "ripe outcome" of Wit or Humour (336, 339). The author proceeds to divide his subject into several heads: there is nonsense of story (fairy tales), moral, theological, dramatic, poetical, satirical, parodistic, caricaturist nonsense, that of the comic journal, tendentious nonsense, and finally the "pure" nonsense of Edward Lear (339). It is obvious that this definition of nonsense as a Fine Art, however charming, is much too wide to be workable, and that in fact what Strachey does in the bulk of his article is to give a short history of humorous writing from Chaucer to his own time. Although he states that Lear introduced "a new and important kind" of nonsense, it is not made clear exactly in what way this "pure" nonsense differs from that allegedly discerned in Chaucer's *The Nun's Priest's Tale*, Shakespeare's *Twelfth Night* ("the most perfect piece of Nonsense which Shakspeare has given us", 348) or Sterne's "Nonsense-romance" *Tristram Shandy*. Yet, Strachey does provide what is quite likely to

---

2. But see e.g. *The Athenaeum* (Dec. 16, 1865) as quoted by Petzold (1972: 146) for adverse criticism of *Alice's Adventures in Wonderland* as a children's book. Petzold gives some more examples on pp. 149-52.

3. On the (neo-)Romantic function of escape, see Chesterton (1901: 447).

be the first description of literary nonsense, and one which it is of interest to quote here, since it has become a persistent strain in many later definitions. Strachey says that Nonsense (he consistently spells it with a capital) is a delightful and humorous way of "bringing confusion into order by setting things upside down, bringing them into all sorts of unnatural, impossible, and absurd, but not painful or dangerous, combinations" (335). Topsyturvydom and the lack of emotion are two aspects that keep recurring in later definitions of nonsense,[4] as well as the more unfortunate associations with humour, the grotesque ("unnatural") and the absurd.[5]

One of the first staunch defenders of nonsense was G.K. Chesterton. In a short article that first appeared in 1901, Chesterton remarks that nonsense evokes a sense of the childhood of the world (1901: 446); "some of the greatest writers the world has seen—Aristophanes, Rabelais and Sterne—have written nonsense" (446-7). Like Strachey, Chesterton regards nonsense in its broadest meaning as a timeless phenomenon, but he distinguishes between this satirical or symbolic nonsense, and the "new literature" introduced by Lear and Carroll. It is this new nonsense which is more than "a mere aesthetic fancy", since it has its own version of the Cosmos to offer, namely that the world is not only tragic, romantic, religious, but also nonsensical (449), inasmuch as Creation is itself nonsensical rather than logical. Thus, Chesterton's contribution is to add, in his own words, a "rich moral soil" to this form of art, which, one supposes, justifies its practice, but fails to explain how nonsense "works".

A Nonsense Anthology, edited by Carolyn Wells, and first published in 1902, is the first post-Victorian collection of nonsense poetry. Such collections are of interest because a definition of this type of literature so brought together (at this stage I will not yet talk in terms of mode or genre) can be derived from the items in them. This particular collection contains only verse, well represented by W.S. Gilbert, Lewis Carroll, Gelett Burgess, Edward Lear, Oliver

---

4. Cf. Cammaerts (1925: 15), Jennings (1977: Introduction), Benayoun (1977: 13), Stewart (1978: 63ff.), Sewell (1980-1: 37), Demurova (1982: 81) for the notion of nonsense as topsyturvydom, and esp. Sewell (1952: 138ff.) for nonsense as incompatible with a sense of emotion.

5. See chapter 3 below.

Herford, Oliver Goldsmith, C.S. Calverley, Hilaire Belloc, Peter Newell and Col. D. Steamer, as well as much that is anonymous. Many of these poems belong to the type of poetry generally referred to as "light verse",[6] some of it is parodistic (e.g. of Imagist poetry), much of it is humorous. An interesting omission is that of the nursery-rhyme, which is often discussed in association with nonsense, especially Lear's and Carroll's nonsense verse.[7] In her introduction, Wells justifies this by stating that nursery-rhymes are not strictly nonsense, because they were invented and used for counting out (and one may add, for orther purposes as well, such as mnemonic devices, sending children to sleep or letting them make particular movements etc.).[8] Otherwise, the choice of items for this collection can be accounted for by the editor's characterisation of nonsense as "words conveying absurd or ridiculous ideas", a definition which "expresses the great mass of nonsense literature", with a minor category of written nonsense that comes under the heading of "language without meaning" (e.g. Carroll's "Jabberwocky", xxi). Like Strachey, Wells considers nonsense a "division" of humour (xxxi).

The most interesting kind of nonsense, then, is that which presents "ideas conveying no sense", which is not the same as an absence of sense (xxv). A quite different approach is to be found in the first, short, monograph on nonsense, Cammaerts' *The Poetry of Nonsense* (1925). Cammaerts regards literary nonsense as an "old and widespread" phenomenon, which was perfected by Lear and Carroll (1925: 2). Lear's Nonsense Songs are traced back to the nursery-rhyme (3). The true characteristics of nonsense are found in an atmosphere which is "fanciful and irresponsible", "grotesque and incongruous" (*ibid.*). In as far as Cammaerts adduces a definition of literary nonsense this happens *ex negativo*: "It is far easier to say what is *not* nonsense than to say what is" (8). He correctly proceeds to distinguish nonsense from epigram and parody, and concludes by

---

6. See chapter 3.4 below.

7. Cf. in this respect Rhys (1927), and Cammaerts (1925). See also chapter 3.2 below.

8. Wells (1902: xxi-xxii); perhaps it is better to say that many old poems "lost" the sense they may originally have conveyed and came to be relegated to the nursery for these purposes or simply because of their "musical" effects. For a history of the nursery-rhyme, see e.g. Opie & Opie (1951 [1973]).

stating that nonsense poems and stories[9] are "meaningless" and irrational (15). Cammaerts' remark that what makes Lear's limericks nonsensical is that there is no particular "point" to them (7) is essentially correct but incomplete. As will be shown in chapter 2, the essence of nonsense is that there is no "release", but it is rather facile to equate this with a lack of significance, as Cammaerts does. Another defect of his thesis is that he relates this absence of meaning to the nursery world to which nonsense is said to belong (see his chapter II: "Nonsense and the Child"), and that he sees "Dreamland" as the realm of nonsense (32).

The third chapter, "Nonsense and Poetry", is the most perceptive. Here Cammaerts is the first to illustrate how in nonsense poetry thought becomes the servant of rhyme, instead of the other way round (40ff.).[10] However, this measure for an evaluation of nonsense ("The more liberties he [the nonsense poet] takes, the better his nonsense", 44) is too vague to be really helpful, and the conclusion of the chapter ("If nonsense poetry is poetry run wild, it is a wildness which preserves and even emphasises its essential qualities. It is not necessarily the highest type of poetry, but it is the most poetical", 57) shows Cammaerts' enamouredness of the "musical" school of poetry associated with Verlaine and Mallarmé, rather than a perception of what nonsense entails.[11] In his chapter on "Nonsense and Art", the author completely misses the point of the necessary tension between text and illustration.[12] His thesis that nonsense is particularly English (Chapter V: "Nonsense and England") will be disproved in a later chapter.

The merit of Cammaerts' book is not so much that it takes nonsense seriously (Strachey had done as much before him) as that it is the first to describe some of the peculiar techniques and effects of "pure" nonsense, especially with regard to its more irrational aspects.

---

9. Cammaerts is the first critic to make it explicitly clear that nonsense may occur in prose as well as in verse, without sticking to Strachey's very broad definition (1925: 39).

10. Cf. Sonstroem (1967).

11. Cf. Huxley (1923) and Eliot (1942).

12. For a perceptive discussion of the relationship between nonsense texts and their illustrations, see van Leeuwen (1986; rpt. in Tigges 1987: 61-95).

Between the appearance of Cammaerts' monograph and the standard work by Elizabeth Sewell, *The Field of Nonsense* (1952), little of interest as regards an understanding of literary nonsense was added. These years saw the production of some important biographies of the two grandmasters of nonsense,[13] but hardly any analytical statements (except of a Freudian nature) are encountered here. Thus, for instance, Davidson (1938) closely follows Cammaerts in speaking of Lear's poems as "pure and absolute nonsense" (195) whose "native realm is poetry" (198), emphasizing their musical quality and calling them "the 'reductio ad absurdum' of Romanticism" (200). "Lear's writing is intended to be absurd, whereas that of the Surrealists is not", he states (*ibid.*), thus correctly making a distinction which was not made in much French criticism of the period.[14]

Leimert (1937) starts a German tradition of nonsense scholarship which regards nonsense as a (typically English and particularly Victorian) form of "echter Humor" (369). Her references to the dream-atmosphere which Lear's poems share with the works of Carroll (372), and in particular her use of qualifications like "märchenhaft", absurd and grotesque (373) give rise to that unfortunate confusion of terms that it is one of the main aims of this present study to dispel. A similar confusion is presented by de la Mare, who characterizes nonsense as an "indefinable 'cross' between humour, phantasy and a sweet unreasonableness" (1932: 8), and who does not really answer his own question how nonsense differs "from the merry, the comical, the frivolous, the absurd, the grotesque and mere balderdash" (14-15). He is, however, one of the first writers to be implicitly aware of an elementary tension, when he states that there is (in Lear's limericks) "a sort of vacuum ... where the 'sense' should be" and simultaneously "an abundance of meaning" (16). Nonsense "lies in some celestially happy medium between what is sense and what is not *sense (ibid.)*.[15]

---

13. De la Mare (1932), Ayres (1936) and Lennon (1945) on Carroll, and Davidson (1938) on Lear.

14. Cf. e.g. Parisot (1952: 89-90), who recognizes "pure nonsense" in works by Arp, Schwitters, Savinio, Picabia and Tzara. For a refutation of this view, see Thody (1958), and also chapter 3.7 below.

15. I have been unable to consult Kent (1934), Mégroz (1938) and Graham (1945).

Huxley, in his 1923 article on Edward Lear, mainly celebrated the "spiritual freedom" this poet's work asserts (1928 edn: 167). He defines Lear's nonsense as "the poetical imagination a little twisted out of its course" (*ibid.*). What one wishes to know, of course, is exactly what this "little" consists of. Huxley's distinction between the nonsense of Lear and that of Carroll is of interest, because it points in a direction of the existence of at least two *types* of nonsense. "Lewis Carroll wrote nonsense by exaggerating sense—a too logical logic", writes Huxley, whereas "Lear, more characteristically a poet, wrote nonsense that is an excess of imagination ... His is the purer nonsense, because more poetical" (168).[16] T.S. Eliot (1942 [1953]) enjoyed Lear's "music" for similar reasons. He calls Lear's nonsense "not a vacuity of sense" but a parody of it, and "that is the sense of it" (56). Similar views are still found in Kusenberg (1947). Nonsense has no system. Surrendering to its playful, unpredictable nature is recreation (956). In the realm of nonsense a cheerful anarchy prevails, without a hierarchy. Nonsense is open—it is no more than it appears to be, in contrast with surrealism. It is, finally, a pungent ingredient of humour. "Unsinn treiben, heißt die Bausteine des Denkens spielerisch durcheinander würfeln" (957). Remarkably, Lear is missing from his "canon", which includes Hughes, Morgenstern, Carroll, Ringelnatz, Toepffer, Busch and Oberländer.

In *Here, There and Everywhere. Essays Upon Language* (1950), Partridge devotes an article to "The Nonsense Words of Edward Lear and Lewis Carroll". Although his definition of nonsense is obviously too wide (the limericks by Cosmo Monkhouse quoted on pp. 164-5 are light verse, not nonsense, since they contain a "point" in the punch-line),[17] Partridge is the first to give a detailed analysis of nonsense techniques, such as its preference for neologisms, portmanteau words and puns. He thereby illustrates that nonsense is primarily lexical, a fact that was to be made more explicit by Sewell.[18]

Sewell (1952) basically defines nonsense as a game, which in its turn is defined as *"the active manipulation, serving no useful pur-*

---

16. See esp. Hildebrandt (1962: 74-5), and cf. chapter 2.5 below.

17. See e.g. Cammaerts (1925: 9-10) for a good illustration of the distinction between nonsensical wordplay and witty wordplay. See also Hildebrandt (1962: 50-63) for the relationship between nonsense and joking, and cf. chapter 3.1 below.

18. Cf. also Deleuze (1969: 112).

pose, of a certain object or class of objects, concrete or mental, within a limited field of space and time and according to fixed rules, with the aim of producing a given result despite the opposition of chance and/or opponents" (1952: 27). With Sewell, we move from the concept of nonsense as irrational playfulness to that of nonsense as a rational game with rules of its own. "We can begin ... by describing nonsense as a collection of words or events which in their arrangement do not fit into some recognized system in a particular mind" (3). One must regard "Nonsense as a structure held together by valid mental relations' (4), "a construction subject to its own laws" (5), that is applicable to the works of Lear and Carroll (the two authors Sewell mainly discusses here), different as they are. She later particularizes that nonsense may be "an attempt at reorganizing language, not according to the rules of prose or poetry in the first place but according to those of Play" (25). Nonsense is "not a universe of things but of words and ways of using them, plus a certain amount of pictorial illustration" (17). Since "play consists in establishing mastery over something", nonsense is to be seen as an attempt at mastering language, since language and numbers are the chief sources of mental playthings (28-9).

Sewell opposes the view that nonsense creates disorder out of order as is the case with dreams. She points out that syntax and grammar are not disordered, but only reference is (37-8). Nonsense is in fact created by "the mind's force towards order", and so order is "the principle of organization in Nonsense" (44-5). Nonsense is a game between order and disorder, a *tension* between the two. Unfortunately, at this stage the author introduces a false distinction between nonsense and poetry, adding a further weakness in that she seems to be in two minds about the aesthetics of nonsense, first stating that "Nonsense verse is too precise to be akin to poetry" (23), and later modifying this by remarking that "Nonsense adds to poetry's precision an element of incongruity" (102). There is a clear contradiction here as regards the precision of poetry.

Although Sewell realizes that in order to be considered art, the universe of nonsense must be more than the sum of its parts (cf. p. 53, where she denies that with nonsense "proper" this is the case), she fails in her attempt to bridge the gap between game and dream at the end of her book, where we are meant to reach "the world of religion, magic, alchemy, astrology, poetry and the strange riddles, oracular or monstrous, proposed to human beings as a matter of life and death" (187), a country where "words and play together fringe out into liturgy and magic" (184). Apart from the tone of mysticism in the previous quotations, Sewell's persistent distinction between poetry and play (e.g. 193) to an unnecessary extent confuses the issue of what nonsense is, because we can not be quite sure what is meant by poetry either. I am willing to go along with statements to the effect that the use of simile, metaphor, imagery and figurative speech is different in poetry (112), or that "[i]mages in Nonsense are not allowed to develop, to turn into or mingle with other images as happens in dreams and poetry" (127), if the word "poetry" in these phrases is modified by "other". For it is meaningless to conclude that Lear "never quite reaches poetry" (164), or to be surprised at the "genuine pathos" in the "Dong" and the "Yonghy-Bonghy-Bò" (146).

These criticisms do not alter the fact that Sewell offers many valuable insights into the nature of literary nonsense of the type which earlier critics alluded to as "pure" nonsense, and she contributes a first decisive step on the way to a demarcation of nonsense as a mode in Fowler's sense of the word.[19] Sewell is also the first to discuss its rational nature, and to be struck by the very essential effect of the tension which it upholds.[20] She also discovered and explained many of the techniques and themes of nonsense, such as its preference for seriality (ch. 5), the prominence of number words, thing words, abstracts and gibberish (59, and chs 7ff.),[21] and the resulting interest in clothes, food, furniture, houses and other "normal experience" words (101), the avoidance of beauty (107), and the connections with the dance (189ff.), which is said to be "half a game" (192). Many of the points made by Sewell will be picked up again in the following chapters.

In the 1950s appeared the work of Annemarie Schöne, starting with her 1951 dissertation, which has remained unpublished. The views expressed there ("Ihrer inneren, wie auch ihrer äußeren Struktur nach gehört die Nonsense-Dichtung in die Bereiche des *slechthin Komischen*", 91) had not materially changed by 1954.[22] In the artic-

19. Fowler (1982). See my Introduction, and chapter 2.1 below.
20. See my discussion of Ede (1975), on pp. 29-30 below.
21. Not all the examples quoted by Sewell are "pure" literary nonsense, however.
22. See Hildebrandt (1962) and Petzold (1972) for references to and quotations from Schöne's dissertation, which is really a history, thematic survey and formal treatment of the limerick. Like Leimert (1937) before her, Schöne stresses mainly the comic elements in

les she published in that year she characterizes nonsense as a genre ("Gattung") of comic literature in England, with two main features, playfulness and lack of direction ("Tendenzlosigkeit"; 1954a: 102, cf. 1954b: 132). Its humour is absolute rather than substantial, and is rooted in the world of children. Schöne provides a brief and perceptive history of the origins of nonsense as a literary genre, which will be reverted to in chapter 5.2 below. She explains how Carroll creates humour by means of a manifold shifting of perspective, which follows the law of dreams. Some of the characteristics and techniques succinctly enumerated are useful and will be referred to later, others are equally applicable to fairy tales or fantasy.

The first and only (brief) discussion of nonsense in the Dutch language, that by Morpurgo (1960), reverts to the timelessness of nonsense, which is traced especially with regard to the development of Italian literature. Morpurgo's enumeration of nonsense themes (culinary expressions, geographical names, names of animals etc., [10])[23] adds little to what was already noted by Sewell, although the occurrence of these themes in the fifteenth-century "burchiellesci"[24] as well as in later "nonsense poetry" is interesting. Morpurgo obviously uses too wide a definition: Aldo Palazzeschi's poem quoted in a Dutch translation on pp. [12]-[14] is decidedly dadaist, and Erasmus' *Praise of Folly* is hardly a "masterpiece of nonsense literature" ([1]).

Spacks (1961, rpt. in Phillips 1971 [1974], to which page numbers refer) offers an important step forward in the perception of the role of language in nonsense literature. In her opinion, Carroll shows in *Through the Looking-Glass and What Alice Found There* (henceforth abbreviated as *TLG*) that whereas language has a rigorous logic, the *traditions* of language, i.e. the way we use it, are sloppy.[25] In

nonsense writing (63ff.). Her discussion of the stylistic elements of nonsense verse (sound-play, linguistic play, humorous exaggeration, surprise, topsyturvydom, hidden meaning and imagery are given extensive treatment, 92ff.) entirely overlooks the fact that these features, even "in ihrer Gesamtwirkung" (138) are also characteristic of other types of (comic) literature.

23. The text of this (inaugural) speech consists of 16 unnumbered pages, which I have numbered from [1] to [16].
24. Liede (1963) discusses Burchiello on pp. 432-5 of Vol. I of his monumental work to be discussed below.
25. Cf. Themerson (1987).

Looking-Glass land, on the contrary, language is never used loosely (317-8). Carroll makes his point by the use of four devices: punning; personal discipline imposed on language (by Humpty-Dumpty and the White Knight); emphasis on the importance of names; and the convention that existent sets of words can determine the pattern of events, which Nöth (1980: 35) calls word-magic (323-4). This makes the Looking-Glass world as near to the realm of absolutes as the world of dreams.

Another inaugural lecture, Forster's *Poetry of Significant Nonsense* (1962), is the first to pay extended attention to the German poet Christian Morgenstern within the scope of nonsense literature.[26] Forster defines nonsense as no "sheer absence of logical sense, but the creation of a structure which is satisfying in itself" (cf. Sewell 1952), "without reference to verisimilitude, logical sense or even intelligible words, though it may embody elements of all of them" (6). Forster takes a Chestertonian view, as appears from his discussion of what underlies Morgenstern's nonsense verse: firstly "the fundamental harmony of divinely ordered existence, which can even comprehend the absurd", and secondly "absurdity of existence, pointing to God as the only solution" (25). He sees Morgenstern as a precursor of dada and surrealism (26, 30, 38), and much nonsense he calls "poésie pure" (32); the lecture is little more than an amalgam of the main theses of Chesterton (1901) and Cammaerts (1925), and the mystical findings as voiced in the final chapter of Sewell (1952); its main asset is that it introduces modern nonsense writers as essentially avant-gardists, rather than as the epitomes of a long tradition.

It will have become clear that many of the definitions of nonsense given so far are hard to make mutually compatible, although a certain development can be traced, including an accumulation of nonsense techniques. One of the problems is that the different authors occasionally seem to be dealing with different *types* of nonsense altogether. It is the merit of Hildebrandt (1962) to have presented a viable classification of nonsense. He distinguishes three types: 1st folk or popular nonsense ("Volks-Nonsense"), an early form of which is manifest in particular in the nursery-rhyme; 2nd ornamental nonsense, which includes wordplay and similar devices; and 3rd literary nonsense, where nonsense prevails in form as well

---

26. I have not seen Stählin's "Morgenstern's Spiel mit der Sprache" (1950).

as content, as in the "classic" nonsense works of Carroll and Lear (74-5).

In the course of his perceptive dissertation, Hildebrandt builds up a useful definition of nonsense as an "aesthetic category". Nonsense is a-logical (26), complementary to "common sense" rather than to "sense" (37).[27] As such, it can be clearly distinguished from satire and parody (45), and especially from the joke (50ff.), from which nonsense basically differs in that it is pointless.[28] Following Cammaerts' line rather than Sewell's, Hildebrandt regards nonsense as being closer to the dream than jokes are (56).[29] He also discerns a relationship with the fairy tale ("der Nonsense hat sich ... die Märchen-technik weitgehend anverwandelt", 70). Nonsense is essentially a *formal* phenomenon:

> Rein formal gesehen entspricht der Nonsense als untendenziöse Darstellungsweise den Bedingungen ästhetischer Betrachtung weitgehender als diejenigen Komikarten, die Mittel zum Zweck sind, doch ist er darüber hinaus ein Spiel mit Formen und Inhalten, ein Träger außerästhetischer Werte. Und erst dieser Zwittercharakter—formal Komik-Kategorie, inhaltlich Humor-Kategorie—macht sein Wesen aus (68).

> Im literarischen Nonsense entspricht die absurde Grund-konzeption den stilistischen Eigenheiten, und aus beiden spricht derselbe Geist; im ornamentalen Nonsense äußert sich dieser Geist in der Inkongruenz, die sich aus dem komischen Widerspruch zwischen unsinnigen Extravaganzen und ihnen nicht gemäßen Kontexten ergibt; ... (184).

> In Übereinstimmung mit den Auffassungen von E. Sewell und A. Schöne kann trotz bisweilen hochgradiger Bewußtheit der

---

27. Cf. Stewart (1978).
28. The examples of nonsense quoted on p. 53 are not equally "nonsensical", however.
29. The whole dream-joke-nonsense triangle has been treated from a psychological point of view by Freud (1960 [1976], orig. 1905: e.g. chapters II(2) and VI). The non-analyst in particular no doubt tends to regard dreams as "pointless", hence nonsensical, rather than "witty". The analyst, however, discerns a deeper meaning in e.g. the puns and neologisms (which are prominent nonsense devices) that occur in dreams.

Gestaltung der Nonsense als emotionsarmes intellektuelles Spiel mit Formen und Inhalten charakterisiert werden, bei dem das Hauptaugenmerk fast durchgängig auf die von der Sprache gebotenen Möglichkeiten zu zweckfreier geistiger Betätigung gerichtet ist (242).

Nonsense ist eine ihrem Wesen nach alogische und sinnlich indifferente Erscheinungsform der literarischen Komik, in der die Besonderheiten des englischen Charakterhumors in tendenz-freiem schöpferischem Spiel zum Ausdruck kommen, und die mit Hilfe distanzierender Verfremdung und sprachkomischer Effekte ästhetisches Vergnügen ohne emotionales Engagement zu erzielen sucht (244).

Hildebrandt's starting-point is that there is no such thing as a "genre" ("Gattung") of literary nonsense (6, 215, 241), a point of view which it will be one of the aims of my thesis to refute. His discussion of the "classics", Lear and Carroll (119-58), is therefore somewhat disappointing—no close analyses are presented, only descriptions of the various poems and stories. The conclusion that two types of nonsense were founded by Lear and Carroll respectively (158) is not followed up. The description of "ornamental nonsense" in fantasies and comic stories and verses for children (166-215) is perceptive in terms of its largely correct sense of the gradation of the quality and quantity of nonsense present, although I do not agree with all the judgments expressed in these sections. Thus, for instance, I do not find any ornamental nonsense in Tolkien's *The Hobbit*.

In German scholarship on the subject, a useful distinction is made between "Unsinn" (in Hildebrandt's terms: folk and ornamental nonsense) and "Nonsense" (literary or "pure" nonsense). Alfred Liede's monumental *Dichtung als Spiel* (1963) is a history of "Unsinnspoesie" in the widest sense. In his introduction, Liede refers to Blumenfeld (1933), who distinguishes five types of nonsense: semantic, telic, eidic, logical and motivational. Eidic nonsense is of importance in visual art; in literature only semantic and logical nonsense are manifest. In semantic nonsense, there is no relationship between sign and object. In logical nonsense an utterance has no foundation (e.g. "This round table is square"). But Liede emphasizes that "der größte semantische oder logische Unsinn ... offenbar einen Sinn hat, ... der außerhalb der Semantik oder der Logik liegt" (I, 7).

Liede's self-confessed concern with the smallest units of words and sentences only, and not with thematic nonsense, has the disadvantage that the type of nonsense discussed in my thesis, generic or "pure" nonsense, receives only limited attention. A discussion of the works of Lear and Carroll is given under the heading of "Höherer Blödsinn und Nonsense", where they are thrown on a heap with a low level of nonsense in the form of the "poetry" found in students' almanacs. This form of nonsense is regarded as a "liberating" form of poetry as play; the other categories Liede introduces are the *childlike* (subdivided into demonic, cosmic and divine, represented respectively by the works of Mörike, Scheerbart and Chesterton), and the *resigned* (which includes the works of Morgenstern).

Liede's work is an impressive history of playful literature (Volume I) supplemented by a broad survey of all the possible playful devices and (sub)genres (Volume II). "Die englische Nonsensedichtung" Liede calls "der Versuch einer Flucht aus der Bildungsgläubigkeit in den unschuldig reinen spielerischen Unsinn des Kindes" (I, 165), in other words, a type of regression. Morgenstern, on the other hand, links up his nonsense[30] with a playful virtuosity of form, which hides the unsatisfied desire for a higher form of poetry behind the mask of nonsense verse: "Aus einem schwachen Dichter wird ein starker Unsinnspoet" (I, 305). This view of nonsense "en défaut de mieux" pervades the whole book, which practically concludes with the statement that *"Unsinnspoesie ist immer eine Dichtung aus Unvermögen"* (I, 430), a view which I find it impossible to accept. Liede's work is valuable, however, as a historical survey and description of what Hildebrandt would term "ornamental" nonsense. No analyses are provided, and the definition of "Unsinn" is obviously much too wide for my purpose.[31]

A more fairly presented parallel to Liede's view of nonsense as an inferior type of poetry is found in an article by Sonstroem, in which verbal play in Gerald Manley Hopkins' poems is compared to that by Carroll, Gilbert and particularly Lear. Sonstroem points out that nonsense is not senseless, but that it presents double-sense or double-talk: "Nonsense, like *all* poetry, has something to do with both kinds of arranging, of making sense; but, unlike conventional

---

30. Like Hildebrandt (1962: 230), Liede is careful to point out that Morgenstern denied that his Galgenlieder were nonsense (1963, I: 284).

31. For a perceptive criticism of Liede, see Taraba (1968). Taraba objects to Liede's method of "explaining" inexplicable nonsense (236-7), but approves of the section dealing with Carroll.

verse, its first allegiance is to rhyme rather than reason" (1967: 198; italics mine). Moreover: "The strength of nonsense poetry is its tidy self-consistency and its independence from referents" (*ibid.*). Sonstroem's article is important, because it is the first to perceptively analyse some of Lear's verse, and because it provides a meaningful distinction between nonsense poetry and "conventional" poetry:[32] nonsense:conventional verse::mathematics:physics (198-9). As will appear later (ch. 2), I do not think that sound always lords it over meaning in nonsense; I prefer the notion that in the best nonsense it only appears to do so.

Gray's perceptive article "The Uses of Victorian Laughter" (1966) is of importance because of the distinction it makes between nonsense and humour. The characteristic quality of nonsense is said to be its "rigorous control" (168).

> Consonance, integrity, its pretense to be complete and conventionally coherent: that is what makes nonsense. Like other entertainments which furnish release from the imperatives of ordinary experience, nonsense amuses by failing to achieve the coherence expected of sounds and sentences and literary forms like those it uses. But the writers of nonsense also amuse by being careful to make their poems and tales so coherent in their own terms that they seem to be making sense, so entire and satisfying in their logic and motion that their order seems to be free-standing, and completely independent of the conventional orders of language and literature against which they are in fact playing (171-2).

Victorian nonsense and humour begin on the same ground (168), but whereas much humorous wordplay frustrates expected significance *throughout*, nonsense creates an illusion of autonomy with a pretence to seriousness that is lacking in parody, burlesque or mere wordplay, so that "nonsense is different from other varieties of the Victorian laughter of release in its carefully fashioned coherence and its stubbornness in keeping in view some profoundly disturbing actualities" (175). Implicitly, Gray comes very close indeed to the notion of a balance between meaning and non-meaning.

As verbal nonsense is one of the traditions that are displayed by the theatre of the Absurd, Esslin (1961 [1968]) devotes part of his

---

32. I will revert to this in more detail in chapter 2.3.4.1.

chapter on "The Tradition of the Absurd" to this phenomenon. He speaks of a "lustful release from the shackles of logic" (330), but emphasizes that "[t]he literature of verbal nonsense expresses more than mere playfulness" (331). "Verbal nonsense is in the truest sense a metaphysical endeavour, a striving to enlarge and to transcend the limits of the material universe and its logic" (331-2), a view which seems to be contrary to that of Chesterton. Like Liede, Esslin stresses the liberating effect of nonsense, but with a rider:

> Most nonsense verse and prose achieve their liberating effect by expanding the limits of sense and opening up vistas of freedom from logic and cramping convention. There is, however, another kind of nonsense, which relies on a contraction rather than an expansion of the scope of language. This procedure ... rests on the satirical and destructive use of the cliché—the fossilized débris of dead language (338).

In as far as this use of language is satirical it is not, of course, purely nonsensical, but at most a form of "ornamental" nonsense.

In her biography of Edward Lear, Vivien Noakes adheres to Sewell's definition of nonsense (1968: 330, note 7); her own tentative suggestion is that "perhaps it could be said that incongruity of characters, situations, or words, plus a predictable, stable element such as numbers, choruses, alliteration or, paradoxically, an insistence on the correct use of words, equals nonsense" (223). She agrees with Sewell that "Nonsense is a universe of words" and that "[o]ne of the characteristics of pure nonsense is detachment" (224), and also that humour is not a necessary ingredient (225).

The most notable contribution on the part of Deleuze is that he considers Carroll's novel *Sylvie and Bruno* a masterpiece, and a successful continuation of techniques first introduced in the Alice books (1969: 58). I know of hardly any Carroll scholar who holds a similar view.[33] More valid, because an essential addition to Sewell's main thesis, is his view that a "pure game" is a game *without rules*: each turn multiplies the chances by ramification (cf. Huxley 1976).

---

33. For adverse comments on the *Sylvie and Bruno* books, see e.g. Alexander (1951: 565), Sewell (1952: 149), Petzold (1972: 67), Ede (1975: 148), Henkle (1976: 72), Sutherland (1978: 18, 171), Kreutzer (1984: 58-9). Favourable views are given by Gattégno (1976) and Miller (1976).

Such a game can only be mental, and then only as "non-sens", and the result of such thought-play is a work of art (75-6). In reading a work like *Alice's Adventures in Wonderland* (henceforth abbreviated as *AW*), one indeed has the impression that the rules of the game are continually and randomly modified rather than consistently adhered to.

Deleuze's pretentious and highly metaphysical, not to say esoteric work does little to contribute to a better understanding of the working of "non-sens".[34] In the eleventh "series", "du non-sens", he defines nonsense as "[l]e nom qui dit son propre sens", the normal thing being that the "sens" of a noun must be expressed (defined) by another noun, and so *ad infinitum* (84). In a portmanteau word, which in another place he calls "disjunctive", each element defines the other.[35] The absurd, on the other hand, is that which *lacks* sense or which presents merely a vicious circle (86).[36] "[L]e non-sens ne possède aucun sens particulier, mais s'oppose à l'absence de sens ... en opérant la donation de sens" (89). Nonsense belongs to the surface, in contrast with "sous-sens", which is a deeper meaning (111). This will prove a useful criterion to distinguish nonsense from surrealism.[37]

Holquist (1969/70) bases his article on the works of Sewell and Liede (149). Nonsense is "a closed field of language in which the meaning of any single unit is dependent on its relationship to the system of the other constituents" (150), "a system in which, at its purest, words mean only one thing, and they get that meaning through divergence from the system of the nonsense itself, as well as through divergence from an existing language system" (151). Meaning in nonsense, then, is dependent on the field it constructs; the difference between nonsense and gibberish is that nonsense is a system that can be learned, which also explains why it is highly abstract. "[T]he absurd is basically play with order and disorder. Nonsense is play with order only" (152). It contrasts one system of order with another.

34. His main aim seems to be to present a "theory of sense" based on a series of paradoxes inspired by Stoic philosophy.
35. Cf. Reichert (1974: 184), who calls the portmanteau word the quintessence of nonsense.
36. See chapter 2.3.4.2 below ("The Portmanteau"); also chapter 3.9.
37. See chapter 3.7 below.

In Holquist's approach there is too little space for the more "poetical" or "musical" type of nonsense as created by Lear, but then the aim of Holquist's article is to explain the origins of modernist literature, just as Parisot wished to explain the tradition of surrealism and Esslin that of the absurd. The more "hermetic" a text is, the more nonsensical, and hence the more "Modernist", according to Holquist. In a discussion of Carroll's *The Hunting of the Snark*, which he finds more nonsensical than the Alice books (150), Holquist enumerates six instances of "systematic arbitrariness" (156ff.). The most interesting of these is the "rule of three", semantically introduced by the Bellman in Fit One of the poem,[38] and exemplified by the rhyme, which is a "rule of three" in that two words which are different in meaning result in a new meaning when bound by rhyme. "Like the syllogism, two disparate but related elements originate a third" (162). This, however, is said to be *un*true of nonsense verse, where there is no meaning to begin with (163). Unfortunately, Holquist seems to be begging the question here, and we will have to revert to the function of rhyme in nonsense verse in a later chapter.[39]

Both Flescher (1969/70) and Sutherland (1970) investigate the way language works in nonsense, in particular in the works of Carroll. According to Flescher, "Nonsense bears the stamp of paradox" (128). "An adequate definition must embrace both language and reference, order and disorder" (*ibid*.), combining the approaches of Sewell and Cammaerts. At the core of nonsense is the total coincidence of word and reference, "the power of meaning is reduced to a minimum" (137). Thus, in nonsense conversations, no argument is ever developed: "The principle is one of deflection" and "Puns are one way of deflecting meaning" (138, 139).

Nonsense, then, is more than a formal structure, a pattern of rhyme, metre, alliteration etc., that provides a framework obliterating the actual meaning; rather, meaning itself is constantly shown to be arbitrary: "Each new statement is met with a contradiction" (139). "Reality remains implicit behind every manifestation of nonsense, but it is never explicitly represented. The nonsense world is a world of fantasy which shies clear of reality, yet indicates its existence" (141).

38. See Carroll/Gardner (1962 [1967]: 46).
39. See e.g. chapter 2, pp. 59-60; chapter 4, pp. 162-3.

According to Flescher, it is the *incongruity* between the terms of the paradoxes that are constantly found to exist between language and meaning, order and disorder, formal patterns and imagination of language (142), which define the relationship, rather than any *tension* (143). This is were I beg to disagree. The incongruity may be there in the detail, and it may certainly explain the humorous effect of much nonsense, as Flescher points out (143); however, the complete context must present a tension between meaning and non-meaning which is not resolved, or otherwise the nonsense can be at most "ornamental" (see chapter 2).

Sutherland detailedly illustrates the point that Flescher generally makes. His kernel thesis is that "[i]llustrations of non-understanding and misunderstanding occur throughout Carroll's literary works" (1970: 227), and he primarily deals with Carroll's linguistic insights and notions. The most striking aspects of Carroll's play are "his use of linguistic symbols as mere counters to be conjured with" and "his exploitation of linguistic phenomena (...) to create situational humor" (21). Sutherland is not concerned with manipulatory linguistic play, but with "functional play", play that arises from the communication function of language.

"Carroll saw that humor could be derived from treating ordinary discourse as though it were amenable to the rules of logical discourse" (69). He explicitly stated that most words are ambiguous, that words mean more than we mean to express when we use them, that no word has a meaning inseparably attached to it, and that word-meanings are totally arbitrary (98). Sutherland proceeds to illustrate these various aspects of Carroll's linguistic nonsense, thereby greatly illuminating its workings. Obviously, however, few literary-aesthetic insights are to be gained from a book primarily concerned with Carroll's linguistic theories.

Laffay, in a unique, unfortunately rather elementary, little monograph on literary nonsense and humour in French, defines nonsense as a "forme littéraire de l'absurde" (1970: 10). Like Sewell, he wishes to distinguish it from poetry proper (87). Nonsense describes a non-existent universe in which objects have been replaced by signs representing them (119). Laffay repeatedly emphasizes the verbal nature of nonsense (94, 123, 141). Like the dream, it takes words and metaphors literally, but it does so consciously and intentionally (130). Apart from dreams, the phenomenon is also related to and distinguished from fantasy and the marvellous (120ff.), and humour (140ff.); "... le *nonsense*, c'est l'humour lorsqu'on le dirige vers l'utilisation déréglée, ou du moins l'emploi autonome, du langage"

(153). Contrary to Sewell, Laffay finds the play-element in nonsense to be related to the *disorder* of certain games rather than to their *order*.

Both Phillips (1971 [1974]) and Parisot ([1971]) reprint articles by Elizabeth Sewell, in which a development of her views since *The Field of Nonsense* can be traced. In "Lewis Carroll and T.S. Eliot as Nonsense Poets" (orig. 1958) she still adheres to the thesis already voiced in 1952 that "Nonsense is by nature logical and antipoetic", and that it is a game with strict rules (Phillips 1971 [1974]: 155-6). In Eliot's *The Waste Land*, "[t]he Nonsense rules procure the necessary working conditions—detachment of mind from subject matter, analysis of material, manipulation of patterns of unfused images" (159).

In "Lewis Carroll, poète du Nonsense" (in Parisot [1971], transl. J. Gattégno, orig. 1970) nonsense and poetry are no longer stated to be distinct matters, but "le Nonsense est et n'est pas poésie" (225), a view which she states had already transpired in the final chapter of *The Field of Nonsense*. The paradox voiced here is by no means Sewell's latest position. In Guiliano (1976) appeared her article called "The Nonsense System in Lewis Carroll's Work and in Today's World", in which a rather pessimistic view is put forward. Carroll's nonsense is a system, and, Sewell argues, many modern institutions (in particular religion, education and politics) have adopted similar systems. She now states poetry to be an alternative to nonsense (66).

Apart from the article by Spacks already referred to, which is reprinted in Phillips, neither Phillips' nor Parisot's collection of essays contains any material that offers new views on the nature of literary nonsense.

Haight (1971) doubts the possibility of defining nonsense at all, but like Laffay he sees absurdity as its keynote (247). In various directions nonsense shades off "into pure fantasy, pure farce, the grotesque, the Surrealist, and so on" (255). Nonsense can only be literary within a meaningful context (247ff.), and it seems that Haight considers nonsense as a form of parody of words, grammar and style in general (rather than of specific texts). "Its characteristic effect is parody of a playful, fantastic kind, carried out at several linguistic levels" (255). My objection is that if this statement is true, this parody must be the "point" of the exercise, which, as will be shown, goes against the grain of nonsense.

In his comprehensive study of 1972 Petzold's ultimate definition of nonsense is "conservative":

> Nonsense ist eine besondere Erscheinungsform der spielerischen, unkritischen literarischen Komik. Seine komische Wirkung basiert vorwiegend auf einem Lustgewinn, der durch eine radikale Durchbrechung von Denkgewohnheiten zustande kommt, was sich äußerlich in einer charakteristischen Spielhaltung gegenüber sprachlichen Konventionen, Logik und/oder empirischer Realität manifestiert. Nonsense-Dichtung erweist sich somit als eine komische Form der Unsinnsdichtung. Sie hat ihre klassische Ausprägung in den Werken Edward Lears und Lewis Carrolls erhalten (241).

Although he defines nonsense as a "Sondergebiet des literarischen Humors" (2), he later modifies his view by admitting "[daß] es ... keineswegs ... als gesichert gelten kann, daß Nonsense tatsächlich als Komikkategorie zu betrachten ist" (21). "Nonsense-Dichtung" as "*komische* (bzw. humorvolle) Unsinnsdichtung" is however retained as an *ad hoc* definition for convenience's sake (24).[40]

Petzold's method is to consider in particular the reception of nonsense in the Victorian period, beginning with an analysis of the works of Lear and Carroll. By considering these from the comical point of view, he is able to demonstrate that the humour is not only evoked by linguistic play or logical incongruity, but also by such elements as surprise (31), a sense of superiority (48f.) and irony (50ff.). "Eine Stimmung wird mit großem Geschick aufgebaut und gleichzeitig vernichtet dadurch, daß der Gegenstand durch den enthaltenen Nonsense komisch erscheint" (55). The *intellectual* appeal of nonsense lies in its play with logic (59-61), and in its use of philosophical problems (61ff.).[41] He comments adversely on Sewell's thesis, also followed by Schöne and Hildebrandt, that "emotional" nonsense is a failure, by pointing out that many passages appeal to the reader's emotion (65ff., and cf. 187ff.).

In the second chapter, which presents a survey of Victorian nonsense outside the works of Lear and Carroll, Petzold states that purely formal categories are not sufficiently essential. Nor is it

---

40. Petzold perceptively states: "Eine Aussage, die ... sowohl komisch als auch unsinnig sein will, muß sich in einem Schwebezustand zwischen dem Sinnvollen und dem Unsinnigen befinden" (22).
41. Petzold mentions the problems of identity, time, the conventions of language, death and (non-)being.

enough to establish "absurd and incongruous actions on the part of the principal characters" (94, quoting Langford Reed). He agrees with Hildebrandt that nonsense is not a logical category,[42] and points out that playfulness and lack of seriousness are characteristics of other genres as well. His pragmatic conclusion about the possibility of defining nonsense is: "[Es wird] in der Regel möglich sein, einen Text dann als Nonsense zu betrachten, wenn er mehrere dieser Elemente in auffallendem Maße enthält" (95), and thus arrives at his definition quoted above.

Henkle (1973) defines nonsense as play "often deliberately restrained by an arbitrary order of rules invented by the player" (103). He gives a succinct psychological explanation of the phenomenon: "Ambivalence and indirect attack, *angst* and muted self-assertion are beautifully accommodated in nonsense. The virtue of nonsense is its obliqueness" (115).[43] He ends up by calling nonsense a "rigidly controlled anarchy, in a straightjacket of conventional verse forms and rhyme schemes" (116).

One of the consequences of a psychological reading of nonsense literature has been that nonsense became historically limited to a particular period in time. As an accepted way of criticizing one's social surroundings and of voicing one's personal anguish it has been linked up in particular with the Victorian age. Petzold, indeed, already gave warning of the ahistoricity of a general study of nonsense (1972: 225), but he was able to trace the nonsense-tradition into the twentieth century, for children as well as for adults (227ff.). Reichert (1974) is much more categorical: in his opinion, English nonsense literature was a transitional phenomenon (7), that began with the appearance of Lear's first *Book of Nonsense* in 1846, and ended with the death of Carroll in 1898 (103). After that "kann es keine Unsinnliteratur mehr geben, weil es sie nicht mehr zu geben *braucht*: alles, was gerade für sie typisch ist, wird nun legitim in der Literatur selber, die Entwicklung hat sie gleichsam eingeholt" (*ibid.*).

42. Cf. Deleuze (1969) for a different view.

43. For other psychological approaches to nonsense, see e.g. Empson (1935), Nock (1941), Lennon (1945 [1962]), Andersen (1950), White (1966), Reichert (1974), Hark (1978), Prickett (1979), Sewell (1987). I have not seen Miller (1973), reviewed in Ede (1975: 11). See also chapter 5.3 below.

Victorian nonsense is more than a mere game. It is not the nonsense that is a denial of "sense", but that which enables the construction of "non-nonsense": "das Nicht-Unsinnige als Sinn des Unsinns" (9). "Der Unsinn entwirft eine *neue* Ordnung, vor deren Gesetzen die praktizierten der alten nur noch ein Stück Vergangenheit sind, ohne doch durch befreiendere, nicht-restriktive ersetzt worden zu sein" (10).

Reichert correctly states that there is a resemblance between nonsense and humour rather than an identity (11). The method of nonsense is a repeated alternation between the presentation of a norm and its breaking (12). The equation of nonsense with children's literature is seen as a misconception (17). The characteristics of nonsense according to Reichert are isolation, disintegration, detachedness, disconnection—characteristics which it is said to share with such various phenomena as the charade and the tableau vivant, the museum and the dictionary, the exhibition, the newspaper and the city (20). Thus, *AW* is an arrangement of isolated episodes; its continuity is fictional. The same goes for *TLG* (66-9).[44] What is characteristic of nonsense is not its comic nature, but that the author refuses to play along with his cultural surroundings (104).[45] Reichert then arrives at the following definition:

> Mit Unsinn zu bezeichnen, auch um ihn abzugrenzen etwa vom Quatsch, schlage ich all jenes vor, das in sich und aus sich selbst nich verstanden werden kann, potentiell aber gegen eine Übersetzung in seine Signifikate, etwa durch Analyse, nicht versperrt ist. Dort, wo die Vermittlung beider Ebenen absichtlich vorenthalten wird, wo die Bezugslosigkeit hergestellt und einem in sich konsistenten Regelsystem unterworfen wird, gleichwohl aber noch, auf Grund des historisch bedingten mangelnden Konsenses als pathologisch verzerrte Rede mißverstanden werden *kann*, schlage ich vor, den Namen Unsinnliteratur zu gebrauchen (104-5).

Nonsense poetry exists when there is *no longer* any *sense*, and *not yet* any *meaning* (113). Humpty Dumpty's "commentary" on the

---

44. Cf. p. 109, where it is stated that series of which the elements are interchangeable are a characteristic of nonsense.

45. Cf. Liede (1963: I, 165) quoted on p. 19 above.

opening stanza of "Jabberwocky"[46] is to indicate that its sense is *not* in the interpretation (129). Negation, reduplication, opposition (mirroring) derive from Carroll's desire to deny, to take back the statement made (*ibid.*). This seems to be the central point of Reichert's book, and this may well be found to be applicable to the nonsense writer in general.

Tabbert (1975), who otherwise follows Hildebrandt's approach, emphasizes that nonsense is not a genre but a quality, which is characterized by five stylistic characteristics already adduced by Petzold: 1st meaningless accumulation of words and concepts (additive incongruence); 2nd lack of causality in thought and action; 3rd conscious expression of trivialities; 4th conscious misapplication of words; and 5th creation of new words without definable sense (8-9; cf. Petzold 1972: 24-50).[47]

A very important contribution to an understanding of what literary nonsense entails is the unpublished dissertation of Lisa Ede.[48] She begins by saying that "literary nonsense ... might be defined casually as verse or prose which is presented by the author so as to emphasize illogicality or even irrationality" (1975: 3). Building upon the notion already found in Sewell (1952) and elsewhere that nonsense is "a world of words come to life, a world whose insistently self-defined reality is almost completely linguistic" (6), and following a brief survey of critical approaches, whose only shortcoming is that it entirely neglects the bulk of German scholarship on the subject, she argues that "nonsense is, if not a genre, then a sub-genre or type of literature with definite thematic and structural characteristics" (12). She then goes on to define nonsense as

> a self-reflexive verbal construction which functions through the manipulation of a series of internal and external tensions. The basic dichotomies involve illusion and reality and order and disorder, with such further contrasting pairs as fantasy

---

46. Carroll in Gardner's edn (1960 [1965]: 270-2).
47. Petzold's classification is somewhat less orderly, hence Tabbert's concise enumeration is presented here instead.
48. The introduction to this thesis as well as a rewritten version of the chapter on Lear have been reprinted in Tigges (1987: 47-60 and 103-16). References to and quotations from Ede's dissertation are to the original typescript.

> and logic, imagination and reason, the child and the adult, the individual and society, words and their linguistic relations (...), denotation and connotation, and form and content.... The power and fascination of nonsense arise from the successful maintenance of these tensions, and from the wide range of emotions, ideas, and attitudes it is thus free to explore (12-13).

She proceeds to give a perceptive analysis of the works of Lear and Carroll in the light of this definition, including a comparison between the two authors to which I will revert in a later chapter (2.5). An important addition to preceding scholarship is that "even in the simplest forms of nonsense, some degree of plot and structure are necessary if any sustained interest, much less meaning, is to be achieved" (52). She also shows how such a device as punning plays a role in a larger framework of meaning (105). As will appear in the next chapter, my own definition of nonsense will be largely based on Ede's.

In 1976 appeared the volume of essays on Lewis Carroll edited by Edward Guiliano, which has been alluded to already on p. 25. Besides Sewell's article referred to there, this collection contains an interesting paper by Donald Rackin,[49] in which he argues that the comedy in *AW* rests on polarities (15). The tensions created by the polarities of sense *versus* nonsense, consciousness *versus* unconsciousness, waking *versus* dreaming etc. are finally resolved with a dynamically comic solution (*ibid.*). It is interesting that Rackin detects roughly the same tensions that are also adduced by Ede, but that he appears to diametrically oppose her view that the essence of nonsense is precisely that these tensions are *not* resolved. For illustrations of those tensions in nonsense and their failure to be resolved I refer the reader to chapters 2 and 4 of this thesis. Gattégno, in the same collection, comes closer to Ede's view when he states that "[t]he opposition one constantly finds in Carroll's work is ... between two kinds of sense, paradoxically linked ..." (77). Miller, finally, reverts to the Sewellian view that "Nonsense may be said to have a higher order of logical consistency than ordinary reality" and "than the complexities of our everyday language com-

---

49. I have not been able to consult Rackin's 1964 dissertation on *AW*, nor the critical handbook on *AW* that appeared under his editorship in 1969.

monly allow" (134), and that "nonsense is a variety of logic" (140). The other articles have no direct bearing on an assessment of the nature of nonsense.

One of the most curious accounts of (Carrollian) nonsense is undoubtedly Francis Huxley's *The Raven and the Writing Desk* (1976). This book is in fact a demonstration of its own definition of nonsense, which is that "Nonsense ... is a logical game played with feeling by at least two people, in a spirit of self-contradiction, in such a way that one thing leads on to the other to the constant surprise and mutual enthusiasm of both parties" (10). Its basic principle is that of convertibility (*ibid.*). Fancifully associating, Huxley deals with basic nonsense themes and devices: language, reversal, permutation, coupling, space and infinity, time, food, identity and nothingness, doubling, negating, parallelling and circularity.

The first extensive analysis of the works of Edward Lear is given by Thomas Byrom in his *Nonsense and Wonder* (1977). There he expresses the view already found in Reichert (1974: 7, 103) that Lear was the first nonsense poet, and he also maintains that Lear and Carroll became "spiritual fathers" of absurdism, surrealism and related streams (2). It is this view that necessitates my distinction between nonsense and later "schools" presented in chapter 3. After a preliminary and somewhat gratuitous statement that nonsense "resists closed interpretations" (46; which work of art does not?), Byrom proceeds to analyse Lear's limericks and longer poems and stories in a perceptive way, to which I will revert in chapter 4.2.1. Byrom too seems to detect the tensions and their irresolution in Lear's nonsense, as when he calls "The Owl and the Pussycat" nonsense "because of the strange distance, the empty space, between what is said and what is meant" (158).

The late seventies saw the appearance of three large anthologies of nonsense in three different languages: Jennings' *Book of Nonsense* (1977), Benayoun's *Le Nonsense* (1977), and Dencker's *Deutsche Unsinnspoesie* (1978). In their introductions, both Jennings and Benayoun assume the simple position that "Nonsense ... involves seeing reality from the other side" (Jennings), and that it is "[l]'art de demeurer volontairement sur la tête" (Benayoun: 13). That they regard nonsense as a timeless device appears from the scope of their collections, which respectively start with Aristophanes and the thirteenth-century French "fatrasies". The same goes for Dencker, whose anthology starts with Hans Sachs. Benayoun adduces as procedures of nonsense: simulated incompetence, logical errors, and exhaustive treatment or superfluity (20-5).

Dencker, who emphasizes the play element of nonsense (6), stresses its relationship with "poeiesis" in general, referring to Huizinga's views on "poeiesis" as a play-function.[50] He takes issue with Liede in stating that nonsense does not operate at the borders of language, but that it is an essential reservoir of language and ideas, serving the aims of innovation and criticism (15). For his definition he agrees with Baacke, whose paper "Spiele jenseits der Grenze. Zur Phänomenologie und Theorie des Nonsense" is appended by way of Afterword.[51] Baacke's definition runs:

> Nonsense, als eine besondere Spielart der Phantasie, ist nicht sachunangemessenes Reden aus Leichtfertigkeit, pueriler Albernheit oder mangelnder Information, sondern schafft einen Spielraum an der Grenze möglicher Vorstellungen und ihrer sprachlichen, künstlerischen oder realen Darstellung, der nicht nur von üblichen Vorstellungs- und Verhaltenszwängen entlastet, sondern eine distanzierende Heiterkeit und eine neue Optik für Menschen, Gegenstände und deren Konstellationen auf die Räume gestattet, in denen wir leben müssen (356).

He agrees with Sewell that nonsense has its own laws (357). The essence of nonsense is "die Lust an der Verblüffung, Belustigung und Verwirrung des Lesers durch absurde, sozusagen aleatorische und weder logisch noch psychologisch vorbereitete Situationen und Sprachspiele..." (358), but this also occurs in dadaism, surrealism and absurdism. Baacke makes an interesting reference to the linguistics of nonsense as voiced by Kurt Schwitters,[52] who stated that the *letter*, not the *word* is the original material of poesy. Unlike words, letters have no meaning or connotations, only sounds. According to Baacke, nonsense fails to take seriously the phonemic oppositions which distinguish words semantically (e.g. "Rat", "Tat", "Rad" etc., 362). Nevertheless, nonsense cannot entirely divorce itself from

---

50. Huizinga (1938 [1974], esp. ch. 7).
51. I have not been able to consult the collection *mobile* from which this paper has been reprinted, and which also contains essays by Lütgert and Wuthenow.
52. See Richter (1964: 150-2) for the text of Schwitters' "Konsequente Dichtkunst" (orig. 1923). Schwitters, of course, here discusses poetry in a very wide sense.

meaning: "Nonsense bleibt, solange er an Sprache gebunden ist, immer mit Spuren von Sinn behaftet" (363-4).

Baacke makes a correct but not quite clear-cut distinction between nonsense on the one hand and surrealism as well as jokes or anecdotes on the other in the fifth section of his paper (368-70) by showing that, unlike these types of written communication, nonsense never conflicts with logic, for as soon as it does, it makes a "point" or appeals to phantastic associations. Nonsense, on the contrary, "nimmt eine uns allen geläufige Realität als Bezugsebene, erfüllt sie aber mit seltsamen Figuren und Gegenständen und tut so, als sei dies das Alltägliche und Geläufige" (370). The author proceeds to describe a scale of linguistic forms running from the language of logic through objective, scientific language, everyday speech, and literary language to esoteric, hermetic language. Nonsense, which arises from a mixture of fiction and objectivity, finds itself on the middle ground of everyday language—hence it cannot be avantgardist (370-1).

Baacke's article contains some interesting points, but fails to go much beyond the rather circular and unproven statement that nonsense means "itself" and is therefore uninterpretable (365), which ultimately leads him to the facile conclusions that "Eine «Nonsensesologie» [*sic*] ist ihrerseits nur als Nonsense möglich" (376), and that "Nonsense ist Schöpfung ohne Mythos und Logos" (*ibid.*) and "[e]ine Propädeutik für schöpferische Vorstellungen" (377), inasmuch as it only experiments with a reality that is not loaded with any sense.

The most recent monograph in the English language is Susan Stewart's impressive *Nonsense. Aspects of Intertextuality in Folklore and Literature* (1978), in which the author discusses nonsense as a social phenomenon, concomitant with the sense-making activities of human beings in general. The beginning of nonsense is "language lifted out of context" (3). Language is discourse, a social event accomplished in a social process, which is the act of communication. "The discourse of common sense refers to the 'real world'. The discourse of nonsense refers to 'nothing'" (13). There are "provinces of meaning" (meaning being achieved in the course of social interaction, 14), and the relationships between these provinces or domains is intertextual. Commonsense is manufactured in the domain of reality—its intersubjectivity is highest. All other provinces of meaning are "modifications or transformations of the common-sense world" (15-16). Nonsense operates in particular "between" the domains, that is to say in those transformative operations used in moving from one domain to another. "There will be as many varieties of nonsense as there are varieties of common sense" (16).

Stewart proceeds to describe the four aesthetic (as opposed to scientific or common sense) domains, which are those of *realism*, which is symbolic and refers to *real* domains; *myth*, which refers to *possible* contexts; *irony*, which presents *conflicts* between two domains of reality; and *metafiction*, which presents fiction about fiction, and is intimately connected with nonsense. "Each level of textuality ... stands at an increasing distance from common-sense procedures and thereby decreases in realism" (21).

Stewart's theory can be linked to Sewell's in *The Field of Nonsense* where the notion of play is introduced, which is defined by Stewart as "a shift to another domain of reality" (29). Play behaviour is a paradox in communication: for instance, one is "fighting" and yet one is not (30). Such a paradox, too, is the possibility of alternative domains of reality. "The procedures by which the schizophrenic or aphasiac 'fails' to make sense are often the same procedures by which others succeed in making nonsense", in both cases illustrating an "inability to distinguish between a hierarchy of messages and contexts" (32).

Realism depends upon metonymy, which shows reference to context. "Any radical shift towards the metaphoric or metonymic pole will result in nonsense" (33), a metaphor being, like nonsense, a violation of the rules of semantics (34). This shift creating nonsense is accompanied by a "decontextualization" of the utterance. Nonsense is "an overlapping of two or more disparate domains". It is only the (re)contextualization that saves metaphor as such from being nonsensical. "In nonsense, metaphor 'runs rampant' until there is wall-to-wall metaphor and thus wall-to-wall literalness.... Once the impossible context is reached, the interpretive possibilities open up and nonsense, like metaphor, is characterized by a multiplicity of meanings" (35-6), thus becoming perhaps "the most multiply-meaningful of fictions", but least meaningful in terms of everyday life (36).

Stewart goes on to show how nonsense resembles humour rather than being a sub-category of it,[53] because of the clashing of intertextual contradictions. In fact, she calls nonsense "humor without a context" (38). By intertextuality Stewart means the relationship between universes of discourse (48). "Nonsense, play, and paradox, as

---

53. For the view of humour being frequently an effect of reversal, see e.g. Milner (1972). Cf. also ch. 2 below.

activities that discourse on the nature of discourse, are built into the generic system as methods for innovation and evaluation" (50). Hence, "the nature of nonsense will always be contingent upon the nature of its corresponding common sense... the forms of nonsense will always be determined by the generic system available to the given set of members" (51). Any genre may or may not be nonsense, according to the valid conventions of discourse.

Part II of the book may be summarized succinctly. In it, Stewart illustrates the five "procedures" or operations that can be applied to create nonsense from common sense, presenting as it were a systematization of the various types of "play" that had already been adduced with lesser or greater emphasis by previous scholars. The first procedure is that of Reversals and Inversions, in which we recognize the aspect of nonsense as "topsyturvydom".[54] The second device is that of Play with Boundaries, among which is given as a type the surplus of signification already encountered in Benayoun (1977). The third operation is Play with Infinity,[55] the fourth Uses of Simultaneity (including e.g. the pun), and the fifth Arrangement and Rearrangement within a Closed Field. To each of these types a separate chapter is devoted, and many subdivisions are given, with illustrative examples. A summary of the five operations is given:

> In realism the frame is hidden, as if the shape of everyday events could form a continuum with the shape of fictive events. In reversals and inversions the frame becomes an articulation of exact difference, of a "proper not" relationship between categories. In misdirection the frame is dissolved into content as the fiction appropriates its immediate context. With infinity the frame becomes self-generating and self-perpetuating and reveals the etymological problem of the frame holding another frame. With simultaneity the frame becomes the very shape of infinity, a place where events converge. In arrangement and rearrangement within a closed field, frames are appropriated and made the absolute and arbitrary boundaries of a content that may be incongruous in its relationship

---

54. Cf. e.g. Cammaerts (1925: 25-7), Flescher (1969/70: 129), Milner (1972: 16), and Benayoun (1977: 13).

55. Note that Sewell (1952: 81, 86) specifically opposes the view of nonsense as a movement of infinite regress, and speaks of the process of *limitation*.

to the frame, or in the relationship between its constituent elements. In simultaneity we saw the infinite possibilities of convergence once convergence was permitted; with nonsense made within a closed field, those possibilities of convergence are themselves combined and recombined within a borrowed structure (172).

The whole theory is summarized as follows:

> I have suggested that the texts of nonsense are produced by appropriating the vertical and horizontal (or any other) organization of categories common to common sense and traversing that organization through procedures such as reversing or inverting them, shifting their boundaries, repeating them to infinity and/or exhaustion, conjoining them in time, or fracturing them into their members and recombining them according to some "contra-sensible" principle. By investigating how nonsense making works rather than what it is about, I have tried to emphasize that the "nature" of nonsense—nonsense's target and focus—is something that is ongoing and emergent in social process. The set of operations itself does not suggest exhaustiveness or universality, since it obviously depends upon a "culture"-specific set of logical principles. Nor are the operations *in themselves* sufficient to produce nonsense. The five operations I have considered are contingent upon a message "This is play", a message that recognizes the contextual parameters of the playground (199).

I have discussed Stewart's book extensively because much of her theory lies at the basis of my own definition of nonsense to be elaborated in chapter 2. However, here some criticism is called for. My main objection is that Stewart does not adduce any literary standards by means of which we may judge either the nature or the quality of the "accomplishment" of, say, Edward Lear, Lewis Carroll and Christian Morgenstern as compared to those of Thomas Hood, Ogden Nash and Wilhelm Busch. Having discovered that both Sterne's *Tristram Shandy* and Cabrera Infante's *Three Trapped Tigers* are novels that score highly on most levels of nonsensical operations, we still have no explanation why the first has considerably more literary quality. Moreover, Stewart does not take away our suspicion that nonsense is at most accidental to literature, a mere device—and in any case, no reader, I presume, would call *Tristram Shandy* a "nonsense novel". At the same time, a text consisting entirely of a palindrome (reversal) or hinging around a pun (simultaneity) is not necessarily literary nonsense.

Some devices Stewart adduces by way of illustration are not nonsensical at all. Misdirection, for instance, of the kind illustrated on p. 105, is not permanent: the reader/hearer must restore his direction, so that tension is resolved, and a point made. Finally, the chapter on the Uses of Simultaneity seems to work largely within a different framework from that of the other operations, and a mixture or overlapping with other types occurs here.

Prickett (1979) reverts to the theory voiced by Reichert that our understanding of the technique is "incomplete without an attempt to see the psychological motivations behind it" (139).[56] Like Reichert, he regards nonsense as "a product" of the Victorian era" (126) and he calls it "the most rigidly controlled of all forms of fantasy" (*ibid.*).[57]

A very interesting semiotic approach to nonsense is presented by Winfried Nöth (1980). Nöth points out that nonsense in Carroll's *AW* and *TLG* manifests itself on seven levels: the linguistic (e.g. the empty lexemes in "Jabberwocky"); the sociological (e.g. a Duchess nursing a baby in a dirty kitchen); the physical (e.g. falling through a rabbit-hole, going through a mirror); the biological (e.g. growing and shrinking); the semiotic, the psychological and the philosophical/ideological. Only if the presuppositions are accepted as fantasy conventions are the results not nonsensical (e.g. talking animals). Speaking of the levels of physics and biology, Nöth states: "Nonsens auf diesen zwei Ebenen beginnt erst dort, wo Anomalien vorliegen, die den erwähnten genrespezifischen Rahmen sprengen" (22).

The anomalies can be created in various ways, namely by means of semiotic transformation, of non-differentiation of levels and of reciprocal determination of levels, especially the determination of "reality" through language (word-magic). In semiotic transformation, properties normally associated with elements of one level are assigned to elements of another level. Non-differentiation of levels is found in particular in the pun, or in phrases like "flamingoes and mustard both bite", where the level of animals and that of vegetables are not differentiated in the zeugmatic use of the verb. An

---

56. Cf. p. 27 above.

57. Cf. Jackson (1981: ch. 6) for a similar view of nonsense as a form of Victorian fantasy.

example of the determination of world through language is Alice's suggestion that pepper may make people hot-tempered, vinegar sour etc. Nöth here makes a sub-division into "sprachlicher Determinismus", "wortspielerischer Determinismus" and "wort-spielerische Magie" (33-5; examples: Tweedledum and Tweedledee having to fight because the nursery rhyme says so; "Mock turtle soup" determining the nature of the Mock Turtle; "drying" people by telling them a "dry" story).

"Nonsense ist ... ein graduelles Phänomen. Der höchste Grad des Nonsens ist in einem Text erreicht, der keinerlei semantische Interpretation zuläßt und damit ein Maximum an Verstößen gegen die Regeln der Textkonstitution aufweist" (37). Thus, according to Nöth "Jabberwocky" is an example of "pure" nonsense, whereas the dialogue in the Alice books is on a lower level of nonsensicality.

Nöth contributes to an understanding of nonsense in pointing out the difference between the fairy tale convention of speaking animals on the one hand and on the other the nonsensicality of the disruption in the actual dialogues, through mishearing, the use of different conventions by each dialogue partner, taking representative statements for declarative ones and so on (42ff.). Thus, the postulates of speech-cooperativeness are often not observed: there is ambiguity, lack of relevance, triviality etc.—those aspects, in fact, also signalled by Benayoun (1977).

Nöth also introduces the interesting term of "meta-nonsense", which consists in the realization of the nonsensicality of one's own words and/or actions (57). After his chapter on the Pragmatics of dialogue in the Alice books, Nöth devotes a chapter to their use of *signs*, as *icons* (which are *like* the objects they denote), as *symbols* (arbitrary but conventional), and as *indices* (referring to single units, focussing attention on their objects). He shows how disorientation in *AW* and *TLG* is mainly due to disorienting symbols ("found *it* advisable", "jam every *other* day", etc.). Syntactic anomalies in these books are scarce, a point already made before and emphasizing the lexical nature of nonsense. In all, Nöth demonstrates how the semiotic nonsense of the Alice books is underpinned by a deeper semiotic sense (101). His semiotic matrix (see p. 16) is a useful addition to Stewart's levels of textuality.

From the plurality of "operations" discussed by both Stewart and Nöth it might be supposed that the ways of creating nonsense are legion. It is of interest, therefore, to consider a recent article by Sewell (1980/1; rpt. in Tigges 1987: 135-48) in which the suggestion is made that "perhaps there are only so many ideas in Nonsense—

platonic forms of what might be called a nonsense universe" (1980/1: 37). Without referring to Stewart, Sewell here comes up with a series of procedures that somewhat resembles that presented by Stewart: inversion, verbally induced contradiction (cf. Stewart's reversals); rhyme of unfitting pairs (cf. simultaneity, its sub-category of discontinuity); disproportion (cf. play with boundaries); and muddling things up (rearrangement). What nonsense does is to "produce by re-patterning of letters in a word or of objects in a seemingly given universe, a dislocation of that given and then a re-location which, slight as it is, may yet permit glimpses of just such other orders beyond and through our usual perspectives. Nonsense may give delight in proportion as it makes possible such glimpses" (41). This explains why some nonsense is "better" than other.

Lang (1982) opens his account with a criticism of Nöth, whom he accuses of failing to distinguish "anomaly" from literary nonsense: "Praktisch kein Thema für Nöth sind allerdings die hermeneutischen Fragen des Unsinns auf Textebene bzw. als Rezeptionskategorie, die Frage nach der literarischen Unsinnigkeit also" (11). It seems to me that this omission can be made good to some extent by combining with Nöth's (and Stewart's) insights those presented by Sewell in her recent article.

Lang's own contribution is the distinction, within a semiotic framework, between *linguistic* (non)sense and *literary* (non)sense. In literary nonsense, language is thematic (14). It must be determined by pragmatic, especially hermeneutic means (16-17). Lang's definitions are as follows:

> Grundsätzlich ist mit sprachlichem Unsinn jede Verletzung der sinnkonstituierenden Regeln, Relationen und sonstigen Zusammenhänge von sprachlichen Ausdrücken bzw. Äußerungen gemeint; solche Verletzungen sind 1. innerhalb einer der drei Dimensionen [viz. of syntax, semantics and pragmatics, WT] möglich und 2. (z.T. als Folge von 1.) als gestörtes Verhältnis der Dimensionen zueinander (23).
>
> Als *literarischen Sinn* sehe ich das Verhältnis eines einzelnen literarischen Werkes bzw. verschiedener Werke eines Künstlers zu dem vorgegebenen Erwartungshorizont der potentiellen Rezipienten seiner Zeit an (30).
>
> Historischer *werkliterarischer Unsinn* liegt vor, wenn ein Werk sich dem hermeneutischen Verstehensprozeß widersetzt, d.h. wenn das Ganze des Textes nich mehr ist als Summe seiner

> Teile und die Teile sich nicht organisch rückbeziehen lassen auf das Ganze (31).[58]
>
> [W]erkliterarischer Unsinn [ist] sprachlicher Unsinn auf Gedichtebene (99).

That this definition of *literary* nonsense is far too narrow is illustrated by the fact that Lang denies the literary nonsensical value of linguistic nonsense after Dada (34). It is clear from this that Lang basically regards literary nonsense as transitory and avantgardist, and he doubts the possibility of its occurring in a "normless" era (cf. 55).

Technically, the emphasis on the important aspect of the episodic nature of nonsense, the stringing together of loose elements, is correct (cf. also p. 67: "Reihung auf Textebene, so lautet die Formel für sprachlichen Unsinn"), but the notion, shared by Sewell, that the nonsense whole is not more than the sum of its parts must be refuted, as will be argued in the following chapters.

Lang also takes issue with Liede, whose approach he considers ahistorical (34-7). A perceptive counterargument is offered on p. 57, where Lang points out that since in the sixteenth century "stringing" as a structural principle was common, the occurrence of this device in texts of that period is not nonsensical. In his discussion of German nonsense literature, Lang states that in as far as they are precursors of the avant-garde, Morgenstern and Scheerbart produced literary nonsense on the edge of literary sense (58), while Lear and Carroll, being self-professed "mere" nonsense-writers, were not in the avant-garde tradition.

In an analysis of some poems by Mörike, Lang signalizes the arbitrariness of interpretation as indicative of "linguistic nonsense". In his comment on the similarities between Wilhelm Busch's *Eduards Traum* and Carroll's Alice books, he introduces the term *partial* nonsense for the former. "Der sprachliche Unsinn [in *Eduards Traum*] bleibt partiell und ist darum immer auf einen sinnvollen Kontext beziehbar" (63). Lang's conclusion is that literary nonsense is not a closed phenomenon in literature, but that it is a historical process which has been isolated in surroundings of neo-romantic streams,[59]

---

58. Cf. Sewell (1952: 53).

59. Cf. Mellor (1980: esp. chs 1 and 6), and see ch. 5, esp. 5.2, below.

increasingly reflecting alienation in language. Its contents cannot be generally characterized (110). It is indeed useful to start out with a suggestion of the multifariousness of literary nonsense.

Hofstadter (1982) too notes that the style and tone of nonsense have changed over the centuries (19). But it soon appears that in fact he mixes up nonsense with surrealism and absurdity, as appears when he characterizes as nonsensical the "tiny surrealistic vignettes" by R. Edson (25). It is simply not true that the story from *The Clam Theatre* quoted on that page "leaves one with a host of unresolved images", and the idea that "Nonsense stresses the incomprehensible face of the universe" is not so much Chestertonian as reflective of Esslin's definition of the absurd.[60] Like Benayoun (1977: 9, 11) Hofstadter sees a relationship between nonsense and Zen Buddhism, which he states "is perhaps the archetypal source of utter nonsense" (25). Hofstadter calls Gertrude Stein "[p]erhaps the greatest nonsense writer who ever lived" (20), but I prefer to classify her work as prototypical absurdity, since, as Hofstadter himself writes on the same page, "there is nothing to grab on to".

Hark (1982), following the paths trodden by Sewell and Stewart, adds little to their theories of nonsense as play with language, which she regards as "a central technique of nonsense" (102). In pointing out the closed and balanced nature of Lear's nonsense verse, in particular the limericks, she makes a distinction between nonsense and "mere light verse" (29).

The year 1982 also saw the appearance of yet another collection of essays on Carroll edited by Guiliano. This volume contains quite a few interesting analyses of Carroll's *oeuvre*, but none of these deal with the texts on the basis of a nonsense-oriented theory. A concurrent collection of Carrolliana edited by Kincaid and Guiliano mainly concentrates on biographical and artistic subjects.

A literal "discussion" (between the author and Lear's cat Foss) about the poeticality of nonsense is conducted in an article by Susan T. Viguers (1983). In her own voice, she points out that figurative language and nonsense are both "play": "Like nonsense, metaphor and other figures of speech are 'playing' with language, and thus with the normal, ordinary perceptions of the world" (145), and "nonsense can contribute to the creation of meaning" (146). Earlier on, a metaphor had been discussed: "At the heart of every metaphor is a merging of two apparently mutually exclusive worlds" (142). Both

---

60. Cf. Esslin (1968: 23-4).

serious poetry and nonsense avoid sentimentality, and neither is complacent (144). The differences between nonsense and poetry are adduced by the voice of Foss: nonsense must be approached literally, whereas the language of poetry is approached figuratively. Nonsense offers "the cadence of meaning without the content" (139), and it "takes great pleasure in long lists of things that have nothing to do with each other" (141). The suggestion, then, is that the difference is thematic (and possibly formal) rather than aesthetic.

A similar view is expressed in Kretschmer's monograph on *Die Welt der Galgenlieder Christian Morgensterns und der viktorianische Nonsense* (1983). Although Kretschmer does not give a definition of nonsense of his own but confines himself to a short survey (218ff.; cf. Kretschmer 1985: 114), his analysis of the Galgenlieder and the works of Carroll and Lear yields many new insights into the themes and techniques of nonsense literature.

Discounting the first part of the book, which deals with the world of the German Empire which roughly covered Morgenstern's lifetime, Kretschmer, in the second part, discusses the Galgenlieder in terms of four "worlds": that of unreality, that of humour, that of play and game, and that of dreams. In "Die Unwirkliche Welt" the author demonstrates how Morgenstern uses the freedom of thinking as he wishes, in four "stages" (46-53): firstly, the stage of the unusual in a real world (example "Das Huhn"); secondly, the impossible in a real world ("Der Gaul"); thirdly, the (im)possible in an unreal world ("Das Nasobēm"); and fourthly, unreal language in an unreal world ("Das große Lalulā", "Fisches Nachtgesang").[61]

Morgenstern thus created a world of *fantasy*, which develops a life of its own, and in which for instance inventions play an important role (63-4). In "Die Welt des Humors", Kretschmer distinguishes humour (as an attitude) from the comic (its product). He demonstrates how the characters in the Galgenlieder are shown to be independent, keeping distant from the world, in a sovereignty which is typically expressed by humour (81). Quite correctly Kretschmer points out that Morgenstern's nonsense poems lack a "pointe", and are therefore to be distinguished from jokes. Also, there is no frustrated expectation as there is in jokes (144-6). Perhaps it would be clearer at this point to put forward the suggestion that nonsense frustrates the expectation of frustrated expectation which is charac-

---

61. See ch. 4.3.2 below for a more detailed account of Kretschmer's analysis of the Galgenlieder. See also ch. 2.3.7.

teristic of the joke or anecdotal humour, which also incidentally explains why the "shaggy dog story" with its anti-climax comes much closer to being nonsensical than the ordinary joke.[62]

In "Die Spielwelt", Kretschmer starts out with a summary of the views of Liede and Walter (1966) on Morgenstern's nonsense poetry. Walter had stated that "[d]as Spiel der Galgenlieder ist kein Spiel mit der Sprache, sondern 'ein Spiel der Sprache in sich und mit sich selbst'. Kern des Sprachspiels ist das Wortspiel, 'das eigentliche Spielfeld der Sprache'" (156, quoting Walter 1966: 59). This opposes the view of Liede, who regards Morgenstern's play as a destructive and resignatory game with worldly things (155-6).[63] The most important addition that Kretschmer presents here is that the poet of the Galgenlieder created a world free from reality, in which any rule kept is kept *voluntarily* (150). Thus, he retains the verse rules of lyrical poetry, its rhyme and metre. "Im Spiel der Galgenliederwelt werden Worte als Bilder von den ihnen herkömmlich zugeordneten Dingen getrennt" (170).

In "Die Traumwelt", finally, Kretschmer remarks that the language of dreams is often fantastic, comic and playful. It makes use of the same shifts or displacement, condensation, and representation[64] that we find in the Galgenlieder. Kretschmer gives examples of lapses and reconstructions of language (e.g. "Anto-logie", "Der Lattenzaun"), displacement in making use of homonymics, homophony, polysemy etc. ("Der Werwolf"), condensation (portmanteau-like constructions, which can be compared to "mixed persons" in dreams), and representation (taking metaphors literally, or turning abstract notions into concrete ones, as in "Lebenslauf") (172-203).

In the third and last part of his book, Kretschmer compares similar elements in the poetry of Morgenstern and of the Victorians, especially Carroll and Lear. Thus, he notes a similarity of motifs (manipulation of time, mirroring of space, 221, 223), and of the use of language (both Morgenstern and Carroll make the relationship

---

62. See further chapter 3.1 below.

63. For definitions of game and play Kretschmer is indebted to Huizinga and Sewell.

64. Kretschmer here makes use of the Freudian terms "Verschiebung", "Verdichtung" and "Bildlichkeit", which Strachey translates as "displacement", "condensation" and "representation" respectively. See Freud (1960 [1976]: 221-3).

between things and the signs that determine them into a theme). In some of Morgenstern's, Carroll's and Lear's poems, unknown or nonexistent words are used to create an effect of (mild) horror (234, 240). Words are treated as individuals, they are "entbürgerlicht" and given a new dignity. In this respect Carroll and Lear are precursors of Symbolism. But where Mallarmé is serious, Morgenstern remains comic, and for Lear writing was a secondary activity altogether (249-50).

Next, Kretschmer considers the various types of play used by Morgenstern and the Victorians. He calls *TLG* an epic "großes Lalulā": literature designed as a game of chess (253). Edward Lear plays within the framework of the rules of the limerick (255). The various devices used by Carroll, Lear and Morgenstern (framework-play in alphabets, botanies etc., repetition-play in refrains and first lines, wordplay in games of displacement, condensation and representation) are compared (257ff.).

"Die Literatur des Nonsense verhält sich den Erfordernissen der Logik gegenüber indifferent" (274). Morgenstern's Lieder seem to have a more logical "sense" than much of Carroll's writing. Morgenstern sets "problems", Lear on the other hand does not, he just sets situations. The Galgenlieder possess a "Grund-idee", they are communicative. Lear's limericks are "provocative" (276-9). In this section on "Sinnvergleich", Kretschmer finally notes that whereas Lear and Carroll wrote primarily for children, Morgenstern wrote for adults, which accounts for the essential irony of the Galgenlieder, which is not found in Victorian nonsense (284). To what extent this is a valid statement remains to be seen.

In the last section Kretschmer compares the similar uses made of fauna, flora and objects. The animals, plants and things are neither the beings of a fairy tale nor those of a fable, though they have some elements in common with either, such as personifcation and antithesis. There is, however, no antithesis between good and evil, no moral attached (305-6). Kretschmer concludes:

> Christian Morgenstern, Lewis Carroll und Edward Lear sind Nachbarn oder gar Verwandte in "typologischer" Hinsicht. Ob der Dichter der Galgenlieder darum auch der Kleinfamilie "Nonsense" angehört, bleibt eine Schubladenfrage (314).

In his monograph on Christian Morgenstern Kretschmer is more explicit. There, although admitting there may be some nonsense in the Galgenlieder, he states: "Dem »Unsinn« der Galgen- Gingganz-

und Palmströmlieder ist eine Qualität eigen, die dem Nonsense Lears und Carrolls fehlt und die man mit Morgenstern »Geistigkeit« nennen könnte" (1985: 116).

Kreutzer (1984) treats the Alice books as what they originally are: children's books, which he places within the context of the rise of the literary fairy tale, the nursery rhyme, the fantasy etc., as well as the culture of light entertainment (89). After presenting a survey of Victorian reception and twentieth-century interpretations and imitations of the books, he defines nonsense as a system of rules. For more detailed characteristics of nonsense, Kreutzer leans heavily on the work of Petzold and Reichert, and in speaking of "die spielerischen Sprachkomik des Nonsense" (74) he places himself firmly in the tradition of Sewell and Stewart.

The principal characteristics of nonsense in his opinion are incongruence of a text leaving the expectations of sense unfulfilled, visual distortion of observed reality, and pseudo-logical connections, arising from a playful delight in abnormality.

In a recent article which I invited for my collection of papers on literary nonsense (Tigges 1987), Stefan Themerson brings up a useful distinction between sense and nonsense as means and as result. Poets make sense by means of nonsense, such as the use of rhyme (5). Lewis Carroll is regarded as the quintessence of sense (8). He used Symbolic Logic to detect nonsense, and he used *AW* fiction to unmask it, thus establishing himself as the "Great Master of Logic-Fiction" (9). In this view, Themerson follows to the extreme the steps of Sutherland (1970), and also those of Laffay (1970), who regards *AW* and *TLG* as reflections *on* nonsense, stories written in the style of nonsense, rather than as actually *being* nonsensical (1970: 129).

In the same volume, Anthony Burgess begins by reverting to the simple definition of nonsense as "a lack of sense" (1987: 17), distinguishing it from both logic and dream. In his conclusion, however, he characterizes the phenomenon as "a bizarre way of making sense" and as "a playful pragmatic way of interpreting the universe" (21), and he ends by stating that "there is as much sense in nonsense as there is nonsense in sense" (*ibid.*), which, taking us full circle back to the early Chestertonian vision, seems an appropriate statement with which to round off this historical survey of nonsense scholarship.

Without a pretence to have been completely exhaustive, the above survey is presented as a fair summary of the extant scholarship on nonsense literature in so far as it offers an attempt at a definition of the phenomenon or contributes to its better understanding by adducing characteristics, features or techniques.

It will become clear that the elements shared by most if not all discussions summarized in the foregoing pages are those of game or play, with language and logic playing important thematic as well as structural roles. Frequently mentioned devices are those of inversion (topsyturvydom), incongruence and simultaneity (unfitting collocations, puns). The absence of emotion is often noted.

Rather than lengthening this chapter by discussing the merits and demerits of the various views expressed in greater detail than has already been done, I will proceed in the next chapter with a definition of my own, for which the indebtedness to earlier scholarship will become evident. Of even greater importance will be to show what nonsense is *not*, which will be possible once a viable definition of nonsense has been provided.

The main shortcoming, however, of practically all the works discussed in the present chapter is that hardly any attempt at a literary analysis is made. Whenever, that is, such analyses *are* presented, they almost invariably start from a point of view that leaves aside any theory about nonsense, simply leaving the question what nonsense is unanswered. It will be the main aim of this study to present the beginnings of an analysis which is based on a theory of literary nonsense. Before that is possible, a definition and typology of literary nonsense must first be provided, which will be attempted in the following chapter.

CHAPTER 2: DEFINITION AND TYPOLOGY

In an earlier publication I defined literary nonsense as:

> a genre of narrative literature which balances a multiplicity of meaning with a simultaneous absence of meaning. This balance is effected by playing with the rules of language, logic, prosody and representation, or a combination of these. In order to be successful, nonsense must at the same time invite the reader to interpretation and avoid the suggestion that there is a deeper meaning which can be obtained by considering connotations or associations, because these lead to nothing. The elements of word and image that may be used in this play are primarily those of negativity or mirroring, imprecision or mixture, infinite repetition, simultaneity, and arbitrariness. A dichotomy between reality and the words and images which are used to describe it must be suggested. The greater the distance or tension between what is presented, the expectations that are evoked, and the frustration of these expectations, the more nonsensical the effect will be. The material may come from the unconscious (indeed, it is very likely in many instances to do so), but this may not be suggested in the presentation.[1]

In this chapter I intend to clarify and refine this definition, beginning with a discussion of the question whether nonsense can indeed be considered as a genre, or whether one ought to prefer the term "mode" or even "device".

2.1 Genre, mode and device

A large majority of the scholars discussed in the first chapter describe nonsense in terms of a quality which can be shared by various types of text, or of a device which may feature in a text as one of its aspects. Texts in which this nonsensical quality is found to be dominant are included in Anthologies of nonsense, and can be referred to as "nonsense verse", "nonsense poetry", "nonsense stories" and so on. These appellations, however, must be rejected as imprecise, because "nonsense" here is often used as the equivalent of

---

1. Tigges (1986a: 166-7; rpt. in Tigges 1987: 27-8). My particular indebtedness to Sewell (1952), Ede (1975) and Stewart (1978) will be obvious.

other terms, such as "funny", "comic", "ludicrous", "topsyturvy" and the like.

To my knowledge, Annemarie Schöne (1954a; possibly already in 1951)[2] is the first scholar to define nonsense straightforwardly as a genre, a view which is shared by the present author. It is evident that the viability of such a view depends on one's definition of "genre". As has been announced in my remarks on methodology in the Introduction, I do not intend to enter into a regressive argument as to the merits and demerits of various definitions of this term, but I wish to make my position quite clear. Hempfer (1973) has sufficiently demonstrated the existence of a veritable "anarchy of concepts", and his own dialectic constructivist approach seems a safe enough middle road to follow (1973: 124-5, 221). The question whether the determination of a genre is to be argued inductively or deductively can thereby be shelved. Two other questions adduced by Hempfer, whether a corpus of texts belonging to a specific genre can be discerned, and whether it is possible to determine an archetype of the genre (130, 132) can, with regard to the genre of literary nonsense, be answered in the positive without necessarily leading to the "Aporien" this author foresees (130). As will be shown in chapter 4, a corpus of nonsense does indeed exist. There is no need to be so illiberal as to require a concretely labelled membership of the corpus. As archetypal nonsense one may safely designate the works of Edward Lear and Lewis Carroll. The possible earlier occurrence of a stray text containing enough of the characteristics shared by these works, and to be discussed in the following sections, to warrant the generic label of "nonsense" can be taken in stride, if one is willing to accept that a dividing line, however arbitrary, has to be drawn. The proviso here is that such a dividing line can be justified by the data, without thereby necessarily obtaining an absolute status. About this dividing line there will be more in chapter 5. In any case, it seems wise policy to avoid following the nonsensical device of moving around in circles of definition.

Hempfer's preferred approach, as set out on pp. 135ff. of his book, is quite convenient. One's starting point is a historically limited text-corpus which has been "received" as belonging to one genre. From this corpus one determines the genre norms, which had

---

2. See 1951: 8-11, where a "corpus" of nonsense texts is presented. In what follows, however, her unit is the device rather than individual texts.

perhaps better be termed more neutrally its characteristics. Subsequently, irrelevant texts are rejected from the corpus, and relevant other texts are introduced into it. In one's ultimate definition one must see to it that elements and structures discerned are strictly hierarchical (137). It is largely on the lines of this theory that I intend to approach my subject-matter in this chapter. In a later chapter, I will briefly go into the relevant aspects of the development of the genre from the early nineteenth century to the present day.[3]

The fact that what I define as nonsense has not been consistently "received" as a corpus is only an apparent problem. Very few readers have failed to detect nonsense in the works of Lear and Carroll. The similarities between their works have been discussed. However, the similarities between their works and those of others have not been intensively investigated, except inasmuch as linguistic play and situational fantasy featuring in Lear and Carroll have been discovered to feature in other works as well. In so far as they do, it may legitimately be stated that we are dealing with nonsensical "devices", or that a novel, a short story or a poem has a greater or lesser nonsensical quality. In this respect "nonsense" is like "satire" in its usage, since the latter term too can refer to a genre (the Roman verse satire) as well as to a quality.

Fowler uses the term "mode" to indicate a category of genre where certain features of the "generic repertoire"[4] have been subtracted (1982: 56). Fowler uses the word "genre" to include this modal category, but the term "mode" in Fowler's sense is a convenient label to define nonsense by, since "a nonsense" may very well be in prose or verse, it may have a sonnet form or that of a ballad or another lyrical type, or be in the shape of a short story or a play. It cannot, however, be a satire or a burlesque or a parody (other

---

3. I agree with Nies (1973), who discusses the equally heterogeneous genre of the "historiette", and with Fowler (1982), that the changes and developments of a genre must be taken into account. However, the chronological limits of nonsense are not so wide as to preclude a more synchronic or static treatment in this chapter and the following one (cf. Fowler 1982: 47).

4. The repertoire is defined as "the whole range of potential points of resemblance that a genre may exhibit" (Fowler 1982: 55). "Every genre has a unique repertoire, from which its representatives select characteristics" (*ibid.*). See also Hempfer (1973: 211).

genre labels), since it is the prime characteristic of nonsense not to make a "point" or draw a moral, not to satirize, to ridicule or to parody, and not even primarily to entertain. Since it is only as to its formal characteristics that nonsense may belong to different kinds of literature, I prefer to retain the term "genre" for the corpus of texts discussed in this study. Only in so far as the features of the nonsense repertoire can in some cases be labelled as "nonsensical" is nonsense also a device. As such, it may occur in satire, parody, burlesque, tragedy, comedy and so on. With this qualitative type of nonsense, which has been amply and aptly analysed by Liede (1963) and Stewart (1978) I will not, however, be mainly concerned.

Fowler's genre definition is based on the notion of the conventionality of literature (21). In the following sections I will try to establish the convention of nonsense, its generic repertoire, not indeed to define the genre once and for all, but rather in order to "identify the genre to [be able to] interpret the exemplar" ("Fowler 1982: 38). Like Fowler (41-2), I shall therefore understand by a genre simply a group of texts showing a family resemblance, and leave it at that.

As has been said, one must allow for the fact that genres may change and develop over the years. They may in fact develop from or originate in other types of literature, and new genres may arise from them, causing the old ones to develop according to different patterns, or even to die off. In this thesis I will not describe, let alone stipulate, a firmly normative genre of nonsense literature, to which certain texts must exclusively belong or from which they must be completely rejected. It has been my intention to define the genre in such a way that the definition will enable the critic to group together a set of texts which have thus far been either classified otherwise (and under a variety of labels), or not at all. On the basis of my definition it is possible to discern a kernel corpus of texts, whose members resemble one another to such a degree that a sensible comparison and evaluation can be made.

If in this study I will seem to treat the notion of genre as a rather fixed and static phenomenon, this is merely done for the sake of convenience. I have no quarrel with those who regard most of the texts I discuss here as arising from nursery rhymes, fairy tales, light verse or parody, or as lying at the basis of dadaism, surrealism, absurdism or modernism. What I will do is show how they *differ* from these types of literature. Nor do I have an *a priori* objection to interpretations of some or all of these texts in terms of a different genre. My point is not that if something is "a nonsense", it cannot also be a novel, a play or a lyric; but if something is "a nonsense", it cannot *simultaneously* be an allegory, a satire or a joke.

2.2   *The Essence of Nonsense*

As will have become evident, the genre of nonsense is not so much circumscribed by formal characteristics, metrical features or even a preferred standard scale (although the most successfully sustained nonsense tends to come either in shorter verse or prose forms) as by its basic type of communication. Its most essential characteristic is that it presents an unresolved tension, which in my definition I refer to as a balance between presence and absence of meaning. This balance has to be prevalent in the work as a whole, but frequently it also features as a device on a smaller scale within the work. Once this type of balance or dialectic is signalled, it cannot be confused with that of irony, where meaning is also frequently negated. An illustration may serve to elucidate this point.

In the Marx Brothers' first movie, *The Cocoanuts* (1929), Groucho Marx plays the role of Mr Hammer, the owner-manager of a large hotel in Florida as well as the owner of some real estate which at a certain stage he tries to auction. In a famous scene he attempts to instruct Chico in how to play the role of a shill. At one point in the dialogue Hammer says: "... when the crowd gathers around, I want you to mingle with them. Don't pick their pockets, just mingle with them", to which Chico replies: "I'll find time for both." Hammer then retorts: "Well, maybe we can cut out the auction" (Anobile 1972: 37). Out of its context, Hammer's remark is ironical, conveying a reflection on Chico's stupidity. Within its context, however, it is nonsensical: Hammer simultaneously considers the possibility of having the auction (he goes on to instruct Chico about it) and not having it (the suggestion being that more money can be obtained out of the crowd by having Chico picking its pockets).

Edward Lear's nonsensical limericks, when considered separately, are perfect samples of texts in which the balance between meaning and non-meaning is consistently maintained. At this stage, one example may suffice:[5]

---

5. The example, taken from Lear, ed. Jackson (1947: 4), is discussed in Tigges (1986b), which deals more extensively with the

> There was an Old Man with a nose,
> Who said, "If you choose to suppose,
> That my nose is too long, you are certainly wrong!"
> That remarkable Man with a nose.

In "The Limerick: The Sonnet of Nonsense?" (1986b: 223) I suggested that "for the limerick in question to be nonsensical at all we need the information provided by the drawing. Here both the size of the nose and the dismay of its beholders are turned nonsensical by means of an exaggeration which does not appear from the text." The tension between meaning and its absence thus works between the text and its illustration. On second thoughts, I think it also operates in the text on its own. The first line, which introduces the theme, is nonsensical in that it does not actually present an unusual fact: we would expect any man, young or old, to be provided with a nose, however long or short. An old man *without* a nose would be unusual and, indeed, "remarkable", but might evoke an emotion which in nonsense is undesirable, as my next paragraphs will show. The man is subsequently reported as denying that there is anything wrong with his nose. As the text provides no evidence of the contrary, this statement is gratuitous or trivial, although it is presented as meaningful information. The man himself only states that his nose is *not* too long, upon which the poet proceeds to offer the judgment that this "Man with a nose" *all the same* is "remarkable ".

The requirement of unresolved tension, so clearly fulfilled by Lear's limerick (Is the man remarkable or not? Is his nose too long or is it not?) rules out clever verbal trickery as well as wordplay for the sake of a comic effect. It also rules out the presence of emotion. This characteristic of nonsense has been most extensively discussed by Sewell (1952: 107, 129, 144). Because of the tension between presence and absence of meaning, any suggestion of an emotion is at the same time withdrawn, so that puzzlement is all that remains.

By its very denial, the emotion is not made to disappear altogether; it is rather that one's expectations in this respect are

---

limerick as a nonsense form, and by Ede (in Tigges 1987: 104-5). This particular quality of Lear's limericks is also noted by Cammaerts (1925: 7), Byrom (1977: 120), Hark (1978: 121) and Lang (1980: 40). See also Ede (1975: 21-49).

persistently frustrated. Again, the Marx Brothers come to mind, in particular the ambivalence of the repeated wooing scenes between Groucho Marx and Margaret Dumont. In their recurrent "love affairs", whatever happens to the emotions of love and affection, the emotions are not ignored. Very often, if not always, these scenes serve to offset the sentimentality of the "serious" affairs that are going on at the same time. The validity of these affairs, as well as the insincerity of the feelings of the upper-class world against which the Marxes are in permanent (but nonsensically ineffective) rebellion, are thereby debunked.[6]

Nonsense, then, is never lyrical in the true sense of the word—it does not express the personal feelings of the author, nor a communal feeling through his mouth. The nonsense writer or poet rarely writes in the first person at all. If he does, this is a deceptive device, as is the use of a "lyrical" form. Consider Mervyn Peake's nonsense poem "O'er Seas that have no Beaches":[7]

> O'er seas that have no beaches
> To end their waves upon,
> I floated with twelve peaches,
> A sofa and a swan.
>
> The blunt waves crashed above us
> The sharp waves burst around,
> There was no one to love us,
> No hope of being found—
>
> Where, on the notched horizon
> So endlessly a-drip,
> I saw all of a sudden
> No sign of any ship.

Any emotion suggested in this poem ("There was no one to love us,/ No hope of being found—") is enervated by the nonsensicality of the

---

6. See Tigges (1986a: 166). For the nonsense in the Marx Brothers films, see Eyles (1974) and Galestin (1986). See also ch. 4, pp. 196-201 below.
7. In Peake (1974: 37). A slightly different version is found in Mervyn Peake, *Mr Pye*, Harmondsworth: Penguin, 1972 (orig. 1953), p. 230.

situation: the beachless seas which cannot therefore exist to float upon, the inconsequentiality of the "twelve peaches" (why peaches? why twelve?) accompanied by a sofa and a swan—objects, none of which are ordinarily associated with the sea, and so take away its associations and connotations, except those of wetness and vastness. Nor are waves ordinarily said to be either blunt or sharp, so that a false contrast is suggested. And how can a beachless sea, if taken figuratively, be surrounded by a "notched" horizon, *from* which waves are dripping? The last two lines, in all their amazingness, are not a "point". One would *expect* the sense of solitariness to be broken by the sign of a ship, but there is no sign of one. However, this absence of a ship is presented as a *positive* sign—as if the poet has so far seen nothing but ships around him. If that were the case, the "sudden" view of "No sign of any ship" would have to imply that all these ships suddenly and simultaneously vanished or that the absent-minded seafarer had never noticed them before, which would make nonsense of his complaint about "no hope of being found". The only emotion, if any, that remains is that of isolation, which has been stated to be possibly the only emotion that nonsense allows for.[8] Not being lyrical, nonsense must of needs prefer the narrative mode, as has been perceptively noted by Lisa Ede (1975: 12).

A third essential feature of nonsense, and one that has also been most aptly discussed by Sewell, although it is the aspect that crops up in most discussions of the subject, is its playlike character. I refer the reader to chapter 1 for a plethora of sources in which this aspect of nonsense has been treated, and will only mention here the particular nature of play that I consider to be essential for nonsense, which is not only that the "game" of nonsense has its own rules or laws, but that it adheres to its self-appointed rules only voluntarily.[9] It is not, as Deleuze puts it, a "pure game", a game *without* rules (1969: 75), but the simultaneous presence and absence of rules, the feeling that arbitrary rules are meticulously adhered to, but might be abandoned at any moment, is one ever-present aspect of the balance of meaning and non-meaning which is an equally essential characteristic. Yet, at the same time the play- or game-like quality of nonsense also reinforces its avoidance of emotion, since

---

8. Sewell (1952: 145); Ede (1975: 14-15).
9. For this point I am indebted to Kretschmer (1983: 159). Cf. Henkle (1973: 103).

Sewell among others has pointed out (1952: 131) that the counters of a game preclude emotional attachment.

According to Sewell, these counters in the game of nonsense are words, or, more generally, the elements of language, and this leads me to the fourth essential characteristic of nonsense, its predominantly verbal nature. It has been said about Morgenstern's Galgenlieder, which I include in the canon of nonsense, that there the language creates the fantasy rather than representing it, that it is the language that creates a nonsensical reality, rather than, as in the absurd, a nonsensical reality being verbally represented.[10] Here too the notion of balance, if one likes of paradox, has to be introduced. For this is where the aesthetic quality of nonsense, to be more extensively discussed in chapter 4, comes to the forefront. If the language material of a nonsense text were not to suggest that a reality, however absurd or fantastical, is presented or described, it would not rise above the level of empty wordplay, which is one of the things from which I wish to distinguish literary nonsense. As Walter rightly observes of the Galgenlieder, wordplay is not the aim but the initiator of these poems (1966: 96). As long as this is realized, one is entitled to say that in nonsense the word has precedence over reality.[11] One has, of course, to take into account that this may legitimately be stated about literature in general, just as it may be said that nonsense is no more or less a game than is literature in general, with its rules and conventions. The main distinction here is that the game of nonsense is played for its own sake rather than with a transcendent aim.

To summarize, literary nonsense is characterized by four essential elements: an unresolved tension between presence and absence of meaning, lack of emotional involvement, playlike presentation, and an emphasis, stronger than in any other type of literature, upon its verbal nature. In the following section I will investigate the repertoire of nonsense, its semiotic and stylistic means or "procedures" that nonsense makes use of to create its effects and to signalize its presence.

10. Walter (1966: 50, 68).
11. This is made explicit in Morgenstern's poems "Das Böhmische Dorf", in which von Korf accompanies Palmström "nur des Reimes wegen", and "Das ästhetische Wiesel", whose actions are stated to be "um des Reimes willen" (Morgenstern 1933: 102, 36).

2.3   The Nonsense Repertoire

2.3.1   *Mirroring*

In view of the strong predilection of nonsense for paradox and dialectic, for a sustained balance between opposites, it will not be found surprising that the first of Stewart's five "procedures" for turning sense into nonsense,[12] Reversals and Inversions, or mirroring, as I have called it in my definition, is a prominent stylistic feature in this type of literature. On a large scale it operates in the presentation of a "topsyturvy" world, a world beyond the looking-glass, where in addition cause and effect may be reversed. Depending on whether the emphasis lies on the effect-side (absence of effect or aim) or on the causal side (absence of cause or motivation), this may be seen as an extreme form of Blumenfeld's telic nonsense ("Zweckunsinn") and motivational nonsense ("Motivationsunsinn"),[13] but it should be noted that a "sensical" description of a telic or motivational nonsense situation is not in itself constitutive of literary nonsense. Sisyphus' labour is sensible when viewed as a punishment, but nonsensical from the point of view of an expected result (Blumenfeld 1933: 42). Since the myth is presented as the former, it is not a nonsense story.

In view of the lexical nature of nonsense, mirroring is often on the lexical level: letters may be reversed or even mirrored (as in the version of "Jabberwocky" that Alice first discovered), words may be reversed or acquire their opposite meaning. Stewart lists the following devices under this heading: anomaly, ambiguity, ambivalence, proper-nots, taking things back, inverting classes, reversible texts, self-denying discourse, and the inversion of metaphor (1978: 60-81). Thus, the trickster hero systematically violates categories and norms of behaviour, by means of negation, reversal and inversion. He presents the "proper-not" of every category (63). The inversion can be symmetrical, hierarchical or fragmentated (66). Under "inverting classes" comes for instance the treatment of human beings as animals or the other way about (*ibid.*). Reversable texts include reversal of phonemes, spoonerisms, palindromes, conundrums and mirror writing (68). Ironic footnotes are a form of self-denying discourse

---

12.   Stewart (1978: Part II). For a summary, see ch. 1, pp. 33-7 above.

13.   Blumenfeld (1933: 40ff., 65ff.).

(72), and the inversion of metaphor is obtained when the metaphor is taken literally, as in the shaggy dog story or the Wellerism (77).

I believe that the primary requirement of unresolved tension, that of the absence of a "point", rules out many of these devices as belonging to literary nonsense proper. Thus, the point of the trickster hero is that he breaks a taboo, or uses deception in order to survive, and therefore the trickster story is not nonsensical, as a moral is clearly drawn from it; neither are fables, where humans are presented as animals to point a moral, or Spoonerisms, Wellerisms and palindromes, where the point is the clever play with letters or sounds. The mirroring device is thematic, but not absolutely essential to nonsense. In the Peake poem considered earlier, the phrase "No sign of any ship", negating the reader's expectations, is a device that contributes to the creation of literary nonsense by means of inversion.

2.3.2 *Imprecision*

The second device is imprecision or mixture, which Stewart refers to as "play with boundaries". This occurs when separate elements are not so much mirrored, or contrasted as one another's negation, but glide into one another without quite overlapping. As types of this procedure Stewart mentions misdirection, surplus of signification (including spelling riddles, rebuses, echo verse, trick questions, acrostics, calligrams, false contrasts in language—as in "Mots d'heures, gousses, rames" to "translate" Mother Goose's Rhymes—so-called Jonathanisms, exaggerations and miniaturizations), deficiencies of signification (blank pages, lipograms, hiatus), and manifestations of the implicit (commentary on non-existent books, or dissolution of boundary between fiction and reality, as when the author becomes a character in his own book).[14]

Here again it must be obvious that no literary nonsense is created if these devices are used for ulterior purposes or merely for their own sake, and that in fact they stop being nonsensical if and when "the 'magic' is solved" (Stewart 1978: 105), that is to say, when the recipient is set a puzzle which he is both meant to solve and is able to do so. My additional requirement would be that here too the imprecision or mixture must be maintained. In *AW* a baby is

---

14. Stewart (1978: 89-112).

turned into a pig, but it never becomes clear whether we have not been dealing with a pig all along.

For this device of play with boundaries to be nonsensical, the misdirection or deficiency or surplus of significance must be presented as a meaningful direction or a sufficient signification. In Lear's limerick "There was an Old Man with a nose", the information is deficient in so far that in order to judge how remarkable this nose is we need a modifying adjective, which the text does not provide. The modifyer "Old", on the other hand, is superfluous. The "magic" is solved, of course, by the accompanying illustration, but then we know that the illustration is not always to be trusted.[15] It is therefore impossible to come to a conclusion about the meaning of the poem.

Play with boundaries is particularly prominent in what Blumenfeld refers to as "eidic nonsense" ("Gestaltsunsinn"; 1933: 52ff.), where the recipient fails to let the parts of what he observes arrive at a meaningful whole, or where a part is taken for the whole, as in Morgenstern's "Das Knie". It features in visual nonsense, of which Saul Steinberg is a prominent representative.[16]

2.3.3 *Infinity*

A third device is that of stringing or seriality, or in Stewart's terms: play with infinity (1978: 116-43). Stewart links up this procedure with the playlike quality of nonsense: the movement of play becomes a movement of infinite regression. Play time is paradoxical. Like play, "the work of nonsense is reflection and self-perpetuation".[17] A nonsensical series is a series without cause and effect. Nonsense verse often comes in such series, as in Alphabets, limerick sequences, picture stories etc.

---

15. The man looks middle-aged rather than old. Cf. also the Old Man of Peru, who is *said* to be baked by mistake, but *seen* to be shoved into the oven intentionally (Lear, ed. Jackson 1947: 28).

16. For an extensive discussion of visual nonsense, including an account of Steinberg's *oeuvre*, see van Leeuwen (1986).

17. Stewart (1978: 119). But cf. Sewell (1952: 81, 86) for an opposing view. According to Sewell, nonsense, like any game, "can have no truck with infinity", which is why it is "dangerous" for nonsense to play with numbers (81).

Besides serializing (also exemplified in counting and listing), Stewart mentions under this heading nesting (the Chinese box or text-within-the-text effect), circularity (seasons, months of the year, days of the week as organizing devices), and infinite causality (chain verse, and even the picaresque as a string of adventures).

The same provisos that were applied to inversions and reversals, and to boundaries, hold good here. In nonsense literature, the required tension between meaning and non-meaning can be held unresolved by the arbitrariness of closure (Stewart 1978: 143; cf. Reichert 1974: 20), as well as by the frequently episodic nature of the text, both of which fall under this category.

2.3.4   *Simultaneity*

The strongest semiotic device of nonsense literature is that of simultaneity. It is strongest because the tension between two disparate elements is most strongly present. Stewart (1978: 154-68) lists five varieties: simultaneity and form (footnotes, table of contents, index, chapter headings, as well as the cento or collage), discontinuity (combination of disparate elements), riddles and puns, portmanteaux, and macaronic texts.

Simultaneity, then, includes the device of the ill-matched pair or set of objects, as when twelve peaches, a sofa and a swan are brought together from their various spheres (garden, living-room, and lake or river) into one sphere which is in itself incongruent with them (the sea). Of course, Peake's poem can be interpreted, and a new, consistent "boundary" or "horizon" be established (see Stewart 1978: 85) by reading it as the reminiscence of a child who is or feels himself to be "afloat" or "at sea", unloved, in a sitting-room with peaches on the fruit-dish, a sofa it is sitting on, and an ornamental swan on the table or mantlepiece, on a rainy day (the "notched horizon" of the window-lintel being "endlessly adrip" with rain)—in other words, as a child's fantasy. But there are no clues in the poem to "re-direct" the reader from a nonsensical reading to this "sensical" interpretation.

According to Stewart, "rhyme works as a principle of simultaneity and convergence" (1978: 158), and so does alliteration. One often has the impression that in nonsense verse the rhyme determines the contents instead of the other way about.[18] Holquist in particular has

---

18. See e.g. Cammaerts (1925: 40). Cf. footnote 11 for references

noted the way in which rhyme, as a kind of "rule of three", binds two words which are disparate in meaning "in a new meaning which was not contained in either of them alone" (1969/70: 162). Sewell, on the other hand, characterizes rhyme, together with refrain and alliteration, as "pseudo-series" (1952: 77). Redfern, finally, suggests that there are arguments for its kinship with punning (1984: 99). In the same place he states that "[t]he pun *is* like the rhyme, in that it calls the sense by the sound; it brings together words which often are thought separate". As the pun, the portmanteau and the neologism are very important lexical devices in nonsense, I will proceed to discuss them in separate sections.

2.3.4.1 *The Pun*

Hammond and Hughes (1978) make a distinction between puns and wordplay that is not always adhered to by other writers on the topic. In their first chapter (this curious little book has no page-numbering) they define *homophones* as words which sound the same but are spelled differently and have different meanings (e.g. "intense" and "intents"), and *puns* as ambiguous sentences which are created by using the sound of two different words (e.g. "The excitement of the circus is *in tents*"). *Wordplay* on the other hand is the creating of an ambiguous sentence by using *homonyms*, words that are spelled and sound the same, but have different meanings (e.g. "An architect in prison complained that the walls were not built *to scale*"). In wordplay, then, the requirement is that the meanings of the word played upon are etymologically linked.[19]

Both sentences given above (taken from Hammond & Hughes) are examples of what Hausmann (1974: 16-19, following Wagenknecht 1965: 20-1) refers to as *vertical* wordplay. In vertical wordplay, the word (or phrase) in question is used only once, with a scintillation between its two (or more) meanings. Should the sentences have run "The excitement in the circus was intense as well as in tents", or "The architect complained that the prison walls were built to scale but not to scale", the pun or wordplay would be *horizontal*.[20] As-

to self-confessed examples from Morgenstern.
19. Hammond & Hughes present a critical study of various dictionary meanings of these and related terms in chapter XXVI.
20. Hammond & Hughes (1978: X) call this an "untangled pun", which they compare to a simile, whereas the pun proper is more like

suming, as I do, that nonsense requires the non-resolution of the tension between the two meanings, or rather, between the possible meanings of the word and the absence of meaning created by their incompatibility, it will be readily seen that nonsense can only make use of the type of pun or wordplay called vertical. The exception is when a clear non-sequitur is presented, as in the ("proper") pun: "We called him Tortoise because he taught us" (Carroll, ed. Gardner 1960 [1965]: 127).

Incidentally, neither Hausmann nor Wagenknecht wishes to make the distinction between punning and wordplay that is insisted on by Hammond and Hughes, nor does Redfern (1984), who otherwise praises Hammond and Hughes as the "best study" on the subject (5). Hausmann calls the distinction between homonymy and polysemy a diachronic distinction, which is superfluous in a synchronic approach of wordplay (1974: 104). In fact, there is not so much a distinction between homonymy and polysemy as one between plurivalence and context-variance (108, and see the model presented on p. 106). "Mit verschiedenen Meinungen eines Semems kann man ein Meinungsspiel machen, mit verschiedenen Sememen eines Zeichens aber ein Wortspiel" (110). Wordplay must fit a context, and not be merely situational-linguistic; it must be a means to an end, not an end in itself (113). In my view, what is of importance in nonsensical wordplay or punning (I will presently revert to the distinction) is that it is the plurivalence that counts, and not the context-variance. There are, one might say, three reasons for punning: firstly to make a (good or bad) joke, as in much nineteenth-century punning; secondly to create a literary effect, excluding nonsense (as e.g. in Shakespeare's works); and thirdly, to create nonsense. In the first and second instances, there is either no tension at all to begin with, or the tension is resolved (I assume that the initial puzzlement presented to the recipient of a pun or wordplay is a form of tension, which the recipient is intended to see through and so resolve). In the third instance, although the recipient is aware that he is presented with a pun or a wordplay, he cannot come to a conclusion as to what is the point of the game, except that it is to continue to puzzle him. In this respect, I do find Hammond and Hughes' distinction useful, in as far as they state that the characteristic of the pun (in their limited definition) is irrational, and that of the wordplay rational (1978: I; cf. ch. XVI).

a metaphor. See also pp. 63-5 below.

In any case it will be clear that punning as one of the types of ambiguity discussed in Empson (3rd edn, 1955) (mainly as the Third Type) must here be left out of consideration, since the point about this type of ambiguity is that the ideas are connected by their mutual relevance within the context (117). Incidentally, Empson does touch upon nonsense very briefly on p. 21, where he ascribes the works of Carroll and Lear to the cult of vagueness adhered to by nineteenth-century poetry in general.

With Empson, we can also ignore for our purposes the otherwise very interesting classifications of the pun presented by Mautner (1931) and Brown (1956), neither of whom are relevant to the functioning of the pun in nonsense. The latter, in particular, makes it quite explicit that a pun which fails to link the contexts of either meaning is a "bad" pun (16). Indeed, "[t]he power of the pun-phrase lies in its simultaneous assertion of all its meanings" (24), but for nonsense this statement ought to be modified into the assertion of the tension between meaning and non-meaning.[21]

More relevant to our purpose is Gray's discussion of the pun in "The Uses of Victorian Laughter" (1966). He distinguishes two main uses of punning in Victorian humour: one of them is "to strengthen a serious point" (168), the other to reduce or frustrate significance "by preparing or recalling serious responses which turn out not to be required" (169). When puns are "frequent and forced, the pleasure lay not in relaxing an expectation of a serious meaning, but in recognizing throughout that this time the response ordinarily required will be inappropriate" (*ibid.*). He then goes on to say that "nonsense went a step further ... A pun requires a conscious awareness of the ordinary and expected meaning of the sound on which the pun is made. The writers of nonsense often play with the sounds of words, but they rarely pun" (170). I do not think the facts bear this out. What happens, in fact, is that the successful nonsense pun *simultaneously* strengthens a point *and* frustrates it.

The most useful approach to the pun as a nonsensical device is found in Nöth's *Literatursemiotische Analysen zu Lewis Carrolls*

---

21. Petzold, who as we have seen defines nonsense as a subcategory of humour (1972:2), denies that punning is a typical stylistic device of nonsense, since it does not lead to "nothing" but to another sense (41). Obviously, this view is based on the misconception that nonsense is to be equated with absence of meaning.

Alice-Büchern (1980). In two brief sections (27-31, 58-60) Nöth presents a clear semiotic analysis of the working of the pun in nonsense. The polysemy which is characteristic of a linguistic ambiguity, and which is ordinarily resolved ("aufgehoben", 27) in a special context, is used in the comic pun to send the reader to the "other" meaning. But in addition to that, the pun may often present an anomaly between two (or more) semiotic levels.[22] Thus, the "Tortoise"-"taught us" pun from *AW* could be explained as an anomaly of the type PX (biological level) = SZ (sociological level). It is the incompatibility between these levels in the one word/phrase that makes the pun nonsensical, and this also explains why homophonic puns are often preferred to homonymic puns, simply because in etymologically related words the chances that the levels are very different are smaller than in the case of completely unrelated words.[23]

On pp. 58-60 Nöth demonstrates how punning may lead to misunderstanding in dialogue situations, as when the frog-footman in *TLG* fails to understand what Alice means by "to answer the door", as he apparently takes this figurative expression literally. Absence of meaning (for the listener) is balanced with presence of meaning (for the speaker).

This brings me to my final point concerning the pun, its relation to the metaphor. We are here clearly in the field of what Blumenfeld describes as semantic and logical nonsense (1933: 25-30, 59-62). "Was einmal semantischen Sinn hatte, verliert ihn nicht. Auch wenn ein Ausdruck zur Phrase wird, wenn der Sprechende sich 'nichts mehr dabei denkt', der Hörer ihn als abgedroschene, inhaltsleere Hülse hinnimmt, selbst dann ist er *objektiv* Zeichen für einen Gegenstand, wenngleich für einen von beiden Partnern oder beide 'sinnlos', weil der Sinn nicht mehr 'vermittelt' wird" (29). However, when such an "empty" phrase is taken literally, a semantic tension arises, which, when unresolved, leads to nonsense.[24] Also, what is logical to one partner ("to answer the door" logically evokes the

---

22. See ch. 1, pp. 37-9, for a summary of Nöth's semiotic theory.
23. Obviously, this is not to be taken as a hard-and-fast rule.
24. Cf. also *op. cit.*, 30-2 on the relationship between partners in a dialogue. The "other", the recipient, may be oneself, or an animal. Such cases too seem to be nonsense-inducive, since no tension can be resolved. One does not answer one's own questions, nor would one expect one's pet to answer them, except in a very figurative sense.

question "What's it been asking of?") is not necessarily so to the other (Blumenfeld 1933: 58).

Redfern notes that "[l]ike wordplay, metaphor incites us to think, see and hear on more than one level concurrently, or at least with only a slight timelag, the time needed to seek the connection" (1984: 97). From A. Welsh, *Roots of Lyric* (Princeton 1978: 245) he then quotes: "When the pun discovers that two things, two different concepts, or two widely separate experiences bearing the same name also share deeper affinities, it is a metaphor." In nonsense, of course, this connection must *not* be made, and the time-lag must be of infinite length, or at least until the reader gives up.

Hammond and Hughes (1978: IX) demonstrate how puns can revitalize clichés, proverbs or truisms ("Any stigma will do to beat a dogma", or cf. Carroll's famous dictum, through the mouth of the Ugly Duchess: "Take care of the sense, and the sounds will take care of themselves"). Misunderstanding or reinterpreting an expression, word or phrase is very close to this. We are simultaneously invited to note the similarity, and to note that it should not be there.

A favourite quarry for nonsense in this respect are dead metaphors. An explanation for this can be found in a remark by Landheer (1984), who notes that dead metaphors possess a denotative plurivalence, whereas living metaphors contain a connotative plurivalence (23; cf. 26: "*La métaphore morte est un mot polysémique*", and 27: "La métaphore morte, lexicalisée, se prête ... facilement à des ambiguités intentionelles ..."). One has to choose, in fact, between a metaphorical and a non-metaphorical reading (30), which can be taken even one step further by positing that nonsense is frequently presented as a metaphor that "does not work", as literal meaning and figurative meaning are not allowed to meet by means of overlapping connotations. One could also say that the pun is the metaphor of nonsense.[25]

Hausmann distinguishes four types of metaphor: the poetical or "new" metaphor; the ritual metaphor (which is affective and vague); the historical or "dead" metaphor; the diachronic metaphor. Wordplay is only possible with the last three types, because these are "Bedeutungsmetaphern" (1974: 117-8), that is to say, they feature on a

---

25. Stewart classifies the dead metaphor taken literally as a form of inversion (1978: 77-80). Because of its proximity to the pun I prefer to deal with it here.

higher level (meta)linguistically speaking than the "Bezeichnungsmetapher" which is new. In nonsense one is bound to meet metaphors of these three types, but not those of the first type, for reasons which will have become evident.

2.3.4.2 The Portmanteau

Another common device in nonsense texts is the "portmanteau word", a phrase coined by Carroll, or rather by Humpty Dumpty in *TLG*.[26] Reichert (1974: 184) calls this device the quintessence of nonsense. It is a self-realization in the form of synthesis, prefiguring the ultimate self-realization of death, which is in its turn seen as a symbol or sublimation of the (failed) sexual act.[27] Deleuze has pointed to the disjunctive nature of the portmanteau (1969: 62). Divergence can be synthesized in three manners: connectively ("if ... then ..."), conjunctively ("both ... and ...") and disjunctively ("either ... or ..."). With the proviso that a balance, an unresolved tension between divergence and synthesis of meaning is maintained, one can regard these forms as three ways of creating nonsense as well. Connectively by means of neologisms or nonsense words (a non-existent word to indicate a non-existent being, quality or action, such as "Dong", "brillig" or "to galumph"),[28] conjunctively by means of the pun, and disjunctively by means of the portmanteau. If this "series" of Deleuze is to be taken any further, I would prefer to reverse the two latter, and take the pun as an example of disjunction, the suggestion being that either one or the other meaning must apply, and the portmanteau, in which two meanings are "melded" into one, as a form of conjunctivity.[29] Deleuze, however, is quite

---

26. Carroll, ed. Gardner 1965: 271: "You see it's like a portmanteau—there are two meanings packed up into one word."

27. Reichert is referring to the ending of Carroll's *The Hunting of the Snark*. The psychological aspects will be left until ch. 5.3.

28. See sections 2.3.4.3 and 2.3.7 below.

29. Hammond and Hughes in fact relate the portmanteau very closely to the "meld pun" (1978: XI, XXII), which they also regard as a form of neologism (XI). The rather arbitrary distinction hinges merely on the question how much of the compounding words is still retained in the meld. Thus, "alcoholiday" is called a "meld pun", whereas "brunch" (from "breakfast" and "lunch") is called a portmanteau. Holquist (1969/70: 160) regards the portmanteau also as a

explicit about the nature of the "mot-valise" as corresponding to a disjunctive synthesis (1969: 84). He fails to convince me of the validity of his statement that in a portmanteau each element defines the other ("Chaque partie virtuelle d'un tel mot désigne le sens de l'autre", 84). In as far as the portmanteau actually defines an existent phenomenon, as "slithy" is explained by Humpty Dumpty to apply to a creature which is both "lithe and slimy" (Carroll, ed. Gardner 1960 [1965]: 271), it is not nonsensical. I suspect that this word is in fact a neologism, and that the explanation that Carroll puts into Humpty Dumpty's mouth is itself nonsensical; after all, the creatures which the word is modifying, "toves", are themselves nonexistent, and their characteristics, if Humpty Dumpty is to be trusted, are nonsensically incompatible.

Hausmann mentions the portmanteau (the German term, quoted from Wagenknecht 1965: 21, is "Kontamination" or Hausmann's own more positive term "Wortverschmelzung", 1974: 64) under the heading of the complex lexeme (80), which is by its very nature a form of "vertical" wordplay (63, 79).

Terminologically, it seems most convenient to regard both the pun or paronomasia and the portmanteau as subcategories of (vertical) wordplay, the distinction being that whereas a pun is a word with two meanings, a portmanteau is two words which are collapsed into one meaning, so that a portmanteau is itself as it were the "inversion" of the pun. At the same time they seem to be identical. Sewell comments on Humpty Dumpty's definition of a portmanteau word that it would equally well fit that of the pun, since two meanings are packed up in one word (1952: 119, cf. 35-6). One might therefore regard the pun as the perfect portmanteau: instead of

combination of language and logic, in that it offers the precision or "truth" of the conclusion to a syllogism, which contains both its premises. "Carroll's portmanteaux are *words* and not gibberish because they operate according to the rule which says that all coinages in the poem ["Jabberwocky"] will grow out of the collapse of two known words into a new one" (161). For an analysis of the poem and a concentration on neologisms, portmanteaux and puns in Carroll and Lear, see Partridge (1950). See Redfern (1984: 82-102) for a survey of the types of wordplay related to the pun. For a classification and discussion of various types of "Wortverschmelzungen", see Hansen (1963).

linking or "melding" up two different words, the pun links or melds two identical-sounding words.

We will save up the neologism for the following section. At this stage we may draw the conclusion that wordplay is the most obvious form of play with language. As Walter puts it: "Das Wortspiel ... ist das eigentliche Spielfeld der Sprache" (1966: 59). Both the pun and the portmanteau create a tension, which is only resolved when and if the wordplay is the point of the statement, as in the works of Karl Kraus discussed by Wagenknecht or the satirical texts in the *Canard enchaîné* treated by Hausmann. The disparity of meaning rules out the connotations and associations of each single denotation, and so contributes to a lack of emotional involvement as well. They are by definition both playful and verbal. In other words, the pun and the portmanteau are to be considered prominent devices of nonsense literature.[30]

2.3.4.3 *The Neologism*

The neologism has the advantage that no connotations or associations are attached to it; it could combine *all* meanings—and *none*. Petzold, in fact, calls the neologism the only type of wordplay or linguistic humour (he also lists homophony, "word-splitting", ambiguity, grammatical analogies, puns, malapropisms, and witty interpretations; 1972: 40) which is typical of nonsense (41). Once again, this is a logical inference from his view of nonsense as the absence of meaning.

According to Petzold, the neologism must seem to make sense, it must appear to be a "normal" word, keeping to the laws of syntax, morphology and phonetics. Variants of the neologism proper are words used in an "original" (etymological), no longer current sense, in impossible collocations, or with suggested meaning (44). By way of example Petzold analyses Lear's "The Cummerbund" (45-6), a poem in which Indian words are used in a sense that has nothing to do with their original or actual meanings, and is merely suggestive of a would-be exoticism which the poem partly parodies.

---

30. Interestingly, Freud's three categories of dream-technique, "Verschiebung", "Verdichtung" and "Bildlichkeit" correspond exactly to the verbal use of punning, portmanteaux and taking metaphors literally. Cf. ch. 1. p. 17, n. 29 above.

It is in the realm of these "meaningless" words that the nonsense writer is omnipotent, since he can assign his own preferred meaning to the words he has himself created, or, as in the case of Lear's favourite "runcible", revived. The word "runcible" which is recorded in *Webster's* but not in *The Oxford English Dictionary*, is used by Lear of a hat, a goose, a spoon, a raven and a wall. Each time the modifyer is used a meaning is suggested, but since the word is used to modify completely disparate and unrelated nouns, the meaning is simultaneously denied.

Very often neologisms are used to denote non-existent creatures (a "Dong", a "Snark", a "Nasobēm"), which are subsequently described in more or less mimetic terms. Poems like "Jabberwocky" or "Das große Lalulā" are rare, because if used too accumulatively or even exclusively, the neologisms tend to turn into gibberish, with which the reader loses patience as there is too little semantic information to hold on to.

Strictly speaking, "neologism" is not quite a correct term, because it suggests the introduction of a new word into the language, which acquires a well-defined denotation, and subsequently may develop the connotations and associations which any word in a language is subject to. This more general use of the word is, of course, not applicable to nonsense.

Kretschmer has aptly illustrated the "logic" behind some of the nonsense neologisms introduced by Morgenstern, as in the poem "Anto-logie" (the title, of course, is a pun), where the series "Gigant - Zwölef-ant - Elef-ant ... Nulel-ant" is generated (1983: 172f.). The series itself is a fine sample of nonsensical play with infinity.

Redfern rather mixes up the categories of neologism and portmanteau (1984: 99), understandably, because the portmanteau is indeed a neologism in the sense that it is a "new" word. There is, of course, a clear distinction, in that portmanteaux can be traced back to the root-words of which they are composed, whereas the neologism proper is an entirely made-up word, without an etymological history, so to speak, as it is freely invented by its first user. As soon as it acquires a fixed meaning, as happened with Gelett Burgess' famous neologism "blurb" (see Jennings 1977: 75), it is no longer nonsensical, unless it is used, as any other word may be, in a nonsensical context.[31]

---

31. For a more detailed discussion of the nonsense neologism, see Sewell (1952: ch. 10) and Partridge (1950: 162-88, esp. 171-8, 182ff.).

2.3.5 Arbitrariness

The fifth "procedure" is that which Stewart has called "Arrangement and Rearrangement within a Closed Field", and which I more succinctly refer to as arbitrariness, or even more simply shuffling. As Stewart herself realizes, simultaneity is one of the effects of arbitrariness (1978: 171). The boundaries of the event are fixed (in contrast with play with boundaries or imprecision, where they are shifting, *ibid.*), and content is subordinated to form, the latter creating a spatial playground; this is the inverse of play with boundaries, where form is subordinated to content. Defined in this way, neither of these procedures can be properly nonsensical within the scope of my definition, because nonsense requires an unresolved tension between form and content. In any case, when form clearly dominates it is unrealistic to expect literature of any kind to emerge. What one does expect under this heading is a lot of "weak" wordplay (as opposed to the "strong" wordplay encountered under simultaneity), which is indeed the case. The devices listed by Stewart (1978: 173-93) are: the medley; variation and repetition (anagrams); syntagmatic and paradigmatic allusion (i.e. rearrangement of syntax or lexis, as in substitution, secret languages, texts appropriating the metonymic structure of a game—on p. 182 these are said to be the most nonsensical; examples of the latter are "doublets"); travesties (perversions of proverbs, parodies), and ready-made systems (mnemonic devices, alphabetical arrangement,[32] or arrangement by days of the week, months of the year etc.; ceremonial institutions such as tea-parties, law-courts etc.).

In my definition, the word "arbitrariness" is used in a very general sense, and it is perhaps the most general nonsense procedure in that it establishes the "playing field" of the nonsense poem or story: the serial form of the alphabet or of the geographical limerick, the quest or journey, and indeed the orderly setting of a law-

---

Curiously, Stewart does not mention this category at all; the only oblique reference seems to be given under the heading of the "sound poem", discussed in her chapter on Play with Boundaries (1978: 92).

32. Stewart speaks of "those two great nonsensical enterprises, the dictionary and the encyclopedia" (1978: 190; cf. Reichert 1974: 20). In fact, one would expect these arrangements to come under Play with Infinity.

court, a tea-party or even a labyrinth. It often features as a linking device, rather than the conventional devices of character-development or the unfolding of a feeling or of a plot, which is a history based on cause and effect. Simultaneity and infinity are closely linked with it, but subordinated in the sense that the rearrangement may lead to the collocation of the most unexpected objects or events, what Lautréamont has called "the chance juxtaposition of a sewing machine and an umbrella on a dissecting table".[33] Imprecision derives from the arbitrariness of the boundary itself, while negativity, as the extreme form of otherness, is perhaps the only aspect of a thing that is not *arbitrarily* different from it, so that it becomes a very precise manifestation of change of identity. And of course negativity or mirroring takes care of the dialectic, the tension which always operates between opposites, between objects or ideas and their negations or reversals.

If I have paid overmuch attention to the "procedures" discussed by Stewart, this is not because I agree on all scores with her classifications and sub-divisions nor because I agree that all these devices are equally contributive to what constitutes literary nonsense, but because the elements of arbitrariness and imprecision, infinity, simultaneity and mirroring do play an important role, and, as chapter 1 will have demonstrated, many scholars have hit upon the same devices, although they give different names to them or place different emphases. Thus, to give only one example, Sewell's seminal discussion of the topic is largely in terms of seriality within closed boundaries.

2.3.6 *An Illustration*[34]

At this stage, an illustration of what has been argued thus far in this chapter is called for. The following text is a posthumously published sonnet by Edward Lear:[35]

> Cold are the crabs that crawl on yonder hills,
> Colder the cucumbers that grow beneath,

---

33. *Maldoror*, tr. P. Knight, Harmondsworth: Penguin, 1978: 217.
34. This section is, with slight modifications, reprinted from Tigges (1986a: 167-70).
35. Lear, ed. Davidson & Hofer (1953: 63). For discussions of this poem see Liede (1963, I: 171) and Byrom (1977: 229-31).

And colder still the brazen chops that wreathe
    The tedious gloom of philosophic pills!
For when the tardy film of nectar fills
The ample bowls of demons and of men,
There lurks the feeble mouse, the homely hen,
    And there the porcupine with all her quills.
Yet much remains—to weave a solemn strain
That lingering sadly—slowly dies away,
Daily departing with departing day.
A pea green gamut on a distant plain
When wily walrusses in congress meet—
    Such such is life—

In this poem, so many images are offered that a multiplicity of meaning is clearly suggested. The sonnet form prepares the reader for a lyrical utterance, but no personal feelings are recorded. It is the crabs, the cucumbers and the chops (the first two linked by alliteration) that are cold, not the poet. All the same, a feeling of sadness, if not despair, seems to be clearly suggested by the repetition of "cold" and "colder" in the first three lines, followed by references to "tedious gloom", "tardy film", "demons", "feeble", "a solemn strain", "lingering sadly", "slowly dies away", "departing", and culminating in the exclamation "Such such is life". Lear makes use of the formulas of Romantic poetry and the Victorian ballad, to make it appear as if the state of nature reflects or is indicative of the poet's mood. "Quotations" from or at any rate echoes of and allusions to Pope, Tennyson, Wordsworth, Keats, Burns, Gray and Arnold have been traced by Byrom (1977: 230). The poem is not, however, primarily a parody of traditional lyrical poetry, but a certain amount of "arrangement and rearrangement" of a near-parodistic nature is present.

    The first quatrain, as the word "chops" indicates, is not so much a reflection on a cold landscape as on a cold supper. The crabs, cucumbers and chops, but also the nectar suggest simultaneously the remnants of a meal ("Yet much remains"), the effects of which must be neutralized perhaps by means of pills, and the animal, vegetable and liquid ("chops" in the sense of breakers of a choppy sea) aspects of a landscape which is only present in the mind of the poet, who surely cannot actually observe the crabs and cucumbers from his dinner-table, or from the homely surroundings suggested by the mouse, the hen and the porcupine, which are more likely to inhabit a garden. The key-phrase in the first quatrain is "brazen chops", which can be interpreted as "brass-coloured choppy waves", "impudent jaws", and even, one may wonder, "saucy slices of meat"? For this is how the nonsensical pun works. The reader wishes to know what are these "brazen chops" that "wreathe / The tedious gloom of philosophic pills!" In what sense can "chops" be said to "wreathe"? In what sense can anything be said to "wreathe" "pills"? And what are "philosophic pills"? The pills, perhaps, prescribed by (love of) medical wisdom? It could be that this wisdom is gloomy, then, or that the pills look gloomy, or cause gloom. These, and subsequent phrases are sonorous, but they are mere concepts and lack coherence. The rules of semantics are played with, and the first quatrain offers a new metaphor, creating a multiplicity of meaning, which is killed by any attempt at a "sensible" interpretation.[36] Is the gloom of cold nature presented in terms of a cold supper or is it the other way about? Is it either or neither?

The second quatrain consists mainly of a suggested contrast ("For when ... There lurks ..."), and an implicit series of disproportionality: things are too slow ("tardy"), too large ("ample"), too weak ("feeble"), too simple ("homely")—and too prickly, as witness the porcupine with *all* her quills. If the first quatrain is an extended pun, wordplay based on simultaneity of meaning, the second offers the arbitrary simultaneity as well as the seriality of a catalogue.

The first, sad and sentimental terzet is a return to the clichés of Victorian diction (cf. "yonder hills", "wreathe / The tedious gloom") and prosody, with its inner rhyme ("remains"—"strain", suggesting "pain" as well), the hesitant midline collocation "sadly"—"slowly", and the chiasmic conclusion ("Daily departing"—"departing day"—the first phrase more appropriate perhaps to a solemn *train*). Any meaning these lines may still convey is completely eliminated by the con-

---

36. Stewart (1978: 35) states that "nonsense results from a radical shift towards the metaphorical pole accompanied by a decontextualization of the utterance ... nonsense can be seen as an activity that replicates the activities of both play and metaphor in that it has to do with common-sense relationships brought into a paradoxical is/is not status." Metaphor, she continues to argue, is "rescued" from nonsense by contextualization. Without this contextualization, the metaphor ("like most nonsense ... a violation of the rules of semantics", 34) becomes a "dead" metaphor. Any "new" metaphor creates a multiplicity of meaning, but once it is interpreted literally, it is "killed".

cluding terzet: the "solemn strain" proves to be a "pea green gamut", a monochromatic scale, possibly produced by "wily walrusses" that meet in "congress", which may well present a *double entendre*, but is not supported by any such other textual evidence. The expectations of the probable collocations of the first terzet are frustrated by the completely unpredictable sequence of "pea green", "gamut", "distant plain" (to mirror "yonder hills"?), "wily", "walrusses", "congress" and "life", and, of course, by the fact that the poem is unfinished. Or is it? In view of the rhyme scheme, what is required at the end of the last line is a rhyme on /i:t/. In view of the abundant food-imagery (see section 2.4) "it's all the things we eat" would be a suitable conclusion, and we may wonder if the solemn strain that lingers sadly and daily departs after a cold supper on the terrace of Lear's San Remo villa, with a sound that is reminiscent of peas and resembles a meeting of walrusses, may have something to do with the poet's digestion.

If this is considered too far-fetched (or too nonsensical), I would suggest, by way of alternative ending, "—a poem incomplete". Such a statement, of course, would be "true", and therefore not to be included in a nonsense poem. But it would also be untrue, because if included, it *would* in fact make the poem complete. Could one think of a better example of empty space (both infinity and its reversal, nothingness) as a nonsensical device?

It will be clear, I hope, that in this poem, a fairly random sample of nonsense, meaning is suggested and taken away, leaving only the sense of isolation, which Sewell considers perhaps the only emotion permissible in nonsense (1952: 145). The expections of a Victorian sonnet, its sentimentality and wistfulness, are frustrated and shattered by its ultimate lack of coherence. This lack is created by Lear's play with thoughts rather than with words: none of the tricks of language that Stewart enumerates occurs in a direct form; the wordplay is the reader's activity, if he attempts to obtain any meaning at all from the poem. The sonnet does not feature as a secondary device, but is nonsensical as a whole: it is, in fact, "a nonsense".

2.3.7 *Some Final Notes on the Use of Language*

That the nonsense world is largely, if not purely, a verbal one is a conclusion which many authors have arrived at. Many of the devices enumerated by Stewart are purely verbal, such as palindromes, anagrams, lipograms, but also puns, portmanteaux and neologisms.

They are also frequently metafictional, in that they draw attention to the text as an artefact rather than a representation of reality.

I hope to have made it clear that nonsense "proper" requires a balance between form and content, between the words it uses and the reality, however nonsensical, behind these words. Needless to say, this balance can be of various natures, and I found an interesting "scale"-division relating to this aspect in Kretschmer's book on Morgenstern's Galgenlieder and their relationship with Victorian nonsense (1983). In a section to which I have already briefly referred on p. 42, the author discusses the Galgenlieder in terms of four, or rather five categories, which Kretschmer considers as "stages" of increasing freedom of thought. The first stage is that of the unusual in the real world, as when a chicken is signalled in a railway-station, where its appearance is indeed unusual, but not of course impossible. The second stage is that of the impossible in a real world, as when a horse enters a house, mounts the stairs and addresses the inmates. The third stage I wish to divide into two: the possible in an unreal world, and the impossible in an unreal world. The "Nasobēm", an "impossible" creature (which walks on its noses) is created from language ("Es trat aus meiner Leyer", Morgenstern 1933: 71). Interestingly, Kretschmer skips the stage of the possible in an unreal world, presumably because this would be a world of fantasy rather than one of nonsense.[37] The very reality of the possible would give some sense of reality to the unreal world.[38] Kretschmer's fourth state is that of unreal language in an unreal world.

In his further discussion of the Galgenlieder Kretschmer makes it quite clear that he regards Morgenstern as a poet who creates his own world (63, 159, 168-9), and that the Galgenlieder fulfil the basic rules of nonsense in that they are not satirical (114), nor parodistic (130), that they lack a "pointe" and are therefore not "jokes" (144). "Das Spiel der Galgenlieder ist kein Spiel mit der Sprache, sonder 'ein Spiel der Sprache in sich und mit sich selbst'" (156, quoting

---

37. On p. 217 Kretschmer lists eight scholars who all characterize Morgenstern's Galgenlieder as nonsense. The whole point of his book is to compare the similarities to the works of Carroll and Lear (218-20).

38. Perhaps the "astral" works of Paul Scheerbart, discussed by Liede (1963: I, 73-92) and Lang (1980: 65-82) belong to this category. I find them just short of being nonsensical.

Walter 1966: 59). Yet, in the first two stages this play with language is hardly noticeable. At the same time, in the third stage the reality of the world in which a "Nasobēm" can stride onwards on its noses is more than merely linguistic—one does not have the impression that one is the victim of a verbal trick. Where then lies the boundary of nonsense in these poems? If one tends to place it before State I, so that it includes "Das Huhn", I assume this is because the emphasis on "unpoetical" words like "Bahnhofhalle" and "Stationsvorsteh'r" seems to impress the reader with a strong sense of verbality. On the other hand, these are exactly the words which provide the realistic setting, clashing in their incompatibility with a quite different setting in which a "Huhn" may occur. Another nonsensical effect this poem has is its lack of connotation: neither the feelings associated with a station nor those accompanying a farmyard are evoked. The same goes for "Das Nasobēm". The words "Nase", "Kind" and the names of Brehm and Brockhaus are simultaneously indicative of reality and lacking in connotation because of their association with a non-existent, purely linguistic creature. The nonsense effect is reinforced by the inconsequentiality of the event (the creature is just striding, that is all), as well as by the circularity in the virtual repetition of the first stanza in the last.

I have enlarged a little upon this discussion brought up by Kretschmer, because it illustrates that language may work very differently in nonsense from what is suggested by Stewart's approach, and in fact very similarly to the way it operates in "regular" literature. I wish to make this statement here, so that I shall not have to touch upon it in my fourth, largely analytical chapter.

There is another omitted stage, which I want to discuss by way of conclusion to this section, and that is the stage of *unusual* language in a real or unreal world, a stage between that of the Nasobēm or Jabberwocky, where new words are created in an otherwise syntactically and lexically "correct" language pattern, and the stage of unreal language that features in "Das große Lalulā" or "Fisches Nachtgesang". I am referring to the type of language that occurs in Lennon's "Own Write", in the letters of Edward Lear, in Queneau's *Zazie dans le Métro*; the type of language which Sewell in her most recent article on nonsense refers to as "little languages" (1987: 185ff.), a term based on the language that Swift used from time to time in his journal-letters to "Stella". Oomen, in an article on the texts by John Lennon, introduces the concept of "nonsense English" (1967: 173)—one may, of course, theoretically just as well speak of nonsense French, German or any other language. Oomen's hypothesis is that the similarities between Standard English and Nonsense English are bound by regularities, which she proceeds to analyse (175ff.), and her conclusion is that Lennon's nonsense has become predictable by the second volume (192). I believe that Oomen misses a very important point here, which relates to the literary quality of Lennon's nonsense. One example will have to suffice. In "Araminta Ditch" (Lennon 1965: 53-6), Lennon spells the word "people" consecutively as "peofle", "peokle", "peojle" (53), "peoble", "peotle" (54), "peochle", "people", "peodle" (twice), "peomle" (55) and "peouple" (56). The heroine's name is consistently spelled the same, and her activity, which is to laugh, is consistently spelled as "larf". The effect this creates of contrasting a stolid personality whose behaviour is unaccountable to a vague and fickle crowd, comparable to the "they" in Lear's limericks, is not noted by Oomen, who merely lists the various changes of phonemes.[39]

Landheer briefly discusses Queneau's "zazismes" (1984: 89), which are "phonetic" spellings resembling the practice of Lear in his letters—Lear hardly ever used the device in his nonsense poems or stories.[40]

In my view, neither "little language" nor phonetic spelling is characteristic of nonsense literature, although it may be used, as by John Lennon, to underpin the nonsensical contents of a text. In fact, by drawing the reader's attention to the odd spelling, especially if it is (as good as) consistently odd, one invites him to apply a simple key or code, and thereby to resolve this tension between the expected spelling and what one finds on the page. With James Joyce, whose "Joysprick" resembles a "little language" in many respects, we are at the other extreme of a literary scale. His aim is a universality of language and meaning which meets nonsense at its opposite end, perhaps, but is certainly not meant to do so.

---

39. In any case, Oomen only discusses texts from Lennon 1964, which she considers superior to 1965.

40. As I do not consider Queneau's works as nonsensical in the strict sense, I have not investigated the secondary reading on his use of language. For references, see the bibliography in Landheer (1984), and cf. Redfern (1984: *passim*).

2.4 The Themes and Motifs of Nonsense

Several critics have noted the predilection of nonsense literature for certain themes and motifs, and its avoidance of others. Rather than summarize the views of earlier scholarship, I will in this section briefly enumerate the themes and motifs which I consider significant, providing references and brief examples as I go along. It will be seen that many of those themes and motifs are particularly conducive to the nonsense "procedures" discussed in the previous section.

To begin on the most abstract level, we find that nonsense has a great predilection for numbers and letters. Numbers with a highly symbolical value, such as three, seven or twelve, are usually avoided, or they are collocated with words containing no "sacred" or symbolical value of themselves ("twelve peaches", "If seven maids with seven mops ..."). More often the numbers are obviously random (the 4207 soldiers of the White King's army in *TLG*) or inordinately large ("In a moment the beautiful boat was bitten into fifty-five-thousand-million-hundred-billion bits, ...", Lear ed. Jackson 1947: 104-5). Another favourite is what Sutherland has referred to as the "Existential Treatment of the Null Class" (1970: 198ff.), as in the famous altercation between Alice, the Messenger Haigha and the White King about the running speed and visibility of Nobody in *TLG*, or as in Richard Hughes' story "Nothing" (1972: 65-7). This last aspect corresponds well with Sewell's view that nonsense tends to avoid nothingness (as it does everythingness; 1952: 124).[41] Like numbers, letters and even words can be put into series, reversed or negated, or shuffled around. Language itself is frequently a topic in nonsense, especially in that of the Carrollian kind.

On the physical level, prominent themes are those to do with cause and effect, with time and with space. These too can be reversed or rearranged. Beyond the Looking-Glass, time is reversed, and so the punishment precedes the crime, and pain the wound. In Flann O'Brien's *The Third Policeman* time is made circular and space flattened out. The voyage is normally a procedure in time and space; if one returns to the place of departure it is even circular in that respect. A voyage is episodic. The nonsense voyage or quest is

---

41. It does so, apparently, by giving it an identity. The use of number in nonsense has been amply discussed by the same author (1952: esp. 61-96).

therefore a very common motif in nonsense; both *AW* and *TLG* are examples of it, as is Lear's poem "The Jumblies", and as are his two nonsense stories.

Special forms of "rearrangement" of space are the labyrinth and the uncanny house—the latter is very common in the works of Edward Gorey, the former features often in Borges' *oeuvre*. Calvino has presented a series of "invisible cities" and a "castle of crossed destinies".

As to the matter of cause and effect, Hark has correctly stated: "In nonsense the link between cause and effect is always tenuous and frequently nonexistent" (1978: 117). In Lear's limericks, for instance, a motivation for the eccentric behaviour of the protagonists or for the specific reactions of "them" is hardly ever convincingly presented.

A crucial element in nonsense is that of identity. In establishing an identity, one by definition avoids both nothingness and everythingness. But in nonsense identity is highly insecure and erratic, and changes take place frequently: metamorphosis (baby into pig, or, linguistically but not less threateningly, cat into bat),[42] malformation ("There was an Old Man with a nose"), meeting oneself (or a hostile world) in a mirror,[43] and especially violence are frequent motifs. On the latter topic Sewell in particular has had a great deal to say.[44] It is characteristic of nonsense that all these threats to the identity are presented as a matter of course. The same goes for the common motifs of animals and things that are personified, or living creatures that are treated as objects. Consider for instance the Dutch nonsense poet Daan Zonderland's Marienbad Cook in doubt about whether to marry a mermaid or to stew her ("Zal hij haar stoven of zal hij haar huwen?").[45] Reichert associates the frequent occurrence of animals in the Alice books with a reference to aggression, and draws a link with the theme of metamorphosis (1974; 76-7). We have already seen that Stewart regards the personification of animals as a form of the inversion of classes (1978: 66).

---

42. On the theme of metamorphosis in *AW*, see Massey (1976: 76-97).
43. See Ede (1975: 71-2) for the different ways in which Lear and Carroll make use of mirror images.
44. See Sewell (1952: 138ff., and esp. 1987).
45. Zonderland (1982: 41).

Inwardly and outwardly the identity is sustained and modified by respectively food and clothing, two more nonsense motifs, which Sewell moreover links up with nonsense's preference for concrete nouns to play with (1952: 101; she also mentions furniture and houses here—furniture, of course, provides an identity to a dwelling-place). Curiously, both Deleuze and Blake, from entirely different angles, make a connection between the phenomena of eating and other nonsense activities, notably speaking (both being oral activities) and playing games. Blake, who discusses Carroll's manifold game-inventions, states that "[t]he model can be ... epitomized as follows: play—spontaneous, disinterested, non-utilitarian—is characterized by a fundamental urge to mastery through incorporation of experience to the ego rather than by adjustment or accommodation of the ego to experience ... the difference is between eating up life—for the pleasure, not the hunger—and being digested by it" (1974: 18).[46]

Inventing things is to change them, and to change the world. The invention therefore is another motif which is current in nonsense. To mind come Carroll's White Knight and Morgenstern's inventive characters Palmström and von Korf.[47] A neologism, of course, like a portmanteau, is a verbal invention. A particularly popular invention is that of the game, and this phenomenon features frequently as well,[48] as do other things that have to do with rules or laws, such as rituals, law-systems and law-courts, and logic. Language and mathematics, which have already been alluded to, come under this heading as well, as do the laws of nature, which are often flaunted. It is most interesting when the laws of gravity, relativity or entropy are upset or reverted, when pigs have wings, time stops altogether

---

46. On the theme of food, cf. also Empson (1935, in Phillips 1971 [1974]), who attributes the importance of rich foods in *TLG* to the fact that "it is the child's symbol for all luxuries reserved for grown-ups" (409). Boelens states that "[e]ating, but especially being eaten plays an important role in nonsense" (1987: 236). This theme needs further investigation.

47. See Kretschmer (1983: 64ff.) for a discussion of Morgenstern's inventors in the light of late 19th/early 20th-century science, and see ch. 5 below.

48. In games, the mirror motif is also often present in that one finds oneself mirrored in one's opponent, and one's pieces or cards in his.

(at "T-time"?) and a cake need only be cut up to be made whole after having been divided up into slices.

A ritual which nonsense is very careful about is that of courtship—which is always between ill-assorted or nonexistent pairs: an owl and a pussycat, or a Dong and a Jumbly-girl. Often it is avoided altogether, as in Morgenstern: "Weder Korf noch Palmström noch Palma Kunkel verlieben sich" (Kretschmer 1983: 99). Absolutely forbidden grounds are the themes of sex, feeling or emotion, God and religion, and beauty, but not, *pace* Sewell, love or death,[49] as long as they are not treated with emotions of either elation or horror. Kretschmer has noted the love of animals that transpires in the Galgenlieder (1983: 89ff.), and Lear's love of all being is very evident, as is Carroll's love of logic and order. It is the love between man and woman, and the whole area of eroticism, which is absent from literary nonsense.

The last theme to be mentioned is one closely related to pairing and courtship, the dance. Sewell devotes her final chapter to this phenomenon (1952: 183-94, esp. 189ff.), and she calls the Dance "half a game" (192).[50] Perhaps the reason why the dance is so important in nonsense is that it is one of the few rituals, if not the only one, which one can perform on one's own.

The purest examples of nonsense, such as Lear's limericks and many of Gorey's picture stories, are very close to the nursery rhyme, and both of these are close to the pure forms of Aristotelian *melos* and *opsis*, as discussed by Northrop Frye (1957: 275-8). These are respectively the aural and visual aspects which in literary art find their harmony as the structure of words: an equilibrium of rhythm and images in the word. Frye translates these terms into "babbles" and "doodles". In the "babble", rhyme, assonance, alliteration and wordplay develop from the free association of sounds. In this view, one first associates, for instance, "hills" with "pills" and "quills", which occur as rhyme-words in Lear's sonnet discussed in section 2.3.6, before a context is thought of in which these concepts are somehow brought into contact.

Rhythm, on the other hand, is a "physical pulsation close to the dance" as well as to the heart-beat, and is often filled with nonsense words, as in the refrain of a ballad. This also seems to be the

---

49. See also White (1969: 283).

50. Cf. Huizinga (1974: 161), who refers to the dance as constituting one of the purest and most perfect forms of play.

case with many of Lear's limericks. Here we find the recurrent rhythm of the anapaestic measure, the Old Men and Young Ladies from all over the world are chained in a chorus of absurd behaviour. The "dancing" quality often appears in the illustrations which are vital complements to the texts. The Old Man of the Nile, who cut off his thumbs when sharpening his nails with a file (note the motif of mutilation) makes a dance-step as he says: "This comes / Of sharpening one's nails with a file!" Dancing the laudable cook fishes the Old Man of the North out of the basin of broth (food and the threat of death) he had fallen into, and many other samples can be found (Lear, ed. Jackson 1947: 33, 25). Again and again, feet can be seen to be slightly raised from the ground, or just touching it with the tips of the toes, arms being thrown backward. Music and dance also play an important role in the texts themselves: the Old Man from Whitehaven dances a quadrille with a raven, others are dancing with a cat, or teaching ducklings to dance, thereby also exemplifying the motif of humanized animals. Someone plays the harp with her chin, another plays the lyre with a broom (she actually "sweeps" it, one of Lear's fairly scarce puns), yet others play the flute, the fiddle and the gong. It is not surprising that in his lecture "The Music of Poetry" T.S. Eliot thinks of Lear first (1953: 56).

2.5 *A Typology of Literary Nonsense*

Thus far I have described and analysed nonsense literature as if it were a homogeneous phenomenon, which is not quite the case. Any scholar who excludes the works of either Lear or Carroll from the nonsense canon (although he may have his preference) would have a hard job proving his case. Yet, the nonsense of Lear differs materially from that of Carroll, as has been noted by many critics.

Edmund Strachey in his pioneering survey mentions Carroll and Lear in one breath (1888: 339), but discusses only the latter at length, which may be because he had died in the year of publication, whereas Carroll was still alive. The first to actually compare the two grandmasters of nonsense was Chesterton, who notes in his "In Defence of Nonsense" that whereas Lewis Carroll's Wonderland is purely intellectual, Lear introduces an element of the poetical and even emotional (1901: 448). Similarly, in "How Pleasant to Know Mr Lear" he states that "Lewis Carroll's nonsense was merely mathematical and logical. Edward Lear's nonsense was emotional and poetical" (1953: 123-4).

Carolyn Wells has an opposing preference, but like Chesterton she regards both Lear and Carroll as nonsense writers. "Although like Lear's in some respects, Lewis Carroll's nonsense is perhaps of a more refined type. There is less of the grotesque and more poetic imagery. But though Carroll was more of a poet than Lear, both had the true sense of nonsense" (1902: xxvii). Most creative writers, like Eliot, Huxley, Orwell and Auden, seem to prefer Lear.

Emile Cammaerts (1925), who deals with both Lear and Carroll as nonsense poets, does not discriminate between them, and is attacked on this score by Alexander, who says that "if Edward Lear and Lewis Carroll are both purveyors of nonsense, then there is a very great difference between their kinds of nonsense" (1951: 554). On the same page he explains this attitude by noting that whereas Lear's nonsense as exemplified by the limericks "throws overboard all rules except the minimum ones of verse structure", Carroll's nonsense on the other hand "obeys rules, but rules which are different from our normal ones". His emphasis, of course, is on the logical basis of Carroll's humour (551).

Elizabeth Sewell too speaks of their "respective brands of Nonsense" (1952: 7). Lear's nonsense she calls "simple, concrete, descriptive and unconversational for the most part, with far more verse than prose. Carroll's Nonsense takes the form of consecutive narrative, with much more prose than verse, essentially conversational (...), and at times highly abstract and complex in its language." But she also notes their similarities, some concrete examples of which are adduced on pp. 8ff. Most of these are thematical rather than structural. The linking element, according to Sewell, is that of the nursery rhyme (12), to whose world both poets' works are said to be akin, albeit in different ways (14).

Further differences and similarities are commented on in the rest of the book. Thus, Carroll's nonsense is correctly stated to be more concerned with the process of language itself than is Lear's (18), which would explain why Carroll uses the pun more frequently than Lear does (20). The main similarity, of course, is that both Carroll and Lear are playing a game, which is the main theme of Sewell's book.

> The game of Nonsense may ... consist in the mind's employing its tendency towards order to engage its contrary tendency towards disorder, keeping the latter perpetually in play and so in check. The apparent disorder in the Nonsense World may be the result of such an encounter.

> ... It has already been suggested that order in the mind tends in the direction of number and logic, while disorder moves towards dream and nightmare (48).

Perhaps the main distinction between the Carrollian type of nonsense and that of Lear is that in the former the elements of number and logic are more prominent, whereas the latter is more dreamlike and, if not necessarily night-marish, is more fantastic and occasionally grotesque.

Hildebrandt too notices a difference between Lear and Carroll, which has not in his opinion been sufficiently emphasized by previous critics (1962: 136). As characteristics of Lear's nonsense Hildebrandt enumerates play with language, absurd reasoning, exaggeration, logical and material indifference, free association and total lack of direction (126). Carroll's nonsense is called the nonsense of the *ratio* (136).

On pp. 158-66 Hildebrandt extensively compares the nonsense of Carroll to that of Lear, mainly touching upon mutual influence. Some of the statements made here are unproven, as for instance the influence of Carroll's "Jabberwocky" upon Lear's "The Cummerbund" assumed on p. 164. An important statement, however, is that it is considered advisable to trace the nonsense of later authors to that of one of the two "grandmasters", although he is hesitant to speak of two "Hauptstränge" of nonsense (158).

Liede (1963, I: 157-204) treats Lear and Carroll as close relatives. Petzold, however, notes roughly the same differences observed by Sewell: "So wie Carrolls charakteristische Qualität auf dem erzählerischen Moment liegt, besteht Lears Stärke in der Bildlichkeit seines Nonsense" (1972: 29). Elsewhere he comments on the difference in style: "Während Carroll in der Regel eine sehr lebendige, abwechslungsreiche und natürliche Sprache zu verwenden bemüht ist, wirken Lears Sätze oft gewollt schwerfällig und schematisch" (47).

Ede contends that "[t]here are many distinctions that need to be made between the nonsense of Edward Lear and Lewis Carroll" (1975: 70). She mentions the different choice of literary genres, the different ways in which they use motifs (e.g. the mirror image), the fact that "[t]he world of Lewis Carroll's nonsense is more concerned with ideas than with action" (72), and that "[c]onversation is an essential weapon in Carroll's nonsense" (73). Similarities are noted as well:

Both present a fractured universe, one where "normal" causal [corrected from "casual", WT] relations are dislocated, where time and space fail to conform to ordinary expectations. A few of their characters do form social bonds, but these are almost always problematic; the majority exist in isolation, either literal or psychological. Although real or threatened violence plays an important role in their nonsense, the strongest threat to their characters involves mental suffering, despair, and the fear of the loss of identity. Ultimately, by questioning the adequacy of rational thought, Lear and Carroll challenge the possibility of meaning itself (73).

Prickett states: "Whereas the structure of Carroll's work is nearly always logical, in Lear's the structure is primarily *emotional*" (1979: 126). Later on he notes that "[t]o a twentieth-century observer, the apparent similarities of language and style may be more those of a period than of specific individuals" (130). However, "the actual bases of Carroll's nonsense were strikingly different from those of Lear. ... Whereas Lear's nonsense is one of emotion, nostalgia, and sheer buffoonery, Carroll's is one of undeviating rationality pushed to its furthest and wildest extremes" (131).

Kreutzer, finally, notes that "neben offensichtlichen Gemeinsamkeiten treten die Unterschiede zwischen ihnen [Lear and Carroll] mindestens ebensosehr hervor" (1984: 93). Lear's nonsense, he continues, "besitzt die stärkere Anschaulichkeit (...) und in seinem formelhaften Stil besonders sprachklangliche Qualitäten; Carroll operiert stärker mit logischen Verrätselungen und semantischen Spielereien" (93-4). He too discerns more emotional excitement in Lear, and a more rationalistic distance in Carroll.

All these critics, then, count both Lear and Carroll as the masters, if not the grandmasters or fathers of nonsense. The similarities as well as the differences are partly of psychological origin, a point which will be left until chapter 5.3. What is of interest here is that many critics have established a contrast between two basic types of nonsense, represented in particular by the purely intellectual, mathematical and semantical prose nonsense by Lewis Carroll on the one hand, and the emotional, musical and phonetical poetic nonsense by Edward Lear on the other. Must we in fact adhere to a binary typology?

That it is indeed a viable option to distinguish literary nonsense into a "Learic" and a "Carrollian" type is underlined if we consider the typology presented by Hildebrandt (1962). As has been mentioned before (p. 16), Hildebrandt distinguishes three types: folk nonsense, ornamental nonsense and literary nonsense, to which last category the works of Carroll and Lear are said to belong (74-5). I would like to re-align these categories as follows: literary nonsense finds its origin, or if one prefers to put it differently, its inspiration, in two earlier types of nonsense, which are less timebound: the popular type of irrational nonsense found in nursery rhymes, topsyturvy tales and similar ancient samples of inconsequentiality, in which the sound frequently does not care about the sense at all, and the ornamental, rational type of nonsense which plays around with the logic of language, and manifests itself in particular in the various types of word- and letter-play. In diagram form my main typology would look roughly as follows:

literary nonsense	
Lear-type	Carroll-type
↑	↑
folk	ornamental

What precisely constitutes the literary element in each type of nonsense can only be demonstrated hermeneutically, by means of concrete examples, and this will be done in chapter 4, where the dichotomy presented here will be largely adhered to. One of the aspects that is of relevance with regard to literary-aesthetic value has to do with a second dichotomy of nonsense, that between linguistic nonsense and situational nonsense. By linguistic nonsense I mean both the type of nonsense in which the tension between meaning and non-meaning is created by means of play with language elements and that in which a nonsense language is actually created (John Lennon's "Nonsense English"). Situational nonsense entails the creation of a nonsense-world—Wonderland, the land beyond the Looking-Glass, Morgenstern's world of Palmström and von Korf, where, unlike in fantasy (see ch. 3.5 below) no consistency is offered by way of foothold to the reader. The worlds of Kafka and Beckett, because of their heavily satirical or symbolical overtones, are just across the border of nonsense, while that presented in Flann O'Brien's *The Third Policeman* is just inside. Calvino's *In-*

visible Cities and *Castle of Crossed Destinies* could be said to be too purely ornamental to be nonsensical. The art is to combine the "popular" and the "ornamental", the linguistic and the situational in such a manner as to create that prefect tension, perfectly unresolved, which I consider the hall-mark of genre. In the next chapter I will demonstrate where in my opinion the border to another type of literature has been crossed.

At this stage the question arises whether a more refined typology than that of "Learic" versus "Carrollian" or "situational" versus "linguistic" is significant. Ignoring mixed forms as possible labels, and realizing that there will tend to be a fairly strong overlap between Carrollian ("ornamental") and linguistic nonsense, one could arrive at a rough mode, indicating the border-lines of the field of nonsense as well as its adjacent areas, most of which are to be discussed in chapter 3. This model, presented on the next page, should be regarded as a rough indication how the scales develop, rather than as a fixed and firm categorization of a handful of nonsensical authors. In any case, the best nonsense, as I intend to demonstrate in chapter 4, does not adhere to a fixed place on any scale.

There is one category I have not mentioned so far,[51] that which following Lang (1982: 62) I conveniently wish to call "partial nonsense". This term I would like to reserve for those literary works in which nonsense takes a considerable, but not a dominant part, as most prominently in those works where nonsensical devices serve a "sensible" aim. Partial nonsense may occur in parodies, satires, trickster stories and so on, and the occurrence of partial nonsense is less limited to a particular period in time than is nonsense "proper".

2.6 *Conclusion*

Except for more convincing readings and analyses, which are to be presented in chapter 4, I now hope to have made it clear what nonsense is and how it works. In nonsense, a fictional reality is created through language, which simultaneously represents this

---

51. Since the five categories presented by Blumenfeld (1933) are psychological rather than literary, I will not use them in this thesis to distinguish types or categories of literary nonsense.

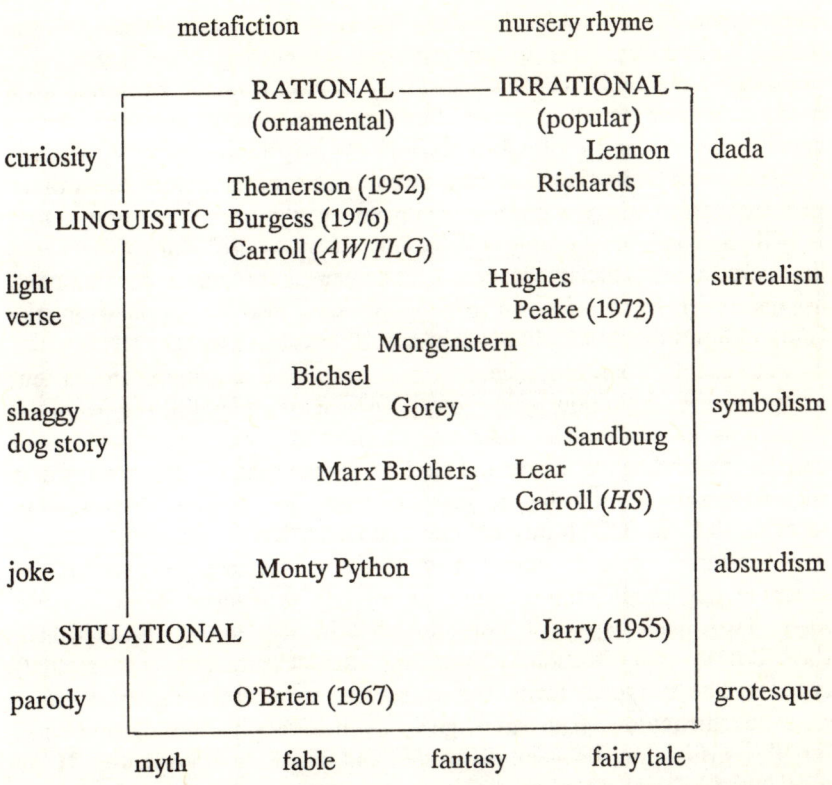

reality. The tension between reality and language, which is at the same time a tension between meaning and non-meaning, is what distinguishes nonsense literature from purely linguistic wordplay on the one hand, and from realistic or mimetic literature on the other. Moreover, as will be demonstrated in chapter 3, it distinguishes nonsense from types and genres of literature which are sometimes so closely related to it as to be confused with it.

One may call nonsense a form of ambiguity, as long as it is realized that this ambiguity is not between two or more related meanings only, but between meaning and its absence. In mimetic literature, the ambiguities that occur are resolved by relating the various possible meanings within the context, or by letting the context rule out meanings which are not desired. This is why it is more commendable to discuss nonsense in terms of genre than of a mode or device, each item being a context of its own, to which the rules of nonsense apply. Needless to say, in a wider sense of the word, the concept has to be regarded as moving on a scale from nonsense as a more or less subsidiary device through nonsense as a mode to nonsense as a genre. Fowler's requirement that one should regard genre as a flexible term, as a phenomenon constantly changing and adapting its own rules[52] can be adhered to without problem. By analogy with his treatment of the term "pastoral" (107) I will henceforth use the expression "a nonsense" for a nonsense limerick, sonnet, ballad, story etc. The stages of genre development, as discussed by Fowler on pp. 160ff., can also be applied to the genre of nonsense, but I will not explicitly discuss this aspect.

An "ideal" nonsense, then, is a text which conforms in its entirety to the definition given on p. 47. It must fulfill the essential conditions of unresolved tension, absence of emotional involvement and an upgrading of its verbal and/or formal nature. Its presence is signalled semiotically by at least one of the devices discussed in sections .3.1 to .3.5 of this chapter, and also by the predominance of one or more of the themes and motifs enumerated in section .4; these motifs should not acquire an overtly symbolical or associative load. Two main types of nonsense, finally, are to be distinguished, the "Learic" (or irrational) type and the "Carrollian" (or rational) type.[53] These types form the extremes of a scale rather than a clear-cut dichotomy. The same goes, by the very nature of nonsense, for the distinction between linguistic and situational nonsense. If an ideal type of nonsense exists, it is presumably to be sought for in the middle of a field that includes both linguistic and situational nonsense, and both rational and irrational aspects.

If nonsense is a game (but is it really more of a game than any other type of literary fiction?) it should be kept in mind that what is essential about this game has been stated very aptly by Huizinga in his *Homo Ludens*: in games and play ("spel"), it is not the result that counts (in the case of nonsense: to obtain "meaning") but the process (the maintaining of tension in nonsense). For the players themselves, the result does count—the game has to be won (1938 [1974]: 48). Perhaps the nonsense-writer is a *false* player of the

---

52. He states that "to mean anything distinctive in a literary way, a work must modulate or vary or depart from its generic conventions, and consequently alter them for the future" (1982: 23).

53. I prefer the terms "irrational" and "rational" to Hildebrandt's somewhat confusing terms "popular" and "ornamental" in this context.

game of language, but he is not a spoil-sport, who *breaks* the game (cf. Huizinga 1938 [1974]: 51). In a figurative sense, Francis Huxley's definition of nonsense as "a logical game played with feeling by at least two people in a spirit of self-contradiction, in such a way that one thing leads to the other to the constant surprise and mutual enthusiasm of both parties" (1976: 10) comes as close to a summary of my thesis as can be desired.

In this chapter I have been mainly fastidious, and it is high time to become more concrete. My first steps on the road to literary analysis will be on the line of negativity, a solid nonsense procedure, but then it is one of the aims of this study to demonstrate what nonsense is *not*, which, as has been remarked by Cammaerts (1925: 8) is perhaps far easier than to say what nonsense *is*. The next chapter will attempt to clear up a few confusions as to mistaken identities of literary nonsense.

CHAPTER 3: WHAT NONSENSE IS NOT

The table presented on p. 87 was intended to mark roughly the "field" of nonsense, fencing it off from various types of literature which, although in some cases closely related, are not to be confused with literary nonsense. It is the aim of this chapter to make more explicit the delineation between nonsense proper and that which is not properly nonsense, making use of the definition presented in the previous chapter. I will only discuss those terms which have been frequently used in close connection with nonsense or even in, mostly superficial, equations. Thus, terms like "myth", "fable" and "fairy tale" will not be dealt with in separate sections, since these terms, so far as I am aware have not been confused with that of nonsense (except, of course, occasionally with nonsense in the vulgar meaning of "rubbish" or "not to be believed in", "not to be taken seriously").[1]

To avoid infinite regression, in most cases the concepts to be distinguished from nonsense will be taken as understood, and I will mainly use generally accepted, "commonsensical" definitions of them, occasionally culled from or based on standard works on the subject. I will not go into definitional controversies between students of these concepts. Obviously, if the reader wishes to adhere to a basically different definition of what I shall define as a joke, a nursery rhyme, light verse etc., this is quite legitimate, and even in that case the distinction between nonsense and the other term should be clear-cut. Only in the first section, which deals with the relationship between nonsense and humour, will a variety of views be discussed.

3.1 *Nonsense and Humour*

The relationship if not the identity between nonsense and humour have been frequently noted. Strachey called nonsense "the flower and fruit of Wit and Humour" (1888: 336), and Wells accords Nonsense its place between the divisions of Humour (1902: xxxi). Cammaerts states categorically that "Wit and Nonsense are arch-enemies"

---

1. But cf. Hildebrandt (1962: 70) and Kreutzer (1984: 62) for a discussion of the fairy tale techniques featuring in nonsense. See also Cammaerts (1925: 19, 30ff.). For a succinct criticism of Hildebrandt's view, see Petzold (1972: 16-19); see also section 3.5 below.

(1925: 82). Nonsense, according to him, evokes "uproarious laughter" (83), and it is the "broad humour" which the English delight in that predisposes them "to appreciate the freaks of the Nonsense spirit, and to enjoy a joke even if there is no point in it" (74). These three early references make it quite clear that a confusion of terms is to be untangled.

Words like "humour" or "humorous" are associated with nonsense by Alexander (1951), Hildebrandt (1962: esp. 38-68), Sutherland (1970: 15, 69, 183-4), Laffay (1970: esp. 140ff.), Petzold (1972: 2, 19-58), Hofstadter (1982: 20) and Kretschmer (1983: 78ff.).[2] Schöne speaks of nonsense as a genre of *comic* literature in England (1954a: 102; cf. 1954b: 132), but in view of the title of her first article she does not seem to regard "Humor" and "Komik" as separate concepts. Hildebrandt does make the distinction, and so does Kretschmer (1983: 80; see p. 92 below). Petzold calls nonsense at the same time a "Sondergebiet des literarischen Humors" (2) and nonsense poetry "nur *komische* (bzw. humorvolle) Unsinnsdichtung" (24), but on p. 24 he expresses doubt as to whether nonsense is really to be considered as a category of the comic. Tabbert, like Schöne, calls nonsense a special form of the comic (1975: 11), and Rackin finds the Alice books comic (1976: 6, 15). Kreutzer speaks of "die spielerische Sprachkomik des Nonsense" (1984: 74). Harmon classifies nonsense as *witty* (1982: 73).

Contrary views, however, are also held. Thus, Sewell argues that "much that happens in the world of Nonsense is not comic at all" (1952: 6). Walter states of the Galgenlieder that they are not primarily comic or humorous (1966: 118-9). Noakes, discussing Lear's poetry, says that humour is not a necessary ingredient of nonsense (1968: 225). Reichert says that laughing at nonsense is the result of misconception (1974: 14), and he notes a resemblance between nonsense and humour rather than an identity (11, 104), and Stewart shares his view that nonsense *resembles* the work of humour (1978: 37). Baacke says that "Nonsense ist kein Witz oder eine Anekdote", but can be part of one (in Dencker 1978: 369). Lang states that the comic should be distinguished from the nonsensical (1982: 10).

2. Alexander and Sutherland discuss Lewis Carroll's Alice books and demonstrate how humour is created there. Hofstadter notes that nonsense was always funny up to the twentieth century but that "nonsense and humor took widely divergent paths early in this century" (*loc.cit.*).

Before we are able to discuss the merits and demerits of the statements quoted or referred to above, we must first sort out the terminological confusion that seems to surround the words "humorous", "comic" and "witty", a confusion which is partly enhanced by the non-equivalence of these English words with their etymological relations "humeur", "Humor", "Komik" and "Witz".

The problem, in fact, is that no universal definition of humour exists (Kretschmer 1983: 80). It would need a separate dissertation, if not a complete branch of study (Kretschmer, *loc.cit.*, suggests a new discipline under the name of Gelotology) to unravel the nature and variety of humour and related concepts. The humorous elements discussed by Kretschmer in connection with Morgenstern (who often described his Galgenlieder as "humoristisch" or "humoristisch-phantastisch"—Kretschmer 1983: 77-8): sovereignty, or superiority, and love, provide a lot of insight into the nature of these Galgenlieder, which could be similarly applied to the works of Lear, Carroll, and others. They do not, however, explain why these works are nonsensical.

Both Kretschmer (1983: 80) and Petzold (1972: 19) refer to the extensive discussion of the relationship between nonsense and humour by Hildebrandt (1962: 38-68). In fact, Hildebrandt initially creates more confusion than clarification in this matter. Beginning to define the comic as an aesthetic category (following Romantic theorists), he describes humour, irony and wit ("Witz") as forms of the comic (39), and parody, travesty and satire as means to a further aim (40). Thus, for instance, irony must have a "sense", which nonsense lacks (41). The Alice books, he maintains, show an ironical attitude throughout, the moral being that one must be constantly aware of what one is saying (42), and therefore according to Hildebrandt in Carroll's works the nonsense serves an ironic aim (45); in other words, nonsense here features as a quality, it is ornamental. In my opinion, it is just the other way about, and Hildebrandt fails to see that an ironic interpretation of *AW*, as is a satirical or allegorical one, is only one possible reading. That this is so is demonstrated later on, when Hildebrandt comes to talk about satire and parody. He disagrees with Empson's thesis voiced in "The Child as Swain" (1935), that *AW* contains "straight satire", on the unproven grounds that there is no relationship between nonsense and satire (45), whereas nonsense and irony are said to be complementary (*ibid.*). Referring to the poem "To the Looking-Glass World it was Alice that said..." in *TLG* (Gardner 1960 [1965]: 329-30), Hildebrandt says that "Carrolls Verse sind eindeutig eine Parodie auf

Scotts Gedicht" (48), but also that Carroll makes parody subservient to nonsense (49). Why this is not also the case with the irony in the Alice books is not made clear. At the same time, Hildebrandt calls Lear's nonsense exceptionally "pure", whereas the longer poems are regarded as parodies of Romantic and Victorian lyricism.[3]

Matters become clearer when Hildebrandt comes to talk about the joke, the shaggy dog story and the riddle. Nonsense and jokes are both forms of play (52). The difference is that whereas the joke has a "point", nonsense has not, and this, I think, is indeed the essential distinction.[4] This point being established, it is enlightening to consider that the pun, as well as the paradox (respectively play with language and play with logic) are in between the joke and nonsense (55, 58). If the pun or paradox or the surprise they create are the point, what we are dealing with is a joke, and not a nonsense. It also explains why the shaggy dog story, the joke with a "weak" point, is close to nonsense: after all, a weak point is closer to no point than is a "strong" point as made for instance in the witticism. In the same way a riddle can be distinguished from a nonsense: if the riddle has a solution it is not nonsensical; the solution is the point of the riddle (61). It may be a serious solution or a humorous one, as in the conundrum, and it may even be an ambiguous one. Hildebrandt's conclusion is a good starting-point to distinguish nonsense from the joke and the riddle: "Nonsense erscheint eben vielfach als auflösungsloses Rätsel bzw. als pointenloser Witz" (62).

What, then, is the relationship between nonsense and humour? According to Hildebrandt, the eccentric characters that nonsense seems to favour can be seen as "humours" in the sense in which Ben Jonson used this term (64). Following Lipps, humour is defined as an emotionally determined attitude (66). Nonsense, like irony, satire, parody and joke, is a "Komikart", in which humour can but need not be expressed. Nonsense is an "intellectual" phenomenon, rather than an "emotional" one. It is and remains a game, whereas humour is also a philosophy (67).

3. See e.g. Liede (1963: I, 169), and the many echoes noted by Byrom (1977: 151-231).
4. Cf. Walter (1966: 95); Ede (1975: 13). Cf. also Cammaerts (1925: 7), Liede (1963: I, 166), Petzold (1972: 135), Byrom (1977: 120), Prickett (1979: 95) and Lang (1982: 40) on the pointlessness of Lear's limericks, and Walter (1966: 95) and Kretschmer (1983: 144) on the similar effect of Morgenstern's Galgenlieder.

Rein formal gesehen entspricht der Nonsense als untendenziöse Darstellungsweise den Bedingungen ästhetischer Betrachtung weitgehender als diejenigen Komikarten, die Mittel zum Zweck sind, doch ist er darüber hinaus ein Spiel mit Formen und Inhalten, ein Träger außerästhetischer Werte. Und erst dieser Zwittercharacter—formal Komik-Kategorie, inhaltlich Humor-Kategorie—macht sein Wesen aus (68).

Hildebrandt's argument enables us to distinguish nonsense from other "Komik-arten", but it does not explain why nonsense is humorous; neither is a satisfactory answer to this question presented by other theorists. Schöne points towards the shifts of perspectives which Carroll applies to create humour in his Alice books (1954a: 107-13). Laffay states that humour reviews the incongruity or oddity of things or events (1970: 141), whereas "le *nonsense*, c'est l'humour lorsqu'on le dirige vers l'utilisation déréglée, ou du moins l'emploi autonome, du langage' (153). In other words, he sees nonsense as linguistic humour. Carroll, indeed, creates the playful mood in which linguistic as well as logical fallacies, in ordinary conversation or communication a nuisance, become funny (cf. also Alexander 1951: 555-6). Presumably Deleuze means something similar when he labels humour the "coextensivité ... du sens et du non-sens" (1969: 166). Carroll's humour, then, arises from the exploitation of the ambiguities in language.

Petzold first classifies nonsense as a "Sondergebiet des literarischen Humors" (1972: 2), but later he argues that it is not at all certain whether nonsense is really to be considered as a category of the comic (21, *contra* Hildebrandt). On p. 24, however, it is stated that nonsense poetry is "nur *komische* (bzw. humorvolle) Unsinsdichtung". Petzold's contribution to our understanding of the comic is his insight that an utterance can be comic only when it is addressed to a subject who is able to recognize something as comic (20). Nonsense can only create this effect if it shows a relation with the sensible world (22); hence, "[e]ine Aussage, die sowohl komisch als auch unsinnig sein will, muß sich in einem Schwebezustand zwischen dem Sinnvollen und dem Unsinigen befinden" (*ibid.*). To overcome this dilemma, Petzold introduces the distinction between "Unsinn" and "Nonsense"; the latter is "diejenige Art von Unsinnsdichtung, die zugleich komisch ist" (24). Since Lear's sonnet "Cold are the Crabs" is not comic at all (23, 74), this poem is presumably "Unsinn" but not "nonsense", a qualification which I am unwilling to accept, as my analysis of this poem on pp. 70-3 will have made clear.[5]

I have given a quite extensive survey of the most important studies of the relationship between nonsense and humour, to demonstrate that a juxtaposition of terms like humour, comic, wit, irony etc. to nonsense and "Unsinn" is not a very fruitful way to elucidate their relationship, because the conclusions arrived at by the various authors depend on a subjective definition of these terms. If my definition of nonsense is valid, it will be easy to see how "a nonsense" can be distinguished from an ironical statement, a satire, a parody, a joke, a shaggy dog story, a riddle and a conundrum. Nonsense, as has been argued in the previous chapter, presents a balance between meaning and non-meaning, and therefore lacks a point or unambiguous explanation. In irony, the balance is between a meaning and its opposite, which is not the same as non-meaning. "You're a fine fellow" ironically means "you're *not* a fine fellow". Satire has the point of attacking or showing up an undesired situation or event. Parody satirizes a subject-text, whose weaknesses (usually formal) come under attack. A joke, and even a shaggy dog story, has a point; the tension is released when we see what the joke is about, just as the tension in a riddle is released when we see what the solution is.[6] Compare the following two texts:[7]

(1) HOUSEWIFE: "Have you the time?"
    ICEMAN: "Yes, if I can find somebody to hold the horses."

(2) GROUCHO MARX: "I would horsewhip you if I had a horse."

The first sample is a joke. Our expectation (ICEMAN: "Yes, ma'am; it's twelve o'clock" or something like that) is frustrated ("I have the

---

5. In his discussion of the comic element of nonsense in this narrow definition (pp. 19-58), Petzold deals with many of the devices also found in Stewart's description of nonsense, such as incongruity, failing causality, triviality, play with language. Petzold also distinguishes nonsense from parody, to which it has a closer affinity than to irony or satire (53).

6. For completeness' sake one should also make mention of Irish bulls and malapropisms. These clearly differ from nonsense in that they have points, albeit (pretendedly) non-intentionally.

7. The examples are from Eastman (1937: 55, 26-7).

time for making love"). The "taboo" element enhances the humorous quality. Sample (2) is nonsensical. Here too, our expectation ("whip" for "horse") is frustrated, but the whole statement comes to nothing. Why a horse? Why-a-no-duck? Why is a raven like a writing-desk? It is, as Eastman rightly says, "the holding out of a meaning and then snatching it away" (1937: 27).

The distinction is clear, but the examples also illustrate the relationship between nonsense and humour. In both cases, expectations are frustrated, and this in itself is a hall-mark of humour. We do not need Bergson's superiority theory or Freud's relief theory[8] to see that, once we have heard the joke, the "fun" or "humour" of sample (1) will only remain when we retell it to another person, whereas the tension in the nonsense of sample (2), being unreleased, keeps us spell-bound. To call nonsense a form of "economy of mental effort", as Nicolson does (1956: 36-7) is plainly begging the question. It is equally clear that in order to appreciate either sample as humorous we must be in a playful mood.[9] If one is not, the frustration of one's expectations may be far from humorous.

Since the tension in a nonsense text is not released, laughter need not necessarily be the result of our contemplation of a nonsense, and I suspect it is this fact that has caused some confusion as to whether or not nonsense is a humorous or comic category. If we see that the point of Lear's "Cold are the Crabs" or Peake's "O'er Seas that have no Beaches" is that there is no point, we may laugh at that fact, but neither the events recounted nor the language in which they are described is humorous, comic, witty or ironic. We are delighted by the clever play with language and logic in Carroll (at least Schöne, Alexander, Hildebrandt and Kincaid among others are). Rackin (in Guiliano 1976) even argues that Alice's escape at the end of *AW* is a "comic resolution" (6, 15). Unless Rackin means this in the medieval sense, where "comic" practically amounts to showing a happy ending (Carroll had to let Alice reenter

---

8. See Bergson (1900), Freud (1905 [1976]) for early authoritative discussions of humour. It is beyond the scope of this thesis to enter into these interesting theories. For a brief but comprehensive survey of the most important theories of humour and laughter see Milner (1972).

9. Nicolson is right of course in emphasizing the playfulness of nonsense (27, 46). Cf. Sewell (1952 *passim*). For a perceptive criticism of Nicolson's essay see Martin (1974: esp. n 35).

the normal world to soothe his child audience) I cannot see the truth of this remark at all. Alice just literally stops "playing the game", when she exclaims: "You're nothing but a pack of cards!" Rackin, like Ede, notes the polarities which Carroll creates, "polarities of sense vs. nonsense, consciousness vs. the unconscious, waking vs. dreaming, reality vs. fantasy, adult vs. child, narrator vs. protagonist, teller vs. doer, delight vs. fear, order vs. chaos, humor vs. wit,[10] and laughter vs. tears" (1976: 15; cf. Ede 1975: 12). The point is not that these tensions are humorous—Rackin admits that to most child readers they are not (3)—but that they are unresolved: we do not know whether to laugh or to cry. In fact, one could very well turn Rackin's theory upside down. The puns and similar "jokes" in the Alice books are obviously meant to amuse children. They are bound to find the linguistic "point" of altercations like "to answer the door"—"what's it been asking of?", or statements like: "Lessons are called lessons because they lessen" very funny, whereas most adults may feel these jokes are rather stale, and in any case exemplary of the "atrocious pun". But Rackin admits that "few children find the book [*AW*] amusing" (3). The adventures, which children are said to find frightening (which is indeed frequently the case), Rackin calls "witty", and these are supposed to appeal to the adult reader (7). The point, however, is that they are not so much horribly comic or comically horrific, but realistic in spite of the fact that they are almost entirely based on linguistic trickery. The plot and plot-episodes are "there", and yet they are "only language"; they come to nothing when the language changes. It is *that* tension that we may find humorous, and which constitutes the nonsense of the Alice books.[11]

"Cruelty, pain, irrationality, death, the savagery of nature beneath civilized man: these are recurrent topics in Victorian humor" (Gray 1966: 167). This tallies with Eastman's view of the joke, which he states is a process "composed of unpleasant experiences playfully enjoyed" (1937: 57). If we consider the themes and motifs of non-

---

10. Humour is said to be warm and sympathetic, whereas wit is the opposite (1976: 7). Cf. Martin (1974: 3), where humour is associated with feeling, and with with reason; humour laughs *with*, wit laughs *at--(ibid.:* 30).

11. Cf. also Flescher (1969/70: 143). There she states that according to her investigations "[t]he children who appreciated the fantasy [of *AW*] also tended to appreciate the humor".

sense as enumerated in chapter 2.4, we see that indeed nearly all those themes are to do with unpleasantness: the disorder of mathematics, language and logic, the labyrinth and the uncanny house, time reversing, stopping or flying by, changes and uncertainty of identity, including malformations of the body and death, violence, ill-matched couples, personification of animals and objects and reification of human beings, unlikely foodstuffs ("Put cats in the coffee and mice in the tea"), eccentricity and queer dancing—all these are very often covered by humour as well.[12] The only theme not shared by nonsense and humour alike is that of sex.[13] Apparently this is a topic nonsense refuses to set up as a game, and which it is in any case difficult to sustain in unreleased tension.

From the above it should have become clear that humour and nonsense are not identical (a position which no one holds in its extremity), but that there may well be certain overlaps. The essential question when considering a text is whether the humour is subservient to the nonsense or the other way about. In the first case the ultimate tension between meaning and non-meaning is not released, in the latter it is. Nonsense need have neither comic form nor humorous content, as Lear's "Cold are the Crabs" easily demonstrates. Thus, one may distinguish "nonsense jokes" and "humorous nonsense" as special categories of the joke and the nonsense. It may even be in rare cases that the two are completely balanced, thus creating a new tension of polarities. Consider the following poem by Morgenstern (1933: 153):

> Palmström legt des Nachts sein Chronometer,
> um sein lästig Ticken nicht zu hören,
> in ein Glas mit Opium oder Äther.
>
> Morgens ist die Uhr dann ganz "herunter".
> Ihren Geist von neuem zu beschwören,
> wäscht er sie mit schwarzem Mokka munter.

---

12. See Gray (1966: 167ff.) for a very perceptive analysis of the close correspondence between Victorian humour and Victorian nonsense.

13. But cf. of course the psychoanalytical approaches of various nonsense works and their authors. See e.g. Lennon (1945 [1967]), and various articles in Phillips (1974, section 7) on Carroll, and Byrom (1977) and Hark (1982) on Lear.

Is this a nonsense or a joke? One might consider it as a literary joke on the silliness of supposing that one can silence the ticking of a watch by dipping it in ether, and bring it back to consciousness by washing it in black coffee. The logic of the second terzet resolves the tension created in the first, the very point being reserved for the very last line, even the last two words. One is reminded of Carroll's Mad Hatter, who more inconsistently oils his watch with butter, so that it runs two days slow. Dipping it in tea does *not* help (Carroll ed. Gardner 1965: 96). Carroll's episode is more obviously nonsensical than Morgenstern's, yet in the latter's poem too there is an inordinate amount of incongruity.[14] Palmström's action is trivial in its over-exertion; he might just as well have covered up his watch, or bought one which does not make a sound. But the main inconsequentiality lies in the fifth line: why is restoring a watch to consciousness referred to as conjuring up its spirit? The word "beschwören" is ambiguous, meaning "to allay, to charm" as well as "to conjure up". In any case the watch is given a spirit of its own, which means that putting it to sleep with opium or ether and waking it up with black coffee is not so silly after all. Is the tension ultimately released or not? Morgenstern has apparently created a tension between taking the poem as a joke or not taking it so, and *this* tension is not released. A borderline case like this one falls to the side of nonsense—and we may well find that humorous.

Nonsense is meta-humour in the sense that the expectation that an expectation will be frustrated is frustrated. As Gray remarks, "nonsense does end in laughter" (1966: 175), but not because the paradox has been solved or the point seen. Laughingly, we give up—to return another time to the same puzzle.

3.2 The Nursery Rhyme

"It is to the nursery rhyme that we owe the nonsense songs", states Cammaerts in *The Poetry of Nonsense* (1925: 3). Cammaerts, who considers the child the best judge of what is nonsense (17), describes in his second chapter how the origins of nonsense literally lie in the nursery (19). Schöne too finds early samples of nonsense in

---

14. Flescher (1969/70: 143) calls the incongruity of the nonsense paradox rather than its tension the key to the humour in *AW*.

the nursery rhyme (1954a: 103; cf. 1954b: 133). Hildebrandt classifies the nursery rhyme as an early type of nonsense under the heading of "Volks-Nonsense" (1962: 74). "Der Volks-Nonsense der Nursery Rhymes ist die entscheidende Vorbedingung für die Ausbildung des literarischen Nonsense" (243). Petzold agrees with Hildebrandt (1972: 81), and moreover points out how the inconsequential maxims and morals attached to the nursery rhymes in John Newbery's *Mother Goose's Melody* (1760) lifted the collection to the level of nonsense for adults. He goes on to state categorically that "[d]ie Bedeutung der Nursery Rhymes für den literarischen Nonsense kann kaum überschätzt werden" (83). Both Lear and especially Carroll were clearly inspired by them (83, 180).[15] Since Lear and Carroll wrote primarily for children this need not be surprising. Benayoun also draws the link with children and their "sens inné de l'incongru" (1977: 16) which is expressed in counting rhymes and nursery rhymes (17). Dencker, referring to Liede (1963), places the nursery rhyme ("Kindervers") more precisely in the historical development from meaningless refrain through sign without significance to play with language material (1978: 6). Stewart mentions nursery rhymes as fitting into a "nonsense tradition" in folklore and literature, and like Cammaerts she points to the occurrence of nursery rhymes and their characters in *AW* and *TLG* as well as in more modern literary works (1978: 51-2). Kreutzer situates Lear's and Carroll's works within the context of the rise of the literary fairy tale, the nursery rhyme and the fantasy as well as the culture of light entertainment (1984: 89). The nursery rhyme, then, seems to represent an early stage of nonsense writing.[16]

Another relationship between nonsense and nursery rhyme than a historical one is occasionally observed. Thus, Walter notes the similarity of Morgenstern's Galgenlieder to the nursery rhyme (1966: 120-2), and Byrom, discussing Lear's "The Owl and the Pussycat", states that Lear turns its ballad-form "into a sort of literary nursery rhyme" (1977: 157). Sewell remarks on the affinities between nursery rhymes and Lear's verse (1952: 12). In the previous chapter it was already remarked that in its purest form nonsense is very close to the nursery rhyme (p. 80). Stewart adduces them to illustrate various

---

15. Cf. Sewell (1952: 12).
16. See Hildebrandt (1962: 105-19) for a history of the nursery rhyme. The standard work on the English nursery rhyme is Opie & Opie (1950 [1975]).

procedures of nonsense (1978: 91-2, 134-5, 142, 159, 162, 185, 189). What then is the distinction?

We have already seen (p. 9) that Wells excludes the nursery rhyme from her anthology of nonsense because it was used for specific purposes other than to present "nonsense for nonsense' sake" (1920: xxii), such as counting out or familiarizing children with quantity and metre of verse, and one could well add such uses as lulling children to sleep, familiarizing them with the letters of the alphabet, teaching them the parts of the body or the months of the year etc. Besides these, as the extensive annotations to Opie & Opie (1975) show, there are many nursery rhymes that are relics of meaningful texts, which have reached the nursery in a garbled and therefore often nonsensical or rather pseudo-nonsensical form. Others (like no. 10 in Opie & Opie) are riddles to which an answer can be given, and which are therefore not nonsensical. If we discount obvious instruction songs, riddles, counting verses, alphabets, lullabies, finger games, ballads, moral verse, tongue-twisters, jokes, street-cryers' tunes, garbled obscenities and "mad" songs, there are among the 550 nursery rhymes given by the Opies only some 22 that are also "nonsenses", that is, primarily nonsensical.[17]

It is certainly true that nonsense is often a quality of the nursery rhyme, but only relatively few are purely nonsensical. The most famous nursery nonsense is without any doubt no. 213 in the Opies' collection:

> Hey diddle diddle,
> The cat and the fiddle,
> The cow jumped over the moon;
> The little dog laughed
> To see such sport,
> And the dish ran away with the spoon.[18]

With this nonsense poem, whose incongruities are not solved, compare the following:

---

17. At a cursory glance (i.e. without being extremely categorical about some of these), I would include the items 7, 26, 51, 56, 58, 64, 72, 88, 131, 137, 160, 213, 219, 244, 318, 331, 348, 360, 460, 486, 487, and 523.

18. For some curious "explanations" of this verse, see Opie & Opie (1975: 203-5).

Ride a cock-horse to Banbury Cross,
To see a fine lady upon a white horse;
Rings on her fingers and bells on her toes,
And she shall have music wherever she goes (No. 29).

Apart from being far more obviously a "galloping song" than no. 213, this verse is more realistic as well as more associatively poetical, and an interpretation such as is given by Opie & Opie (1975: 66) more likely to be acceptable.

The relationship between the nursery rhyme and literary nonsense is clear. Carroll used several nursery rhymes in his Alice books, in some cases making them serve as the basis of a nonsensical variant with a tinge of parody (e.g. "Twinkle twinkle little Bat"), in other to create characters in the story (e.g. Humpty Dumpty). The nursery rhyme shares many themes with the nonsense (numbers and letters, food, clothing, music and dance, personified objects, ill-matched pairs, violence and death). Nonsense poems can easily become or at any rate be used as nursery rhymes. However, to see an indulgence in (or simply an appreciation of) nonsense verse as a way "to evoke the spirit of the nursery", as Cammaerts does (1925: 37) is to take too limited a view of the essence of nonsense.

3.3 *The Curiosity*[19]

At least as old, if not older, than the nursery rhyme is what I would like to label the "curiosity", most frequently the pure form of the fifth transformation type adduced by Stewart (1978), arrangement and rearrangement in a closed field, but also occasionally that of other types. Many samples can be found in C.C. Bombaugh's *Oddities and Curiosities of Words and Literature* (ed. M. Gardner 1961). One of them is the following "snow-ball sentence", in which each word has one more letter than the preceding word, thus presenting a pure form of Play with Infinity:

> I do not know where family doctors acquired illegibly perplexing handwriting; nevertheless, extraordinary pharmaceutical

---

19. This and the following sections are an expanded version of section 2 of Tigges (1986a).

intellectuality, counterbalancing indecipherability, transcendentalizes intercommunications' incomprehensibleness (350).

The cleverness of the author, and so the "point" of the phrase, is in his ability to make as much "sense" as possible out of his material. Obviously, the aesthetic quality is negligible. The same goes for the following limerick, also from Gardner's annotations to Bombaugh:

> Said the chemist: "I'll take some dimethyloximidomesoralamide
> And I'll add just a dash of dimethylamidoazobensaldehyde;
>   But if these won't mix,
>   I'll just have to fix
> Up a big dose of trisodiumpholoroglucintricarboxycide (359).

Many other chemical terms could be substituted here, without adding or diminishing the meaning.

The appearance of any of the transformations in their pure form is not sufficient to justify the appellation of nonsense.[20] In the curiosity, the balance between form and content is awry: it is at the opposite end from Dada (see section 3.8) in that its form has been made entirely dominant over whatever content has been forced, no matter how ingeniously, into its Procrustean bed. Any tension is absent, and the text itself is its own point, as in much of the work in this line by H. Brandt Corstius under the pseudonym of Battus (*Opperlandse Taal- en Letterkunde*). A more literary presentation of the curiosity can be found among others in the works of Robert Desnos (e.g. the puns and spoonerisms in *Rrose Sélavy*)[21] and Raymond Queneau (e.g. *Exercices de Style*, Paris, 1947). These works are not, however, nonsensical within the scope of my definition.

What the curiosity in particular shares with nonsense is the element of play; it is this playful aspect that is dealt with extensively by Liede (1963), who quite explicitly states that he is only concerned with the smallest units of words and sentences (I, 7). Many of the examples discussed by Liede and also by Stewart (1978) are texts in which the play has become either an aim in itself, or a means to obtain a humorous, rather than a nonsensical effect. To these types of text I would like to append the label "curiosity", so that they may be distinguished from the nonsense. Depending on the

---

20. Cf. Petzold (1972: 94).
21. In *Corps et Biens* (1953 [1968]: 33-46).

device used, the curiosity may be subdivided into types like the palindromic, the acrostic, the anagram and all the others expounded in particular by Liede and Stewart. The nonsense is a separate category altogether.

3.4 *Light Verse*

The confusion between nonsense and light verse arises mostly in the contents of anthologies of nonsense, or of comic or humorous verse or prose.[22] The confusion is, however, also a terminological one. In A.F. Scott's *Current Literary Terms* (1979) we find the following entry for light verse:

> Verse written to entertain. It usually deals with "the everyday social life of its period or the experiences of the poet as an ordinary human being." Light verse includes parodies, limericks, epigrams, and lyrics in French fixed forms, such as the triolet, ballade, and the rondeau. Nonsense verse is represented by nursery rhymes, and the poems of Lewis Carroll and Edward Lear (163-4).

In a separate entry, nonsense verse is defined as "A form of light verse in which the sound and movement are more important than the sense", and as "entertaining absurdity" (196). Harmon, who edited the *Oxford Book of American Light Verse*, equates Lear's nonsense limericks with light verse as well (1982: 73).

With all but the last line of Scott's definition I have no quarrel. But unlike nonsense, light verse, if it is to be more than mere doggerel, cannot afford to be without wit. To mind come poems by Hilaire Belloc or Ogden Nash, for instance the latter's "The Turtle":

> The turtle lives 'twixt plated decks
> Which practically conceal its sex.
> I think it clever of the turtle
> In such a fix to be so fertile.[23]

---

22. See also the accompanying introductions, e.g. to Wells (1902), Rhys (1927), Jennings (1977). The relationship discerned by the respective editors is rarely made explicit—the aim seems to be to collect non-serious texts.

23. Quoted in Cohen (1952: 50). This collection, and its sequel

There is wit in the rhymes, culminating in the American pronunciation of "fertile", which is forced upon the reader, and in the humanized turtle, but the poem is not nonsensical, as the question proposed is legitimate enough. There is, in fact, a point, which proper nonsense lacks. Light verse is often an epigrammatic joke in verse, a joke which may serve a further aim of parody or satire. Samuel Butler's *Hudibras* (1663-78) is a long satire in light verse; Hilaire Belloc's *Cautionary Tales* (1907) are parodies of moralistic children's poems of the Struwwelpeter kind. Even W.S. Gilbert's *Bab Ballads* (1869), so often mentioned in one breath with the poetical works of Lear and Carroll,[24] are mostly humorous parodies, burlesquing the Victorian melodrama and sentimentalism of the post-Romantic lyric and ballad.[25]

Where light verse comes very close to nonsense is in its playful use of the verse-form (often a strict metre and rhyme-scheme are adhered to, such as those of the limerick or one of the medieval French lyric forms mentioned by Scott), and in its playing down or avoidance of emotional overtones. Usually, however, emotion or feeling is made fun of rather than omitted. In Gilbert's "Story of Prince Agib" (Gilbert 1920: 518-22), from which Petzold quotes a few stanzas to demonstrate an exceptional use of nonsense metaphor (Petzold 1972: 125-6), the poet admits having committed the serious crime of listening "at the keyhole in the door", to overhear two musical Tartars playing a sonata to the protagonist and subsequently revealing their true identity as "Aleck" and "Beth", a crime for which the poet is duly punished. The opening stanza of the poem is facetious rather than nonsensical:

> Strike the concertina's melancholy string!
> Blow the spirit-stirring harp like anything!

(Cohen 1956), contain many more examples. Nonsense is here treated as a sub-category of comic verse.

24. E.g. by Gray (1966: 147ff.). Cammaerts rightly notes that some of the Bab Ballads, "without being sheer nonsense ... are very close to it" (1925: 11-12). Cf. also Petzold (1972: 124).

25. For a survey of this type of poetry in the nineteenth and early twentieth centuries the reader is referred to Hildebrandt (1962: 199-215).

> Let the piano's martial blast
> Rouse the echoes of the past,
> For of AGIB, Prince of Tartary, I sing! (518).

Gilbert here as elsewhere pokes fun at the clichés of Victorian balladry ("melancholy string", "spirit-stirring harp", "martial blast" etc.) by introducing incongruity between verb and direct object ("strike"—"string", "blow"—"harp") or noun and modifyer ("the piano's martial blast"). Later on he does a similar thing with the "violence" of the punishment:

> Oh! the horror of that agonizing thrill!
> (I can feel the place in frosty weather still.)
> For a week from ten to four
> I was fastened to the floor,
> While a mercenary wopped me with a will! (521)

The narrative has the inconsequentiality of a nonsense story, but the parodistic element is much stronger than that present in Lear's "Cold are the Crabs".

We must agree with Liede that "[e]in nur witziges Gedicht fällt ... nicht ... unter unsern Begriff von Unsinnspoesie" (1963: I, 15). The distinction becomes particularly clear in the limerick form, as I have demonstrated in "The Limerick: the Sonnet of Nonsense?" (Tigges 1986b).[26] Wilhelm Busch's Max und Moritz poems, and much of the poetry by Joachim Ringelnatz is to be classified as light verse rather than as nonsense. Ringelnatz's poems in *Die Schnupftabaksdose* and some of those in *Kuttel Daddeldu*[27] are borderline cases. "Die Geburtenzahl" is taken from the latter collection:

> Die Geburtenzahl
> Ging herunter,
> Traf den Pfarrer im Tal
> Nachts noch munter.

---

26. See also Hark (1982: 29) on Lear's limericks, which are there explicitly distinguished from "mere light verse". The above discussion does not of course imply that I adopt Hark's derogatory qualification of light verse.

27. Collected in Ringelnatz (1950).

Heidel da diedel dum
Wie war das schön im Tal!
Aufwärts steigt wiederum
Bald die Geburtenzahl.

Und dann lächelt alles froh
Im statistischen Büro (1950: 103).

This poem is based on a literal reading of the figurative expression "ging herunter", which is certainly a nonsensical device; the question is whether lines 3-4 are inconsequential, or whether Ringelnatz is here satirizing the "wakeful" sexuality of the parson, which causes the birth-rate to "rise" back to its original hight. It is difficult to say whether "alles" in l. 9 refers merely to the personnel of the statistics office, or to everything in it, and so the poem may be taken as a sample of light verse or as a nonsense, depending on whether the tension created by the original words is felt to be released or not.

One of the advantages of distinguishing light verse from nonsense is that it prevents us from losing sight of the fact that nonsense also features in the form of prose, and that prose and verse nonsense are more closely related than are nonsense verse and light verse, adjacent as the latter two areas may be. Two adjacent areas of prose are those of prose nonsense and fantasy, to which we will now turn our attention.

3.5 *Fantasy*

Of the various types of literature discussed in this chapter, that of fantasy is perhaps the most controversial and elusive. Like nonsense, it has been defined as a genre and as a mode.[28] Jackson (1981: 144) agrees with Prickett (1979: 126) that nonsense is a form of fantasy.[29] The former calls it "a fantasy of extreme logic, of ration-

---

28. See resp. Manlove (1975: 1, 10-11); and Rabkin (1976: 41), Jackson (1981: 3, 32). For a comprehensive survey of the various definitions of fantasy, see Jackson, ch. 2, and Hume (1984: ch. 1).

29. Cf. Baacke in Dencker (1978: 356): "Nonsense, ... eine besondere Spielart der Phantasie ...". Prickett regards nonsense as "an alternative language for coping with the conditions of a world at once more complicated and more repressive" (146) than the late

ality pushed to its limits." To those to whom fantasy offers "the anti-expected, the dis-expected, ... the not-expected" and "the irrelevant" (Rabkin 1976: 13), or for whom its themes "revolve around th[e] problem of making visible the un-seen, of articulating the unsaid" (Jackson 1981: 48, where the preoccupation of fantasy with its limits is also stressed), there may indeed well be places of overlap. Rabkin's definition of fantasy, which is centred around the notion of a 180° reversal of the ground rules of a narrative (12, 41), would seem to tally very well with the "topsyturvy" view of nonsense as voiced by Benayoun (1977: 13) and Jennings (1977: Introduction).[30]

Walter de la Mare speaks of nonsense as an "indefinable 'cross' between humour, phantasy and a sweet reasonableness" (1932: 8); Orwell calls Carroll "less essentially fantastic" than Lear (as well as funnier; 1950: 183); Quennell categorizes Lear as one of the "great Victorian fantasts" (1952: 95; cf. 100). Flescher states: "The nonsense world is a world of fantasy which shies clear of reality, yet indicates its existence" (1969/70: 141). Kretschmer, finally, speaks of "die Morgensternsche Galgenlieder-Phantasie" (1983: 63). The question to be answered is: do Lear, Carroll, Morgenstern and other representatives of the nonsense genre create a world of fantasy?

Only in the sense that the world of nonsense is not realistic, naturalistic or mimetic can this question be answered in the affirmative. "The fantastic ... pushes towards an area of non-signification" (Jackson 1981: 41), and so, indeed, does nonsense. But whereas Jackson defines nonsense also as a "literature of semantic play" which "provoke[s] no ambiguity of response in the reader" (144), Manlove rejects the Alice books as fantasies because in them "the supernatural is seen as a symbolic extension of the purely human mind", since "the happenings are presented as Alice's dreams" (1975: 6). This, I think, blurs the issue. Those who define fantasy in one way or another as imaginative literature, creating a consistent new "world" (as is the case in fairy tales as well as in many utopian and science fiction novels, and also in the works of renowned "high fantasists" like George MacDonald, C.S. Lewis and J.R.R. Tolkien), can only reject nonsense from their canon if they can prove that it

eighteenth and early nineteenth centuries. In this view, nonsense is a form of fantasy that replaced the Gothic convention, and preceded the allegorical fantasy of Charles Kingsley and George MacDonald.

30. Rabkin in fact includes Lewis Carroll in his canon of fantasy writers (1976: 37-8, 109-13). He makes no mention of Edward Lear.

is not only inconsistent (which is not the case) but also non-imaginative (which is not the case either). What then is the distinction between nonsense and fantasy?

Let us assume with Manlove that fantasy is: "*A fiction evoking wonder and containing a substantial and irreducible element of supernatural or impossible worlds, beings or objects with which the reader or the characters within the story become on at least partly familiar terms*" (1975: 10-11).[31] In fairy tales, utopian novels and science fiction, which all fit into this definition, a brave or not so brave new world is presented, which only at first sight evokes wonder. Once the story is on its way, and after we have willingly suspended our disbelief, the reader becomes familiar with the situation and any original "hesitancy" disappears. More importantly, the fantasy has a point to make; each fairy tale has a "moral", and so have utopias, dystopias and science fiction novels. The point these modern forms of fantasy make is often satirical; frequently an "idea" is propounded. The distinction from nonsense is apparent. In fantasy, a tension created is not left unresolved, the meaning is evident.

Accepting a narrower definition of fantasy, such as Rabkin's ("The fantasy is a quality of astonishment that we feel when the ground rules of a narrative world are suddenly made to turn about 180°"—1976: 41) or that of Todorov (permanent hesitancy between the natural or supernatural quality of the events described) obviously brings fantasy somewhat closer to nonsense, but still enables us to make a distinction: fantasy, in Todorov's view, wavers between two meanings: the natural and the supernatural, the marvellous and the uncanny (Todorov 1970: 49). Nonsense, as we have seen, hovers between presence of meaning (of whatever kind), especially of

---

31. The last phrase of this definition tallies with Lee T. Lemon's statement that the purpose of fantasy is "the creation of an endearingly imaginative world" (1971: 12). An opposing view is held by T. Todorov, who requires three conditions to be fulfilled by fantasy: hesitancy on the part of the reader as to whether the events and characters are natural or supernatural; a similar hesitancy on the part of a character (optional); the inability of reader and persona to give an allegorical or a "poetical" interpretation (1970: 37-8. See also Jackson 1981: 28). Todorov's definition comes close to that of the grotesque (see section 3.6 below).

poetical sense (which Todorov explicitly excludes), and its utter absence, but it embraces both extremes rather than excluding them.

Fantasy is obviously a more "serious" type of literature than nonsense, as has been noted by Cammaerts (1925: 32), Morpurgo (1960: [15]) and Hildebrandt (1962: 166ff.). The last-mentioned, who of course mainly concentrates on children's literature, presents a very useful discussion of the relationship between nonsense and fantasy.[32] However, in view of his point of departure (see p. 10) he mainly looks for nonsensical elements ("ornamental nonsense") in fantasies such as *The Water Babies, The Wind in the Willows, Peter Pan, Winnie-the-Pooh* and *The Hobbit*. In view of our generic definition of nonsense, many of his findings are questionable. When in Milne's *Winnie-the-Pooh* the hero hears (and fails to understand) "Crustimoney Proseedcake" for "customary procedure" (quoted by Hildebrandt, 79), this is not so much a matter of creating nonsense as of poking fun at the use of difficult words by the pompous adult-like Owl, and at the animal (and child-like) tendency of Pooh to understand everything in terms of food, and a similar thing happens when Christopher Robin assumes that the North Pole is a tangible pole, a piece of wood. The pun here has quite a different function from the one it has in nonsense, and in any case it provides a suitable closure to the "expotition" adventure (see Milne 1926, ch. VIII).

The same goes for the thematic comparison. Similar themes (food interest, personified animals and toys, counting and spelling, the nature of time) occur in many children's fantasies as well as in nonsense, but the function is different. In *The House at Pooh Corner* (1928), the "Spotted or Herbaceous Backson" derives from Christopher Robin's misspelling of "Back Soon", but does not become a reality as the Bread-and-Butterfly does in *TLG*—it stays in the mind of Owl and remains part of a conversation (ch. V). The Mad Hatter and the March Hare have indeed managed to stop time (a thing the Red King could not even do for a minute!) by beating it and perhaps even killing it—their "reality" has arisen from verbal play, but it *has* become a nonsensical reality. In Pooh's world, after Pooh's clock has stopped "some weeks ago", it is always five minutes to eleven and hence it is always "time for a little smackerel of something" (Milne 1928: ch. I), but we immediately sense that it is merely an

---

32. "Nonsense in der Nachbarschaft der Fantasy" (1962: 166-82). For some critical remarks, see Petzold (1972: 16-19).

excuse: "The clock was still saying five minutes to eleven when Pooh and Piglet set out on their way half an hour later." The author's irony is undeniably present here.

The point about distinguishing the nonsense world as a verbal or linguistic one from that of fantasy proper is well made by Laffay. Nonsense "décrit un univers inexistant où on a remplacé les objets par les signes qui les représentent" (1970: 119), and: "Les aventures y sont des aventures du *langage*" (124). It is not only correct (as Hildebrandt otherwise does) to regard the Pooh books as a form of fantasy, but this label should also be appended to works that have been occasionally confused with nonsense. A notable example is the *oeuvre* of Paul Scheerbart, to whom both Liede and Lang devote some attention. Liede regards his work as the prime example of cosmic play (1963, I: 73-92), whereas Lang discusses those parts of Scheerbart's work in particular that can be regarded as linguistic nonsense (1982: 65-82). Indeed, the famous "Kikakóku! Ekoraláps!", which is one of the episodes of *Ich liebe dich*! (1897: 249), much resembles Morgenstern's "Das große Lalulā", but the context makes it clear that, like a few similar episodes, it is a "drunk" song. In fact, much of the "nonsense" in Scheerbart's oeuvre is explicitly ascribed to overmuch drinking. In *Ich Liebe dich*!, the connecting theme is stated to be that of "anti-eroticism" and the love of the "Weltgeist". *Immer mutig!* contains some quite nonsensical sequences in Part II (see e.g. pp. 48-96), but some of the "Intermezzos" are closer to surrealism (see section 3.7). Part I is more mystical and lyrical, although the purpose of the whole set-up is less clear than that of *Ich liebe dich!* Here too a lot of the nonsense is connected with the use of alcohol. Some of the stories composing *Astrale Noveletten* (2nd edn 1912) edge on the nonsensical, but the whole has a clear moral point, and the asteroidal novel *Lesabéndio* (2nd edn 1913) is definitely a fantasy and not a nonsense novel.[33] The work of Scheerbart is fascinating enough to deserve further study, but as a whole it is not to be included in the canon of nonsense.[34]

---

33. Lang in fact calls it "utopisch phantastisch" (1982: 76).

34. Lang points to the influence of Scheerbart's sound-poems on the work of Morgenstern, who referred to his Galgenlieder as "Scheerbartiaden" (106).

3.6 The Grotesque

"The grotesque impression" of nonsense, writes Cammaerts, "is produced, not by ignoring the general laws of good poetry, but by upsetting them purposely, and by making them, so to speak, stand on their heads." (1925: 40). Elsewhere he describes Gilbert's *Bab Ballads* in terms of his "grotesque imagination" (12). Prickett mentions the grotesque as one of the sources for the rules of "Nonsense" as discovered by Lear and Carroll (1979: 114). De la Mare puts the question how nonsense is to be distinguished for instance from the absurd and the grotesque (1932: 14-15), but he does not provide an explicit answer. One of the problems is that the word "grotesque", like "absurd" and "nonsensical" itself, is often used in a vague, general sense, in this case that of "bizarre", "uncanny", "extravagant" or "ridiculous".

Thomson, who summarizes the history of the concept, defines it in its present-day use as the simultaneity of the laughable and the horrifying or disgusting (1972: 3). He also stresses the importance of the unresolved nature of the grotesque conflict (21). In this respect, the grotesque seems to be close to nonsense, in its persistent ambiguity of the expectation evoked. Thematically too there seem to be close connections: we have already seen that violence, death and physical deformity are important nonsense themes, and these are the topics one also frequently finds in the grotesque. Kayser emphasizes the monstrous mixture of the animal and the human (1957: 25), which is a common device in nonsense. In fact, one might consider the grotesque as a specific form, in Stewart's terminology, of "play with boundaries". Like Kayser, Thomson mentions the names of Carroll, Lear and Morgenstern in this connection (Kayser 1957: 132-3, 162-9; Thomson 1972: 65), the latter speaking of "playful grotesque", the former dealing with Morgenstern in terms of a "Sprachgroteske". Morgenstern, who according to Kayser called himself a writer of grotesques (but cf. Walter 1966: 115-6 and Kretschmer 1983: 148), "will in seinen Grotesken das naive Vertrauen in die Sprache und das von ihr getragene Weltbild erschüttern" (166). The difference between grotesque and nonsense has been discussed by various German authors who deal with these concepts from the "nonsensical" angle, so to speak. Liede, founding himself amongst others on H. Schneegans and F. Th. Vischer, and referring to Blumenfeld's category of "eidic nonsense", makes the distinction by questioning the comic aspect of the grotesque, which Thomson regards as essential to it.[35]

Walter, in his discussion of Morgenstern, prefers calling the Galgenlieder "Arabesken" rather than "Grotesken" (1966: 97-8):

> Das Element des Spielerisch-Heiteren aber underscheidet die Arabeske wesentlich von der grotesken Ornamentik, die zwar weitgehend gleich geartet ist, hinter deren Welt sich aber letzten Endes eine Unheimlichkeit öffnet, ein Abgrund, in dem alle natürlichen Ordnungen zerbrochen sind und dem fremde, fabelhafte und monströse Wesen aller Art entsteigen können (*loc.cit.*: 98).

The playful nature of the guirlandic ornamentation circling round and round itself is what makes the Galgenlieder like arabesques. On pp. 112-6 Walter demonstrates that they do not fit into the tradition of the grotesque, thereby opposing Kayser's view. His argument is that the Galgenlieder are not the expression of a complete alienation from reality and sense. If Morgenstern called himself a writer of grotesque, he used this term in its harmless, lighthearted sense. Walter's view is shared by Petzold, who holds that nonsense writing belongs to the comic category of the immediately noticeable incongruity, which is of the harmless and not of the grotesque or nightmarish kind (1972: 24-5). Kretschmer, likewise, agrees with Walter in the main, but compares the stylistic devices which are common to the Galgenlieder with the grotesque (1983: 146-53).

Thomson's thesis of a balance between two opposing emotions, laughter and horror, is enlarged upon by Van Buren, who describes the grotesque as a clash between pairs of incompatible codes: it may clash with the classical canon of beauty, with the conventions regulating the representation of reality, and with the rules of tragedy. Violations of these "codes" result respectively in physical distortion, in fantasy and in comedy (1981: 52-3). I would still take the

---

35. 1963: I, 11-14. See Thomson (1972: 50), and cf. Blumenfeld (1933: 103): "Reine *Gestaltkomik* finden wir in allen Formen der *Groteske*." Blumenfeld here also makes mention of a form of *kitsch*, which is the amalgamation of eidic and telic nonsense (p. 104). The ash-tray in the shape of a frog which is at this moment on my writing-desk is a treasured sample. The object is not so much nonsensical as grotesque.

first of these as the primary characteristic of the grotesque: the distortion or fantastic combination of physical forms, which evokes horror rather than laughter. Because in nonsense the suggestion is made that all words and images have been pared of their emotional associations, the cruelty and violence frequently exhibited in nonsense are made to appear rather harmless. There is, that is to say, a tension between the presence of cruelty and the absence of the expected emotions, while in grotesque art the distortions are presented so as to illustrate the "lowest" aspects of reality.[36] Unlike the physical oddities in Lear's limericks, grotesques are usually depicted quite "realistically", as witness the cartoons of Roland Topor or the stories of Roald Dahl. Sewell refers to the strict avoidance of beauty in nonsense (1952: 107, 126). The grotesque not only avoids beauty, but it evokes ugliness, including all the emotions (disgust, pity, fear) associated with it; it must be clear that it belongs to an altogether different category from that of nonsense. Compare for instance the following limerick by Edward Lear:

> There was an old person of Pinner,
> As thin as a lath, if not thinner;
> They dressed him in white, and roll'd him up tight,
> That elastic old person of Pinner (Lear, ed. Jackson 1947: 201).

to Roald Dahl's account of Violet Beauregarde in *Charlie and the Chocolate Factory*. Lear's nonsense is contained in the tension between an ordinary expression about thinness ("thin as a lath") and the lack of emotion with which "they" first inconsequentially dress the old person in white and then proceed to roll him up, so that the man can literally be called "elastic". No horror is evoked by the text. The accompanying illustration (Fig. 1) shows how it is at all possible to roll the thin man up: because he is not only excessively thin but also extremely long. The doodle-like quality of the drawing creates a distance from reality. Here too, although the face of the thin person clearly expresses apparently blissful madness, that of the left-hand spectator stupidity and that of the man on the right placidity and possibly cunning, no emotion is conveyed. No canons are offended in either text or illustration, because nowhere is there

---

36. Cf. Thomson (1972: 47), where it is stated that the grotesque is primarily emotional.

Fig. 1   Fig. 2

a reference to what should be a normal state of affairs.

In Dahl's story, the little girl who swells up to the shape of a giant blueberry clearly evokes horror in author, characters and readers alike:

> Everybody was staring at Violet. And what a terrible, peculiar sight she was! Her face and hands and legs and neck, in fact the skin all over her body, as well as her great big mop of curly hair, had turned a brilliant, purplish-blue, the colour of blueberry juice!
> "It *always* goes wrong when we come to the desert," sighed Mr Wonka. "It's the blueberry pie that does it. But I'll get it right one day, you wait and see."
> "Violet," screamed Mrs Beauregarde, "you're swelling up!"
> ...
> But there was no saving her now. Her body was swelling up and changing shape at such a rate that within a minute it had turned into nothing less than an enormous round blue ball... (Dahl 1964 [1973]: 89).

The only person who does not seem to be greatly concerned about the metamorphosis is Mr Wonka, because he knows what the outcome will be, since what happens to Violet must be regarded as a punishment for indulging in chewing-gum. The accompanying illustration (Fig. 2) is just that—no information is added, no further tension created. Even more than his children's books, Dahl's short stories for adults often contain grotesqueries, as in "Jelly Royal" (in *Kiss, Kiss*, 1962), in which a baby is changed into a queen bee. The suggestion that all these events, though horrible, are real, excludes the effect of nonsense.

3.7 *Surrealism*

Although historically the origins of Dada precede those of surrealism, I will deal with the latter phenomenon first, because whereas surrealism shares the suggestiveness and emotional impact of the grotesque[37] and fantasy, Dada approaches more closely to the meaninglessness conveyed by the absurd.

Surrealism originated in France, in 1924, in the wake of the symbolist movement.[38] If much symbolist poetry strikes some readers as "nonsensical", this is presumably because of its frequently somewhat aimless appearance. Presenting images and sensations, it does not so much describe or recount as evoke feelings. Whereas nonsense pares each concrete noun or adjective of its connotations and associations by making them incompatible with other parts of the text, symbols in poetry cannot suggest enough of these, so that a deeper sense or "higher" reality can be discovered by the reader. Surrealism adds to this in particular the expression of the subconscious, which can only be effected by discarding the curbing force of reason. Sewell rightly distinguishes nonsense from surrealism by pointing at the latter's attempt to "suppress any conscious control of the mind's flow of images" (1952: 5; cf. Bigsby 1972: 37, quoting from Breton's first Surrealist Manifesto), and Stewart mentions the arbitrariness of surrealist art (1978: 141), also quoting Breton's unambiguous definition.[39] "The surrealists made the simultaneous convergence of disparity into a conscious poetic principle..." (159), which is seen as an element which they share with nonsense writers; so is the fact that

---

37. For the relationship between the grotesque and surrealism see e.g. Kayser (1957: 180ff.).

38. For the literary history of surrealism see e.g. Balakian (1947).

39. See Breton (1962: 40).

"Surrealism" itself can be seen as splitting into a pun, or being the answer to a riddle" (161). Breton, who is quoted as defining sur-reality as a resolution of dream and reality, implicitly shows why surrealism may not be equated with nonsense. The dream is no denial of reality, but an extra layer of it, except of course for those who consider dreams as by definition meaningless. If nonsense is a dream, it must be a dream stripped of all its symbolism—not a wish-dream, nor a day-dream or a nightmare.

All the same, the connection if not the equation between nonsense and surrealism has been frequently made. Kusenberg, in his very brief but perceptive article, could still point out that nonsense is "open", that it is no more than what it appears to be, in contrast with the work of the surrealists (1947: 957). "Aus zehn von ihnen [viz. the surrealists] kommen neun, die blanken Unsinn hervorbringen, immer aber in der stillen Erwartung, es sei vielleicht doch ein Sinn dahinter verborgen, oder es finde sich Einer, der ihn nachträglich hineinlege" (*ibid.*). Presumably under the influence of psychologically and theologically interpretative works on Lewis Carroll by such authors as Lennon (1945 [1962]) and Taylor (1952), later scholarship began to recognize the symbolic meaning of the Alice books. The relationship between Lewis Carroll and surrealism may have been noted first by Breton himself,[40] a view which was followed up by another surrealist, Louis Aragon, in 1931, and apparently echoed by later Freud criticism.[41] In spite of Thody's objection to this view—a mild one, because he found Breton's alleged statement that Carroll is surrealist in nonsense not untenable—a spate of scholarship has continued to draw the link between nonsense and surrealism.

---

40. See Thody (1958: 428). There is a reference to Lewis Carroll in "Du surréalisme en ses oeuvres vives" (1953), in Breton (1962: 356). Breton here states that Carroll, like Lautréamont, Rimbaud and Mallarmé, reacted to the "dépréciation du langage". In his introduction to the Carroll fragment collected in the *Anthologie de l'humour noir* (1939 [1966]), Breton links this nonsense with the absurd, and he fails to see a satirical intention behind the Alice books (183-4).

41. Aragon (1931: 25-6). Cf. Thody (1958: 428-9). The latter rightly questions the appropriateness of seeing Carroll as a revolutionary precursor of the surrealist movement.

Hildebrandt, noting Kayser's remark that Lewis Carroll has been emphatically mentioned as one of the ancestors of surrealism (Kayser 1957: 132) and Empson's to the effect that Alice has become "a patron saint of the Surrealists" (in Phillips 1974: 420), holds that one could call Carroll "den Surrealisten unter den Nonsense-Autoren" (1962: 238; see also 271, n. 43). Forster, discussing Morgenstern's sound poems, regards these as foreshadowing *avant-garde* experiments such as those made by the dadaists and the surrealists (1962: 25ff.; 37ff.). Indeed, when seen in isolation, "Das große Lalulā" and "Fisches Nachtgesang" are of course quite similar to poems by Hugo Ball, but these Morgenstern poems are neither representative of the Galgenlieder nor of nonsense verse in general.

Liede devotes a brief section of his first volume to surrealism (1963, I: 245-7), from which it becomes clear that it is to be seen as a form of play with literary art in the service of a new order of society. Since Liede includes both nonsense and surrealism (as well as Dada) in his wider scope of "Dichtung als Spiel", with a special reference to their liberating qualities, the relationship in terms of his approach is understandable. Both are different species of a larger genus. A similar "kinship" in a wide sense is recognized by Flescher (1969/70: 144).

Reichert, like Breton, Hildebrandt and Forster, sees nonsense as a predecessor to Dada and surrealism, noting in particular certain aspects of Carroll's "Jabberwocky" (1974: 124). I do not wish to deny that certain nonsense devices and themes feature in surrealism as well. Benayoun, however, not only states that one can discern the nonsense in Desnos, Arp, Soupault, Picabia and many others, but maintains that nonsense is an essential ingredient of surrealism (1977: 25).

Stewart, who has already been mentioned, notes resemblances in the application of various nonsense techniques, in particular inversion in the form of self-denying discourse (1978: 76-7), and simultaneity in that of multiple worlds and the convergence of disparity (153-4, 159-60). However, the differences are also made clear, albeit implicitly. Thus, the "verse" of the surrealists is stated to depend "much more upon the logic of talk than upon a logic of rhyme" (77). More important is her quotation from Réverdy on imagery: "The image is a pure creation of mind. It cannot be born from a comparison but from a juxtaposition of two more or less distant realities. The more the relationship between the two juxtaposed realities is distant and *true* [italics added, WT], the stronger the image will be—the greater its emotional power and poetic reality" (Stewart

1978: 159, quoting Réverdy from Breton's 1924 Manifesto). This statement, endorsed by Breton (see Breton 1962: 34 for the original quotation and Breton's comment), shows what is essential to surrealism: the importance of the *image* and of its *emotional* impact, which is counter to what we have seen is essential to nonsense—the absence of emotion, caused by the impossibility to satisfactorily interpret the images in their connotations and associations.

The most extensive as well as interesting comparison between surrealism and Carroll's nonsense in particular is made by Stern (1982).[42] Discussing "what is Carrollian about surrealism and what is surrealist about Carroll" (132), Stern elaborates on the three methods which the surrealists applied in common with Carroll: the use of material offered by dreams and madness, automatic composition, and the probing of language and logic, space and time. Although Stern overemphasizes the importance of the unconscious dream elements and equates Carroll's unpremeditated composition of the first Alice book and *The Hunting of the Snark* too easily with automatic writing, he has some interesting comments on Humpty Dumpty's way with words, which is said to resemble that of Duchamp with a urinal, and offers an extended comparison of portmanteau words with verbal as well as visual collage (143ff.). But this is really no more than to say that arbitrariness and incongruity are procedures that surrealism shares with nonsense proper—and with kitsch, for that matter (cf. p. 97, n. 35). The merit of this article is that it convincingly argues the importance of Carroll to the surrealist movement, at the expense, however, of showing no awareness of the vital distinction between surrealism and nonsense.

This distinction is aptly stated by Lear's first biographer, Davidson, although in the following quotation he rather confuses the issue by using the word "absurd" in an imprecise way, rather like the way in which Hofstadter, discussing nonsense, speaks of a particular nonsense poet's "surrealistic vignettes" (1982: 25):

> The "automatic writing" of Surrealism, indeed, with its "absence of all control exercised by reason and all aesthetic or moral preoccupation" is a "reductio ad absurdum" of the

---

42. Stern attributes Breton's reference to Carroll as "Surrealist in nonsense" to the 1936 pamphlet *What is Surrealism?* (135, 152, n. 1). It is not in the original 1924 text of the First Surrealist Manifesto, nor in the 1929 revision.

Romantic theory of Inspiration: but Lear's writing is intended to be absurd, whereas that of the Surrealists is not. Lear's effects are deliberate, carefully thought out, selective: there is about him none of the conscious, and self-conscious, irresponsibility that is one of the principal dogmas of the Surrealists (1938 [1968]: 200).

Similarly, Deleuze points at the "sous-sens" (of the schizophrenic) which must be distinguished from the "non-sens" of the surface (1969: 111). In surrealism the "sub-sense" is the ultimate significance of a text (or painting). Less explicitly than Stewart, Ede and Petzold note the surface similarities between surrealism and nonsense (Ede 1975: 5; Petzold 1972: 228-9). Ede in particular concludes that it is the "insistence upon non-transcendence that distinguishes Lear's and Carroll's nonsense from Surrealism", and that "[t]he Surrealists' goal of 'reaching the supreme point of total reintegration of man with himself and with his universe' [quoting Paul Ray] separates them in crucial ways from Lear and Carroll's nonsense" (156-7). The surrealists' subversion was far more explicit than that of the nonsense writers (*ibid.*). Finally, Baacke points at the conflict with logic, which is typical of surrealism but not of nonsense.

An important distinction that has not been mentioned so far is that surrealism was a "movement", which was of course never the case with nonsense. *If* one wishes to regard nonsense as a predecessor to Dada and surrealism (which only in a very general sense it may be said to have been) this does not mean that the latter art forms take over from nonsense and bring it to an end as a type of literature in its own right, as is suggested for instance by Reichert (1974: 7) and Lang (1982: 34).

An example of a surrealist poem is André Breton's "La mort rose", from which I will quote the beginning:[43]

> Les pieuvres ailées guideront une dernière fois la barque dont
>   les voiles sont faites de ce seul jour heure par heure
> C'est la veillée unique après quoi tu sentiras monter dans tes
>   cheveux le soleil blanc et noir
> Des cachots suintera une liqueur plus forte que la mort

---

43. For the full text, see Breton (1948: 71-3). For an example taken from a collection of surrealist poems in the English language, see Tigges (1986a: 176).

> Quand on la contemple du haut d'un précipice
> Les comètes s'appuieront tendrement aux forêts avant de les
>   foudroyer
> Et tout passera dans l'amour indivisible
> Si jamais le motif des fleuves disparaît
> Avant qu'il fasse complètement nuit tu observeras
> La grande pause de l'argent
> Sur un pêcher en fleurs apparaîtront les mains
> Qui écrivirent ces vers et qui seront des fuseaux d'argent
> Elles aussi et aussi des hirondelles d'argent sur le métier de
>   la pluie
> Tu verras l'horizon s'entr'ouvrir et c'en sera fini tout à coup
>   du baiser de l'espace
> Mais la peur n'existera déjà plus et les carreaux du ciel
>   et de la mer
> Voleront au vent plus fort que nous

Bigsby, who quotes the English translation of these lines (1972: 65-6) notes the elegiac tone created by the images used in this poem, but since such a tone could also be detected in Lear's sonnet quoted on pp. 70-1 above, this remark is not sufficient to disqualify Breton's poem as nonsense. What makes the emotion in "La mort rose" more poignant is the direct address to the reader in the second line, and again in l. 8 etc. The poem has a clear meaning, namely the approach of death, and the various images, although at first their relevancy may be in doubt, can therefore be interpreted in this light: the "barque dont les voiles sont faites de ce seul jour heure par heure" is the sun, "guided" as it were by the clouds in the shape of winged octopuses ("pieuvres ailées"). The notion of the sky as a large clock as well as a sea on which the sun sails and in which the clouds swim is fairly commonplace—of course, the specific images chosen ("octopus", "sails made of this day") are new and striking, and therefore create a dreamlike effect, which makes the poem interesting—but not nonsensical. The images that follow ("la veillée unique", the black and white sun rising "dans tes cheveux", the "liqueur" oozing from the "cachots", the "haut d'un précipice" etc.) all underline the earlier ones—and fall in place. The line "Tu verras l'horizon s'entr'ouvrir et c'en sera fini tout à coup du baiser de l'espace" is a marvellous image of death occurring, reminding one of the English Metaphysical Poets and of the French Symbolists rather than of Lear or Morgenstern. What makes the poem forceful is the plethora of connotations and associations which is offered by all these mutually reinforcing (instead of exclusive) images. It is clear that this poem is not a nonsense. Language represents a (sur)reality, but it does not create or determine it.

3.8 Dada

If symbolism and surrealism intended to multiply meaning, Dada, which briefly preceded surrealism and is a far more limited phenomenon, wished to destroy it altogether. According to Bigsby, quoting Jean Arp, the dadaists wanted "to make people alive to the creative possibility of language shorn of its burden of definitive meaning" (1972: 37), hence the prevalence of sound-poems. Schwitters, quoted in Richter (1964: 150-2), wrote: "Nicht das Wort ist ursprünglich Material der Dichtung, sondern der Buchstabe" (150). Words have too many associations, they are not "eindeutig". Abstract poetry has liberated the word from its associations. Each word has the same value (151). "Die konsequente Dichtung ist aus Buchstaben gebaut. Buchstaben haben keinen Begriff" (152). This already makes it clear that Dada cannot be equated with nonsense. Denying both sense and order, Dada manifested itself as anti-art, anti-establishment, anti-everything. Once again, I think that Stewart is mistaken to emphasize the great interest of dadaism (and surrealism, as has been shown before) in simultaneity, one of the transformation processes of nonsense (1978: 153).[44] When she states that dadaism was "characterized by a convergence of languages and cultures" (167), she does not really do more than indicate the growing internationality of the modern world. Apart from its myth-making aspects Joyce's *Finnegans Wake*, which also exhibits this convergence, is a surrealist rather than a dadaist novel. Stewart remarks that "the dadaists and surrealists were willing to invert the rules of poetic form" (77). Not only, indeed, do Dada and surrealism go further than Lear and Carroll in this respect, they belong to different categories altogether.

If anything counts in a Dada text, it is the position and the shape of words and symbols on the page rather than their semantic contents. This appears from the Dadaists' preference, already alluded to, for sound-poetry, collage, the newspaper clipping poetry of Tzara

---

44. On the dadaist belief in simultaneity, i.e. "the simultaneous existence of different levels of experience", see Bigsby (1972: 19-20).

and the automatic poetry of Arp.[45] As Grossman rightly observes, because of the extreme absence of conscious creation in Dada art, every word serves as an image that evokes thought—or it evokes no thought at all to the non-respondent reader (1971: 130-1).

Nevertheless, of all the categories listed in this chapter, Dada comes closest to being nonsense of the Lear type. Grossman notes the similarity when he says that "[l]ike most forms of 'nonsense', Arp's wordplay was a great source of humor as well as a path into the unknown" (139). But his initial defining statement that Dada was a "revolt against language and logic" (19) also shows the difference, because nonsense does not so much revolt against language and logic as make use of their autonomous aspects.

All the same, Dada is, as Kusenberg rightly remarks, "more open" to the absence of meaning than is the case with surrealism (1947: 957). Forster, I think, is too far from the point in equating Morgenstern's nonsense with Dada as both aiming at "bringing art back into life" (1962:42). He regards the Galgenlieder, together with the "inspired nonsense" of magical incantation and the "poésie pure" of the dadaists as comparable forms of a mystical "speaking with tongues" (36).[46]

Liede devotes an extensive discussion to dadaism (1963, I: 216-45). "Unsinn in Form von Gedichten und Bildern, Unsinn mit dem ganzen lebendigen und toten Inventar der Welt: das war Dada" (221). Dencker includes a lot of dadaist sound-poetry in this anthology, and the justification for this is given in Baacke's afterword in the same volume, based on Schwitters' "Konsequente Dichtkunst" referred to above (see Baacke in Dencker 1978: 360ff.). Rudolf Blümner's long sound-poem "Ango laïna" (Dencker 1978: 214-21) is not a nonsense, but a Dada poem; it is actually headed as "Eine absolute Dichtung". Baacke modifies his account of this type of poetry in terms of nonsense theory when he concludes: "Schon hier, im Versuch des absoluten Lautgedichts, wird klar, daß Nonsense die Freiheit von jeglichem Sinn nicht erreichen kann; wollte er das, so schlüge er um

---

45. See e.g. Grossman (1971: 125, 136).

46. I do not intend to discuss the validity of Forster's statements about dadaism, or even about certain aspects of Morgenstern's verse. What I am questioning here is Forster's failure to see the distinction between nonsense and related but essentially different types of verbal art. My whole argument rests on the assumption that nonsense must not have a secondary aim.

in die Unsagbarkeit mystischen Erlebnisses. Das aber ist wiederum als Non-sense nicht mehr diagnostizierbar" (363). But what is offered as the saving grace (punctuation, repetition, associations with Japanese words or Latin declinations) is not sufficient to redeem the suggestion of a reality behind the "pure" language.

The distinction between Dada and nonsense has been explicitly made by Walter and Petzold. The former, speaking of Ball's sound-poetry and the theoretical supremacy of the word, states: "Von einem zweckfreien Spiel der Sprache kann hier also kaum die Rede sein, eher von einem bewußten Sprachexperiment... Balls Lautgedichte haben keinen eigentlichen Spielcharakter, wenn er sie so dem Zweck einer Erneuerung der Poesie durch die Überwindung der vernutzten Alltagssprache unterstellt" (1966: 141). Whereas Morgenstern's sound-poems are extremes, which are not given the status of a new system, those by the dadaists are means to a further end, the ultimate destruction of language (142).[47] Walter's view is succinctly echoed by Petzold (1972: 228).

I agree with Walter that some of the poems of Hans Arp come closer to being nonsense than most dadaist texts.[48] The following poem is quoted in Richter (1964: 53):

Der Poussierte Gast 5

Ihr Gummihammer trifft das Meer
Den schwarzen General hinab.
Mit Tressen putzen sie ihn auf
Als fünftes Rad am Massengrab.

Mit dem Gezeiten gelbgestreift
Drapieren sie sein Firmament.
Die Epauletten mauern sie
Aus Juni Juli und Zement.

Sie heben dann das Gruppenbild
Vielgliederig auf das Dadadach
Und nageln A.B. Zehe dran

---

47. Cf. Ede, who speaks of the "antagonistic view of language" demonstrated by dadaists and surrealists alike (1975: 5).

48. See Walter (1966: 142-5) for a discussion of Arp as somewhat exceptional in the Dada canon.

Und Numerieren jedes Fach.

Sie färben sich mit Wäscheblau
Und ziehen als Flüsse aus dem Land
Kandierte Früchte in dem Bach
Die Oriflamme in der Hand.

But surely this poem is on the borderline between nonsense and Dada, like much of Lennon's work. Walter finds playfulness lacking in Arp's poetry. "Sowohl eine letzte Tiefendimension des Sprachspieles als auch spielerische Weltbildung in dem Sinne, wie sie in den Galgenliedern vorliegt, wird nicht sichtbar. Arps Gedichte haben keine in sich geschlossene, in sich sinnvolle Welt, irgendwo bleibt auch hier die Sprache totes Material." (145). This is surely a matter of feeling. Certainly there is a somewhat "black" atmosphere in the poem, due to the references to soldiery and words like "Massengrab" and "drannageln", but this is not in itself sufficient to disqualify the poem as nonsense. Perhaps the two words I quoted are give-aways—the word "Massengrab" especially seems to evoke too many unpleasant emotions to be nonsensical. One has the feeling that Arp indeed wants to express something about the terrors of war in this poem, just as John Lennon frequently satirizes the bland hypocrisy of organized religion. On the other hand, if Arp had hit upon almost any other word rhyming in "-ab", the urge towards a particular interpretation would have been greatly lessened if not abandoned altogether. For what is one to make of the images of the sea ("Meer", "gezeiten"), of mortaring epaulettes with June, July and Cement, of the "Dadadach" etc.? If the point is that the emphasized last words of each stanza ("Massengrab", "Zement", "Fach" and "Hand") after all force the reader towards a particular horrific interpretation, the poem is obviously not nonsense. The way the images have been used may still be called nonsensical, or they may be considered as being in line with the tenets of Dada. It is obvious that the alignments between this kind of poetry and nonsense need deeper investigation than can be presented within the scope of this exploratory chapter.

3.9 *Absurdity and Absurdism*

In everyday speech, "absurd" and "nonsensical" are often used as synonyms.[49] A similar equivalence is frequently found in discussions of nonsense writing. Thus, Wells states that the great mass of nonsense literature is mainly expressed by the definition of nonsense as "words conveying absurd or ridiculous ideas" (102: xxi). Cammaerts writes that nonsense "invariably brings with it a touch of absurdity" (1925: 8). Davidson calls Lear's poetry "the 'reductio ad absurdum' of Romanticism", and states that "Lear's writing is intended to be absurd", as opposed to that of surrealism (1938: 200). This latter distinction is not made by Parisot, who equates nonsense with the absurd, and proceeds to recognize "pure nonsense" in works by Arp, Schwitters, Savinio, Picabia and Tzara (1952: 89-90), all of whom belong to the Dada movement. Morpurgo points to the absurd, that is incongruous, collocations in the fifteenth-century Burchiellesci, which he considers as early samples of intentional nonsense (1960: [8]).

Hildebrandt merely mentions the occurrence of "absurde Schlußfolgerungen" as one of the essential characteristics of nonsense (1962: 126). Forster refers to the absurdity of existence and the absurd as comprehended by "the fundamental harmony of divinely ordered existence" as underlying Morgenstern's metaphysical nonsense verse (1962: 25).[50] Laffay begins by defining nonsense as "cette forme littéraire de l'absurde" (1970: 10), but later argues that "... dans ce qu'on nomme littérature du *nonsense*, l'absurde [est] toujours affirmé *par rapport à des références parfaitement raisonnables*" (111, original emphasis).

Haight calls absurdity the keynote of the nonsense writers (1971: 247). His canon includes Carroll, Lear, Borges, Beckett, Joyce, Ionesco, Rabelais and Aristophanes. Byrom calls Lear "with Lewis Carroll the spiritual father of a movement in European culture which embraces Flaubert, Jarry, Kafka, Ionesco, Beckett, Pinter and many modern painters' (1977: 2). The last four names mentioned belong to the movement called Absurdism, and it is clear that Byrom regards

---

49. Freud does not seem to make a distinction either. See e.g. 1905 [1976]: 130, 176-7.

50. When stating that "the absurdity of existence, pointing to God as the only solution" underlies Morgenstern's nonsense verse (*loc.cit.*), Forster shares what I would like to call a Chestertonian attitude; "absurd" here means inexplicable and wonderful. This attitude is the reverse of that voiced by the absurdist dramatists to be discussed below.

Carroll and Lear, and nonsense literature in general, as precursors of the absurdists: Lear was "our first absurdist" (*loc.cit.*). Baacke, too, draws the link between the nonsense of Lear and Carroll and the way the absurdists used language (1978: 358-9, with particular reference to Beckett).

Stewart speaks of absurdity and disorder as varieties of nonsense (1978: 16). Hofstadter, after briefly discussing Lear and Carroll, refers to Gertrude Stein as "[p]erhaps the greatest nonsense writer who ever lived" (1982: 20), and goes on to speak of her "experiments in absurdity" (*ibid.*). Subsequently, he extensively discusses speeches from Beckett's *Waiting for Godot*.

To begin with, we must unravel the complication about the use of the word "absurd" in a general, dictionary sense, and in the more specialist, literary sense. Esslin gives the dictionary meaning as "out of harmony with reason or propriety; incongruous, unreasonable, illogical", and its common usage in the sense of "ridiculous" (1968: 23). None of these terms is essential for nonsense, although incongruity is often adduced as such. Samuel Foote's "The Great Panjandrum", frequently referred to as an early if not the earliest nonsense poem, is really an absurd string of phrases which the actor Foote made up on the spur of the moment to test his colleague Macklin's boast that the latter could repeat anything after once hearing it.[51] Printed as poetry, as it is usually found, it runs as follows:

> So she went into the garden
> to cut a cabbage-leaf
> to make an apple pie;
> and at the same time
> a great she-bear, coming down the street,
> pops its head into the shop.
> What! No soap?
> So he died,
> and she very imprudently married the Barber:
> and there were present
> the Picninnies,
>   and the Joblillies,
>   and the Garyulies,

---

51. See Harvey (1967) s.v. "Panjandrum". The text is quoted in many anthologies of nonsense; see e.g. Rhys (1927: 239), and Jennings (1977: 163).

> and the great Panjandrum himself,
> with the little round button at top:
> and they all fell to playing the game of catch as catch can
> till the gunpowder ran out at the heels of their boots.

This is indeed but one step away from mere gibberish, as no part of this text allows itself to be read as an image. The "poem", if it is that at all, can be read in no more than one way, as no ambiguity is suggested. Primary themes (food, traffic, death, marriage, a party and a game) are alluded to and can be linked, but the complete inconsequentiality ("So", "and", also the impossibility of identifying the many characters and their relationships) does not give us any clues as to a possible meaning of the "plot". One may well call this text absurd, for the nonsensical tension between meaning and its absence is lacking, and the "reality" is not primarily created by the language.

It is this last point which allows us to distinguish nonsense from the absurd in the technical sense of the representation of a meaningless reality in a literary text, especially such as represented by the so-called Theatre of the Absurd, but also in the prose narratives of Kafka, Sartre and Camus. Walter phrases the distinction very succinctly: discussing Morgenstern's poem "Der Glaube", he calls this text "ein eindringliches Beispiel dafür, wie sich in den Galgenliedern eine deformierte Wirklichkeit jeweils aus der Sprache selbst und ihren Möglichkeiten ergibt, und nicht umgekehrt die Sprache die Funktion hat, eine zerstörte, sinnleere Wirklichkeit wiederzugeben" (1966: 65). In nonsense, language *creates* a reality, in the absurd, language *represents* a senseless reality.

Deleuze makes the distinction on more philosophical grounds: "...les deux notions d'absurde et de non-sens ne doivent pas être confondues" (1969: 49). The absurd is firstly that which lacks sense, and secondly the paradox (i.e. a confusion of formal levels in regressive synthesis) or vicious circle (86). The word "snark", which expresses its own sense, "Snark", neither more nor less, is nonsensical; "Qdrtso", or "a square circle" is absurd. As Flescher puts it, "[i]t is the existent or implicit order which distinguishes nonsense from the absurd. It is the departure from this order which distinguishes nonsense from sense" (1969/70: 128-9). Emphasizing the paradoxical nature of nonsense, the interplay between order (created by language) and disorder (created by reference) (128), Flescher later on states that the relationship between these terms of the nonsensical paradox is one of incongruity rather than of tension, the incongruity being a key to the humour (143). We must assume, then, that Flescher does not equate absurdity with incongruity, or else her earlier statement falls flat.

Holquist is more explicitly clear in making the distinction between nonsense and the absurd: "The absurd points to a discrepancy between purely human values and purely logical values ... The absurd is a contrast between systems of human belief, which may lack all logic, and the extremes of a logic unfettered by human disorder. Thus the absurd is basically play with order and disorder. Nonsense is play with order only." (1969/70): 151-2). To the implications of this for the relationship between nonsense and modernism I will return in the following section. Reacting to Holquist's article, Ede points out that the absurdist dramatists turned predominantly to extralinguistic means, "using language minimally and then only to reveal its inadequacies", whereas in nonsense "words often exercise a creative power similar to that granted to language in some primitive cultures" (1975: 5-6).

This last point corresponds to Esslin's statement about the Theatre of the Absurd which "tends toward a radical devaluation of language" (1968: 26). This in itself would be enough to indicate the essential difference with nonsense literature. Nevertheless, Esslin fits the tradition of verbal nonsense into that of the absurd. In his section on Victorian nonsense (pp. 330-8), he emphasizes the "lustful release from the shackles of logic" that nonsense literature and poetry have provided for centuries (330). "Verbal nonsense is in the truest sense a metaphysical endeavour, a striving to enlarge and to transcend the limits of the material universe and its logic" (331-2). "As in the Theatre of the Absurd, and, indeed, as in the vast world of the human subconscious, poetry and cruelty, spontaneous tenderness and destructiveness, are closely linked in the nonsense world of Edward Lear" (333).

True as this may be in a wider sense, I think it is not so much the aim of the absurdists to free themselves from logic and conventions, as to describe a world that has lost its meaning for man "[c]ut off from his religious, metaphysical, and transcendental roots" (Esslin 1968: 23, quoting Ionesco).[52] As Hinchliffe summarizes it: "The Theatre of the Absurd is one of the ways of facing up to a

---

52. See Esslin (1968: 389-419) for an extensive philosophical explanation of the significance of the absurd.

universe that has lost its meaning and purpose" (1969: 11). Hinchliffe also quotes Irving Wardle's definition of the Theatre of the Absurd:

> Its characteristics are: the substitution of an inner landscape for the outer world; the lack of any clear division between fantasy and fact; a free attitude towards time, which can expand or contract according to subjective requirements; a fluid environment which projects mental conditions in the form of visual metaphors; and an iron precision of language and construction as the writer's only defence against the chaos of living experience (6-7).

One can easily recognize some of the thematic relationships with nonsense, especially the fluidity of time and space, but the difference should be clear. Absurd drama (but the statements made could be extended to other literary forms as well) "challenges the audience to make sense of non-sense" (12). If the language itself is absurd (whether with "iron precision" or not), this is to illustrate the fact that language, as a part of the human universe, is worn out (see e.g. Hinchliffe 1969: 61, where Ionesco is quoted as using this phrase). Thus, Lucky's famous speech in Beckett's *Waiting for Godot*, quoted by Hofstadter (1982: 20-1) is not nonsensical at all, but absurd. It summarizes the absurdity of Lucky's life from birth ("Given the existence...") to death ("... alas alas abandoned unfinished the skull the skull" etc.) in terms of metaphysics, theology, work, food, physical exercise, economics, geography, history, in that order, as a close reading of this speech will easily reveal.[53]

The absurd, then, is the art form that conveys meaninglessness, which is contrary to the purpose of nonsense to avoid complete absence of meaning. Nothingness rather than monstrosity is its key concept, which separates it from the grotesque, close as the two may otherwise be.[54]

Of the exponents of the Theatre of the Absurd discussed by Esslin and Hinchliffe, the dramatist who comes closest to nonsense

---

53. See Beckett (1956 [1965]: 42-5).
54. See Thomson (1972: 30-2) on the distinction between grotesque and absurd. The absurd, according to Thomson, does not have a formal pattern: "it can only be conceived as content, as a quality, a feeling or atmosphere, an attitude or world-view" (32).

is possibly N.F. Simpson.[55] His plays are less metaphysical than those of Ionesco, whom, according to Hinchliffe, he seems to imitate (1972: 84). Rather than the absurdity of existence or the universe, Simpson shows up the absurdity of bourgeois society and behaviour, of which his characters Bro and Middie Paradock are the prime representatives. More parody, and also more satire, I would say, are involved here than nonsense will allow.

3.10 *Metafiction*

Stewart considers nonsense "the most radical form of metafiction" (1978: 85). Whereas surrealism makes the unconscious conscious, metafiction makes skill conscious. It is fiction that is conscious of its own proceedings. Waugh states that metafiction "is a term given to fictional writing which self-consciously and systematically draws attention to its status as an artefact in order to pose questions about the relationship between fiction and reality" (1984: 2). Linda Hutcheon has called her monograph on the topic of metafiction *Narcissistic Narrative* (1980 [1984]). Her definition is "fiction about fiction—that is, fiction that includes within itself a commentary on its own narrative and/or linguistic identity" (1).

A classic early example is Laurence Sterne's *Tristram Shandy*. More recent instances are novels and short stories by John Barth, Richard Brautigan, Robert Coover, John Fowles, Flann O'Brien, Jorge Luis Borges, Italo Calvino and Vladimir Nabokov, to mention only a few. Many of the devices listed by Stewart are applied in these prose works, which of late have begun to form a genre in its own right. It is more difficult to see, however, how *AW* can be defined as metafiction, even if it is presumably the most linguistically self-conscious nonsense work. The importance of language and its workings and failures do not justify calling *AW* a fiction about fiction, nor does the admiration expressed by some of the above-mentioned authors for Carroll make his Alice books or his Snark poem into the first examples of (post-)modern literature.[56] Holquist's argument that

---

55. Jennings includes his TV-play *The Best I Can Do By Way of A Gate-Leg Table is a Hundredweight of Coal* in his anthology of nonsense (1977: 357-78). I have not seen A.J.P. Froehlich, "N.F. Simpson and the Aesthetics of Nonsense", PhD Diss. Toronto, 1976 (DAI 38-10 (1978), p. 5800-A).

56. See Holquist (1969/70) for a link between Carroll and post-

The Hunting of the Snark "best dramatized the attempt of an author to insure through the structure of his work that the work could be perceived only as what it was, and not some other thing" (1969/70: 147) is of course correct in so far as nonsense in general can (and should) be seen as "a structure of resistances to other structures of meaning which might be brought to it", and applies strategies "which insure its hermetic nature against the hermeneutic impulse" (156). Holquist, however, also sees the poem as initially without meaning (163), and here I beg to disagree. It *is* a quest poem, and that is its meaning. What makes it nonsensical is that it frustrates any attempt towards a coherent allegorical or symbolical reading, whether religious, political or psychological.[57] But that does not make it postmodern or metafictional. Although it may of course well be true that the metafictional writers share with Carroll a distrust of language as a representation of reality, as is noted by Ede (1975: 4-5), it is doubtful whether Carroll's main aim was to show up language as "a mass of dead words which inhibits man from perceiving his essential condition" (*ibid.*).

In my view, the playful aspect of metafiction is a closer ground of resemblance between metafiction and nonsense,[58] and so is the notion of reality as a linguistic construct (Waugh 1984: 84ff.). A good deal of metafictional literature is closer to fantasy, a relation which has been pointed out by Jackson, speaking of Borges' "linguistic fantasies" (1981: 164) and of the "fantasy as fabulation, as metafiction" expressed in novels by Barthelme, Coover, Hawkes, Malamud and Vonnegut (*ibid.*).[59]

---

modernism. See also Peze (1987); in this article a plausible connection is made between the situational nonsense in *AW* and that in some post-modernist American novels. A situation is said to be nonsensical when it is experienced as decontextualized, as when the literary character who finds himself in such a situation expresses a lack of emotional involvement.

57. See further chapter 4.2.2.

58. See Waugh (1984: 34ff.) and Hutcheon (1984: 82ff.) on metafiction as playful creation. Cf. also Schöne (1955b), where Sterne is related to the nonsense tradition, and esp. p. 62: "Das spielerische Nicht-Ernstnehmen der Dinge, das Tristram Shandy auszeichnet, bereitete den Boden, auf dem die Nonsense-Dichtung erwachsen konnte..."

59. See also Hume (1984: 45ff.); Hutcheon (1984: 76ff.).

The distinction between metafiction and nonsense is that the latter does not make itself its own subject. Also, most of the metafictional writers mentioned in this section make their work serve a further aim of social and/or artistic criticism. It is the very self-consciousness of these authors which keeps them, so to speak, out of the pale of nonsense, although some of them, as will be demonstrated in the following chapter, may be considered borderline cases. I will conclude this section by presenting a few brief examples, which all play self-consciously with the order of the limerick form. The first two samples are taken from Gardner's annotations to Bombaugh (ed. Gardner 1961: 362):

> There was a young man of Japan
> Whose limericks never would scan.
>   When someone asked why
>   He replied with a sigh,
> "It's because I always try to get as many words into the last line as I possibly can."
>
> Another young poet in China
> Had a feeling for rhythm much fina.
>   His limericks tend
>   To come to an end
> Quite suddenly.

To this, I suppose, should be added the "limerick" quoted by Fowler (1982: 173):

> There was a young lady at Crewe
> Whose limericks stopped at line two.

These texts are fictions about fiction and that is their point. A further point may well be that the authors found some (if not all) limericks rather insipid.[60] They are quite clearly not nonsensical.

---

60. Cf. the famous non-rhyming limerick ascribed to W.S. Gilbert, quoted in Bombaugh (1961: 361), and also e.g. in Baring-Gould (1968: 57). This text may be called nonsensical only in the sense that its contents are trivial. The parodistic intention is unambiguous.

3.11 Conclusion

In the previous sections of this chapter I may well have created the impression that the various types of literature I have discussed, including that of nonsense, can be easily defined in a simple fashion, and as easily therefore differentiated from one another. The very fact that nonsense has been associated with all these other types shows that the matter is actually highly complex. It would indeed be necessary to devote a complete chapter, if not a book on each of the types that have been discussed, and perhaps on some others as well, to do justice to the variety of phenomena that are here reduced to the same denominator in a rather off-hand manner. The reader will realize that the limited scope of this thesis forces me to be more succinct, and hence more normative than I would like to appear. I am well aware that most of the areas of literature dealt with in this chapter are under constant discussion by experts in the respective fields. I also realize that my samples had to be highly selective and are therefore of a somewhat arbitrary nature.

Unlike Haight, I do not doubt that a (descriptive, not prescriptive) definition is possible (see Haight 1971: 247). I quite agree with him that dividing *lines* indeed cannot be drawn (255). "Nonsense shades gradually, in various directions, into pure fantasy, pure farce, the grotesque, the Surrealist, and so on" (*ibid.*). So, in the spectrum, does green shade gradually into yellow on the one side, and blue on the other. All the same, we are well aware of the differences between these three colours, as well as of the presence of various shades of them. What I have tried to do in this chapter is to concentrate on the differences, without altogether losing sight of similarities. If the reader wishes to make other alignments of characteristics, I have no quarrel with that, as I hope to have implicitly made it clear how that would affect one's ability to distinguish one type of writing from another.

In the Table on pp. 136-7 I have set out the types and genres discussed, as well as some others omitted from this chapter. It will be evident why myth, fable and fairy tale have not been touched upon: these types share none of the basic characteristics of nonsense as given in my definition, nor are they usually confused or associated with nonsense, except in a purely comparative sense. Symbolism is by its very nature incompatible with nonsense, even if its reality is occasionally created by language. The riddle may share all four qualities; we then speak of a nonsense riddle. The prime example is that famous one set by the Mad Hatter in *AW*: "Why is a raven like a writing-desk?" It is not meant to be answered, in contrast with the riddle proper. Parody, like nonsense, is playful, and it occasionally creates a reality out of language. It is never presented so as to take away the meaning it simultaneously suggests. Nonsense *can* be parodied (*pace* Stewart 1978: 186), but the result is no longer nonsense. It is, as Cammaert says, like caricature, a form of satire, not nonsense (1925: 11).

As the table shows, some but not all nursery rhymes may be nonsenses. All the other types can be distinguished from nonsense on at least one of the four basic characteristics enumerated, mostly on that prime characteristic, the tension or balance between meaning and non-meaning. Only the absurd occasionally shares this quality with nonsense, but the absurd never lacks emotion; it always expresses anguish at the human predicament. It is rarely playful.

This chapter will have served its aim if it has managed to set the reader to think about the nature of nonsense as well as of all the other genres and types discussed, and if it has managed to clear away some of the confusion which transpires in earlier scholarship.

TYPES/ GENRES	BASIC CHARACTERISTICS	FEATURING BASIC CHARACTERISTICS OF NONSENSE:			
		TENSION OF MEANING VS ITS ABSENCE	LANGUAGE CREATES REALITY:	ABSENCE OF EMOTION:	PLAY:
nursery rhyme	secondary aim (counting out, putting to sleep)	sometimes	sometimes	sometimes	yes
curiosity	point is play with form or words	no	no?	yes	yes
parody	ridicules source	no	sometimes	no	yes
light verse	wit	no	sometimes	sometimes	yes
joke	*pointe*; mimesis	no	no	no	yes
shaggy dog story	weakened point inconsequentiality	no	sometimes	no?	yes
riddle	invites answer	no	sometimes	sometimes	yes
myth	deep significance	no	no	no	no
fable	moral point	no	no	no	no
fantasy	alternative reality	no	no	no	no

TYPES/ GENRES	BASIC CHARACTERISTICS	FEATURING BASIC CHARACTERISTICS OF NONSENSE:			
		TENSION OF MEANING VS ITS ABSENCE	LANGUAGE CREATES REALITY	ABSENCE OF EMOTION	PLAY
fairy tale	moral point	no	no	no	no
grotesque	evokes horror	no	no	no	no
symbolism	invites associations	no	sometimes	no	no
surrealism	represents subconscious	no	sometimes	no	no
dadaism	anti-art, absence of meaning	no	sometimes	no	sometimes
absurdism	represents meaningless universe	sometimes	sometimes	no	no
metafiction	self-reflexive	no	yes	no	yes

CHAPTER 4: A LITERARY APPRAISAL

4.1 *Introduction: Early Samples and Nonsense as Device*

Nonsense is often said to have originated with Lear and Carroll, that is to say, in Victorian Britain. However, if nonsense is defined as a mode or a device, along the lines set out by Liede or Stewart, this cannot be true. We may safely assume that playing with language is as old as language itself. Stewart refers to an example from ancient Egypt (1978: 66), and many of the devices listed in her book can be found in the Hebrew Bible. In these early instances, however, nonsense devices seem to have served the further aims of satire and numerology respectively. J.G. Frazer, in *The Golden Bough*, offers many examples of how in so-called primitive societies words and sometimes complete languages are replaced because of taboos on names.[1] This is interesting in view of the fact that Stewart refers to nonsense as "of necessity ... a kind of taboo behaviour" (88). In this light, nonsense is seen as a "threat" to society, holding up the processes of social interaction by making the discourse of everyday life conscious of its own procedures, which Frazer tells us is exactly what happened in some of the societies he describes. In some instances the men and women belonging to one community speak two largely different "languages"; in others no history can be recorded, since the names of deceased persons are tabooed.

However, nonsense has also always been a device for "[m]aking the unsaid 'said'" (Stewart 1978: 89). For instance, Shakespeare's numerous puns enabled him to introduce a layer of *double entendre* into his plays, which may have been relished by the "understanders" for its own sake, but which also debunked and showed the relative value of the protagonists' ambiguous noblemindedness. Here too, when nonsense is used as a device in mimetic art, a meaning is suggested and simultaneously taken away, as when the author can ingenuously declare that "that" is not what he meant.

Considered as a literary genre, however, according to the views set out in the previous chapters, we cannot indeed trace the origins of nonsense beyond the nineteenth century.[2] Although in the follow-

---

1. Abridged edn in one vol., London, 1922 [1971]: 321-45 on "Tabooed Words".

2. For a survey of opinions on the socio-historical, cultural and psychological reasons advanced for the rise and prominence of literary nonsense in Victorian England, see chapter 5 below.

ing description and analysis of the corpus of literary nonsense I limit myself to texts that have appeared since Lear's first *Book of Nonsense* in 1846, I do not thereby wish to suggest that there are no incidental "nonsenses" antedating that landmark. I would contend, however, that they are far less numerous than is suggested by the compilers of anthologies of nonsense, such as Benayoun, Dencker and Jennings. I hope to have made it sufficiently clear already that the early samples of nonsense quoted in anthologies or mentioned by critics (names that occur frequently in this context are those of Aristophanes, Rabelais, Shakespeare, Swift and Sterne) are at most nonsensical as device or mode, subservient to other aims such as satire, parody and burlesque.

Henry Coggswell Knight's "Lunar Stanzas", written in 1815 and quoted by Wells (1901: 241) as "irreproachable" nonsense, besides its being titularly presented as a "mad" song, is still in the tradition of an enumeration of incongruous images and events:

> Night saw the crew like pedlers with their packs
>   Altho' it were too dear to pay for eggs;
> Walk crank along with coffin on their backs
>   While in their arms they bow their weary legs,

and so on. This is the tradition of Lucian's true history of the voyage past a series of wondrous isles, but also that of the thirteenth-century French fatrasies, and of the list of unlikely events which according to an anonymous Middle English poet must come to pass before one can trust women. That the "Lunar Stanzas" are just short of being nonsense is not so much because of the give-away title (it has already been stated that *AW* and *TLG* need not be read as dreams, although Carroll presents a similarly "give-away" framework to that effect), as because of the fact that all the untoward images and events are suppositional ("Yet, *'twere* profuse to see for pendant light,/ A tea-pot dangle in a lady's ear", my italics).

It is not suggested that these events take place, even in a nonsensical or topsyturvy world. The poem is reminiscent of the famous nursery rhyme:

> If all the world were paper,
> And all the sea were ink,
> If all the trees were bread and cheese,
> What should we have to drink? (Opie & Opie 1973: 436).

What indeed, *if*? In nonsense, all the world *is* paper and all the seas *are* ink (cf. Sewell 1952: 17). It is legitimate to regard poems like these as the precursors of the nonsense genre, but they should not be included in its corpus.

In the following sections, I will not so much describe the nineteenth and twentieth-century corpus of the genre, as present it in a very broad outline. My analyses of the works of Lear and Carroll, and of later authors writing in their tradition, will necessarily have to be eclectic, that is to say, subjective and incomplete. The main aim of the present chapter is not only to provide further and more detailed illustrations of my definition and of what I consider to be the essential characteristics of nonsense, but also, and in particular, to demonstrate that these texts possess a literary quality which goes beyond the value which is generally ascribed to them. In passing, it will become clear what these texts have in common, as well as what differentiates them. The corpus, as it is, is neither closed nor static. If occasionally I seem to present it as such, this is for economy's sake, but not for that of prescription or proscription. I will start, along the lines of my typology (see chapter 2.5), with the works of Edward Lear and Lewis Carroll—not because they are to be considered as the "Fathers" of nonsense, nor because they are the uncontested grandmasters by whose works other practitioners are frequently tested, but simply because they are the earliest in the chronology of the genre's history.[3]

4.2 *Lear and Carroll*

4.2.1 *Edward Lear*

Edward Lear (1812-1888) and his works are reasonably well documented. There are two major biographies (Davidson 1938 [1968] and Noakes 1968), some minor ones (Richardson 1965, Kelen 1973, Lehmann 1977 and Hark 1982), and a fair number of critical books and

---

3. In what follows I will reduce detailed references to secondary reading to a minimum, in order not to cover the same ground twice. I will also refrain from giving biographical information about the authors to be discussed; for these data, the reader is referred to the criticism indicated in the bibliography, and to further references given in the bibliographies to the standard biographies and monographs.

articles. For a general discussion of his nonsense works, the reader is referred to Cammaerts (1925) and Sewell (1952), both of whom also deal with Carroll, and further to Davidson (1938 [1968]: 186-202), Hildebrandt (1962: 119-36), Liede (1963: I, 165-72), Petzold (1972: 10-78, 144-77), Ede (1975: 21-69), Byrom (1977), Hark (1978), Prickett (1979: 114-31), Sewell (1980/1 [1987]), Hark (1982) and Lang (1982: 39-44). I have not been able to consult Liebert (1975). For a recent, extensive bibliography, see Hark (1982), who also announces a forthcoming two-volume edition of the complete nonsense by V. Noakes and C. Lewsen. Unless otherwise indicated, quotations from Lear's nonsense are from Jackson's 1947 edition of the *Complete Nonsense of Edward Lear*.

Sufficient attention has been paid to the limericks,[4] which are generally considered the most nonsensical of Lear's verses, and to which Lear himself actually attached the appellation of "nonsenses". I have already demonstrated (pp. 51-2) how the tension between meaning and absence of meaning is left unresolved in these self-reflexive little poems. For a start, there is the tension within practically each of the separate items, preventing a point from being made. Then, there is not infrequently a further tension between the text and its illustration, so that if one were to look for a point in the text after all, the illustration enervates this option. Finally, the limericks are not isolated, but presented in a series, the order of which appears to be random. The effect of this serial presentation is to prevent any method from being found in the madness. It is all very well for Lisa Ede to write that in *More Nonsense* the first four limericks "present in rapid succession ... images of regression and despair, madness, physical deformity, and social repression" (1975: 60), but it should not be overlooked that the fifth item deals with a "romantic" old person who happily feeds himself on roast spiders and chutney, unhampered by any criticism (Jackson: 159-61).

This last text is perhaps as good an example as any other to show the odd mixture of nonsensical devices and those of "regular" poetry—and art.

---

4. See Cammaerts (1925: 5-8); Schöne (1951); White (1966 [1969]); Ede (1975: 21-49); Harrowven (1976: 34-45); Byrom (1977: 49-150); Prickett (1979: 120-5); Hark (1978: 114-8); Hark (1982: 39-41); Kretschmer (1983: 255-7); Tigges (1986b: 222-9); Ede (1987b).

There was an old person of Putney,
Whose food was roast spiders and chutney,
Which he took with his tea, within sight of the sea,
That romantic old person of Putney (161).

Note that, just as the left half of the doodle is "romantic", and the right half absurd, the top half, so to speak, of the text is absurd, and the bottom half romantic. The rhymes on "tea" and "sea" are perhaps just short of being Victorian clichés, and in any case these open vowels effectively link a symbol of domesticity to one of nature. Lear himself must often have taken his tea in the garden of his San Remo villa, which was within sight of the Mediterranean. The romanticism of the rhymes is underlined by the alliterative pattern in the third line. In the picture, with only a few lines of the pen, Lear has drawn a similar collocation of domesticity (the tea-urn and cup on a three-legged table) and its opposite, travel by sea (the sail on the horizon—a recurrent theme in Lear's nonsense).[5] The same collocation is presented in that of exotic (but edible) chutney, and domestic (but inedible) spider (another common motif, as witness "Mr. and Mrs. Discobbolos", who, as no one seems to have noticed, are of course spiders). In the text, the playful inconsequentiality of chutney and spider is stressed by the strident sounds of the phrase "roast spiders and chutney", and in the picture by their being two arms' lengths apart; perhaps east is east (chut-

---

5. Cf. e.g. "The Owl and the Pussycat" and "The Dong with a Luminous Nose".

ney) and west is west (spiders) and never the twain shall meet—except in the stomach of the old person.

Why is this person called romantic? Because he takes his strange food (of course, the spiders are "roast"; who would be so mad as to consume a raw one?) in that romantic environment? He does not seem to be interested in it—his blissful look, if it is directed outward at all, seems to derive rather from involvement with the food he clasps. Why spiders and chutney? The latter is a "preserve" and so, like the jar it is in, it suggests durability. Like life, a jar can be broken however, and so can the spider's thread. What other contrasts are involved? Art and nature, vegetable and animal? Or does the man take chutney merely because he is from Putney—in other words, is his nourishment based on rhyme? In many of the limericks the situation described is ultimately based on language: "There was an old person of Slough,/ Who danced at the end of a bough" (160), rather than bowing at the end of a dance, one supposes. Lear has turned about a phrase (Stewart's inversion or mirroring), and created a new reality, which is depicted in the illustration. But the inconsequentiality is not in the word-play, but in "them" commenting on his possibly damaging the trees, *if* he should happen to sneeze. *That* is what makes him "imprudent", not his dancing as such. The word-play features here, but not as the point of the limerick. In fact, it has, as far as I am aware, escaped the critics' attention. It needed Anthony Burgess to notice that the young lady who "swept the loud chords of a lyre" (42) with a broom did so because she took the cliché phrase literally (Burgess 1986: 301).[6] Lear brings these and similar phrases to life, and that is the power of his art.

Lear's longer poems have only been discussed at some length (but not in great depth) by Byrom (1977: 157-231) and Hark (1982: 52-100), and, more briefly, by Ede (1975: 61-8). Lack of space forces me to limit myself to one sample, and the choice is not easy, especially as Hark's contention that "the Nonsense songs together constitute a related body of myth-making" (1982: 53) evokes comment which would require a close comparison of all the poems. A fuller literary-aesthetic study than those offered by Byrom and Hark, who mainly discuss the Songs in terms of Lear's life-history, is called for, but cannot be presented within the scope of this thesis.

---

6. Burgess is mistaken to see it as the "point" of the limerick (*ibid.*).

My favourite is "The Dong with a Luminous Nose" (henceforth "Dong"), one which is not generally recognized as being "pure" nonsense,[7] and which may consequently be regarded as a fair and unbiased example. The text of the "Dong" is given by Jackson on pp. 225-8. Liede quotes it in full (1963, I: 167-9), and warns us that we must not take it as a parody on the romantic ballad (169) so much as in terms of a poem reflecting Lear's hankering after love and companionship (171)—a "Blues" (170).[8]

The "Dong" is different from nearly all the other Songs in that its stanza form is irregular. Byrom calls it an ode rather than a ballad (1977: 175). In irregular phases, there are two different refrains, each repeated twice: that of the Jumblies, repeated from the poem of that name, and that of the Dong himself, which embraces the other. The two refrains contrast the hysterical awe of the Dong's beholders with the wistful wonder evoked by the Jumblies, who travelled over sea *from* unknown parts rather than *towards* them, as is the more sensible state of affairs. They came in a sieve, which is less absurd than it may seem, because a Victorian sieve, as depicted in the illustration (71), does in fact float; Jarry's pataphysician Docteur Faustroll was to explain the principle a few decades later.[9]

The world of the Dong, the Gromboolian plain and the Hills of the Chankly-Bore, are lacking in colour—it is a world of black and white. It is the same with its sounds: if there is no awful silence, one hears angrily roaring breakers, wailing animals, or the discordant sound of the Dong's squeaking pipe. The world of the Jumblies, on the other hand, is colourful, and feminine. Their arrival even affects the surroundings: the otherwise stormy shore with its towering heights is transformed into a fertile plain were "Oysters grow,/ And the rocks are smooth and gray". The reader's attention is drawn from the threatening Bong-trees to the woods and valleys,

---

7. See e.g. Sewell (1952: 159); also Byrom (1977: 177). Sewell considers the Nonsense Songs in general as beyond the pale of "Nonsense proper" (164ff.), and speaks of Lear's "Nonsense failures" in this context (155). Cf. Laffay (1970: 87-90) for a similar view, presumably based on that of Sewell.

8. For treatment elsewhere, see Ede (1975: 62-5); Byrom (1977: 175-8); Hark (1982: 76-8).

9. Jarry (1955: 21-4). See also section 4.3.1 below.

ringing with the Jumbly Chorus. It is here that the Dong falls in love.

Lear honours the poetic conventions in a masterly fashion. The Jumblies are known for their blue hands and green hair. Needless to say, the beloved's hands are sky-blue, and her hair sea-green, as a Victorian beauty's might be rosy pink, and honey gold, or possibly snow white and sloe black. What Lear does here is to paste the conventions of Romantic love poetry on to non-existent creatures. A sieve may float, but it sinks when filled up, and so its crew must be creatures of the imagination. Are the Jumblies a figment of the Dong's sick mind? Has he become mad with love, or has he been mad all the time? Or is the Dong himself a figment of the imagination and fear of "those who watch at that midnight hour/ From Hall or Terrace, or lofty Tower"? That the Dong is mad is proven not so much by his own confession ("What little sense I once possessed/ Has quite gone out of my head!") as by the fact that he looks for a girl whom he has seen departing from the "cruel shore", "[b]y lake and forest, marsh and hill", where he is not very likely ever to run into her. Apparently, he does not wander very far, for he can always be observed in the same place, and in the same manner.

It is not very difficult to read into this poem, as Byrom and Hark have done, an allegory of the unappreciated artist, whose surroundings fail to see that his art (playing his plaintive pipe) is his form of love-making, an allegory also of the lifelong bachelor who may have given vent in this nonsense to a "displacement of sexual fear" (Byrom 1977: 177). But this does not explain the effectiveness of the poem as a poem, or of the nonsense as nonsense. Byrom points out that in the "Dong" the nonsense is in "the failure of the conventionally wonderful to make sense" (178). The irony is that to the Dong himself it is the *un*conventionally wonderful that makes sense; who else would fall in love with a woman with sky-blue hands and sea-green hair? Unless, of course, the Jumblies are to be seen as an allegory of nature. Might they originally have been little sea-animals, which Lear scooped out of the Mediterranean with his sieve and fell in love with, just as the Yonghy-Bonghy-Bò was originally an ordinary chestnut (Noakes 1968: 244)?

The point is that we cannot know these things, and should be able to appreciate the nonsense without these and similar suppositions and guesses, often based on ignorance or at most half-knowledge of what may have moved Lear.

Let us take our main characteristics of nonsense, and see how they fit this poem. To begin with, the balance of meaning and absence of meaning. Ede has discerned a balance of sentimentalism by parody (1975: 63), of romance by irony (65). But both sentimentalism and parody, both romance and irony, carry a meaning—there may be ambiguity here, but no suggestion (as yet) of absence of meaning. If a romantic meaning in the style of Tennyson or Arnold is suggested,[10] and at the same item a parody of such a meaning, centred in the device of the fabricated, red, luminous nose, the absence of meaning is the result of the way in which these two codes clash. They fail to reinforce one another as in Byron's romantic irony. Lear's rhyme, rhythm, and diction are conventional—there is no parody here. Note for instance the four weary stresses on "long, long wintry nights" in the first stanza, the choppy rhythm of the "angry breakers" roaring and beating on the rocky shore, and then the return to the earlier rhyme in a longer, threatening line, of the storm-clouds brooding on the towering heights, which are linked by alliteration to the Hills of the Chankly-Bore. The /ai/-rhyme of the hovering nights and the heights, supremely sovereign, as against the /ɔ/ in the low-down roar and shore, are just right. The odd words are the names: Gromboolian and Chankly-Bore. Like the places around Oxford in Arnold's "Scholar-Gypsy", these names carry associations, since they occur elsewhere: the Gromboolian plain is where Mr Daddy Long-legs and Mr Floppy Fly play at battlecock and shuttledore (note the inversion here), and the Hills of the Chankly-Bore are familiar to the Jumblies in their homelands far and few. Unlike Arnold's Oxford, however, this world is a closed one, as the connotations evoked come to nothing. It is like being sent from one entry in an encyclopedia to another, in an eternal cross-reference, like a veritable shuttlecock.

    The Dong himself is characterized by the things mentioned in the poem: his happy and gay past, his frustrated love for the Jumbly girl, his playing the pipe, his weaving of a wondrous nose. There are no external references to hold on to. In a subtle way this is a reality created by language. The emotions presented in the poem are enervated by the lack of involvement. Perhaps the Dong would not be the Dong if his love had been returned. The Dong is not more lively or plaintive than breakers are angry or storm-clouds brooding. Lear puts our noses to the grindstone of his imagery, and then we find there is nothing there.

    10. Ede has discerned a similarity between the "Dong" and Arnold's "Scholar-Gypsy" (1975: 63-4).

What seems to be lacking in this poem is the use of the procedures listed by Stewart. These are more common to the limericks, and to the other nonsenses, notably the Alphabets.[11] These are based on the seriality of the twenty-six letters. The texts themselves may be quite sensible at first sight, as happens on the whole in the first "Nonsense Alphabet" in *Laughable Lyrics* (263-9), although Davidson has detected the "perfect 'non sequitur'" in the G-verse (1938 [1968]: 211). What is nonsensical is the odd collocation of objects, animals and foodstuffs, whose only merit is that they begin with a particular letter, so that a clear example of language (spelling) creating reality is presented here. If read as a unity, the nonsensicality of the whole text becomes more prominent. What is striking is the sense of exaggeration, occasionally incongruously so, that is subtly but persistently maintained, often in one little word. It begins with the (three) washerwomen underneath an Area Arch, making "a *lot* of lovely starch/ To starch Papa's Cravat" (263, my italics, as in the following)—all that starch for one cravat—and where does the Arch come in at all? Then "B was a Bottle blue,/ Which was *not very small*;/ Papa he filled it *full* of beer,/ And then he drank it *all*" (*ibid.*). Papa's gray Cat pulls a mouse "*All about* the house", Papa's white Duck eats a "*great fat* frog,/ Besides a *leetle* snail" (*ibid.*), Papa eats his *little* egg "*As fast as he was able*" and hysterically admonishes the cook to bring a dish and cook the fish (264), and so on. This eccentric Papa carries an Inkstand in his pocket, sees a Kite flying "Above a *thousand* chimney pots" (265), makes sagacious remarks about Nuts, Owls and Pigs (266), thumps "*extremely* wicked boys" with his *new* Stick, drinks a Tumble *full* of Punch in the *middle* of a wood (267), wishes to make the acquaintance of King Xerxes (himself not unknown for exaggerating behaviour) and thinks he would like a ride on the back of a Zebra (268-9). The funny thing is that as some of these things are more regular than others, they tend to become all equally sensible, like wearing a black Hat, wrapping oneself in a warm Railway Rug and disapproving of the bad conduct of a screaming Youth, or equally nonsensical, like some of the events mentioned before. Some of the texts are trivial, like the W, which "was a Watch of Gold:/ It told the time of day,/ So that Papa knew when to come,/ And when to go away" (268).

11. For discussion of these, see Hildebrandt (1962: 127ff.); Ede (1975: 49-52); Hark (1982: 103-10).

In these Alphabets the themes of nonsense are prominent, especially personification, of the very letters to begin with ("A once was ...", "A tumbled down", 138, 270), but also of animals, objects and foodstuffs; and neologisms, which occur in the "Twenty-Six Nonsense Rhymes and Pictures" (209-221), which are indeed "marvelous nonsense" (Hark 1982: 107), as witness "The Fizzgiggious Fish, who always walked about upon Stilts, because he had no legs" (210) and "The Dolomphious Duck, who caught Spotted Frogs for her dinner with a Runcible Spoon" (211). The nonsense here is that Lear alternates words like Fizzgiggious and Dolomphious with familiar ones such as Abstemious, Bountiful, Comfortable and Enthusiastic, which become as meaningless as the made-up ones because of the way they are used. The Ass is indeed Abstemious, living only on Soda Water and Pickled Cucumbers, but what it is that makes Bountiful the Beetle who carries a green Umbrella when it does not rain and leaves it at home when it does escapes me, unless we have to assume that the Beetle is Bountiful to its Umbrella. Surely, it is not the Cow which is Comfortable, but the Red Morocco Arm Chair in which it is sitting. By mixing up in this fashion existent and non-existent words, and using the former in a relevant as well as irrelevant way, Lear makes what little sense these verses once possessed go quite out of one's head, to adapt the Dong's phrase. Meaning is suggested and simultaneously taken away, in a game played with the letters of the alphabet, which clearly determine the "reality" to be described. Emotional involvement is played down by the very device of the alphabetical presentation.

Lear also wrote two nonsense stories (not to mention the nonsense in his letters and journals, where it mainly consists in odd spellings, as when he speaks of "a Nin or a Pharmouse"), where the nonsense works largely similar to that of the poetry.[12] In "The Story of the Four Little Children Who Went Round the World" (91-106), all the nonsense devices are found: mirroring or inversion ("an island made of water quite surrounded by earth", 93), play with boundaries or imprecision ("So they bought a large boat to sail quite around the world by sea, and then they were to come back on the other side by land, 91), infinity or seriality ("the island was quite

---

12. The Nonsense Stories are discussed in Ede (1975: 52-9), Hark (1982: 117-24). For a discussion of the linguistic nonsense in Lear's private communication, see Partridge (1950), and Sewell (1987, esp. 186-9). See also section 2.3.7 above.

full of veal-cutlets and chocolate drops, and nothing else ... they loaded the boat with two thousand veal-cutlets and a million of chocolate drops", 93), simultaneity ("they pursued their voyage with the utmost delight and apathy", 93) and arbitrariness (the randomly episodic nature of the story as a whole). The ultimate inconsequentiality of the story, in which the meaning of the whole undertaking is affirmed and denied at the same time, is very well demonstrated by the last two paragraphs:

> Thus, in less than eighteen weeks, they all arrived safely at home, where they were received by their admiring relatives with joy tempered with contempt; and where they finally resolved to carry out the rest of their travelling plans at some more favourable opportunity.
> As for the Rhinoceros, in token of their grateful adherence, they had him killed and stuffed directly, and then set him up outside the door of their father's house as a Diaphanous Doorscraper (106).

Lear, by tempering joy with contempt, and grateful adherence (the four children and their companions had literally "adhered" to the Rhinoceros by sitting on its back) with killing and stuffing (note the theme of emotionless violence), and by turning a Rhinoceros into a Doorscraper, although, being dead, it presumably could not even scrape the door, forces his readers to question the meaning and value of each of these phrases, and to do so from both angles. Unable to satisfactorily reconcile joy with contempt and gratefulness with killing, as we sometimes are in real life, we must come to the conclusion that the whole adventure is meaningless, but not without significance. In the beginning of the story, the four children "thought they should like to see the world" (91); at the end they have indeed seen a world, but one which does not allow the unravelling of its marvels. Obviously, at one level, Lear is parodying the travelling accounts popular in his days, with children as with adults. He pokes fun at the pedantically accurate didactic style, "tempered with" romantic description: "... it [an island] was bordered by evanescent isthmusses with a great Gulf-stream running about all over it, so that it was perfectly beautiful, and contained only a single tree, 503 feet high" (93). But the Story rises above the level of mere parody, because the description creates its own reality. In the next section I will attempt to demonstrate how Carroll, using language in a somewhat different manner, reaches a similar nonsensical effect.

4.2.2 *Lewis Carroll*

On the life and works of Lewis Carroll (pseudonym of Charles Lutwidge Dodgson, 1832-1898) a spate of literature exists. There are now more than a dozen biographies in English, as well as a few in other languages. The most important of these are those by de la Mare (1932), Ayres (1936), which I have been unable to consult, Lennon (1945 [1962]), Taylor (1952), Hudson (1954 [1976]), Gattégno (1970) and Pudney (1976). Essays on various aspects of his life and works have been collected by Phillips (1971 [1974]), who includes an extensive "Checklist" bibliography (511-24), Parisot (1971), Gray (1971) and Guiliano (1976; 1982). I have not been able to consult D. Rackin's *Alice in Wonderland: Essays in Criticism*, Wadsworth 1970. Useful critical studies are Cammaerts (1925) and Sewell (1952), which also deal with Lear, Alexander (1951), Schöne (1954a), Hildebrandt (1962: 136-58), Liede (1963, I: 172-204), Sutherland (1970; on Carroll's use of language), Petzold (1972: 10-78), Blake (1974; on Carroll's games), Reichert (1974), Ede (1975: 70-152), Huxley (1976), Sale (1978: 101-25), Prickett (1979: 131-49), Nöth (1980), Lang (1982: 44-53), Kincaid & Guiliano (1982) and Kreutzer (1984). Needless to say, a short section on Carroll's works must be highly selective in the use of earlier scholarship; I have mainly consulted those works which deal with Carroll as a writer of nonsense.

In chapter 2, pp. 81-5, I have already touched upon the differences between Lear and Carroll, which have been frequently noted, and on which I in fact base two distinct branches or types of nonsense. The differences are most noticeable when we regard the works of Carroll and Lear as units rather than in detail. Writing on *AW* and *TLG*, Alexander speaks of the "framework set up at the very beginning of each book" (1951: 552), and he goes on to say that "[w]hat the principle amounts to is that the assertion of a false proposition allows the *possibility* of every other proposition being deducible from it" (*ibid.*). Whereas Lear "throws overboard all rules except the minimum ones of verse structure", Carroll's nonsense obeys rules, "but rules which are different from our normal ones" (554). It is certainly true that Carroll's nonsense is based on linguistic and logical fallacies (556); Lear's nonsense, then, may be said to be based on linguistic and logical imagination, a more random variation from the ordinary. Basically, Carroll's incongruity is *initial*, whereas that of Lear is *final*. What this amounts to in the case of Carroll's nonsense is that when we think we have grasped the rules, they are changed again, or a new situation or proposition is introduced ("Suppose we change the subject" is a favourite phrase), and we have to find our bearings anew.

Themerson, in a recent article entitled "On Nonsense & On Logic-Fiction" (in Tigges 1987: 3-16), refuses to give the name nonsense to Carroll's *oeuvre*. His argument is that we must distinguish between sense and nonsense as means, and sense and nonsense as result. Poets make sense with nonsensical means (such as rhyme) (8). Lewis Carroll is "the very quintessence of sense" (11). He used Symbolic Logic to detect nonsense, and used Alice-in-Wonderland fiction to unmask it, which is why he should be called "The Great Master of Logic-Fiction rather than a Representative of the Tradition of Nonsense" (*ibid.*). Apparently Themerson refuses to acknowledge that Carroll in his fiction creates a reality; there are creatures in his fiction which use the rules of a rigid logic, and these creatures, including Alice herself, are not metalogical labels, but characters, and so I beg to disagree with Themerson's categorical objection to reading the Alice books as nonsense.[13]

It is more useful to take notice of the fact that Carroll makes use of nonsensical reasoning (cf. Ede 1975: 70), reasoning which is nonsensical because it *is* logical, whereas Lear describes nonsensical acts, which are nonsensical because they are unmotivated. Lear, so to speak, presents the heart and hands of nonsense, and Carroll its head. In terms of Jungian typology, in Lear the theme is often a tension between elements belonging to the sphere of feeling and that of sensation (the size of one's nose being in the way of love), whereas in Carroll intuition (embodied by the commonsensical Alice) tries to keep rigid thinking at bay. As Ede puts it: "The world of Lewis Carroll's nonsense is more concerned with ideas than with action" (1975: 72). The tension between meaning and non-meaning is usually presented in conversation rather than in description (cf. Nöth 1980: 64: "*Im Nonsens-Dialog verbleibt die Störung im Verlauf des Dialogs erhalten.*"

One of the most striking aspects of the longer nonsense text in general, which is aptly illustrated in *AW* and *TLG*, is its episodic nature. In his discussion of *AW*, Taylor points out that its story "grew out of separate bits and pieces linked together more by the

---

13. Cf. Gattégno (1976: 74-80, esp. 75).

association of ideas than by cause and effect" (1952: 48).[14] Schöne would define this as "Tendenzlosigkeit", one of the two main characteristics of nonsense, the other being playfulness (1954a: 102). Rackin remarks that in *AW* practically all pattern is annihilated (1966 [1971]: 453). Reichert, who calls isolation, disintegration, detachedness and disconnection the characteristics of nonsense (1974: 20), calls *AW* an arrangement of isolated episodes, whose continuity is fictional (66). Ede recognizes that *AW* is episodic (1975: 83) and Sale states that the episodes are the crucial units (1979: 124). According to him this has important implications for a reading of the text as a whole because "... learning to read one scene helps us very little in reading the next one" (111). Kreutzer too speaks of the haphazard combination of disintegrated units (1984: 63).

I am willing to endorse the above statements, in the sense that like Lear's limericks, and like his longer poems taken together, it is quite possible to read *AW* and *TLG* as "series". At the same time, however, like Lear's series, the works of Carroll are also to be seen as nonsensical units. After all, *AW* and *TLG* are presented as complete stories, as novels containing a beginning and an end, a chapter-division, a protagonist and other recurrent characters, all of which suggests unity. This unity or coherence of the Alice books has been noted as well. Levin refers to the genre of the *voyage imaginaire* with which the dream-vision in *AW* and *TLG* has been conflated (1965 [1971]: 231). Flescher points out the unity created by the "consciously regulated patttern" of verse, a law or the rules of a game, which is the backbone of nonsense (1969/70: 128).[15]

It seems, then, that the Alice books can be seen as simultaneously internally disconnected and coherent, and that the tension between coherence and lack of unity is characteristic of nonsense, embodying not only the tension between meaning of the whole and absence of meaning in the parts, but also that between the meaning contained in the episodes but absent in the whole. Since the episodic nature of the Alice books has been extensively discussed in the criticism mentioned in the preceding paragraphs, to which should be

---

14. Taylor present an allegorical reading of *AW* (41-63), but denies that the allegory is consistent. For an entirely associative reading of Carroll's nonsense, see Huxley (1976).
15. Cf. Prickett, who says that the structure of Carroll's work is nearly always logical (1979: 126), and who calls nonsense "the most rigidly controlled of all forms of fantasy" (*ibid.*).

added Blake's discussion of Carroll's works in terms of play and games (1974), and Nöth's very interesting semiotic approach (1980), I will limit myself to a more general discussion of *AW* as "a nonsense", to be followed by a brief analysis of *The Hunting of the Snark*.[16]

Spontaneous as *AW* may have been (and the evidence of this from the mouth of the author himself may be taken as incontestable),[17] yet a certain order can be detected. Ede speaks of a tripartite structure:

> The first four chapters initiate the reader to Wonderland, establish Alice's essential reliability as a guide, and introduce language as a crucial element in the dialectic between order and disorder. Chapters Five through Seven clarify the relationship between language, identity, and meaning ... The final chapters of the work, which occur inside the long-anticipated garden, elaborate on what Alice has both lost and gained by her rejection of Wonderland; ... (1975: 90).

As Ede also notes, change is an important theme in the book,[18] and one could in fact characterize each of the twelve chapters in terms of what aspect of Alice's world is metamorphosed. As Ede remarks, the opening chapters "focus primarily on Alice's frequent and confusing changes of size" (91). The resulting changes of perspective, including Alice's ultimate realization that the world becomes less frightening the larger one is, can be seen as an example of Play

---

16. For a very perceptive interpretation of *AW* as a dream-vision allegorizing an unfulfilled quest for meaning, see Rackin (1966 [1971]). For discussions of *TLG*, which is generally considered more systematically structured and less spontaneous than *AW*, see e.g. Taylor (1952: 94-147), Spacks (1961 [1971]), Kincaid (1973), Ede (1975: 113-44), Polhemus (1980: 245-93) and Kreutzer (1984: 76-83).

17. On the spontaneity of *AW* as compared to *TLG* see Levin (1965 [1971]: 232), Rackin (1976: 2). Carroll's own words on the spontaneous genesis of *AW* are quoted e.g. by Sale (1979: 102-3). See also Carroll's introductory poem "All in the golden Afternoon", Carroll, ed. Gardner (1960 [1965]: 21-3). All page references to *AW* and *TLG* are from this edition.

18. 91; cf. Massey (1976: 76-91) on the theme of metamorphosis in *AW*.

with Boundaries (see Stewart 1978: 101-2), just as the seriality of the growings and shrinkings is indicative of Play with Infinity.

A simple list of the twelve chapters of *AW* marking the main themes or aspects subject to change would look as follows:

I	Down the Rabbit-Hole	Nature (disruption of order)
II	The Pool of Tears	Body, Measures and Mathematics
III	A Caucus-Race and a Long Tale	Language
IV	The Rabbit Sends in a Little Bill	Habitation
V	Advice from a Caterpillar	Communication
VI	Pig and Pepper	Social order
VII	A Mad Tea-Party	Time
VIII	The Queen's Croquet-Ground	Games
IX	The Mock-Turtle's Story	Ethics and Education
X	The Lobster-Quadrille	Dance
XI	Who Stole the Tarts?	Justice
XII	Alice's Evidence	Order (restoration)

From the list in the right-hand column it already becomes evident that what changes is everything that is under normal circumstances, or rather from a rational point of view, subject to rules: the order of nature, the measures of the body, mathematics, language, space, polite conversation and social order, time, games and play, ethics and education, the dance and, ultimately even justice. Of course, these things do not "really" change. Their metamorphosis manifests itself basically in the language which we use to describe and define them (Cf. Massey 1976: 95). I will attempt to clarify this by looking at each of the chapters in more detail.

In the first chapter, all the themes treated in the book are already succinctly making their presence felt. The change in nature and its order is manifested by the White Rabbit, who acquires human speech and carries a watch. Its very first utterance: "Oh dear! I shall be too late!" (25-6) shows its concern with time. From Victorian times onwards not only adults, but also children were coming to be more and more oppressed by time; we are constantly admonished to be "in time": for meals, for lessons, for work, for bed. That this fear of being late is embodied, in a child's imagination, in a rabbit, is only appropriate, because these scurrying animals seem to be in a constant hurry.

The notion of a rabbit, however, leads to that of a rabbit-hole. By falling through the Rabbit-hole, where gravity is suspended, Alice escapes to what will later turn out to be a timeless place, or rather, a place where the tyranny of time is replaced by that of space. The tunnel's walls are covered with foodstores and bookshelves. In Wonderland, food has magical properties: it not only makes you grow, but shrink as well. The more knowledge one possesses, the more stupid one seems to get. Entropy has ceased to move in one direction only. Even language itself is already questioned here, being reduced to empty sound ("Do cats eat bats? ... Do bats eat cats?"—28). But the place where Alice ends up is a Hall with locked doors. There seems to be no way out, not even when a key fits. Ironically, a child finds herself too large rather than too small to escape into the wonderful garden. The inversions are obvious. Alice is still fettered to the correspondence between an object and its name: a bottle not marked "poison" cannot contain poison (31). Words like "Latitude" and "Longitude" lose their sense; their precision on the surface of the earth is useless at its centre. In infinite space, bodily size proves to be a relative concept.

The notion of size is the link between the first chapter and the second, where Alice also becomes conscious of the relative nature of her identity. Carroll here toys with the idea that identity is not so much based on one's size as on the contents of one's individual brain—as if there is no such thing as shared knowledge. The uncertainty about identity is embodied all through *AW* in the helpless way in which the familiar texts of nursery rhymes get changed. Massey describes this as the metamorphosis of the character into the author (1976: 93). Alice becomes a "disembodied voice" whenever she recites poetry, which happens in nearly every chapter. It is the most prominent illustration of the predominance of language over its pretended users. It is ironical that the Wonderland creatures realize that the texts are "wrong", a knowledge which they are constantly rubbing in. In chapter II Alice is still alone, and she must overcome her initial fears, literally escaping from drowning in her tears, once again a manner of speaking given grim embodiment.

In the third chapter, this theme is continued, when the solid text from a well-known history literally becomes a "dry" subject. In this chapter the first pun, that on "tail" and "tale", comes alive. The clever thing is that Carroll constantly makes his puns "appropriate" by adapting reality to language, things to words. In this instance he performs this trick by introducing a mouse who has a "tale" as well as a "tail". But for the fortune of language this reality would not exist.[19] Carroll elaborates another inversion by having animals behave like human beings. The extinct Dodo (the stuttering Do-do-dodgson himself—see Gardner: 44) speaks in a style which is no longer understood as English (47).

The theme of humanized, personified animals is continued in chapter IV, and the way animals send human beings on errands is already a premonition of the reversal of social order, which is here extended to include the whole of creation. In this chapter, words acquire a visual shape, a house becomes too narrow to contain a human being, pebbles turn into cakes.

Chapter V demonstrates how the rules of conversation (polite or otherwise) are suspended. The meeting of Alice with the Caterpillar (a creature which will by nature have to change into a chrysalis and a butterfly) is worth quoting at length:

> "Who are *You*?" said the Caterpillar.
> This was not an encouraging opening for a conversation. Alice replied, rather shyly, "I—I hardly know, Sir, just at present—at least I know who I *was* when I got up this morning, but I think I must have been changed several times since then."
> "What do you mean by that?" said the Caterpillar, sternly. "Explain yourself!"
> "I can't explain *myself*, I'm afraid, Sir," said Alice, "because I'm not myself, you see."
> "I don't see," said the Caterpillar.
> "I'm afraid I can't put it more clearly," Alice replied very politely, "for I can't understand it myself, to begin with; and being so many different sizes in a day is very confusing."
> "It isn't," said the Caterpillar.
> "Well, perhaps you haven't found it so yet," said Alice; "but when you have to turn into a chrysalis—you will some day, you know—and then after that into a butterfly, I should think you'll feel it a little queer, won't you?"
> "Not a bit," said the Caterpillar.
> "Well, perhaps *your* feelings may be different," said Alice: "all I know is, it would feel very queer to *me*."

---

19. As Gardner is careful to point out, in another language these elements of the story would have taken a different form (8-9).

"You!" said the Caterpillar contemptuously. "Who are *you*?" (67-8).

A "normal" conversation, of course, has to start with the (meaningless) question "*How* are you?" On the other hand, "Who are you?" is a very good (and hence usual) question for an adult to open a conversation with a child, as many readers will be aware. The "turn" is then to the child (in *TLG*, Humpty Dumpty actually discusses conversation in terms of a riddling game where partners take turns to "guess" one another's meanings), who should answer "I am Alice". But Alice takes the Caterpillar's question literally, thereby providing it with an existentialist meaning it does not really have when taken as phatic communion. The Caterpillar is only right to ask for an explanation of Alice's answer. By doing so, he plays what he thinks is Alice's game. When she uses the meaningless tag "you see" at the end of a phrase, he retorts with a literal "I don't see", just as later on, when Alice asks him "Is that all?" he simply answers "No", instead of conventionally providing the additional information (69). It turns out that the Wonderland creatures go by an inexorable logic. This is the tyranny set up by language liberated as noted by Massey (1976: 86). It is Carroll rather than Alice who says to language: "If you are real, let me see how you will act when you are left to your own devices" (87).[20]

The fifth chapter also illustrates the relativity of identity from the "other" point of view. For the pigeon it makes no difference whether a predator who eats eggs is called a serpent or a little girl (76).

Chapter VI elaborates on the inversion of social order. In this chapter a Duchess nurses a baby in a kitchen, a Cook throws utensils about, footmen are insolent philosophers and cats are smiling logicians. Alice remains sane, that is she refuses to accept the Cheshire Cat's thesis that she must be mad. All we are left with at this stage is a grin—an abstraction turned into physical reality.

Chapter VII, the Mad Tea-Party, is often considered the central chapter of the book, an epitome of its message. Once again, a conversation is turned into a riddling game, but the riddle has no answer. Another abstract notion, time, is personified, and killed—it

---

20. Massey uses a striking image to epitomize the working of language in nonsense, when he says that words in nonsense behave like strikers "working to rule" (88).

has stopped. For some it is perennial tea-time (some children's wish-fulfilment, perhaps), for others perennial time to sleep. Drawing (in whatever sense—the conversation on pp. 102-3 contains a marvellous extended pun) becomes an endless business, if one draws *everything* that begins with an M. The Dormouse's enumeration appropriately ends with the all-inclusive "muchness". It is at the end of this chapter that Alice shows the loss of her fear by walking off in disgust. What she does not lose is her yearning for companionship. Instead of calling after her as she *half* hopes (note the balanced ambiguity of her feelings), the March Hare and the Mad Hatter occupy themselves by putting the Dormouse into the Teapot (103).

That Alice now feels herself to some extent in command of the situation is proved by her remark in chapter VIII that after all "they" are only a pack of cards (108). But it is not yet time to leave this world; after all, she has only just reached, through the initial Hall full of doors, the desired rose-garden. In the eighth chapter, it turns out that games like cards and croquet have their rules changed, as well as their implements. It is also a chapter full of violence, with the Queen of Hearts randomly shouting "Off with his/her/its/their head(s)" with the unquestionable authority of a mother or a governess with her "Off to your bed!"[21]

Ede has convincingly argued the importance of holding up the story in chapters IX and X. They form a break, "providing a reasonable degree of suspense during the trial" (1975: 104). The subjects of these chapters are morals and lessons, in other words, education in its widest sense, and the dance, that supremely orderly, almost ritual activity which is a beloved nonsense theme, as has been mentioned before.[22]

21. As the game of croquet is a game of physical skill, so the card-game is a game of chance or fortune. Is it accidental that Carroll started the adventure with a "fall"? In *TLG*, where Carroll introduced a third type of game, that of chess, which requires intellectual skill, as an organizing structural device, Alice is much more active.

22. See chapter 2, pp. 80-1. The "courting" which follows this dance is that of a law-suit. The Knave of Hearts (the symbolic epitome of a "suitor") is accused (of stealing "tarts"), and Alice is a witness for the defence. The psychological implications of the final chapters of *AW* are simultaneously "suppressed", like the guinea pigs, because it is precisely at this stage that Alice reduces the court to

Once again, in chapter IX the numerous puns are appropriate. They belong in fact mostly to the type of wordplay which Hammond and Hughes call the assonant pun (1978: VI). They are appropriate in the sense that addition is indeed often distorted to Ambition in the materialist Victorian world, just as to lose material wealth as well as spiritual health becomes Distraction, multiplying (what Karl Marx called "accumulation") led to Uglification, and dividing (losing one's social status by becoming bankrupt) to Derision. Drawling, Stretching and Fainting in Coils were of course as much the Victorian young person's preoccupation as Drawing, Sketching and Painting in Oils, although Lear might have disagreed here (129).

In chapter X, Carroll in fact *creates* puns and other wordplay. Only under the sea does Whiting shoes and boots become a viable alternative for Blacking them, and does it become appropriate for shoes to be made of "soles and eels" (136-7). The only objection is, as Lear already noted, that fish have no feet and so are more likely to walk on stilts. It is in this chapter that it becomes clear that it is not the Gryphon and the Mock Turtle (the latter creature being an obvious creation from language) but we ourselves who live in a "Wonderland": a place where animals are actually eaten. Alice takes this phenomenon too much for granted, but for obvious reasons the Wonderland creatures, being animals, find this a frightening prospect. In this context it is highly ironical that the Gryphon is a non-existent composite of existent predators, whereas the whole "purpose", not to say "porpoise" of a Mock Turtle is to serve for artificial food.

If in chapter X it is the nature of the dance that is transformed, in chapter XI we find a final metamorphosis, that of justice. Ede has noted that justice is one of Alice's main concerns (as it is for most children), in commenting on Alice's earlier statement: "I don't think they play at all fairly" (1975: 103; Gardner 1960 [1965]: 113). It is in the courtroom chapter that the whole of creation is collected; each member becomes a representative of a judicial role: the White Rabbit turns up as a Herald or usher, the Mad Hatter as a witness, Bill the Lizard as a juror and so on. But Alice is already growing, and with her bodily size her judgement increases, as is proven in the final chapter.

Chapter XII begins with Alice answering to her name; there is no longer any doubt about her identity. In the course of the chapter, a pack of cards and the whole adventure to a dream.

she becomes the authority which the King of Hearts, as both King and Judge, fails to embody. His utter inanity and futility are demonstrated in his "reading" of the "Evidence" poem, "They told me you had been to her". The King fails to realize that in this poem, as in any nonsense, meaning is balanced with non-meaning. Having finally achieved her true identity, her true size and her true judgement, Alice pronounces the liberating sentence: "You're nothing but a pack of cards!" (161). The spell is broken, and everything is, perhaps a little too smugly and sentimentally (Carroll's only weakness) explained in terms of ordinary cause and effect, place and time.

The meaning of the whole book is, as it were, taken away by the explanation (it was a "curious dream" after all), but not retracted. It is certainly true that the book does not circle around within its hermetic context as is the case with Lear's limerick cycles. External references, to education, to the adult surroundings of a bourgeois Victorian seven-year old girl, are brought in. These references are, however, consistently reduced to the level of language, which is always predominant. The satire is played down, and the burlesques and verbal jokes are not presented as the "point" of the story. They are part of what I have called, following Fowler's terminology, the "repertoire" of the nonsense genre. The linguistic presentation keeps emotional involvement at bay. The threatening phrase "Off with her head!" is immediately reduced to a mere phrase, as when the gardeners cannot be beheaded because, being "gone", their heads are "gone" as well, and the executioner finds he cannot behead the Cheshire Cat because its head is not attached to a body (110, 116-7). The result of it all is that a perfect balance between meaning and its simultaneous absence is maintained, by sustaining the various polarities as mentioned by Ede (1975: 12) and Rackin (1976: 15).[23]

Concerning the nonsensical nature of Carroll's long poem *The Hunting of the Snark* (henceforth *HS*) opinions differ widely. Sewell regards it as a Nonsense failure, on the grounds that the emotion it evokes, "a slight sensation of distaste and disquiet" causes it to upset the game, which nonsense essentially is (1952: 147). Laffay finds actual proof of the fact that *HS* is not pure nonsense in that it has been translated into various other languages (1970: 11). Curiouser and curiouser! On the other hand, Holquist describes *HS* as "the most perfect nonsense which Carroll created" (1969/70: 150),

---

23. For more extensive references to these polarities, see chapter 1, pp. 29-30 above.

whereas "the Alice books are less perfect nonsense than *The Hunting of the Snark*" (155).

Holquist, who regards *HS* as a precursor to the "immaculate fiction" produced by Modernist writers, is right in concluding that this poem cannot be turned into an allegory, as so many readers have tried to do (147).[24] According to him, the poem achieves pure order, the quest for which dominated Dodgson's life (151; cf. Rackin 1982b). In his argument to prove that "the poem is best understood as a structure of resistance to other structures of meaning which might be brought to it" (156), Holquist presents six indices of its "systematic arbitrariness", which, though valid in themselves, do not really seem to prove the point that *HS* is more nonsensical than *AW* and *TLG*. I have already alluded to them before,[25] and I wish to subject them here to a brief critical discussion.

The first index mentioned is the introductory Dedication to Gertrude Chataway, which because it contains a double acrostic already points to the closed nature of the poem (156-7). If this is any proof at all, which I doubt, one might with all the more justice refer to the pervasive distortion of nursery rhymes and popular poetry within the Alice books as an indication of the hermetic nature of these books. The second index is the Rule of Three, said to be a parody of the logical syllogism (157). This rule, introduced in the second stanza of Fit the First, goes: "What I tell you three times is true" (46).[26] It is applied only three times in the whole

---

24. Taylor mentions identifications of the Snark with Fortune, Social Advancement, Popularity and the Absolute (1952: 55). His own view is that the poem is a satire against modern (i.e. post-1870) education, and more concretely an anti-vivisectionist tract (157-62). Gardner adds to these Business and Destiny, and his own "solution", the atomic Bomb (1962 [1967]: 23-5, 28). Adams states it presents Nothing (1966: 96). Marnat (1971) and Beaver (1976) have seen parallels with Melville's *Moby Dick*. Reichert regards the Snark as a "Proteus" (1974; 148): everybody has his own Snark; the quest is not a private but a public one; for Carroll, the Snark is "the" little girl-friend, and ultimately his own childhood (171). Carroll himself, albeit with tongue in cheek, agreed that "an allegory of the search after happiness" was presumably the best explanation (see Taylor 1952: 155; Liede 1963: I, 199).

25. See chapter 1, p. 23 above.

26. All page references are to Gardner's annotated edition (1962

poem (itself a rule of three?), and it does not feature for instance in Fit the Sixth, "The Barrister's Dream", where it would have served the Snark a useful purpose. In that Fit the Snark takes upon himself a *fourfold* role of defending counsel, prosecuting officer, jury and judge, but I do not think this is a reinforcement of the Rule of Three.

As a third index, Holquist mentions the fact that all the members of the hunting crew begin with the letter B (158), a device which we have already encountered in the Dormouse's story in *AW*, Chapter VII. It is in fact the common nonsensical device of stringing or infinity we are dealing with here. Equally common is the fourth index, the circularity of the "equation" in Fit the Fifth. The fifth index, the use of coinages, in particular the portmanteaux (159-62), which Holquist calls a systematic violence practised on semantics, is not particularly exploited in *HS*. Apart from the two key-words of the poem, "Snark" and "Boojum", which in fact are the sole instrument of turning *HS* into nonsense, as we do not know what they are and the incongruent "explanations" given by the Bellman and the Baker's uncle do not help us out, Carroll uses eight coinages in all, and we cannot even be sure that they are portmanteaux. We only have Humpty Dumpty's word for it, and Carroll's Introduction to *HS* is not to be trusted, as Carroll always refused to give consistent explanations. They all come from that most obscure of all nonsense verses, the renowned "Jabberwocky".[27]

It will be easily seen that, with the exception of the Rule of Three, Holquist's "indices" are really no more than elements from the nonsense "repertoire". As a sixth index Holquist adduces rhyme, which he calls another rule of three (162-3). In ordinary poetry the association of two words in rhyme create a third meaning which is not contained in either of them alone (162). In *HS*, however, rhyme cannot be related to meaning (163). Holquist illustrates this by quoting the repeated opening stanza of Fits Five through Eight:

[1965]).

27. If they are neologisms rather than portmanteaux, they are different from those by Lear in that Carroll uses them with the same (absent) meaning and "connotations". Unlike Lear's "runcible", that is, Carroll's "beamish", "uffish" etc. apparently always mean the same thing—whatever that may be. See Partridge (1950) for a discussion of these nonsense words.

> They sought it with thimbles, they sought it with care;
>   They pursued it with forks and hope;
> They threatened its life with a railway-share;
>   They charmed it with smiles and soap (73, 83, 89, 93).

There are indeed no connotations or associations evoked here, or rather, because of the difficulty of associating care with a railway-share and hope with soap, the reader who attempts to discover them has to give up soon, and one may conclude that Carroll jumbled these concepts together because of their rhymes.[28] There *is* a new meaning, however, which arises from these collocations, and that is that the search is meaningless, as such entirely divergent "weapons" (or are they tools?) can never result in the discovery of one creature, however divergent its habits. It is in fact the Baker, who is careless and desperate, greasy ("His intimate friends called him 'Candle-ends',/ And his enemies 'Toasted Cheese'"—50), and so forgetful that if he owned a railway-share he presumably left it on the beach along with "[h]is umbrella, his watch, all his jewels and rings" (48), who *does* find the Snark—and vanishes away, upon which the poem comes to a sudden end as well.[29]

The stanza quoted above may be considered a form of imprecision or mixture, like the Lear stanza quoted in note 29. The point about the hermetic nature of *HS* is as well made (if not better) by Holquist concerning the use of rhyme. In any case, the problem of rhyme in nonsense verse is an intricate one. The characters in *HS* are to a certain extent determined by initial rhyme or alliteration, but it is not true that they are reduced to integers, as Holquist states (152; cf. Themerson 1987). They are individuals, and to a large

---

28. Cf. however Gardner's ingenious explanation on p. 73, n. 40.

29. By making the word "Snark" rhyme only with "remark" (seven times), "mark(s)" (three times), "dark" (twice) and "hark" (once), Carroll creates the impression that the Snark becomes never more than a (re)mark, a mere word or sign. There is indeed some "binding effect" to these rhymes after all (Holquist 1969/70: 162, quoting Wimsatt), but it leaves the interpreter "in the dark", as no further clues are offered. In this sense, the stanza in question is rather like the items in Lear's "Teapots and Quails" sequence (see Lear, ed. Davidson & Hofer 1953: 15-42). One "stanza" goes: "Mitres and beams,/ Thimbles and Creams,/ Set him a screaming/ and hark! how he screams!" (16).

extent true to their professions, as witness for instance Fit the Fourth. The nonsense is in the incongruity of all these professionals, who would normally only find themselves gathered so closely together in the Yellow Pages, and in the futile context of a Snark hunt.

Lecercle, who interprets the Snark as Language itself (1971: 48) and the whole poem as a metalinguistic text (50), points to the occurrence in *HS* of the commonplaces of the epic, the style and diction of Romantic poetry, and the literal application of automatisms and stereotypes of speech (43-6). I find myself closer to Ede, who detects in its ballad-metre a resemblance to Lear's limericks (1975: 144). The nonsense in *HS* is at least as prominent in its episodic content-matter as it is in its language. Indeed, Carroll does not offend the rules of either grammar or prosody, and a parody, except in a very general way, is not indicated.[30] Unlike Lear in the "Dong", Carroll uses no Romantic poetic diction—the diction of *HS* is in fact much closer to that of Gilbert's *Bab Ballads* and other Victorian light verse.

The poem had best be regarded as "all quests in one", like human life "a voyage from void to void" (Adams 1966: 96, 98). This makes the epic beginning in *medias res* all the more appropriate, although the place where the crew land is not indicated on that most perfect of sea charts, the one that the bellman has provided to the delight of his fellow-travellers. We may never learn what a Snark actually is, except that this one was a "Boojum", but we do learn what it means to be "snarked". That means: to have complete inversion take place, as when one's bowsprit gets mixed up with one's rudder (57), or when travelling by a blank map, forgetting one's own name, perhaps ultimately having one's life exchanged for death. But these are only surmises, to be dropped as soon as picked up. As Beaver rightly puts it, the poem is "symbolically self-contained" (1976: 128)—there is a perfect balance between meaning and its absence.

Although their methods may be different, as regards the essentials of nonsense Lear and Carroll are not so widely apart. In both, the predominance of language is apparent. Both take a word, and turn it into a myth. Lear beguiles us into getting involved in the adventures of his Uncle Arly, who is merely the word "unclearly" spelled differently. The Snark is no more than an empty sound

---

30. Cf. Lecercle: "le poème est avant tout parodie d'un style" (1971: 43).

and fury, signifying nothing, but the quest is real: by disembodying the prey before it even acquires a body, Carroll allows us to probe the essence of the hunt, until we realize that a hunt without a prey, a quest without an aim, is Nothing.

4.3 The Development of the Lear Type

4.3.1 *Survey*

Both Carroll and Lear set a trend in children's literature, and consequently it has been difficult to dissociate their work and that of their followers from the nursery and the juvenile library. This is not in the last place because both grand-masters of nonsense spawned a host of imitators, who on the whole will be left out of consideration in these pages. On the subject of Lear imitators, Carpenter and Prichard (1984: 307) mention Edward Bradley (1827-89, otherwise known as Cuthbert Bede), whose *Funny Figures* appeared in 1858. According to the same source, "arguably [Lear's] only true heir has been Spike Milligan" (b. 1918), but I think most of his children's verse more suitably categorized as funny nursery rhymes and juvenile light verse, than as nonsenses within the scope of my definition.

Unfortunately, Laura Richards' collected poetry, *Tirra Lirra* (1932) is hard to come by in Europe. This prolific writer of children's books (1850-1943) started to write her nonsense verse soon after her marriage in 1871, and the seven poems selected in Cole 1968 and 1972 clearly bear the mark of Lear's influence. "Tom Tickleby and his Nose" (Cole 1968: 63), of which the first stanza runs:

> Little Tom Tickleby,
> Answer me quickleby!
>   Why is your nose so long?
> "I use it," said he,
> "For a flute, as you see,
>   And it greatly improves my song",

features that nonsense organ in all its musical glory. But "Jumble Jingle" (76) is a tongue-twister, and "The Buffalo" (83) light verse of the Hilaire Belloc variety.

As far as nonsense verse is concerned, I think Lear's only "true heir" is Mervyn Peake (1911-68). His *Book of Nonsense*, a sample from which was discussed on pp. 53-4 above, was published posthumously in 1972. The "Aunts and Uncles" poems on pp. 71-5 are a nonsense series comparable to the limerick cycles. On the whole, Peake's nonsense verse is somewhat more lyrical than Lear's, with the occasional introduction of an "I" (e.g. pp. 52, 53, 78ff.). Peake, who illustrated Carroll's nonsense works, also wrote a nonsensical story called *Captain Slaughterboard Drops Anchor*, which was first published in 1939. It features a sailor with a cork nose, as well as such nonsense creatures as the Balleroon, the Dignipomp and the Hunchabil.

Cohen (1956) selected some poems by Alan Crick (b. 1913). In style and diction, "A Chance Meeting" (63-4) resembles Carroll's *The Hunting of the Snark*, but its inconsequentiality is distinctly Learish. The "singular man" featuring in this poem is not only "playing himself at some strenuous chess/ Which he wheeled on a wickerwork frame", but he also posses a "clock/ With triangular dial and a flat-toned chime/ Which he drew from an old puce sock", and he ultimately "pack[s] up his chattels in sieves". The tone of these poems also resembles that of the most nonsensical verses by the German Joachim Ringelnatz (pseudonym of Hans Bötticher, 1883-1934).[31] The Dutch nonsense poet Daan Zonderland (pseudonym of Daniël van der Vat, 1909-77) has possibly been influenced by both Crick and Ringelnatz, as witness a poem like "Ivan de Verschrikkelijke" (Zonderland 1982: 84-5). His main source of inspiration, however, seems to have been Christian Morgenstern (1871-1914), to whom a separate section will be devoted.

French literature, *pace* Benayoun, is not richly endowed with literary nonsense. Neither Alphonse Allais' shaggy dog stories,[32] nor the verbal tricks of Robert Desnos or Raymond Queneau, neither Samuel Beckett's or Eugène Ionesco's absurd drama nor the sick grotesqueries of Roland Topor belong to the nonsense canon. There is a long tradition in modern French literature that ranges from symbolist and imagist poetry through Dada and surrealism to existentialism and the absurd, but nonsense finds little or no place there, although Boris Vian comes close to it in *L'Écume des jours*.

---

31. On Ringelnatz as a nonsense poet, see Hildebrandt (1962: 232-7).

32. Allais' character Captain Cap is somewhat similar to Morgenstern's Korf and Palmström, but the presentation of his "inventions" and ideas is not nonsensical. Lear at one time attempted to create a similar character in "Mrs. Jaypher".

Exceptions are some descriptive texts by Erik Satie (1866-1925), noticeably his "comic opera" *Le Piège de Méduse* (1913), and, more prominently, Alfred Jarry's *Gestes et Opinions du Docteur Faustroll* (1911, henceforth *DF*).[33]

Jarry (1873-1907) is, of course, mainly known for his *Ubu* cycle, but the Ubu plays are not basically nonsensical, although nonsense devices such as neologisms certainly feature in them. *DF*, however, can well be defined as a nonsense. Completed in 1898, it was not published in its entirety until posthumously in 1911. Its incoherent, episodic structure has been ascribed to Jarry's state of (mental) health at the time of writing (Perche 1965: 115). The long, central third book (it comprises nearly one third of the total text), which was published separately in the *Mercure* of May 1898, is a tribute to contemporary authors, painters and composers that Jarry admired, and as such it is not nonsensical, but its presentation as a journey by sieve over land from Paris to Paris is. Beaumont (1984: 183) explicitly attributes the idea of the floating sieve to Edward Lear's "The Jumblies", and to this one may add the islands in the form of lakes surrounded by land (*DF* XX, p. 65),[34] which are reminiscent of "The Story of the Four Little Children...". The "islands" are "literary universes" (Arrivé 1972: 100), but they are neither parodies nor burlesques.[35] From the language and images of the poets and painters whose names are mentioned as epigraphs to the separate chapters, Jarry creates a world which is not indeed "possible" (Perche 1965: 117) but nonsensical. The vegetation on the "Isle sonnante" (*DF* XXIII, 74-7) consists of exotic musical instruments, whose names Jarry uses as Lear uses Indian words in "The Cummerbund".

The account of the journey is framed in the theory of the science of 'pataphysics (the apostrophe serves to avoid a cheap pun (31), which it in fact evokes), of which Docteur Faustroll himself, born at the age of 63, is the veritable embodiment, if not the

---

33. For discussions, see e.g. Perche (1965: 114-20); Arrivé (1972: 99-104); Caradec (1974: 87-98); Gillespie (1983); and Beaumont (1984: 179-203). The latter's book is a recent biography as well as a critical study of Jarry's *oeuvre*, and contains an extensive bibliography.

34. All references are to the 1955 edition.

35. Cf. Arrivé (1972: 102). Caradec calls the whole work a parody of Töppfer's *Docteur Festus*, itself a Faust parody (1974: 87).

inventor (who is said to be Père Ubu—Caradec 1974: 88). 'Pataphysics, of which an etymology worthy of Humpty Dumpty is given in chapter VIII, is defined as the science which studies the laws of the exceptional (31), and also as the science of imaginary solutions (32). It seems to be the very science of nonsense, even if it is also to be regarded as "the absurdist doctrine" (Gillespie 1983: 96). Gillespie points out that Faustroll's very name "exhibits his compounded totality, a synthesis of contradictions" (105), which tallies with our definition of nonsense. The contradictions involved in particular are those of completion and freedom, the universal and the exceptional (106). Arrivé, who presents a brief semiotic analysis, adds to this an oscillation in *DF* between hyper-language and non-language (1972: 103).

The book also contains many elements which recall nonsense themes of the kind found in the Alice books. Chapter IX, in which Faustroll follows William Crookes in demonstrating "the changes which would appear to occur in the laws of the universe following a simple change in the size of the observer" (Beaumont 1984: 193-4) is ouf course highly reminiscent of the changes of size that occur in *AW*. In chapter XXVII it is argued that a head is a head only when it is separated from the body (94), and in chapter XLI there is a circular equation to determine the identity of God, which recalls the Fifth Fit of *The Hunting of the Snark*.

As the science of 'pataphysics fulfils the requirements of inversion as well as infinity and simultaneity, it is not surprising that Stewart's nonsense procedures of that ilk can be clearly discerned in *DF*. There is Play with Infinity in the circular equation just mentioned, but also in the list of Platonic interjections that occurs in chapter X, as well as in the list of Faustroll's confiscated library in chapter IV. Play with Boundaries occurs in the incongruity of much of the imagery used, as on p. 59: "L'amarre de l'as fut enroulée autour d'un grand arbre, balancé au vent comme un perroquet bascule dans le soleil". Inversion (islands appear as lakes) has already been noted. The themes of figures, food and even violence—Faustroll runs berserk when he discerns a horse's head, which he considers the ugliest object in existence (chapter XXVIII)—are present as well.

Beaumont notes that Jarry constantly seems to take away his own meaning: "everything is relative to the human view-point—including demonstrations of its relativity" (1984: 198). Moreover, "[t]otal scepticism, by a supreme paradox which lies at the centre of Jarry's thought and work, opens the door also to total 'belief'" (201). 'Pataphysics, he states, "involves an attitude which is neither one of commitment nor refusal, of acceptance nor rejection, but of a combination of each—a mixture of fascination and detachment akin to the amused playfulness of the child" (203)—which takes us back to the world of children's literature.

Although quite different from *DF* the *Rootabaga Stories* by Carl Sandburg (1878-1967) present, in Sewell's terms, a similar world of words rather than things (1952: 17ff.). Lynn refers to them as "sheer nonsense" (1980: 118),[36] and Carpenter and Prichard, *s.v.* "Nonsense", refer to these stories as "[o]ne of the few really satisfying 20th-cent. nonsense creations for children" (1984: 381). The *Rootabaga Stories* appeared in 1922, and were followed by *Rootabaga Pigeons* (1923) and *Potato Face* (1930). I will only discuss the first collection.

The stories are, as Lynn indicates, modelled on folk-tales, and in them sound and image are more important than plot and character (1980: 121). Consider the beginning of the first story:

> Gimme the Ax lived in a house where everything is the same as it always was.
>
> "The chimney sits on top of the house and lets the smoke out," said Gimme the Ax, "The doorknobs open the doors. The windows are always either open or shut. We are always either upstairs or downstairs in this house. Everything is the same as it always was."
>
> So he decided to let his children name themselves (1924: 3).

The triviality of the second paragraph is one of the more primitive nonsense devices, and to this Sandburg adds the inconsequentiality of the word "So" in the third paragraph. Although the suggestion is that letting one's children name themselves is *not* the same as "it" always was, the link with the house is at the most extremely tenuous. Sandburg uses practically all the tricks in the bag: seriality ("So they sold everything they had, pigs, pastures, pepper pickers, pitchforks, everything except their ragbags and a few extras"—the objects sold all begin with the same sound, and the "few extras"

---

36. Lynn's article is a loving bird's-eye view analysis of the first two Rootabaga books. She does not offer a definition of nonsense, except for the statement that incongruity is a common device in Sandburg's books.

take away the implication of "everything they had"—pp. 5-6); changes in time ("One of the clocks ran fast. The other clock ran slow", 31); arbitrariness (one's luck in love depends on the letters in one's name, 73ff.); shift of boundaries (edible clothing, 82ff.—cf. Lear's "The New Vestments"; personified utensils, 93ff.); puns (on p. 105 "hat ashes", the American pronunciation of "hot ashes", become the material out of which to make a snowman's hat); changes of size (on p. 115 standing in spilt molasses makes three boys shrink).

There are passages in the *Rootabaga Stories* which are not nonsensical at all, such as the stories called "The Two Skyscrapers Who Decided to Have a Child", "The Wooden Indian and the Shaghorn Buffalo" and "The White Horse Girl and the Blue Wind Boy", which are rather sentimental fantasies, but in other places the nonsense is highly concentrated, as in the opening paragraphs of "The Dollar Watch and the Five Jack Rabbits":

> Long ago, long before the waylacks lost the wonderful stripes of oat straw gold and the spots of timothy hay green in their marvelous curving tail feathers, long before the doo-doo-jangers whistled among the honeysuckle blossoms and the bitterbasters cried their last and dying wrangling cries, long before the sad happenings that came later, it was then, some years earlier than the year Fifty Fifty, that Young Leather and Red Slippers crossed the Rootabaga Country.
>
> To begin with, they were walking across the Rootabaga Country. And they were walking because it made their feet glad to feel the dirt of the earth under their shoes and they were close to the smells of the earth. They learned the ways of birds and bugs, why birds have wings, why bugs have legs, why the gladdy-whingers have spotted eggs in a basket nest in a booblow tree, and why the chizzywhizzies scrape off little fiddle songs all summer long while the summer nights last (141-2).

It is about as close as nonsense can get to regular poetic prose without becoming altogether "sensible".

Sandburg's "long ago" is as little the merely formulaic "once upon a time" of the traditional fairy tale as that in the stories from *The Spider's Palace* (1931) by Richard Hughes (1900-76). Hughes' "fairy tales" are more thematically structured around a particular nonsense device than are those by Sandburg. For instance, "Living in W'ales" is based on a pun, "Nothing" and "The King's Legs" on other wordplay, "The Dark Child" and "The Spider's Palace" on reversal, "As They Were Driving" on infinity, "The Three Sheep" on time-change, "The Ants", "The Gardener and the White Elephants" and "Inhaling" on changes of size, and "The Man with a Green Face" and "The Magic Glass" on metamorphosis.

Hughes sometimes presents a curious mixture of nonsense of the Carrollian type with that of a Learish nature. In "Telephone Travel", which describes a girl who can travel by telephone, but who on one occasion loses her way when she "rushes down the wire" to people who have dialled the wrong number, so that she has to stay with these people for some time, the protagonist is presented on Guy Fawkes Day with a sixpenny rocket. Her reaction is: "'That isn't worth a whole "Thank you," it's worth about half.' So she just said 'Than',' without the ''k you'" (53). This is pure Carrollian linguistic nonsense. But when the girl has returned to a water-tank on the roof of her home by means of this magic rocket, the story ends: "And there they found her and took her out, and washed her, and fed her generally on tapioca pudding and cold mutton, and didn't talk to her, and combed her hair *much* too often" (*ibid.*), which is in the vein of Lear, with its rushed listing of events, the inconsequential "generally", and the slightly odd combination of food-stuffs.

The last nonsense writers to be mentioned in this survey of Lear-type nonsense are Edward Gorey (b. 1925) and John Lennon (1940-80). To Gorey a separate section will be reserved (see 4.3.3 below). Lennon, at one time a member of the pop-group The Beatles, wrote two small volumes of nonsense prose and poetry, *In His Own Write* (1964), and *A Spaniard in the Works* (1965). Some posthumous texts of a more miscellaneous nature were published in 1986 under the title *Skywriting by Word of Mouth*.

Lennon was clearly influenced by both Carroll and Lear, as well as by the Joyce of *Finnegans Wake*. His use of odd and inconsistent spelling in the early volumes has been discussed on pp. 75-6 above. Lennon's *forte*, besides his nonsensical spelling, by means of which puns like "a cup of teeth" (1964: 62) are actually created, is the unexpected collocation, such as "It's time to take a bathos" (1986: 47), and the *non sequitur*, like "I smoked my way down to the ground floor, still suffering from a slight case of vernacular" (1986: 53). Unfortunately, the "story" of *Skywriting* is so lacking in unity, that the reader has nothing to hold on to at all, to the detriment of the nonsense. It reads in fact like, what it presumably is, a ragbag of psychedelic odds and ends, scraped together entirely at random, so that there is not even the necessary initial suggestion of a coherent meaning. For the nonsense one has to look at individual passages, such as the mildly Learish first paragraph of p. 70:

> He hated the "criminal element" with a vengeance bordering on discipline, carefully concealed behind a Fisherman's Dwarf. "These parasites must be harassed, until they know the full meaning of consistency, and every last drop has been drained from their never-satisfied conglomerate," he paused, "and furthermore, to be continued."

The only real complete nonsense in the book is the alphabet on p. 43, which begins:

> A is for Parrot which we can plainly see
> B is for glasses which we can plainly see
> C is for plastic which we can plainly see
> D is for Doris
> E is for binoculars I'll get it in five

Lennon has added an original nonsensical notion to the nonsense alphabet, by occasionally (but not consistently) suggesting that it is the *shape* of the letters that counts, as in the B for glasses and the E for binoculars, and similarly in "O is for football which we kick about a bit". In "R is for intestines which hurt when we dance" it is all of a sudden the letter's *sound* which becomes explanatory, and others are entirely inconsequential ("P is arab and her sister will"). The alphabet itself is the backbone that suggests the meaning, which is dismantled in the individual "explanations". This nonsense ends: "This is my story both humble and true/ Take it to pieces and mend it with glue". However one tries to, nothing will work and the puzzle remains, barring, of course, "inside joke" explanations, and a possible parody of Gertrude Stein.

In the early volumes the stories and poems are more tightly organized. Some of the stories are based on taking expressions literally, as in "No Flies On Frank". In others, some satire or parody hovers in the background, but is kept at bay by the sheer exuberance of the verbal nonsense. Gems of nonsense verse are "I Sat Belonely" (1964: 64) and "The Fat Budgie" (1965: 18-19). Carroll's influence has been detected in some of the songs Lennon wrote for The Beatles.[37]

Before turning our attention to the two greatest successors to the Lear tradition, a misunderstanding must be eliminated concerning T.S. Eliot's famous *Old Possum's Book of Practical Cats* (1940). Whether the point about the nonsensical quality of Eliot's poetry has first been raised by Sewell or by Schöne is a moot question.[38] Undoubtedly Eliot (1888-1965) used both Carroll and Lear as sources for inspiration—his autobiographical poem "How Unpleasant to Know Mr. Eliot" is an inverted inspiration from Lear's "Self-Portrait of the Laureate of Nonsense", and both Schöne and Sewell list various parallel themes and devices. But, as has been argued, the use of nonsense devices does not guarantee generic nonsense, and the Old Possum poems, charming as they are, must be dismissed from the nonsense canon. Their musical rhythm and formal spontaneity are indeed very close to similar aspects in the Songs of Lear, but Eliot's poems have clear points (collectively that each cat has its own mysterious, very individual character, which is embodied in a nonsensical name), and the humanizing of the cats is a common fantastic device which, as we have seen, is not limited to nonsense. If, moreover, a deeper meaning is suggested, as is done by Schöne, who calls the cats "symbolic masks" (1955a: 45), as well as by Douglass, who considers the book to be about "the battle between ego and social self" (1983: 115), then there is all the more reason for abandoning the idea that these poems are nonsenses.

4.3.2 Christian Morgenstern

Although the Galgenlieder of Christian Morgenstern (1871-1914) have frequently been associated with the grotesque (e.g. Schuchardt 1915:

---

37. See Roos (1984).

38. Sewell refers to Eliot in *The Field of Nonsense* (1952: 186), and her 1958 article on Carroll and Eliot is reprinted in Phillips 1971 [1974]: 155-63. In that article she calls *Old Possum's Book of Practical Cats* Eliot's "Overt Nonsense Work", and *The Waste Land* his "nearest approach to pure Nonsense practice" (157, 159). Schöne's article appeared in 1955, but was already presented as "Anhang II" to her 1951 dissertation (190-200). Petzold rightly takes issue against their classification of Eliot's poetry as nonsense (1972: 228). See also Douglass (1983).

639; Kayser 1957: 162-9; Neumann 1964: 332; Thomson 1972: 65, Palm 1983),[39] as well as regarded as precursors to the *avant-gardiste* poetry of the Dada and surrealist movements (Forster 1962: 26ff.; Neumann 1973: 54), most critics refer to them in one way or another as nonsense or "Unsinn". Kretschmer (1983: 217) cites Tabbert (1975), Petzold (1972), Homeyer (1947), Kusenberg (1947), Forster (1962), Klein (1954) and Liede (1963). To this list should be added Hildebrandt, who devotes a brief section to Morgenstern's linguistic nonsense (1962: 229-32), P.H. Neumann, who applies the term "Nonsens-Dichtung" (but equates this with comic and grotesque to the 'niederen' poetischen Gattung" in which Morgenstern attempted to liberate himself from the trammels of traditional lyricism (1973: 54), and Lang, whose section on the Galgenlieder (1982: 87-106) is introduced by a statement concerning the "weiteren Zusammenhang der Unsinndichtung Morgensterns" (87).

It seems, then, that most critics agree on the nonsensical quality of the Galgenlieder. A problem is that the criteria of what constitutes literary nonsense in the opinion of these critics do not always correspond. Some critics actually equate nonsense with the grotesque, sometimes including linguistic or word-grotesque (e.g. Neumann 1973), which creates the confusion of terms I have tried to unravel in chapter 3, section 6 above. Hildebrandt writes: "... Morgenstern läßt die Wörter ein assoziatives Spiel mit den Gedanken treiben, das sich dann zu kleinen Szenen formt, die sinnlich und logisch indifferent sind, keine Tendenz—es sei denn die, zu belustigen—und poetischen Ambitionen haben, gefühlneutral bleiben und sprachlich verfremden—mithin also alle wesentlichen Charakteristika des Nonsense aufweisen" (1962: 231). Lang also finds all *his* criteria of nonsense (which he calls childlike, non-literary and private) fulfilled (1982: 91). Rather than taking issue once again with these criteria, in what follows I will present a brief analysis of the Galgenlieder in the light of my own definition of nonsense. My main tenets will be that the Galgenlieder are to be regarded as a nonsense cycle,[40] and

---

39. This is mainly due the fact that Morgenstern himself referred to them as grotesques. See, however, Walter (1966: 112-6), where the confusion is satisfactorily cleared: "Morgenstern gebraucht dieses Wort [*sc.* "grotesk", WT] in einem gleichsam harmloseren Sinne, es enthält nicht die Tiefendimension wie der von Kayser verwendete Begriff" (116).

40. In this section, as elsewhere in this thesis, I refer to the

that as such it is closer to the lyrical nonsense of the Lear type than to the logical nonsense of the Carroll variety.

If the poems that are part of the Galgenlieder collection are regarded separately, it is indeed not unlikely that one will reach extreme conclusions about their nature. At the one extreme there are poems like "Fisches Nachtgesang", which Liede calls "die Krönung aller Lautmalerei" (1963: I, 292): "Es ist sprachlose Dichtung und reinste Unsinnspoesie in unserm Sinne" (*ibid.*). At the other end of the scale we find some of the poems in *Palmström*, which Liede regards as Morgenstern's best work (341). "Die eigentlichen Galgenlieder sind Aufstand der Dinge als Worte gegen ihren Schöpfer, den Menschen; Palmström dagegen bedeutet die heitere Resignation eines Menschen, der durch Mauthners Fegefeuer hindurchgeschritten ist und in der Mystik den Sinn des Wortes wiedergewonnen hat" (342).[41] Wordplay, which according to Liede had never been essential to the Galgenlieder anyway (348), has by now disappeared. This reading allies with Forster's Chestertonian view, which looks upon the Galgenlieder as "a brand of metaphysical nonsense as distinctively German as Lear and Carroll are English" (1962: 10). Although Forster admits that much of Morgenstern's effect "is gained by playing with language, taking metaphor literally and bringing it to life" (12), he also recognizes satirical elements (18-19), and ultimately "Korf and Palmström and similar figures, like the lonely knee, and the rest of them, become alive and credible because of Morgenstern's doctrine of universal love out of which they spring" (23). Underlying Morgenstern's nonsense are "the fundamental harmony of divinely ordered existence, which can even comprehend the absurd; and the complement to this—the absurdity of existence, pointing to God as the only solution" (25).

Liede's approach can be reconciled to the more holistic view of Forster by distinguishing a scale of categories, as is done by Morgan and Kretschmer. The former discerns the categories of sheer non-

---

Galgenlieder as the compilation of poems posthumously published (with some additions and subtractions on several occasions—see Kretschmer 1983: 43-5) as *Alle Galgenlieder von Christian Morgenstern*. References are to the 1933 edition. Originally, the poems were published in four volumes: *Galgenlieder* (1905), *Palmström* (1910), *Palma Kunkel* (1916) and *Gingganz* (1919).

41. Cf. Lang, who calls the later poems *partial* nonsense (1982: 79).

sense, rhyme nonsense, punning fancies, sound effects, printed shapes, satires, philosophic concepts, sensible ideas grotesquely presented, bizarre ideas and superior nonsense, and illustrates these by means of English translations, without further explanation of the terms used (1938: 288-91). Kretschmer presents a far more detailed analysis, which has already been summarized in chapter 1 (pp. 42-5 above; see also pp. 74-5). What is most important in his analysis is that he discusses the prime characteristic of nonsense in the Galgenlieder, namely that they lack a "pointe" (1983: 144), a view he shares with Walter (1966: 95).

Moreover, like Hildebrandt (1962: 231), Liede (1963: I, 305, 324ff.), F. Neumann (1964), Walter (1966), and P.H. Neumann (1973), Kretschmer stresses the play-element in the Galgenlieder (1983: 154-70; cf. 1985: 95-111), although, as has already been indicated on p. 43, the various authors differ in opinion as to the nature of the game. I share the views presented by F. Neumann (1964) and in particular Walter (1966), that in the Galgenlieder not the world, mystic or not, but the word is primary, and I therefore disagree with Schuchardt's attack on Spitzer's thesis that Morgenstern takes language as his starting-point.[42] That it consequently appears as if "[d]er belebten Wortwelt entspricht einer Außenwelt, in der alles verpersönlicht ist" (Schuchardt 1915: 640) is what constitutes the difference between mere wordplay and literary nonsense: the presence of a balance between meaning and its absence.

By way of example I will proceed to discuss "Die Mittagszeitung", a poem Lang analyses (1982: 99), but whose point, or rather, lack of a point, he misses.

> Korf erfindet eine Mittagszeitung,
> welche, wenn man sie gelesen hat,
> ist man satt.
> Ganz ohne Zubereitung
> irgend einer andern Speise.
> Jeder auch nur etwas Weise
> hält das Blatt (1933: 148).

---

42. 1915 [for 1920]: 652, referring to Spitzer's 1918 discussion of Morgenstern's grotesque use of language. This work has not been consulted. Spitzer defended himself in a short article (1921).

Concerning this poem, Lang states: "Eine *Mittags*zeitung, die beim Lesen sättigt, ist eine anthropologisch semantisch anomale Vorstellung (...) mit komisch phantastischem Charakter; sie ist nicht wirklich unsinnig und wird völlig stimmig—"nirgends unlogisch"—entfaltet. Die Konsequenz, daß sich "jeder auch nur etwas Weise" dieses Blatt hält, ist—wie der Satz ja selbst behauptet—höchst sinnvoll." What Lang fails to observe here is that the whole poem is initiated by the play on "Mittagszeitung"—a nonsensical word in a world which is only acquainted (formally at least) with *morning* and *evening* papers, but not with (after)*noon* papers. Morgenstern suggests (indeed, in his own words, "nirgends unlogisch") a parallel between the nature of meals and that of the news, or between eating and reading. As the German midday-meal is indeed much the heaviest of the three, so a "midday-paper", if it were invented, could be supposed to "sate" its reader "ohne Zubereitung/ irgend einer andern Speise"—but the word "andern" here suggests that reading and eating are one and the same thing ("'I see what I eat' is the same thing as 'I eat what I see'", to quote the Mad Hatter—Carroll, ed. Gardner 1960 [1965]: 95), and not only metaphorically alike. Hence, the sense of subscribing to this "paper" is to be doubted. The "point" of the paper, namely whether it is meant to provide the mind with news or to fill the stomach with food or both (the central word "satt" is of course as ambiguous as its English equivalent "sated") is in doubt, as is the wisdom of taking a subscription.

If we consider the poem not in isolation, but in the context of the Galgenlieder as a cycle, we must also take into consideration that (von) Korf, like his colleague Palmström, is a fictive character in any case: Korf's very identity hinges on a rhyme with "Dorf" (1933: 102, "Das Böhmische Dorf", a village which is itself part of a figurative expression), and we are repeatedly informed about the "pro forma" nature of Korf as a human being: "Denn, wie man schon oft erfuhr,/ ist v. Korf kein Mensch wie wir,/ ist ein Mensch pro forma nur" ("Korf-Münchhausen", 136), "schlechterdings ein Geist" ("Korf in Berlin", 143), "nichtexistent im Sinn/ abwägbarer bürgerlicher Kreise ("Die Wage", 158, cf. "Die Behörde", 165-6). These characters are as much figments of the imagination (and presented as such) as are the "Neue Bildungen, der Natur vorgeschlagen" (29), such as the "Ochsenspatz", the "Kamelente" and the "Regenlöwe". Similar creatures play a role in individual poems. That they are creations of the mind is indicated explicitly in a poem like "Der Tanz", in which the "Four Four Hog" and the "Upbeat Owl" meet underneath a column "die im Geiste ihres Schöpfers stand" (31). This poem features that supreme nonsense motif, the dance.

Among the earliest items in the collection are those famous and often quoted poems "Das große Lalulā" (19), "Fisches Nachtgesang" (25), "Die Trichter" (30), and "Das ästhetische Wiesel" (36), in which the predominance of sound, symbol, shape and rhyme over sense is evident.[43] In a certain sense, however, all of the Galgenlieder can be read like "Das große Lalulā"—and vice versa, and this establishes the tension between meaning and its absence in the infinite cycle. The meaning which one gets out of any of these poems must be put in first, and even if one is able to discern a scale with two extremes, it still holds that like Korf and Palmström "[b]eide lassen so die Menschen schenken,/ statt genießen" ("Die beiden Feste", 174). The essential self-reflexivity of nonsense which also characterizes the Galgenlieder is significantly stressed in the last poem of each of the four original volumes ("Wie sich das Galgenkind die Monatsnamen merkt", 97; "Die beiden Feste", 174; "Denkmalswunsch", 242; "Das Mondschaf", 272).

The cyclic nature of the Galgenlieder can also be demonstrated by considering the smaller cycles. First of all, of course, those of the four separate volumes; secondly, all the poems which feature Korf and Palmström, which form a series of nonsensical, primarily verbal "inventions"; finally, small sequences like the "Elster" poems (199-203), or the pair of "Das Wasser" and "Die Luft" (51-2). "Das Wasser", read in isolation, does not seem to be nonsensical at all, since the point of this poem can be read in something like the following way: if water were able to speak it would use language in as meaningless a fashion as human beings do—"Bier und Brot, Lieb und Treu,—/ und das wäre auch nicht neu" (51), and so it had better remain silent. In "Die Luft", the very next poem in the series, this apparent refusal to personify an abstraction is made relative in its opening line:

---

43. For discussions of "Das große Lalulā", see e.g. Liede (1963: I, 287-8, 291); Neumann (1964: 374-5); Walter (1966: 78-9), Thiele (1967), Neumann (1973: 59-60); Lang (1982: 102-3); Kretschmer (1983: 50-3); Palm (1983: 46-50); "Fisches Nachtgesang": Liede (I, 291-2); Walter (81); Neumann (1973: 60-1); Lang (104-5); Kretschmer (54-5); "Die Trichter": Liede (I, 294); Walter (91); Neumann (1973: 62); Lang (105-6); "Das ästhetische Wiesel": Liede (I, 286-7); Walter (82).

Die Luft war einst dem Sterben nah.

"Hilf mir, mein himmlischer Papa",
so rief sie mit sehr trübem Blick,
"ich werde dumm, ich werde dick;
du weißt ja sonst für alles Rat—
schick mich auf Reisen, in ein Bad,
auch saure Milch wird gern empfohlen;—
wenn nicht—laß ich den Teufel holen!"

Der Herr, sich scheuend vor Blamage,
erfand für sie die—Tonmassage.

Es gibt seitdem die Welt, die—schreit.
Wobei die Luft famos gedeiht.

To cure the air the Lord invents the mud-bath, "Tonmassage", with a wordplay on "sound", because the air is said to prosper from the crying of the world. In spite of the emotional associations evoked by the romantic collocation "die Welt, die—schreit", there is no emotional involvement after all. The possible emotion is as it were conducted along the dash before "schreit", which diverts the reader's attention from pity with the crying world to the wordplay on "Ton", and back to the purely material association between the world and its clay. There is no suggestion that this mud is in fact created by the tears of humanity (one of the possible poetic meanings of "Welt"). In a similar way, any religious overtones of "der Herr" are immediately suppressed by the expression of His fear of disgrace.

This last example demonstrates how even in those of the Galgenlieder which in themselves are heavily loaded with emotional affects ("Sterben", "hilf", "Papa", "mit sehr trübem Blick", "dumm", "Teufel", "Herr", "Blamage", "schreit"), the presentation of the poem in itself, as well as its placement in a cycle, destroy these overtones as soon as they are built up. The Lord is called "Papa", as by a bourgeois daughter, and is ashamed of possible disgrace, and so invents an ambiguous "Tonmassage". The disgrace of the Lord, in itself a fearful Blakean image, is detonated by the link (created by the again vulgarly bourgeois Gallic rhymes) between this disgrace and the mud (or tone) bath. The suggestion that this "mud bath" is in fact the world, creation, and the tone bath tearful humanity, is underplayed to such an extent that it becomes a highly unlikely reading—ultimately, the only point is that the air has been cured of its fatal disease (because, paradoxically, it is now being breathed by creation?).

Morgenstern is perhaps the greatest of all nonsense poets exactly because he manages so precisely to keep his poems in a perfect balance between meaning and non-meaning. Every single Galgenlied deserves a more extensive reading than it has received so far (only relatively few poems have been discussed at all), and than can be given in this thesis. If the Galgenlieder are "Dichtung aus Unvermögen" (Liede 1963: I, 430), it is perhaps because some topics are so terrible that they can only be broached in the form of nonsense. I will revert to this point in chapter 5.3.

What remains to be discussed is why these poems are closer to the nonsense of Lear than to that by Carroll. Kretschmer, who has made the most comprehensive comparison of all three nonsense authors, comes to the conclusion that Morgenstern's Lieder seem to have a more logical "sense" to them than much of Carroll's writing, and that whereas Morgenstern sets "problems", Lear just presents situations (276-8). The Galgenlieder, according to him, possess a "Grundidee", whereas Lear's limericks are "provocative" (279). Kretschmer also discovers an essential irony in the Galgenlieder, written for adults, which is not found in either Lear's or Carroll's children's books (284). That the Galgenlieder belong to the "Kleinfamilie 'Nonsense'" (314) in terms of my definition will, I hope, have become clear. In this respect, Kretschmer's doubts can be resolved. The question that remains is: to which category of nonsense does it belong?

The many stylistic similarities and correspondences in motifs discovered by Kretschmer (Part III, pp. 217-314) do not sufficiently answer this question, because they are shared by both the "Learic" and the "Carrollian" types. Statistically, most of the comparisons that Kretschmer adduces are with Carroll's works. Indeed, at first sight there are some important characteristics that Morgenstern seems to share with Carroll rather than with Lear: a greater predilection for wordplay, and a way of building an argument on a false linguistic premiss. A sequence like "Gig-ant - Zwölef-ant - Elef-ant - Nulel-ant" ("Anto-logie", 72-3) is based on an original wordplay on the element "-ant", which is then logically expanded into the series. "Gruselett" (271) reads remarkably like the opening and closing stanzas of Carroll's "Jabberwocky". On the other hand, Homeyer considered Morgenstern's poems a worthy parallel to Lear's (1947: 54), and Walter too compares Morgenstern with Lear rather than with Carroll (1966: 123-4). The similarity may be noted first of all in individual poems. "Neue Bildungen" (29) resembles Lear's nonsense botany (only without the illustrations), although one is also reminded of the bread-and-butterfly, the rocking-horse-fly and the snapdragon-fly in *TLG*, chapter III. "Das Weiblein mit der Kunkel" (39) is reminiscent of "The Dong with a Luminous Nose", and so, of course, thematically speaking, is "Das Nasobēm" (71). In its circularity, the latter poem structurally resembles Lear's limericks as well. The theme of "Im Winterkurort" (130), in which sparrows are attired in human clothing, parallels that of Lear's "Mr. and Mrs. Spikky Sparrow".

In section 4.2.2 I have described the differences between the nonsense of Lear and that of Carroll in terms of "initial" and "final" nonsense (see p. 150 above). The same differences can be observed between Morgenstern and Carroll. Like Lear, Morgenstern describes nonsensical acts, and he creates creatures that actually *are* nonsensical rather than behaving or speaking nonsensically far more often than Carroll does. Morgenstern most certainly writes no "logic-fiction", even if some of his linguistic games are based on logic, such as the impossibility to decline the plural of "Werwolf" (86-7). It is true, however, that in his nonsense books (unlike his letters and journals) Lear is somewhat less linguistically oriented than Morgenstern, whose work is pervaded by creatures like the "Zwölf-Elf", the "Mondschaf", the "Walfafisch" and the "Schildkröte". But in spirit, the Galgenlieder are far closer to the Nonsense Songs than even to the poems in Carroll's Alice books, whose main characteristic is a nonsense dialectic which rarely features in the more rhetorical verse of the Galgenlieder. This is because in the Alice books speech and conversation play such important roles, as well as an interaction between groups of characters that one scarcely finds in the Galgenlieder, where two is already very occasionally company, and three is a rare crowd. The offspring of the "Nachtschelm" and the "Siebenschwein" (46-7) are as isolated in their diversification as are the creatures that assemble on the Quangle Wangle's Hat.

It is clear that Morgenstern is a nonsense poet in his own right, a bit closer to Lear than to Carroll, but with an individual voice. It is interesting to note that the two main representatives of Dutch nonsense in the twentieth century, Daan Zonderland (1909-77) and Cees Buddingh' (1918-85), were more strongly influenced by Morgenstern than by the English nonsense tradition. In Zonderland's Sylvester one recognizes an amalgam of the inventors Korf and Palmström ("Sylvester had een middel uitgevonden/ Dat bedoeld was als remedie tegen jicht,/ maar dat ook zelfs heel slecht proza/ Kon verandren in een wondermooi gedicht"—Zonderland 1982: 52), and Buddingh's "Blauwbilgorgel", "Wasseneushoorn", "Goudopsneevink", "Halvemaanvis" and "Vijfvooreenhoorn" wander in the same fields that are frequented by Morgenstern's "Mitternachtsmaus", "Steinochs" and "Löwenreh" (Buddingh' 1960 and 1985). Morgenstern's "Das Knie" (1933: 32) obviously inspired Zonderland's "Een rechtervoet ging door de laan" (1982: 20), and Buddingh's "De jenk" (1960: 11) ends on a similar phonetic trick that concludes Morgenstern's "Der Lattenzaun" (1933: 54): one may compare "En stopt alleen zo af en toe/ Zijn oren dicht met poetskatoe" with "Der Architekt jedoch entfloh/ nach Afri—od—Ameriko".

I wish to conclude this section by quoting a poem from the Galgenlieder which aptly epitomizes the very nature and essence of literary nonsense:

> Die Brille
>
> Korf liest gerne schnell und viel;
> darum widert ihn das Spiel
> all des zwölfmal unerbetnen
> Ausgewalzten, Breitgetretnen.
>
> Meistes ist in sechs bis acht
> Wörtern völlig abgemacht,
> und in ebensoviel Sätzen
> läßt sich Bandwurmweisheit schwätzen.
>
> Es erfindet drum sein Geist
> etwas, was ihn dem entreißt:
> Brillen, deren Energien
> ihm den Text—zusammenziehen!
>
> Beispielsweise dies Gedicht
> läse, so bebrillt, man—nicht!
> Dreiundreißig seinesgleichen
> gäben erst—Ein——Fragezeichen!! (147)

Reading nonsense is like reading through Korf's spectacles. The meaning suggested by a single poem is reduced to—nothing. Multiply nothing by thirty-three (a sacred number multiplied by a foolish one), and the result of such a nonsense cycle is—a question-mark, which in its turn is followed by two exclamation-marks. One never gets to twenty at that rate, as Alice realized early on in her adventures.

4.3.3 *Edward Gorey*

Very little has been written so far on Edward Gorey (b. 1925). His artistic work has been discussed in two articles in *Graphis* (Gasser 1972; Mason 1983), in the latter of which it is remarked that some of Gorey's imaginary creatures "are obviously inspired by Lewis Carroll" (Mason 1983: 82). In her monograph on Edward Lear, Hark mentions Gorey as one of the graphic artists who have been influenced by Lear's drawing style (1982: 135). I have discussed his limerick cycle *The Listing Attic* (1954) in an article on the nonsense limerick (Tigges 1986b: 229-35), and there is a perceptive study of his picture stories in a recent article by van Leeuwen (1986: 198-209).[44]

Information about Gorey is exceedingly scarce. There is a "Doubtful Interview" prefacing a collection of Gorey posters (1979: 5-7), from which it transpires that the author admits to a general lack of motivation, a B.A. degree at Harvard, total eccentricity, a collection of fur coats, a messy apartment and a *"tiny mind"*, a predilection for the New York City Ballet, a hidebound existence, an admiration for George Balanchine, a tendency to talk to his cats, a moderate dislike of children, and labouring under the most terrible sense of unreality—all the makings in fact of a nonsense writer. His motto is: "Life is full of alternatives, but no choice." For "life" read "nonsense", and we have another perfect definition of our subject.

Although he makes a living by his art work (he illustrated, amongst other things, Lear's "Dong" and "Jumblies" as well as Eliot's "Practical Cats"), Gorey regards himself primarily as a writer: "My ideas tend to be first literary ones, rather than visual ones" (1979: 6). The books, of which he has by now written more than sixty, were primarily meant as children's books, although nobody would publish them as such. Gorey refuses to acknowledge a deeper meaning to them, although he admits they "are about something, not what they seem to be about" (7).

Fifty-two of the stories, the first of which appeared in 1953, have been collected in three compilations: *Amphigorey* (1975), *Am-*

---

44. Both articles are reprinted in Tigges (1987: 117-33; 61-95).

phigorey Too (1977), and *Amphigorey Also* (1983). A perusal of these volumes easily demonstrates a perfect balance between word and image: the pictures are no mere illustrations to the texts, nor are the texts mere captions to the pictures. Van Leeuwen refers to the combination as a "picture story in which text and illustration are indissolubly linked' (1986: 198).

Steven Heller includes Gorey as one of the twenty-two satirical cartoonists in his collection *Man Bites Man*,[45] and adduces Max Ernst, Wilhelm Busch and John Tenniel as his self-admitted sources of inspiration (van Leeuwen 1986: 201-2). Gorey's work is characterized by a predilection for the macabre, a kind of puzzling Gothic of the 1920s and 30s, what van Leeuwen calls "the hollow sound of an echoing well" (202). According to this critic, what distinguishes Gorey's work from the straightforwardly satirical is the total absence of moral comment, and his application of the point of no return (202-3).

Van Leeuwen also notes the obvious similarities between Gorey and Lear: "the sing-song musicality of the verse, the use of playful rhymes, and the (nonsensical) limerick form", as well as the fascination with dance (204). Moreover, there are the nonsense creatures, the encyclopedic collections and arrangements of words and objects, the alphabets (205). Yet, van Leeuwen is hesitant to classify Gorey's complete *oeuvre* as pure nonsense, because, as he phrases it, Gorey "does not exhibit the hilarity of paradoxical reason, but rather the nullity of paradoxical emotion" (206). This, however, is precisely what brings Gorey far closer to Lear than to Carroll, and in what follows I hope to be able to demonstrate that he is in fact in the very centre of the field of nonsense.

His very first story, *The Unstrung Harp* (1953), is characterized by van Leeuwen as an introspective satire on the incrowd-novelist, a "satire too upon the doubt about the sense of writing at all", as well as "a self-portrait of Gorey" (202). Without doubt, these elements are there, but they are greatly underplayed by the introduction of a spate of nonsensical details. The story consists of thirty paragraphs with accompanying pictures. It begins:[46]

---

45. London, 1981, quoted by van Leeuwen (1986: 201f.).

46. All texts and illustrations in this section are from the *Amphigorey* collections, which do not have numbered pages.

Mr C(lavius) F(rederick) Earbrass is, of course, the well-known novelist. Of his books, *A Moral Dustbin, More Chains Than Clank, Was It Likely?,* and the Hipdeep trilogy are, perhaps, the most admired. Mr Earbrass is seen on the croquet lawn of his home, Hobbies Odd, near Collapsed Pudding in Mortshire. He is studying a game left unfinished at the end of summer.

The tension between meaning and its absence is built up from the start. The reported fame of the "well-known novelist" and his books is undercut by the phrases "of course" and "perhaps". The play on names is a bit facile in this early piece, but the utter inanity of the "studied" croquet game, in any case one of the most static games ever devised, and a favourite Victorian pastime (compare its occurrence in *AW*), is sublime. The story develops into an account of a ceremonial emptiness which becomes paradoxically frantic; it is itself like an "unstrung harp", a musical instrument that cannot be played, but which is, as the illustration on the title page shows, all the same held ready for a recital. Mr Earbrass begins writing "his new novel" on every alternate 18th November, and for writing he "affects an athletic sweater of forgotten origin and unknown significance; it is always worn hind-side-to". What is striking in the rest of this story is a mannerism that is to pervade all of Gorey's further writing, namely the drily reported ornamental but slightly irrelevant detail, frequently echoed in the picture. A few examples from the text of *The Unstrung Harp* may serve by way of illustration (the italics are mine):

> Several weeks later, *the loofah trickling on his knees*, Mr Earbrass mulls over an awkward retrospective bit ...

> ... he broods over it [a sentence] indefinitely *while picking up and putting down again small, loose objects*; ...

> Out for a short drive before *a supper of oysters and trifle*, Mr Earbrass stops *near the abandoned fireworks factory* ...

> How did he get in the *unused room on the third floor*?

> Masses of brown paper and then tissue have reluctantly given up *an unnerving silver-gilt combination epergne and candelabrum*.

> In the blue horror of dawn the *vines in the carpet appear likely to begin twining up his ankles*.

> He wanders through the house, *leaving doors open and empty tea-cups on the floor*.

And so on. Within the italicized phrases occurs a telling word or phrase: the almost decadent precision of the "loofah", the vagueness of "small, loose objects", the slightly odd combination of oysters and trifle (a nonsense meal without a main course), a similarly odd combination of epergne and candelabrum, and so on. As the story proceeds, through these and similar details we become aware of an accumulation of nonsense motifs: from the game alluded to in the very first paragraph, as unplayable as the croquet game in the Queen of Hearts' garden, through food (the oysters and trifle; "his mind will keep reverting to the last biscuit on the plate", "The jelly in his sandwich is about to get all over his fingers"), the materialisation of objects (the "vines in the carpet") and even novel characters, the presence of useless objects, a Restoration tragedy with five plots, a "fantod" under a glass bell (and in the accompanying picture one unnoticed on a cupboard), a list of words that drift through Mr Earbrass' mind ("*anguish turnips conjunctions illness defeat string parties no parties urns desuetude ...*") to, in the end, an unmotivated journey ("Before he knew what he was doing, Mr Earbrass found he had every intention of spending a few weeks on the Continent").

We are informed about the developments of the "novel" ("He cannot help but feel that Lirp's return and almost immediate impalement on the bottle-tree was one of his better ideas"), but, as the pictures show, this fantastic book, which needs much correction and rewriting, cutting and pasting, begins and ends on the same static lines: "It had begun to snow" ultimately leading up to "It was still snowing". Has anything happened at all? We have our suspicions, when the story itself finishes off with: "Though he is a person to whom things do not happen, perhaps they may when he is on the other side".

The story proceeds sensibly enough at first sight, but in the course of its development more questions are evoked than answered: Why was the game of croquet abandoned, and whose game was it anyway? Why the 18th of November? Why has Mr Earbrass bought the stuffed fantod, and why is this not mentioned in the text?

The Listing Attic (1954), a sequence of sixty limericks, also begins with an abandoned croquet game, and surfaces the aspect of drily reported violence that is so characteristic of much nonsense literature, and which in *The Unstrung Harp* had already been referred to as elements in the plot of that mysterious novel. The cruelty is unmotivated and unexplained, and no emotional involvement is evoked. The unaccountable event is Gorey's *forte*, as in *The Doubtful Guest* (1957). The emotion of fear which is occasionally suggested in the verse is denied by the illustrations, in which the late Victorian or Edwardian upperclass family that is afflicted with the Guest is seen to be listlessly resigning itself to its inexplicable fate. The Guest is mainly employed in presenting itself in odd but only slightly disruptive vignettes, as standing on top of an urn, or with its nose to a wall, eating "All the syrup and toast, and a part of the plate", peering up flues, tearing chapters from books, or simply lying on the floor "Inconveniently close to the drawing-room door". It is clear that in the verse the "story" is largely propelled by the exigencies of rhyme, as well as by the need to "explain" pictures which should themselves be explanations of the text. "It came seventeen years ago—and to this day/ It has shown no intention of going away"; in the picture accompanying this final text the family have aged, but they have not changed their attitude of powerless resignation. The Guest, looking away from them, looks as puzzled as any reader.

The next story in *Amphigorey* is *The Object Lesson* (1958). This story, which contains one line of text to each of the thirty pictures (the same number as before), is a complete *non sequitur*. The whole text runs as follows:

> It was already Thursday,/ but his lordship's artifical limb could not be found;/ therefore, having directed the servants to fill the baths,/ he seized the tongs/ and set out at once for the edge of the lake, /where the Throbblefoot Spectre still loitered in a distraught manner./ He presented it with a length of string/ and passed on to the statue of Corrupted Endeavour/ to await the arrival of autumn./ Meanwhile, on the tower,/ Madame O_____ in conversation with an erstwhile cousin/ saw that his moustache was not his own,/ on which she flung herself over the parapet/ and surreptitiously vanished./ He descended, destroying the letter unread,/ and stepped backwards into the water for a better view./ Heavens, how dashing! cried the people in the dinghy,/ and Echo answered: Count the spoons!/ On the shore a bat, or possibly an umbrella,/ disengaged itself from the shrubbery,/ causing those nearby to recollect the miseries of childhood./ It now became apparent (despite the lack of library paste)/ that something had happened to the vicar;/ guns began to go off in the distance./ At twilight, however, no message had come from the asylum,/ so the others retired to the kiosk,/ only to discover the cakes iced in a peculiar shade of green/ and the tea-urn empty/ save for a card on which was written the single word:/ Farewell.

This text borders on the absurd (cf. "The Great Panjandrum", quoted on pp. 127-8 above), but a meaningful mystery is suggested, and reinforced by the pictures. We feel that we could solve the riddle if we had a few more clues.

The Fatal Lozenge (1960) is the first of six alphabets. As in the case of Lear's Nonsense Alphabets, the nonsense mainly lies in the odd collocation of twenty-six unrelated scenes concerning an Apparition, a Baby, a Cad, a Drudge, up to and including a Xenophobe, a Yegg and a Zouave. The scenes frequently are full of innuendo: children are threatened, people obliged to go through a routine that will last their wasted lives, Governesses and Visitors are forgotten in attics or halls, Hermits and Tourists equally patiently suffer the mouldering of their reason and the departure of their trains.

The Curious Sofa (1961) is "a pornographic work by Ogdred Weary" (Gorey delights in anagrams on his own name, to which the present writer would add "God reward ye!"), which leaves everything to the reader's imagination. The suggestive but meaningless phrases like "an extremely well-endowed young man", "something Alice had never done before", "to perform a rather surprising service", are echoed in the pictures by equally suggestive and non-expressive screens, car-doors and branches. The terrible things happen just ousdide the framework of the picture, and so Gorey suggests that they happen just outside the frame of the texts as well. Again, one wonders if they happen at all. It has been stated that in nonsense sex is a tabooed subject, most recently by Sewell (1987: 199), but the fact that sex is avoided in nonsense may have more to do with a Puritanic attitude which foreclosed the subject to Victorian writers and their contemporaries. When separated from its emotional aspects (as it usually is in pornography) it makes a perfect theme for the more liberal modern nonsense-writer, provided it is treated in a nonsensical atmosphere.

The Ugly Wump (1963) is reminiscent of Lear's nonsense creatures, except that Gorey's monsters are more threatening, which means that they are only nonsensical by the grace of their threat remaining unperceived. In fact, an important difference between Lear and Gorey is that the former's characters are heroes who cross the sea in a sieve or make themselves wondrous noses, whereas the latter introduces his monsters as intruders, doubtful guests from an alien sphere, perhaps only that of creative language. They are threatening, but only in so far as their provenance, activities and intentions are utterly unfathomable—which is why they can be nonsensical. The victims, on their part, contribute to this effect by remaining blissfully unaware of any danger, or else by resignedly and only occasionally tearfully accepting their fate. The reader is not given an impetus to identify or get emotionally involved; the distance between the story events and our everyday lives is too great.

Gorey never describes an absurd reality. His landscapes, and especially what I would term his housescapes, are creations of the imagination. In *The Sinking Spell* (1964), which once again starts off with a croquet game, a "thing" slowly descends through the lives of a family, until it sinks down through the cellar floor. We never learn what "it" is, and it does not seem to affect its victims very much. The theme that curiously pervades the sixteen drawings of this story is that of sight: the characters are looking, staring, gazing, peering—the "spell" itself remains invisible, and yet the draughtsman-author suggests that we know from day to day on what height to look for it.

In *Amphigorey Too* we find *The Nursery Frieze*,[47] which is a series of sonorous words spoken by a nondescript four-legged animal, whose figure is infinitely repeated in the "frieze". The words appear in thirty-two rows of three ("Archipelago cardamon obloquy / tacks Ignavia samisen ..."), but can be read as twenty-four lines of anapestic rhyming couplets. Incidentally, the anapest, which nonsense delights in, is frequently used by Gorey. The rhyme words are mostly fairly ordinary monosyllabics ("tacks"/"wax", "baize"/"maze"), but the other items are rare dictionary words, such as "Gavelkind", "turmeric", "quincunx" and "Corposant", marvellous, especially to children unaware of their meanings, for their sound, rhythm and spelling. It is in fact a sound-poem, made up of existant but randomly used lexicographical titbits. There is another, more "primitive" sound-poem in the same volume, entitled [*The Untitled Book*], which is in itself a titular paradox. This latter poem, of which the text runs: "Hippity wippity,/ Oxiborick;/ Flappity flippity, Saragashum;/ Thip;/ thap;/ thoo./ Thumbleby stumbleby,/ Ipsifendus;/ Ramblebly rumbleby,/ Quoggenzocker;/ Hip,/ hop,/ hoo.", describes a wonderful dance of five weird creatures, showing distant resemblances to an insect, a frog, a dog, a bat, and a rag-doll, silently watched from a window by a little boy, and interrupted by what looks like a black comet. The creatures appear and disappear, being as it were created, not by language so much as by each consecutive drawing. In other words, the pictures do not *depict* a reality, however fantastic, but they *create* it; the verse is a spell, which sounds and does not explain anything; perhaps it is the spell by means of which the little boy calls the creatures from the shrubbery, from beyond a wall, from the house (the dog looks very domestic in its lozenged sleeping-suit), from the air and from underground, to present their ritualistic dance. Except when the "comet" hits to interrupt the dance, the boy's face expresses no emotion, either of expectation, of surprise, or of joy or fear.

47. As the colophon to this collection erroneously gives the titles from the first volume, the correct dates of the first appearance of the separate items cannot be given. Nor are any dates provided for items from *Amphigorey Also*.

The Inanimate Tragedy, which describes, once again in sixty pictures and captions, the plottings and misunderstandings between a No 37 Penpoint, a Glass Marble, a Two-Holed Button, A Half-Inch Thumbtack, a Four-Holed Button and a Knotted String, in a Featureless Expanse on the edge of a Yawning Chasm, is like Lear's nonsense in its personification of simple objects, and features a good amount of linguistic non-sequitur. The Pins and Needles, who provide a chorus-like comment on events no less than six times before joining all the other objects into the Chasm in the last picture, do so in sets of four words always beginning with a D ("Death and Distraction!" said the Pins and Needles. "Destruction and Debauchery!"). Unfortunately, we never learn what the communications are all about.

The Iron Tonic is a compilation of hardly related couplets. In one drawing clocks, mirrors and vases (beloved nonsense objects) are seen to be falling unaccountably out of the sky. (A later picture adds a bicycle, which seems to be *the* nonsense vehicle.)

Incidentally, a common device in Gorey's picture stories is the unexplained recurrence of an irrelevant object, like a wad of crumpled paper in the alphabet called *The Chinese Obelisks* ("A was an Author who went for a walk/ B was a Bore who engaged him in talk"). In this poem twenty-six unrelated and largely unexplained happenings befall the Author, depicted in his inseparable fur coat and sneakers.

The Osbick Bird is, again, very Learish. To give the reader an idea of the unity of a Gorey story, I will reproduce it in reduced format on the next three pages. As is so often the case, a strange creature, this time an Osbick Bird, joins an inhabitant of our world to stay with him until his death, rather like the Cricket which adhered to the nose of Lear's "Agèd Uncle Arly" (Lear, ed. Jackson 1947: 275-6). Note how the bowler-hat of the first picture changes into the cap of a tomb-stone in the last. Note also the nonsense themes of the ill-matched couple who find a mode of living together, and who indulge in musical exercises, have tea together, play card-games ("double solitaire"!) and go on distant journeys.

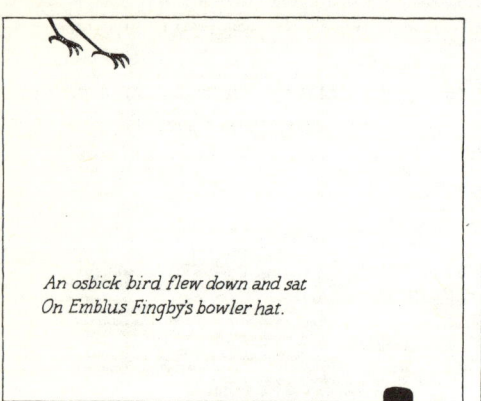

An osbick bird flew down and sat
On Emblus Fingby's bowler hat.

It had not done so for a whim,
But meant to come and live with him.

On Fridays Emblus played the flute;
The bird now joined him on a lute.

The top of the zagava tree
Was frequently where they had tea.

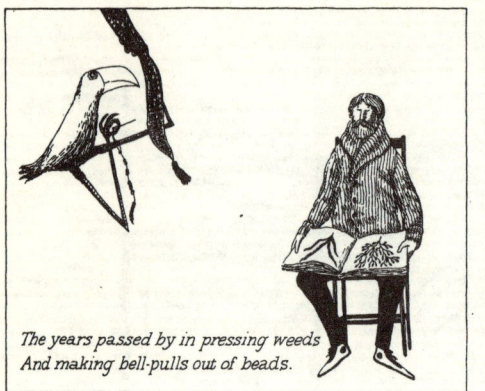

*The years passed by in pressing weeds
And making bell-pulls out of beads.*

*And when at last poor Emblus died
The osbick bird was by his side.*

*He was interred; the bird alone
Was left to sit upon his stone.*

*But after several months, one day
It changed its mind and flew away.*

In *Ampigorey Also*, Gorey occasionally plays with the language of phrasebooks in a manner reminiscent of Eugène Ionesco's *La Cantatrice Chauve*. This happens for instance in *The Sopping Thursday* and in *The Grand Passion*, in the latter case complete with printing errors. In the latter story, objects change unaccountably in the pictures. In this volume too, we find another nonsense alphabet, *The Utter Zoo*, which features descriptions of such fabulous creatures as the Ampoo, the Epitwee, the Ippagoggy, the Ombledroom (which "is vast and white,/ And therefore visible by night") and the Ulp, to limit ourselves to the vowels. "The Yawfle stares, and stares, and stares,/ And stares, and stares, and stares, and stares." This is Play with Infinity in optima forma. In *The Glorious Nosebleed* the alphabet hinges around adverbs for a change ("She danced on the sands Giddily").

In some of these late stories, such as *The Loathsome Couple* and *The Green Beads*, the untoward happenings are ascribed to insanity, which detracts a little from the nonsensical effect. The large majority, however, of the stories in the three collections can be regarded as pure samples of the nonsense. What mainly distinguishes Gorey's nonsenses from those by Lear are the former's somewhat greater predilection for topics that suggest (but do not really convey, for reasons already explained) horror, and the association of violence and cruelty with women and particularly children. From Morgenstern, Gorey mainly differs in that the ultimate lack of meaning in the latter's stories is more predominant from the start; the emptiness, to speak in van Leeuwen's terms, meets the eye straight from the beginning, the senselessness is too oppressive, the echoing well fails to provide even an echo, "an ominous nocturnal gleam" is all-pervading (1986: 204-6).

Gorey's nonsense is "black nonsense". It is the static, sombre black-and-white atmosphere of the drawings, together with the phrasebook style of the texts, and the constant suspicion that time has stopped, and we have entered a world as isolated from our own as Peake's Gormenghast or Lear's Gromboolian Plain and the land where the Bong-tree grows, that all the same impress us with the feeling that this is the realm of nonsense rather than an absurd or grotesque distortion of our own known world. Like Alice staring through the looking-glass, we suspect that things might be very different just around the corner.

Gorey's *oeuvre* is self-reflexive and narrative rather than communicative and lyrical; it turns in upon itself rather than moving outward. It invites one to enter but does not say how to set about it. This world is, in its fashion, as recognizable as Wonderland or the linguistic world of Korf and Palmström. The balance between meaning and its absence is indubitably there, but there is even a further balance between the language and the situation it describes, between the rational play with words and their sounds, and the irrational abandonment to a world that borders on dream and nightmare without ever toppling over. There is even, I would say, a perfect balance between the presence of humour and its absence. What to think for instance of a sentence like "Over the next two years they killed three more children, but it was never as exhilarating as the first had been" (*The Loathsome Couple*, in *Amphigorey Also*)? There is a clash between the words "killed" and "exhilarating", and one simply cannot make up one's mind to say whether it is funny or perverse.[48]

4.4 *The Development of the Carroll Type*

4.4.1 *Survey*

Far more than was the case with Lear's nonsense, the works of Carroll, in particular the Alice books, have been copiously imitated. Petzold lists no fewer than 98 works that were influenced by these classics for the period 1869-99 alone (1972: 252-4), and this stream has continued ever since. The measure of success, both from the point of view of nonsense theory and from that of the history of children's literature, deserves a study of its own. A quite successful attempt of recent date to present a sequel to *AW* and *TLG* is Gilbert Adair's *Alice Through the Needle's Eye*, subtitled "A Third Adventure for Lewis Carroll's 'Alice'" (1984).

Alexander, writing about Carroll's creation of nonsensical humour, not only perceptively points out that what is essential about Carroll's type of nonsense is that it obeys rules which, however, are different from our normal ones (1951: 554), but also that the Marx Brothers constructed their humorous films on a similar principle. Characteristic of this type of nonsense is the use of verbal ambiguities as well as the exploitation of inconsistency and logical fallacy (551). Just as Carroll in both *AW* and *TLG* constructed an initial framework by asserting a false proposition as if it were true, and then built on "the *possibility* of every other proposition being deducible from it" (552), the Marx Brothers are said to have done precisely that in their films (565).

The thirteen Marx Brothers films appeared between 1929 and 1949. Far more than was the case with Karl Valentin's humorous sketches, which also made use of linguistic humor, but which are rarely pointless, in these films the tension between meaning and non-meaning is kept in balance. Some instances of this have already been given (see pp. 51-3 and 95-6 above). It is not difficult to recognize in the scripts, which were collective efforts of various text writers such as S.J. Perelman and Morrie Ryskind, as well as

---

48. Cf. for a contrast the definitely humourless and therefore disgusting grotesque "jokes" by Roland Topor.

the Marxes themselves,[49] a plethora of nonsense procedures, themes and motifs of the kind we have already met, and especially those reminiscent of Lewis Carroll. The following dialogue from *Monkey Business* (1931) reminds one of the "jam every other day" discussion between Alice and the White Queen in *TLG* (ed. Gardner 1960 [1965]: 247):

> **Chico:** What's the matter with me? I'm hungry. I didn't eat in three days.
> **Groucho:** Three days? We've only been on the boat two days.
> **Chico:** Well, I didn't eat yesterday, I didn't eat today, and I'm not goin' to eat tomorrow. That makes it three days (Anobile 1972: 59).

In *Horsefeathers* (1932), Groucho, as Professor Wagstaff, addresses his student-son in the following words: "When I was your age I went to bed right after supper. Sometimes I went to bed before supper. Sometimes I went without my supper and didn't go to bed at all" (*Ibid.*, 105). Similarly, Carroll's Snark "frequently breakfasts at five o'clock tea,/ And dines on the following day" (ed. Gardner 1962 [1967]: 59).

As in Carroll's books, expressions are taken literally, as in the following dialogue from *Duck Soup* (1933):

> **Minister of War:** Sir, you try my patience!
> **Firefly (Groucho):** I don't mind if I do. You must come over and try mine some time.
> **Minister of War:** That's the last straw! I resign. I wash my hands of the whole business.
> **Firefly:** A good idea. You can wash your neck, too (163).

An unanswerable riddle is presented in the same film:

> **Firefly (Groucho):** ... Now, what is it that has four pair of pants, lives in Philadelphia, and it never rains but it pours?
> **Chicolini (Chico):** 'At'sa good one. I give you three guesses.

---

49. For a complete and perceptive account of the films, including the matter of authorship the reader is referred to Eyles (1966 [1974]).

> Firefly: Now, lemme see. Has four pair of pants, lives in Philadelphia. Is it male or female?
> Chicolini: No, I no think so.
> Firefly: Is he dead?
> Chicolini: Who?
> Firefly: I don't know. I give up.
> Chicolini: I give up, too ... (168-9).

Much more, of course, goes on here than a regular riddling game. The person questioned, Chicolini, takes over from the person who originally poses the riddle and who is now no longer able to guess his own riddle. Chicolini answers the counter-question "Is it male or female?" as if "male or female" is *one* characteristic instead of being a choice, and in the next question he does not realize what the other might be referring to. Firefly's answer to "Who?" should of course have been: "The person I think the riddle is about", but instead he gives up. In what follows, Chicolini appropriately changes the subject by asking another riddle, to which the answer must be "Firefly". Instead of guessing, Firefly shows he realizes that Chicolini is having him on, and "punishes" the latter by ... appointing him to the job of Secretary of War. We then remember that Firefly's original riddle was one of the "important questions" he wanted to ask to find out whether Chicolini was suited to the job.

An even finer example of wordplay turning in upon itself so as to result in nonsense is the following dialogue from *Horsefeathers*:

> Wagstaff (Groucho): Why don't you forget about the money? Go to college, meet all the beautiful girls, get yourself a co-ed.
> Baravelli (Chico): Hah! I got a co-ed. Last week for eighteen dollars I got a co-ed with two pair of pants.
> Wagstaff: Since when has a co-ed got two pair of pants?
> Baravelli: Since I joined the college (119).

In his first reply, Baravelli misunderstands the word "co-ed" (American slang for a female student) and takes it to mean "coat". Wagstaff, however, continues to talk about a "co-ed", upon which Baravelli resumes its actual meaning, his second answer implying that since he joined the college (which we know is not the case) the girls had better wear an extra pair of pants in order, one assumes, to be safe from his advances. Has Baravelli joined the college or not? Is he aware of the meaning of "co-ed" or is he not? There is no answer to either of these questions, and so a perfect balance between meaning and non-meaning is maintained. Wagstaff understandably concludes this dialogue by saying: "Baravelli, you've got the brain of a four-year-old boy, and I bet he was glad to get rid of it." Nonsense is added to nonsense.

Like wordplay, of which (near-)punning takes a prominent part,[50] the standard nonsense motifs and themes accumulate as well. A lot of the action centres around numbers (the auction in *Cocoanuts*, 1929), food (usually in association with the mute Harpo, who also takes care of the musical element, featuring the nonsensical instrument of the harp), beards (Hackenbush-Groucho in *A Day at the Races*, 1937: "And don't point that beard at me—it might go off!"), and clocks and mirrors (e.g. the famous "mirror scene" in *Duck Soup*). In the last-mentioned film, the trio also exchange hats. Travel is a recurrent theme, by sea (*Monkey Business, A Night at the Opera*, 1935), air (*A Night at the Opera*) or land (*Go West*, 1940). In *Animal Crackers* (1930), Groucho is first introduced as the intrepid explorer Captain Spaulding, who sings that marvellously nonsensical opening line: "Hello, I must be going" (One should hear the timbre of his voice to obtain the full effect). In the same film, as Eyles puts it, Groucho "throws himself about and leaps around in a madly athletic dance. Part of the time he is hopping around on one leg, rotating the other like a corkscrew" (1974: 35). His very gait, as Galestin points out, is dance-like (1986: 246).

Instances of violence are listed by Eyles (1974: 58-9, 71, 75, 116, 137). Galestin has noted the pervasiveness of physical violence, usually mild as well, rightly associating it with the unemotional cruelty that is characteristic of nonsense (1986: 245). Love and women play prominent roles in all thirteen films, but the emotions associated with them are greatly underplayed (cf. p. 53 above). Harpo chases women indiscriminately, but whenever he comes near one he either offers her one of his legs, or flits himself asleep, as

---

50. For a survey of the various types of linguistic play in the Marx Brothers' films, see, besides Eyles (1974), esp. Tiersma (1985). In this brief monograph the author distinguishes the categories of simple punning, context reversal, decomposition (esp. of idioms), inversion (e.g. Spoonerisms), ethnic humour (Chico's fake Italian accent), violation of pragmatic conditions (thwarting presuppositions of ordinary conversation), faulty parallelism, and some miscellaneous minor categories. See also Galestin (1986).

happens at the end of *Animal Crackers*. Groucho "woos" society ladies, frequently personified by a voluminous Margaret Dumont, but always in a highly ambiguous way, for instance as Hammer in *Cocoanuts*: "I'll meet you tonight under the moon. Oh, I can see you now—you and the moon. You wear a neck-tie so I'll know you" (Anobile 1972: 35). His insults are never taken up, but neither are his compliments. In fact, Groucho always manages to keep compliment and insult in perfect balance.

That the features discussed so far are more than mere partial nonsense can be easily ascertained when considering the films in their entirety. As Eyles points out, the Marxes always "live for the moment, without any long-term objectives" (1974: 31). Their characters are largely established in the first film, *Cocoanuts*, and they do not materially change. No matter what "roles" they play in the individual movies, they are always immediately recognizable. Of course, they can be seen as complementary "archetypes": Groucho is the thinking type, whose nonsense is basically verbal; the "mute" Harpo is the intuitive type, who often creates reality by producing and so visualizing all kinds of objects which have been mentioned verbally; Chico is the mediating sensation type: his nonsense is both verbal and situational, depending largely on whether he is interacting with Groucho or with Harpo (significantly, Groucho and Harpo rarely interact as a pair in any of the films). The fourth Jungian archetype, the feeling type, is usually represented by a colourless lover, in the earlier films embodied by the fourth brother, Zeppo. The sentimental love scenes, rather than being the main course, are clearly intermezzi, to some extent a concession to that part of the audience for whom entire irrelevance and complete nonsense would be too offputting, but the unresolved contrast between "serious" plot elements and utter absurdity is exactly what constitutes the nonsensical tension in the films.

Although some of the movies include satirical elements (notably *Horsefeathers* and *Duck Soup*) as well as parody (*Go West, A Night at Casablanca*, 1946), these aspects never get the upper hand (cf. Galestin 1986: 238). Eyles, who recognizes especially surrealist and absurdist elements in the films (see e.g. 1974: 48, 59-61, 72, 92; 156)[51] rather deprecates the fact that as time proceeds they become increasingly inconsistent (115)—an "excessive nonsensicality" which

---

51. On p. 154 he mentions that Salvador Dali considered their films to be surrealism applied to the cinema.

he regards as a weakness and even a stupidity, thereby missing the point of the essence of nonsense. Nevertheless, he does realize that like the Alice books, much of the Marx Brothers' work shows "how tricky a means language is for communicating what we have to say" (41). It is this utterly inconsequential aspect of the Marxes' films, itself possibly inspired by early vaudeville, that has influenced the post-war British radio and television sketches of the Goons and Monty Python's Flying Circus. Indeed, it is especially in dialogue that the Carrollian type of nonsense is most successfully applied.

The Carrollian type of dialogue is prominent in some of the more playful works of two modern British authors, Stefan Themerson (b. 1910) and Anthony Burgess (pseud. of Jack Wilson, b. 1917). I will limit myself here to a brief discussion of two works in which the Carrollian influence is most evident.

The first of these is Themerson's *The Adventures of Peddy Bottom* (1951). This book is obviously inspired by *AW*. The protagonist, who resembles a human being, a dog and a fish at the same time, goes in search of his identity, a search which takes him on a journey that greatly resembles Alice's wanderings through Wonderland and the Looking-Glass world. Like Alice, Peddy has many episodic adventures, including a fair amount of conversation between personified animals, conducted along the lines of a logical argument based on false premises. The book has been aptly analysed by Boelens (1987), who arrives at the conclusion, not quite warranted I think, that most of the nonsense serves an ulterior purpose, so that it turns out to be what I have labelled partial nonsense. As has already been mentioned, Themerson himself, whose concerns with semantics and logic are well-established, prefers to speak of his works as "logic fiction" (see p. 151 above). Indeed, one cannot always escape the feeling that more than Carroll Themerson is harping on the problems that arise when partners in a dialogue argue along different lines of thought, indicated by their use of language and its logic. Thus, for instance, Peddy Bottom has a delightfully "sensible" conversation with King Penguin consisting entirely of arithmetical sums. It is indeed without either argument or insults, until King Penguin states that nine multiplied by nine equals eighty. When Peddy Bottom begs to differ, the King declares the talk over (1951: 91).

What redeems the nonsense as nonsense in this book is that not all the motivation for action can be explained in terms of a deeper meaning, such as a stone running away from captain Metapherein because the latter is unhappy (35). Nor does Peddy ultimately find out who he is, and so the whole undertaking seems to be pointless after all. Besides containing a number of nonsense devices and motifs, many of which are discussed by Boelens, the book fulfils the criteria of a balance between meaning and non-meaning, a reality created by playing with language and logic, and an absence of emotional involvement.

Much the same can be said for Anthony Burgess' children's book, *A Long Trip to Teatime* (1976). The hero of this book is a schoolboy by name of Edgar, who during a boring history lesson about the Anglo-Saxon kings, falls through a hole in his desk to enter another world. The rest of the book relates his attempt, in an episodic adventure which takes him to the Easter Island and to "Edenborough", to find his way back home, where tea will await him. The blurb on the cover of the book informs us that Burgess "is convinced that our salvation lies in understanding ourselves" and "that such an understanding depends on a concern with language". In its episodic structure *A Long Trip* resembles the Alice books, but also *HS*, which consists of Eight Fits (*A Long Trip* has eight chapters, and so, by the way, has *Peddy Bottom*), and with which it shares the quest theme as well as the importance of words beginning with one particular letter of the alphabet. As in *HS* the members of the crew all begin with the letter B, so *A Long Trip* contains many words beginning with an E, or carrying associations with it, so that the world of this book resembles that of an Encyclopedia. Thus, Maria the Mouse, with her Irish accent, who is "in the middle of me moral tales and me belindas" (35) is Maria Edgeworth. Albert, another mouse, is presumably Albert Einstein, as he helps out Edgar with an explanation of the theory of relativity, which is of course epitomized by the formula $E=mc^2$, and which has important bearings on the nature of "T-time". Chapter I also contains a "song" on Sir Arthur Eddington (another "E"), known "for his contributions/ To the theory of relativity" (24). In fact, in a manner presumably inspired by Joyce's *Finnegans Wake*, one of Burgess' favourites (see also Burgess 1987), the book seems to have ransacked the E volume of an encyclopedia.

There are many reminders of the Alice books: the descent through a hole, the dreamlike shift from episode to episode, and the nonsensical conversations between the hero and the creatures he meets, many of them personified animals and even talking flowers. The brothers Eckhart and Eckermann, quarrelling about trifles, remind one of Tweedledum and Tweedledee. Burgess does not create portmanteaux or even use puns (although Eckhart makes it clear that Eckermann and he are brothers and not "Germans"—16), so much as "misapply" words. Thus, "hamadans" and "vatheks" are stated to be types of coins (21), and a "load of old rubbish" is described in terms of "bucolics and eclogues and barclays and sylviuses and economics and bagehots and darwins and ector and kays and seneschals, all very dusty" (*ibid.*). Play with Boundaries and Infinity (seriality) is rife here. Violence is treated in a Berkeleyan manner as existing only "in the mind" (27), thereby furnishing a very good account indeed of its lack of emotional involvement.

A drink tastes like cold ice "flavoured with currants, raisins, candied peel, chocolate, vanilla, nutmeg and a cut off an overroasted joint of roast pork" (45), which directly imitates the flavour of the contents of the "DRINK ME" bottle in the first chapter of *AW* (ed. Gardner 1960 [1965]: 31). In a very Carrollian manner it is explained that "to help yourself to" a bottle is not the same as to drink it (45). "Changing BLACK to WHITE" in seven moves (88) is based on one of the parlour games invented by Carroll (see Carroll, ed. Green 1965: 1016ff. "Doublets"). As at the end of each of the Alice books, the final chapter of *A Long Trip* has all the characters reassembling in a sort of grand finale previous to Edgar's return from what is ultimately explained as a nap during a lesson (thus proving the relativity of time). Even more obviously than *Peddy Bottom*, *A Long Trip* is an imitation of Carroll, complete with nonsense songs and garbled versions of familiar poems. Like *Finnegans Wake*, it is a combined dream and history lesson, but at the same time it is an encyclopedia come to life, and as such ultimately pointless.[52]

Less clearly influenced by Carroll, but belonging to the Carrollian type of nonsense are the seven short stories by Peter Bichsel (b. 1935), collected under the title *Kindergeschichten* (1969). The first story, "Die Erde ist rund", contains an extensive catalogue of human knowledge. In this story, the futility of empirically testing any knowledge, like that of the roundness of the earth, is demonstrated. In "Ein Tisch ist ein Tisch", a man creates a new language by shifting around the verbal labels of the objects surrounding him, thereby isolating himself from the rest of society. The story effectively explores the nature of an idiosyncratic language. In "Der Erfinder" another man, who is already isolated from society, invents

---

52. For my account of *A Long Trip* I have made grateful use of findings orally communicated by Ruud Hisgen and Mary Boxen.

objects which already exist. "Der Mann mit dem Gedächtnis" describes a man who knows all of a railway directory by heart, and is convinced that the directory is the "real" thing rather than any actual trajectory. When he discovers that his book knowledge is shared by any railway official, he shifts to memorizing the number of stairs he comes across, sure that this knowledge is not to be found in any book in the world. "Jodok läßt grüßen", which is briefly analysed by Tabbert (1975) is about the tyranny of names. "Der Mann der nichts mehr wissen wollte" is a counterpart to the "man with a memory". This story illustrates that in order *not* to know something one must first know it. All these stories hinge around logical paradoxes that would have delighted Lewis Carroll. The stories share the notion of the primacy of the word over the concept it denotes; thus, the inventor writes the word "Automobil" on a sheet of paper, and then proceeds to "invent" it.

Finally mention has to be made of two books by Russell Hoban (b. 1925). In *How Tom Beat Captain Najork and his Hired Sportsmen* (1974), this author devises three games that are as nonsensical as the Queen of Hearts' Croquet game in *AW*. The games are "womble", "muck" and "sneedball".

> Womble turned out to be a shaky, high-up, wobbling and teetering sort of a game, and Tom was used to that kind of fooling around. The Captain's side raked first. Tom staked. The hired sportsmen played so hard that they wombled too fast, and were shaky with the rakes. Tom fooled around the way he always did, and all his stakes dropped true. When it was his turn to rake he did not let Captain Najork and the hired sportsmen score a single rung, and at the end of the snetch he won by six ladders.

The book is not entirely nonsensical in as far as it points the moral that "fooling around" teaches a boy things that may turn out to be more useful than having to learn off pages 65 to 75 of the Nautical Almanac, but the hero's linguistic logic is as irrefutable as that of Alice:

> "I had better tell you," said the Captain to Tom, "that I played in the Sneedball Finals five years running."
>
> "They couldn't have been very final if you had to keep doing it for five years," said Tom.

In his adult novel *Kleinzeit* (1974), Hoban has his eponymous hero suffer from asymptotes, after initial trouble with his hypotenuse and diapason. These, however, are examples of partial nonsense. In the same novel, abstract notions, such as Hospital, Undergound and even Word, take human shape. A hospital form refers to the patient filling it in as "the undesigned" (79). But the account of Kleinzeit's Orphic double life, playing the glockenspiel in the Underground in between stretches of hospital treatment is too suggestive of being pregnant with a deeper meaning to properly qualify as generic nonsense.

4.4.2 *Flann O'Brien*

A separate section should be devoted to the Irish author Flann O'Brien (pseud. of Brian O'Nolan, 1911-66). As has been demonstrated by Lanters (1987), O'Brien uses nonsense devices, especially word-play, in many of his satirical pieces he wrote for the *Irish Times*, but his only truly nonsensical work is his novel *The Third Policeman*, written as early as 1940, but posthumously published in 1967.

J.C.C. Mays, who contributed a critical article to the largely biographical collection of essays edited by O'Keeffe (1973), says that in this novel "[t]he norm of fantasy is tinged with the grotesque" 90). Clissmann, in the most extensive discussion of the works of O'Brien to date, writing about *The Third Policeman* (henceforth abbreviated to *TTP*), notes its affinity with the Drama of the Absurd (1975: 354, n. 23). O'Donoghue places O'Brien, and especially *TTP*, in the tradition of Irish humour, noting for instance the parallel of Policeman MacCruiskeen's diminutive boxes and the "minute observation of detail" as well as the "extreme and often unhelpful specificity", with similar effects in Swift's *Gulliver's Travels*. Lanters, in an earlier publication, discusses the book together with *At Swim-Two-Birds* (1939) as a forerunner of the metafictional genre, the "fiction about fiction" (1983). In that view, the "omnium" discussed in chapters VII and XI is to be seen as the writer's imagination, and the bicycle, which plays an important role in this novel, as a symbol of the novel itself (276, 278).

TTP is indeed a borderline case, as I said in chapter 2 (p. 85 above), in that it combines elements of fantasy, grotesque, absurd, metafiction and humour, but perhaps it is because these adjacent "fields" are so distinctive amongst themselves that the ultimate classification of *TTP* as nonsense is justified. In the model on p. 87

I have placed the novel in question at the "bottom" of the field, bordering close on fantasy, but in any case the model is presumably multi-dimensional, and the more one investigates the nature of nonsense, the more one comes to suspect that in a sense the whole "field" is no larger than a single point, or, if one dislikes such a deflation of the model, a no-man's-land overlapping all the other categories at the same time as being distinct from them. I will revert to this point in section 4.5 below.

What is of interest in comparing the relatively scarce previous accounts of *TTP* is that what they all seem to agree on is O'Brien's "relentless logic" (Lanters 1987: 164), which places the novel firmly in the Carrollian tradition. Mays draws the comparison quite explicitly, but fails to make the proper distinctions: "Elizabeth Sewall [*sic*] has pointed out how the nonsense world of Edward Lear and Lewis Carroll makes the same attempt to render language a closed and consistent system of its own, which is the aesthetic of modernism" (1973: 84), referring however to *At Swim-Two-Birds* (which is obviously a metafictional novel and not a nonsense) rather than to *TTP*. Clissmann, who repeatedly uses the terms "nonsense" and "nonsensical", both in her discussion of *TTP* (e.g. 157, 163) and elsewhere (187, 197), speaks of "a travesty of logic" (163), and points out how in *TTP* logic is turned into nonsense (164). Her remark that "O'Brien generally achieves comic effects by a combination of ideas which, by themselves, are not comic but which, in totality, become incongruous and surprising" (169) can be related to this notion of nonsense-logic or logical nonsense, and her statement that "the narrator is in the same emotional position as the child who feels that the whole world is against him because he cannot understand its rules" (170) provides a clear link between the narrator in *TTP* and Alice. O'Donoghue confirms this by stating that what the techniques of Irish humour share is an ignoring of obvious realities in favour of logical observation or development (1982: 36).

A closer look at some of the logical "theories" in *TTP* easily bears out the above conclusions. These theories are embodied by the characters of de Selby, who in this book (he also features in a slightly more mundane role in a later novel, *The Dalkey Archive*, 1964) is only referred to indirectly, mainly in the footnotes, and of Sergeant Pluck, whom Lanters rightly calls "the master of the sylllogism" (1987: 165). In the course of the novel references are made to de Selby's theories about houses (19)[53], night (28), roads (33-4), names (35-6), journeys (44-5), time and eternity (56-7), life and the shape of the earth (80-3), night and sleep (101-3), air and water (125-8), and the sexes (144-5), all of them based on false logic. By way of an example of perfect Carrollian logic in *TTP* I quote de Selby's account of his investigation of the nature of time and eternity by means of mirrors, notions which like many of the others referred to are recognized at once as common nonsense motifs:

> If a man stands before a mirror and sees in it his reflection, what he sees is not a true reproduction of himself but a picture of himself when he was a younger man. De Selby's explanation of this phenomenon is quite simple. Light, as he points out truly enough, has an ascertained and finite rate of travel. Hence before the reflection of any object in a mirror can be said to be accomplished, it is necessary that rays of light should first strike the object and subsequently impinge on the glass, to be thrown back again to the object—to the eyes of a man, for instance. There is therefore an appreciable and calculable interval of time between the throwing by a man of a glance at his own face in a mirror and the registration of the reflected image in his eye.
>
> So far, one may say, so good. Whether this idea is right or wrong, the amount of time involved is so negligible that few reasonable people would argue the point. But de Selby, ever loath to leave well enough alone, insists on reflecting the first reflection in a further mirror and professing to detect minute changes in this second image. Ultimately he constructed the familiar arrangement of parallel mirrors, each reflecting diminishing images of an interposed object indefinitely. The interposed object in this case was de Selby's own face and this he claims to have studied backwards through an infinity of reflections by means of "a powerful glass". What he states to have seen through this glass is astonishing. He claims to have noticed a growing youthfulness in the reflections of his face according as they receded, the most distant of them—too tiny to be visible to the naked eye—being the face of a beardless boy of twelve, and, to use his own words, "a count-

---

53. All page references are to the 1967 Picador edition.

enance of singular beauty and nobility". He did not succeed in pursuing the matter back to the cradle "owing to the curvature of the earth and the limitations of the telescope." (56-7).

If in his experiments de Selby reminds us somewhat of Morgenstern's Korf and Palmström,[54] the "rational" logic of the former's reasoning seems to have the upperhand over the more intuitive nature of the experiments which is characteristic of Morgenstern's inventors.

The epitome of Sgt Pluck's syllogizing is, of course, the Atomic Theory, voiced extensively in chapter VI. The whole argument, explaining how men change into bicycles and *vice versa*, is not only logically conducted, but leads to a different view of identity and reality as well. Having just heard the theory explained, we are not surprised to find the narrator walking "nimbly and lightly on [his] toes in order to prolong life" (78)—he is obviously afraid of losing part of his identity to the earth. That he is already dead, the whole novel being an account of "life" as a cyclic hell, naturally is ironic. Later in the novel a Police Inspector is noted to have been "leaning by one elbow on the counter" (according to Pluck the sign of a sizeable bicycle component in a man), still later we get an account of a bicycle being hanged, and yet further on the Sergeant himself recounts having once suffered from a slow puncture, not of his tyre but of his own person (84, 91, 105). Thus, the originally false premiss that a man can gradually change into a bicycle is indeed relentlessly pursued in the rest of the novel.

Instances of logical fallacies, which all the same create a backcloth of surprisingly convincing reality in the novel can be easily multiplied, and to anyone familiar with the Alice books the resemblances in technique are striking: time, space and language change in *TTP* as they do in *AW* and *TLG*, and we are not surprised to hear Pluck say: "This is not today, this is yesterday" (53). Chapter V is a veritable mine of logical impossibilities, such as invisible sharpness, boxes within boxes receding to nullity, and inaudible music. In chapter VII we learn how light can be "mangled" into sound by literally "stretching" the length of the waves (92-5); the incomprehensible shouts representing this sound are interpreted in a way that

---

54. Cf. e.g. the poem from the Galgenlieder discussed on pp. 98-9. There certainly is some logic in "waking up" a chronometer by means of black coffee, once one has assumed that one can send it to sleep by dipping it in opium or ether.

resembles the incongruity of the Baker's names in *HS*, or of the objects and concepts with which the Snark is pursued and threatened in that poem. In chapter VIII a machine produces indescribable objects, and a magnifying glass magnifies objects to invisibility (117-8).

It will already have transpired that the five prime procedures of nonsense are well exemplified in this novel.[55] De Selby's mad theories are a reversal of ordinary logic, symbolized by the scientist's predilection for mirrors. "The combination of sheer ordinariness and sheer unpredictable fantasy" that Mays generally discerns in O'Brien's work (1973: 84), and especially the merging of things, persons and places into one another, is the play with boundaries exemplified in Pluck's Atomic Theory. Infinity is played with in the discussion of the infinitely sharp spear and the infinitely receding boxes in chapter V, but also in the very circularity of the book. Simultaneity features in the "collapsing of time" (the term is Stewart's—1978: 150) during the visit to the underground "Eternity" in chapter VIII, and in the characteristics of the mysterious "omnium", contained in the black box, which is itself a means to infinite arbitrariness as it can create any imaginable object. This is explained as follows by Policeman Fox (the third Policeman) in chapter XI: "... if you had that box here, ... you could have a bucket of strawberry jam for your tea and if that was not enough you could have a bathful of it to lie in it full-length and if that much did not satisfy you, you could have ten acres of land with strawberry jam spread on it to the height of your two oxters" (161). The food motif, so prominent in nonsense, is here found in a play with both infinity and arbitrariness, the latter because jam is an utterly inconsequential example.

Another nonsense motif that prevails in *TTP* is that of the body, linked with the concept of identity as well as with the theme of violence. Jacquin has noted the ever-presence of "the body" in *TTP* (1975-6: 189) and her argument is that the novel mainly reflects the characters' attempts to overcome gravity, the primal force of the universe. The narrator has a wooden leg, but so, as it turns out, have many other characters, notably the "tricky man" Martin Finnucane whom the narrator meets in chapter III. The policemen are

---

55. Lanters (1987) discusses the novel, as well as other works by O'Brien, in terms of these procedures.

described as either extraordinarily fat (Pluck and Fox) or lean (MacCruiskeen), and Fox possesses the face of a dead man. Mays comments on O'Brien's "strain of cruelty" (1973: 108), which transpires in the very first sentence of the novel: "Not everybody knows how I killed old Phillip Mathers, smashing his jaw in with my spade" (7). The sentence continues: "but first it is better to speak of my friendship with John Divney ...", illustrating the absence of emotional involvement on the part of the narrator. As Jacquin remarks, O'Brien "consistently shrinks from emotion" (1975-6: 195).[56]

Jacquin also establishes the author's urge to play with words (187), which, as Lanters rightly observes, is much more prominent in his other works, largely for satirical and generally humorous purposes. Punning, for instance, is most rife in the satirical "Cruiskeen Lawn" columns (Lanters 1987: 172), and forms the *"pointe"* of the Keats and Chapman stories (*ibid.*). In *TTP* the relatively scarce punning is more directly relevant. There is a significant ambiguity of the word "lift" on p. 109. The narrator's soul, "Joe", who has become split off from the narrator's personality, doubts the verity of eternity's being reached by means of a lift, but on second thoughts he considers that the word "lift" may have a special meaning: *"I suppose a smash under the chin with a heavy spade could be called a 'lift'"*. Of course, the smashing of old Mathers' skull with a spade by the narrator in the first chapter of the book has triggered off the whole story, sending the protagonist to the "eternity" of a cyclic hell.

There is some Learish word-play in *TTP* as well, as in the following conversation between Sgt Pluck and the narrator on p. 49:

> "What is your pronoun?" he inquired.
> "I have no pronoun," I answered, hoping I knew his meaning.
> "What is your cog?"
> "My cog?"
> "Your surnoun?"
> "I have not got that either."

---

56. Emotional involvement becomes rather prominent, however, in the last two chapters of the book, especially in the meetings between the narrator and Policeman Fox, and between the narrator and John Divney. The balance is maintained, I think, by the onsetting of complete forgetfulness soon afterwards.

The Sergeant elsewhere repeatedly demonstrates his predilection for a neologizing speech-habit which reminds one of Lear rather than of Carroll: "'A constituent man,' said the Sergeant, 'largely instrumental but volubly fervous'" (71). It is, I think, too facile to regard this as mere parody of the pompous officialese one might expect from the average constable.

A perfect combination of wordplay and false logic is the so-called Irish Bull, which according to Butler "provides a set of facts which initially appear to be perfectly logical but which are unacceptable to reason. The mind is then discharged between the polarities of sense and nonsense until the paradox is resolved and the whole thing collapses in the catharsis of laughter" (1974: 39). The last phrase of this definition explains why the Bull as such is not nonsensical. Again, an example comes from the mouth of Sgt Pluck. When the narrator questions him as to the time of his hanging, the Sergeant replies: "Tomorrow morning if we have the scaffold up in time and unless it is raining. You would not believe how slippery the rain can make a new scaffold. You could slip and break your neck into fancy fractures and you would never know what happened to your life or how you lost it" (105-6). Even more paradoxical is the narrator's statement "I was dead" (104).[57]

A final element of the predominantly verbal nature of *TTP* is that of the reversed comparison or simile. Lanters discusses the "strikingly unnatural feature" of the landscape descriptions in *TTP*, and quotes several examples, demonstrating the artificiality of what is presented as beautiful scenery (1983: 275-6). This setting is not merely "man-made" (276), it is entirely verbal, suggesting, without entirely taking away the mimesis of the scenes described, that all the marvels are ultimately the creation of the omnipotent authors. Figures of speech can thus be transformed into meaningful statements. What is nonsensical is that instead of a supposedly "real" phenomenon becoming merely figurative or even "dead" cliché, the metaphor becomes mimetic. When Sgt Pluck interrupts his account of the Atomic Theory by saying "... you would be surprised at the number of people in these parts who nearly are half people and half bicycles", the narrator reacts: "I let go a gasp of astonishment that made a sound in the air like a bad puncture" (74). His soul thereupon remarks: "*Apparently there is no limit ... Anything can be said*

---

57. For the relationship between O'Brien's humour and the Irish Bull, see O'Donoghue (1982: 37-8).

in this place and it will be true and will have to be believed" (*ibid.*). It is the side-by-side presentation of two opposing views of reality, in the mind of the narrator, and hence in the whole novel, that in the end preserves the required balance between (multiplicity of) meaning and absence of meaning, and this leads me to the final point, concerning the nonsensicality of the book as a whole, an issue which is not touched upon by previous critics, who have tried rather to find a principal theme in it.

Jacquin, as has been mentioned, emphasizes O'Brien's obsession with gravity, and hence with the image of the fall (1975-6: 194) as well as with the helplessness of the human body (188). I do not think that these themes are really much more prominent than they are in *AW*, nor do I think the book can really be "explained" in these terms. In a recent article, which is ingenious but somewhat forced in its (intentionally?) nonsensical conclusion, Kemnitz describes the novel as the creation of "a literary locale controlled by atomic theory" (1985: 56). There is indeed some justification in remarking that "The parish of *The Third Policeman* exists beyond th[e] zone of middle dimensions [viz. that of Newtonian physics, WT], at the extremes of quantum mechanics and general relativity" (60), and that in *TTP* O'Brien "dramatizes" various aspects of both quantum mechnics and relativity (62, 64),[58] but his conclusion that "Bicycles represent subatomic particles" (65) and that the utterly inconsequential "Readings" in chapter VII can be "explained" in terms of three spatial and one temporal coordinates (71), thereby reflecting *TTP* as a "four-dimensional" novel, the four levels of narrative being dramatized by the female bicycle (72), is really altogether unwarranted. The presentation of "Eternity" in chapter VIII in terms of a black hole, where time comes to a standstill and gravity is immense (see the description on pp. 115ff. of the novel) is a side-effect, and surely not "the meaning" of the book. I would prefer to say that O'Brien here and elsewhere in *TTP plays* with the concepts of time and space in a fashion similar to Carroll's in the Alice books.

Lanters, as we have seen, in her first essay regards *TTP* as a fiction about fiction (1983: 267-8), but if this is true, and omnium is indeed the writer's imagination, the effect remains very implicit. The

---

58. O'Brien was greatly interested in physics and chemistry. See e.g. O'Keeffe (1973: 26). See also Clissmann (1975: 153) on his interest in Einstein's theory of relativity, and cf. Burgess (1976) discussed in section 4.4.1 above.

irrevocable "reality" of the policemen's world is constantly reaffirmed. All the same there is certainly some resemblance between the theories sparked off by de Selby and the unwritten but recorded fictions by the character Kilgore Trout in some of the metafictional novels by Kurt Vonnegut Jr.[59]

Clissmann points out that the original title of the manuscript was "Hell goes round and round" (1975: 152). This would have indicated a serious link with the Absurd.[60] In the end she calls *TTP* "perhaps a comedy of negation, nullity and abstraction" (181). Like Carroll's *HS*, *TTP* indeed abounds with images of nothingness, as when Mathers answers "No" to every question put to him by the narrator in chapter II (it is presumably the answer Mathers would have given to the question "Would that be your parcel on the road?" which John Divney asks him to divert his attention—p. 15). Soon afterwards, the narrator, like the Baker in Carroll's poem, forgets his name. Although the book begins with the word "Not", the answer to the question put on the last page, "Is it about a bicycle?", must now be "Yes", because the narrator has in fact lost a bicycle, the one we assume is again now behind lock and key in the police station. But simultaneously, as the cycle is to repeat itself, thus becoming a "bicycle" and presumably a "tri-cycle" and so on, the narrator, like old Mathers, is forced to answer "No" as he did on p. 48.

In view of the nameless state of the narrator, which reminds us also of Alice temporarily losing her name in the Looking-Glass forest or her questioning whom she may have turned into in *AW*, the theme of identity and the problems involved with it is perhaps altogether the most pervasive one.[61] If human beings can change

---

59. Clissmann states that O'Brien felt Joyce had been, as it were, wiping his nose with "our beloved tongue" (1975: 222), and a parodistic element cannot be excluded altogether. In a sense, O'Brien's early novels are an attempt to burlesque the Joyce of *Finnegans Wake* and to outdo him at the same time.

60. Cf. Kenner (1968), esp. the chapter entitled "The Cartesian Centaur" (117-32), where the relationship between a (lame) man and a bicycle is also commented on in connection with Beckett's *Molloy*. There seem to be interesting thematic links between Beckett and O'Brien, which deserve further investigation.

61. Mays believes that "de Selby" is related to German "der selbe", thus suggesting the theme of selfhood: "The book's method is its theme: the dizzying indulgence in the abyss of selfhood (*der*

into bicycles by transferring atoms, the crucial question "Is it about a bicycle?" also comes to imply, "What or who are you?" and even "What does it mean to be?" Is the narrator alive or is he dead? What does it mean to be, or not to be, when time stops, when gravity is suspended, when one is a fictional character at the mercy of its author (or, as in *At Swim-Two-Birds*, an author at the mercy of his characters)? There seems to be, moreover, a strong ethical quality to the book, which goes counter to the requirements of nonsense. The novel, which like *AW* and *TLG* consists of twelve chapters, is framed by crime and punishment, which acquire as dreamlike a quality as does Dostoyevsky's novel, and we begin to wonder if the story of the search after a black box full of omnium is the precipitation of the narrator's feeling of guilt, as in the case of Raskolnikov, or of the actual punishment. The most curious, least nonsensical feature of *TTP*, which I think is connected with this issue, is that the narrator has an obvious sense of beauty, a notion which Sewell teaches us is incompatible with nonsense proper (1952: 107, 126; cf. also 1980/1: 39).

There is indeed a great deal of beauty in *TTP*, which makes the novel bearable, if not to the narrator, then at least to the other characters, and to the reader as well. The policemen's world, even if it is cyclic and so becomes a Sisyphus-like round of punishment (or guilt) for the narrator, is not altogether unpleasant. Like Alice, to a large extent the narrator in *TTP* manages to adapt himself to his surroundings. Realizing that the "revived" Mathers answers "No" to any direct question (chapter II), the narrator rephrases his questions so that he obtains the answers he desires. This may be self-deceptive, but it offers him the hope he needs to keep him going. When he has left Mathers' house, the natural scene strikes him agreeably: "The dawn was contagious, spreading rapidly about the heavens. Birds were stirring and the great kingly trees were being pleasingly interfered with by the first breezes. My heart was happy and full of zest for high adventure" (33). It is true he has lost his name, but that does not bother him overmuch. As Lanters has pointed out, there is something mechanical in the phrase "interfered with", but

selbe), the regardless pursuit of omniscience (*omnium*)" (1973: 91). It was one of de Selby's beliefs that life is illusory. As Clissmann observes, in "hell" the theories of de Selby, the only theoretical frame of reference that the narrator seems to possess, do in fact apply (1975: 155).

there is no threat to sanity or happiness. If dawn is described in terms of a contagious disease, it affects the heavens, not the narrator. Lanters comments on the purposefulness of nature in *TTP* (1983: 275)—it literally reflects the narrator's mood; affective fallacy has become a truth in this world. But things which are really artificial (and impossible to boot), like MacCruiskeen's set of boxes, are also described in terms of exuberant beauty:

> He went to the little chest and opened it up again and put his hands down sideways like flat plates or like the fins on a fish and took out of it a smaller chest but one resembling its mother-chest in every particular of appearance and dimension. It almost interfered with my breathing, it was so delightfully unmistakable. I went over and felt it and covered it with my hand to see how big its smallness was. Its brasswork had a shine like the sun on the sea and the colour of the wood was a rich deep richness like a colour deepened and toned only by the years. I got slightly weak from looking at it and sat ⁿ on a chair and for the purpose of pretending that I was disturbed I whistled *The Old Man Twangs His Braces* (62).

Surely the "punishment", if that is what the narrator is undergoing, is considerably diminished if these experiences of beauty, no matter how artificial they are, are to be had cycle after cycle. At the same time, the greatest despair that the protagonist suffers from is when he finds out he cannot take any of the conjured riches away from "Eternity" (chapter VIII), and when he cannot leave the mystery of the burning light in Mathers' house alone (chapter XI). The last scene rather resembles Alice seeing the egg disappear through the ceilling of the little shop and later finding the dream-rushes fade at her feet in *TLG*, chapter V.

It will be obvious that both the variety of meanings, of actual interpretations evoked by *TTP*, as well as its repeated moments of beauty and fear with their concomitant emotional impact can be said to detract from the ultimate nonsensicality of this book. My own interpretation of the novel, without denying the aspects of the nature of being and eternity, and of reality and imagination, in particular the imagination of the creative writer, is that it is about the impossibility of an understanding between the hubristic character of the narrator, who is only interested in the precious contents of the elusive black box, and that of the simple-souled and sensitive policemen, who find omnium (which can be interpreted both as energy and as imagination) mainly convenient for boiling their eggs or taking the muck off their leggings. They are content with their world, which the narrator would prefer to rid of muck altogether and to fill instead with golden bicycles and "unbelievable commentaries on de Selby" (see pp. 162ff.).

That *TTP* is all the same a nonsense is partly because no clear "message" of this kind is explicitly conveyed, but mainly because in the whole of the novel a constant shifting and reshifting of perspectives takes place, and a balance between various polarities is kept up. Because the world is circular, cyclic, all the hopes and fears, the beauties and the cruelties, being and non-being, men and bicycles, remain in a perennially static balance. The conclusion of each syllogism leads back to the premise. O'Brien displays just sufficient playfulness in this novel to keep it from crossing over into the absurd, and just enough inconsistency to prevent it from becoming a fantasy. But it is also clear that we have reached the borders of nonsense.

4.5 *Borderline Cases and Partial Nonsense*

In what has gone before I have mainly acted on the assumption that, by offering a fairly simple definition of literary nonsense, it is possible to tell what nonsense is (Chapter 2), and how it can be distinguished from other types of literature with which it has been confused (Chapter 3). As a result, I have been able to describe and analyse what appears to be a kernel corpus of literary nonsense in the previous sections of the present chapter. In this section it is my aim first of all to acknowledge the fact that this approach even so has had to be limited; this chapter, lengthy as it is, is to be seen as exemplary rather than exhaustive. By means of my definition I have been able to reduce the hundreds of names included in the various nonsense anthologies, and the scores of names discussed in the secondary literature, to what is indeed to be conceived of as a kernel corpus of about twenty names, without suggesting of course that no further names or items are to be enrolled. Before offering a conclusion to this chapter, however, I first have to show my awareness of the existence of borderline cases, not so much between what I have labelled Carrollian and Learic nonsense, but rather between nonsense on the one hand and other types of literature discussed in chapter 3 on the other.

As has been remarked before (p. 134), I disagree with Haight's conclusion that defining lines regarding nonsense cannot be drawn to the extent only that this precludes a descriptive definition, and I certainly agree with him that "Nonsense shades gradually, in various directions, into pure fantasy, pure farce, the grotesque, the Surrealist, and so on" (1971: 255). This "shading off" can, I think, be attributed to two causes, the first of which may be the prevalence in a text of nonsense as a device, so that we can speak of a nonsense fantasy, fairy tale, joke etc. As Stewart (1978) and to some extent Liede (1963) also have described this aspect of nonsense extensively, I will not cover this ground once again. Needless to say, here too, what one regards as nonsensical is largely dependent on one's initial definition.[62] A second cause is the overlapping of two (or more) types which are adjacent to the "field" of nonsense, in particular if that field lies in between, according to the model I presented on p. 87 above. Thus, for instance, surrealism and symbolism, or parody and light verse, may easily shade off into one another without necessarily crossing the border into nonsense, but what happens if a work is at the same time surrealist and a fairy tale (some of Hughes' stories seem to have this quality, cf. pp. 170-1), or metafiction and fantasy, as in some of the stories by J.L. Borges? It seems reasonable not to pass by some authors here simply because they do not easily fit into my definition of nonsense.

As the model on p. 87 is to some extent tentative (some critics might like to readjust some of the categories I introduced there), I will not go through a systematical discussion of all the possible combinations, trying to fill slots with forced examples. Rather, I will very briefly discuss a few authors, mainly limiting myself to single

---

62. To be included under this heading are those texts in which one nonsense device, procedure or even theme is particularly dominant. Thus Sewell has suggested the possibility of regarding Flannery O'Connor as a nonsense writer, mainly because of the prevalence in her works of emotionless violence (1987). For comparable approaches, cf. Elderhorst (1987) on the anamorphosis as a nonsensical form in Donne's "First Anniversary", Peze (1987) on the situational nonsense in some postmodern American novels, and also the various accounts of partial nonsense in works by Aristophanes, Rabelais, Shakespeare, Cervantes, Swift, Sterne, Thackeray, Thomas Hood, G.M. Hopkins and T.S. Eliot. Needless to say, it is quite clear in all these cases that their works primarily served other aims than presenting nonsense, and that they are rarely if ever read as "nonsenses".

texts or collections of texts, that have occasionally been mentioned in connection with nonsense literature, or that cannot always be categorically excluded from the nonsense corpus. I will take the names (and again it should be emphasized that the list is far from exhaustive) in more or less chronological order.

Gertrude Stein (1874-1946) has been called "[p]erhaps the greatest nonsense writer who ever lived" (Hofstadter 1982: 20). Quoting a fragment from *How to Write*, Hofstadter classifies it as "simply an absurd string of non sequiturs" (*ibid.*). Indeed, much of her work is presumably to be categorized as absurdity rather than as nonsense. Kostelanetz, in his introduction to *The Yale Gertrude Stein* (1980), emphasizes the close relationship between Stein's writing and abstract painting (see esp. pp. xvi, xxiii, xxiv) as well as atonal music (xxiii). That we do not have nonsense here, except perhaps to those to whom her voluminous writings appear to be a mere purposeless logorrhea, is proven by the fact that Stein's favourite devices, those of repeating words or word-groups, and of separating lexical items from conventional syntax, serve to evoke connotations rather than to evade them (xvii). In so far as her mature works lack any purposeful ulterior subjects (xxiii), they do not offer a balance between meaning and non-meaning so much as an initial non-meaning or non sequitur, to which the reader is invited to attach what sense and connotations he pleases. All the same, many of the devices enumerated by Stewart (1978) are to be found in her works. Thus, "A Birthday Book" uses the separate days of the calendar as its basic pattern. Stewart remarks that "Stein's writing is an extreme example of the metaphorical turned literal" (1978: 80). I would say that it only shares this characteristic of inversion with nonsense, but is not to be equated with it.[63]

An important name that cannot be left altogether out of consideration in a discussion of nonsense is that of Franz Kafka (1883-1924). Petzold quotes Gardner on the latter's comparison between the Alice books and Kafka's longer works such as *Der Prozeß* and

---

63. I have not been able to consult Rieke's unpublished dissertation on "Sense, Nonsense, and the Invention of Languages: James Joyce, Louis Zukofsky, Gertrude Stein" (1984). According to the Abstract, Rieke considers nonsense to designate "privileged speech and plurality more than lack of meaning" (*DAI* 45/9, 1985, p. 2871-A).

Das Schloß (1972: 229; cf. Gardner 1960 [1965]: 15).[64] I think that what keeps Kafka ultimately just out of bounds is not so much the "consciousness" of his dream visions, as Petzold suggests (*loc.cit.*), but the fact that in most stories, and especially in the novels, Kafka applies what Hume refers to as the "skewed world" principle (1984: 125, 137-9). Another category discussed by Hume is that of the contrastive interpretation of reality (94-101), and this is where our overlapping comes in. *Die Verwandlung*, besides containing that important nonsense procedure of Play with Boundaries, the actual metamorphosis, is at once a mimetic story, a fable and a grotesque. However much tension there may be between the contrastive poles of Gregor Samsa "as bug versus his family" (Hume 1984: 83), so that one is reminded of Ede's definition of nonsense as basically a manipulation of tensions (1975: 12), this tension seems to be ultimately resolved in terms of the sad condition of man-as-bug. In other words, the story has an undeniable point.[65]

This may seem to be not so much the case with the incomplete "Beschreibung eines Kampfes", which at one stage contains a nonsensical discussion about "nobodies",[66] emotionless violence and command over reality ("Die Steine verschwanden nach meinem Willen ..."), so that a certain amount of metafictionality is present here as well. But as in the case of Beckett's plays and novels, the diction is too associative to be ultimately nonsensical. Miniature stories such as "Eine Kreuzung" (1970: 302-3) and "Gibs auf!" (358) may have influenced Buddingh's *miniaturen* (1982), which show the same mixture of surrealism, grotesque, absurdity, symbolism and humour, and therefore create a certain nonsensical impression, especially when a point seems to be lacking.

---

64. Cf. also Liede (1963: I, 201), where the lawcourt-scenes in *AW* and *TLG* are compared to those in Kafka's works.

65. That many theorists classify Kafka's works, notably *Die Verwandlung*, as fantasies (see e.g. Todorov 1970: 177ff.; Rabkin 1976: 28, 180; Jackson 1981: 159ff.) does not really serve to distinguish them authoritatively from nonsense, as these critics would include the work of Carroll under the same label. As so often, the confusion is due to divergences in genre definition.

66. "Ritt", Kafka (1970: 206-7). See the English translation in *Description of a Struggle and Other Stories* (1979). This passage is not found in *Sämtliche Erzählungen*, whose editor apparently uses another manuscript version of the fragment (see 1970: 403).

Much of Kafka reads like the account of a dream, and so do the miniature stories of the Russian Daniil Kharms (ps. D.I. Yuvachev, 1905-42). Here too we find such nonsense devices as a self-denying story ("Blue Note Book No. 10"—see Gibian 1971: 53); in most of the stories people get wounded or die without evoking any emotional reaction. Still, one feels that there is a "point" here consisting in the message that the crowd is heartless and gormless in its sensationalism, which is different (because more realistically presented) from the reaction of "them" in Lear's limericks, where the events described are far more incongruous. "Falling-Out Old Women" is pretty nonsensical:

> An old woman fell out of a window because she was too curious. She fell and broke into pieces.
> Another old woman leaned out the window and looked at the one that had broken into pieces, but because she was too curious, she also fell out of the window—fell and broke into pieces.
> Then a third old woman fell out of the window, then a fourth, and then a fifth.
> When the sixth old woman fell out of the window, I became fed up with watching them and went to the Maltsevsky Market, where they said a blind man had been presented with a knit scarf (54).

Compare, however, "A Lynching" (62), which ends more explicitly in its authorial comment with: "The crowd gets excited, and for lack of another victim seizes the man of medium height and tears off his head .... The crowd, having satisfied its passions, disperses." Some of these stories are more pointless than others.

According to Gibian, the "Oberiuty", a movement to which Kharms belonged and which suffered from Stalinist censorhip, had the intention of conveying the jarring of component parts (1971: 17-18). The movement was rounded up in 1930 on the grounds that "nonsense poetry" was found to be "a protest against the dictatorship of the proletariat" (21). Gibian also discusses the clearly satirical elements, and the differences with the absurdists (28-9). It is in particular the pointlessness which is found to be the keynote to the nonsensical elements in Kharms' work (29), and both Kharms and Vvedensky, another member of the same movement, are said to have been influenced by Carroll and Lear,[67] as well as by the nonsense of "Kozma Prutkov".[68]

As a counterweight to this Eastern European tradition of near-nonsense, which on the whole tends to verge upon the areas of the absurd, the grotesque and the parodistic, there is a more "intellectual" Latin tradition, which has a strong admixture of the metafictional, the fantastic and the mythical, and which includes the important names of Jorge Luis Borges (1899-1986) and Italo Calvino (b. 1923). In as far as these works are nonsensical, the nonsense is of the Carrollian rather than of the Learic type.

67. His poetry is said to be reminiscent of "Kharms' favorite English author, Edward Lear" (35). It seems to be "untranslatable" (34), and my knowledge of Russian is insufficient to test their nonsensicality—obviously this topic requires more expert investigation. For the complete poetical works, see the volumes edited by M. Meilakh and V. Erl (Kharms 1978-80).

68. Prutkov too deserves further investigation. According to Mirsky this fictive poet "flourished" from 1853 to 1863. The poems and prose works in question were composed by A.K. Tolstoy and his cousins, the Zhemchuzhnikov brothers. "Kuzma Prutkov became the founder of a whole school of nonsense poetry", notably the works of V. Solovyov and F.L. Sollogub (1926 [1958]: 232, 234). The twenty poems translated by Monter (1972: 121-38) are mainly parodies, but the works are stated to "contain both nonsense and parody" (xiii). There is an "Alphabet for Children" (for the original text, see Prutkov 1955: 328) which Monter associates with those by Lear (1972: 55), but which reminds me more of Lennon's alphabet discussed on p. 172. The aphorisms, discussed by Monter on pp. 56ff., are often less nonsensical than they appear at first sight. Aphorism 155: "A good cigar is like the globe: it turns for the contentment of man" (58-9) is not really "irrelevant": the connoisseur frequently applies a turning movement to the cigar while smoking, in order to stimulate the aroma. My impression of Prutkov's poetry, which is more accessible than that of Kharms, is that it is generally to be classed as parodistic romantic irony, resembling Carroll's "Rhyme? And Reason?" poems rather than Lear's Nonsense Songs (see Carroll, ed. Green 1965: 755ff.). I have not investigated the plays and the prose, which from Monter's account of them seem to be more obviously farcical and parodistic, with a strong admixture of mainly anti-bureaucratic satire.

The Argentine Borges is included among the writers of nonsense by Haight (1971: 247), who quotes from the story "Tlön, Uqbar, Orbis Tertius"[69] to illustrate the author's "Nonsense Philosophy" (254-5). Borges' work is certainly rich in the use of nonsense devices, and his writings convey a strong impression of the predominance of words and syllogistic reasoning. However, he does not so much *create* a nonsense reality as *discuss* one, even if Jackson refers to some of his stories as "linguistic fantasies" (1981: 36, 164). Mostly, Borges' stories are referred to as metafictions (Waugh 1984: 15; Hutcheon 1984: 18, 72, but cf. 47, where she speaks of them as "fantasy fictions").

In the stories nonsense procedures and motifs abound; examples of the latter are the mirror, the labyrinth, non-existent languages, the lottery, dreams and numbers, a complete memory. Waugh, in discussing various stories, discovers the procedures of infinity (1984: 31, referring to "The Library of Babel"), inversion (84, in "Death and the Compass") and simultaneity (137, in "The Garden of Forking Paths").[70] I would regard the stories primarily as symbolic-fantastic descriptions, or rather allegories, of the universe. In his presentation of philosophical and metaphysical notions such as infinity, time, space, fate, chance, identity, allegorized in terms of labyrinths, libraries and lotteries, Borges turns the whole universe into a kind of metaphysical Wonderland, but this is not quite the same as creating a nonsense reality. In "The Library of Babel" Borges makes explicit his view that ultimately everything must have a meaning: "The impious maintain that nonsense is normal in the Library and that the reasonable (...) is an almost miraculous exception. ... In truth, the Library includes ... not a single example of absolute nonsense" (1970: 84).

In "Funes the Memorious" Borges presents the life history of a man who amongst other things gives individual names to numbers (1970: 93). Here Sewell's principle of "one and one and one and one

---

69. All quotations from Borges are from the 1970 Penguin translation of *Labyrinths*. I have not consulted the original texts.

70. These procedures are also discovered in Borges by Stewart, from whom the example of infinity actually seems to be taken (see Stewart 1978: 126-7). Some further examples adduced by Stewart are boundary play in "The Garden of Forking Paths" (106) and arrangement and rearrangement (what I have called "arbitrariness") in "Tlön ..." (187-8).

and one" (1952: 44-54) is applied to perfection, but it is presented as a "philosophy", not as a (nonsensical) reality. In fact, most if not all of Borges' stories have a point (or, in Borgesian metaphor: each labyrinth has at least one way to the centre, if not a way out), except in as far as they explicitly confess to a lack of knowledge or a variety of possible solutions to a problem. As Gibian has remarked of Kharms (1971: 34), Borges presents "What if" stories: what if a man tried to memorize everything that came to his knowledge?[71] What if the world could be compared to an endless library? What if a man "re-created" Cervantes' *Don Quixote*? As Maurois puts it in the Preface to *Labyrinths*, Borges wonders: "If this absurd postulate were developed to its extreme logical consequences ... what world would be created?" (1970: 11). The initial paradox or twist of thought which is consistently elaborated points in the direction of a fantasy rather than a nonsense, but the simultaneous self-reflexivity of Borges' writings causes frequent overlapping on to the field of nonsense.

A similar phenomenon occurs in the works of the Cuban-born Italian writer Italo Calvino, whose writings, especially the short stories collected in *Cosmicomics*, border on the mythical rather than the fantastic, and who combines a Carrollian delight in logic and science with a wistful romanticism reminiscent of Lear. With Kafka Calvino shares what Hume refers to as a departure from consensus reality in western literature (1984: 21). Both Hume and Jackson (1981: 37) count him among the writers of fantasy; Waugh and Hutcheon, who include him among the writers of metafiction, celebrate respectively his "combinative impulse" (Waugh 1984: 44) and his ability to turn reality into fiction (Hutcheon 1984: 79). Again, one is reminded of Ede's (and my own derived) requirement of tension in nonsense literature. Hume reckons *Cosmicomics* together with Kafka's *Die Verwandlung* in the category of "contrastive literature", which confirms the presence of tension (1984: 98-100). On pp. 49-50 she states that "in *Cosmicomics* and *T Zero*, he [Calvino] juxtaposes absurd, homely, human behavior with the physics, chemistry, biology and mathematics of the developing universe", but significantly she goes on to say that he "goes on from there to create a new sense of wonder, a new human scale for measuring and admiring the

---

71. On this theme cf. Bichsel's "Der Mann, der nichts mehr wissen wollte" (1969: 81-91).

infinite" (50), an emotional reaction towards and involvement with the subject-matter that precludes pure nonsense.[72]

In *Cosmicomics*, which I think of Calvino's works comes closest to the spirit of nonsense, the author takes physical facts (such as the closeness of the moon to the earth in an earlier stage of the evolution of the solar system) and translates these in terms of myth: the tides were so high at the time that one could climb up into the moon and collect its "milk". In "How Much Shall We Bet" there is a nonsensical play on words which do not yet have any referents, but the implications of this are very mythical. This story is in a certain sense a nonsensical expansion of an initial linguistic-logical proposition that is strongly reminiscent of Carrollian logic, but at the same time it is quite clearly a satire on cybernetics. A similar ambiguity occurs in "The Form of Space": is this the story of a frustrated three-cornered real life affair in terms of a mathematical metaphor, or is it a fantasy about parallels outside a curved universe, which can therefore never meet? A second collection of similar stories, *Time and the Hunter*, peters off much more obviously into metaphysical speculation represented in terms of fantasy or myth (cf. Barth's *Lost in the Funhouse*), and thus remains constantly "below" the border of nonsense in my model of p. 87. Calvino's other works, which are more purely metafictional, tend to stay "above" it.

My conclusion as regards the borderline cases of literary nonsense would be that they are most striking where divergent but related genres overlap, so that a tension is created between metafiction and fantasy, as in Borges' *Labyrinths*, or between myth and absurdism, as in Kafka's *Die Verwandlung*; other examples can be added to this. Scheerbart's "astral", "hippopotamus" and "railway" fiction combines fantasy, surrealism and grotesque, although, as has been suggested (p. 111), the balance is regularly upset by ascribing this blurring to a holistic cause such as "Weltgeist" or drunkenness. David Lindsay's intriguing fantasy *A Voyage to Arcturus* (1920), which is modelled on AW[73] in its Alice-like quest of the protagonist

---

72. Cf. p. 83 (on Borges and Kafka): "Contrastive works differ from the subtractive dualism seen in heroic black-and-white, in that readers have a foot in both camps. *We are emotionally committed*, or at least intrigued, by both sides in contrastive works" (my italics).

73. The comparison is explicitly made by Rabkin (1976: 47). Cf. also Hume (1984: 160). Like *AW*, and like Flann O'Brien's *The Third Policeman*, this book may be regarded as a "dialogic novel" (see

Maskull across a planet which is subject to sudden metamorphoses, and which contains many prominent nonsense motifs such as the sprouting and disappearance of organs, unmitigated violence and a cyclic time-space structure, is too heavily suggestive of a Nietzschean-Bergsonian message to be nonsensical. Kurt Vonnegut's works are basically satires, but in a novel like *Slaughterhouse-Five* (1968), the mixture of metafiction, absurd and fantasy is striking, and many nonsense features occur, such as the writer being at the same time a character (play with boundaries or imprecision), the way Tralfamadorians read their books (simultaneity), the famous passage of the bomber movie experienced backwards (inversion), and the infinite list of works (extended over other novels) by the fictive writer Kilgore Trout, some of whose plots are worthy of invention by Korf or Palmström. But the message, the senselessness (and certainly not the nonsensicality) of the Dresden bombing ("So it goes") is all-pervasive. The book is too much an indictment to be a nonsense, even if so many nonsense devices are used, presumably to create a distancing effect.

Richard Brautigan's *The Hawkline Monster* (1974) is a mixture of widely divergent genres (its subtitle is "A Gothic Western"), and seems to be a pointless parody. Apparently in accordance with the "Atomic Theory" as voiced by Sgt Pluck in Flann O'Brien's *The Third Policeman*, a monster changes into a set of diamonds. A final interesting case is Joseph Heller's *Good as Gold* (1976), in which it gradually turns out that the strongly mimetic sense of reality in this novel is manipulated by the characters' speeches and conversations, which come to resemble more and more those in *AW* and *TLG*. But here we have clearly arrived in the not less interesting but different field of partial nonsense proper. The book is a satire on the American way of life in general and in that context the Jewish experience in particular. The mad logic of Father Gold and the representatives of American administration is a satirical device using the means of linguistic exaggeration and distortion.

From the foregoing paragraphs it may be clear that the concept of nonsense as a device and as a mode invites more investigation, and especially a more systematic treatment than it has thus far received from scholars like Liede and Stewart. At this stage I would tentatively define nonsense as a genre if it fulfils the requirements of my definition as presented in chapter 2. If these requirements are

Henkle 1982: 98, quoting Michael Bakhtin).

not fully fulfilled, we must speak of *partial* nonsense. This partial nonsense may feature as a *device* in another genre, for instance in the form of the occasional occurrence of one or more of the procedures, themes or motifs described in my second chapter. If one or more of these devices becomes dominant, we may speak of nonsense as a *mode*. Only if this distinction is made can we speak in one breath of Carroll, Lear, Borges, Beckett, Joyce, Ionesco, Rabelais and Aristophanes as writers of nonsense (Haight 1971: 247). Of the writers enumerated by Haight, only Carroll and Lear produced generic nonsense. In all the others nonsense is partial, and features in larger or smaller measures as a device—more so for instance, I would say, in Beckett than in Joyce (and in Joyce more so in *Finnegans Wake* than in *Ulysses*), and in Borges to such an extent that we can speak of modal nonsense. The nature of the nonsense, and the measure of its presence can be ascertained only by a literary appraisal, which is what this chapter has tried to offer.

4.6 Conclusion

Previous scholarship has failed on two scores to bring clarity into what constitutes the corpus of literary nonsense. Firstly, there is very little agreement on what are the contents of this corpus, which can be attributed to a lack of theoretical insight into what literary nonsense is; and secondly, there is an overall lack of critical appraisal, which might have led to such an insight. As regards the corpus of literary nonsense, the only agreement one discovers in a handful of anthologies and a score or so of scholarly works is that Lear and Carroll are very rarely omitted. Morgenstern's Galgenlieder are mentioned quite often—about one third of the critics (all of them Germans) refer to these as nonsense. Less frequently mentioned names are those of W.S. Gilbert (of the *Bab Ballads*), Ringelnatz, T.S. Eliot (*Old Possum's Book of Practical Cats*), Scheerbart and Lennon. Rarely mentioned or not at all are Bichsel, Gorey, Hughes, Jarry, the Marx Brothers, Flann O'Brien, Peake, Richards, Sandburg and Satie. Of earlier writers, one frequently encounters the names of Aristophanes, Rabelais and Sterne, and occasionally Shakespeare, Swift and Cervantes. Scores of writers are discussed in terms of their use of what I have called partial nonsense, and the anthologies, largely due to a confusion of nonsense with curiosities, nursery rhymes, light verse and parodies, include hundreds of writers. Some anthologies include only poetry, others introduce (fragments of) prose texts and plays as well.

This plethora of names is partly due, as I have stated, to a confusion about definitions, and I have tried to solve this in earlier chapters by offering and elaborating a genre definition of nonsense. A second reason seems to be a somewhat nationalistic bias: it is striking that as the nationality of both critics and anthologists varies, the emphasis is shifted from representatives of one language area to another. I have to some extent contributed to this phenomenon by adding the names of some Dutch nonsense writers, notably Buddingh' and Zonderland, and some more names could be added from a handful of Dutch anthologies, most of the items in which however would have to be reclassified as light verse or parody rather than as nonsense. A theory-based survey or history of Dutch nonsense literature is called for, but will not be attempted here. Neither will I draw conclusions here as to possible other national traditions of literary nonsense. In this respect I will limit myself to a few general remarks in chapter 5.

The first conclusion to be drawn from the present chapter is that, on the basis of my definition a corpus of literary nonsense can be drawn up and described. Needless to say, the chapter could have been enlarged by adding some more examples and possibly more authors, but from what has been said the reader should be able to test to the theory texts that have come to his attention and possibly escaped mine. For reasons of accessibility as well as economy I have largely limited myself to examples from English, German and French. With the exception of the Marx Brothers films, I have not discussed combinations of verbal and visual nonsense such as are to be found in the television sketches of Monty Python's Flying Circus or the drawings of Saul Steinberg, as it is doubtful to what extent one can actually still speak of *literary* nonsense in these cases where the visual aspect has become, if not dominant, at least of equal importance with the verbal.

In my discussion of the corpus I have started from a distinction between a Carrollian and a Learic type of nonsense, without suggesting, I hope, that this distinction is always clear-cut. Just as there may be overlappings of nonsense with related genres, so there may be an overlapping between the Carrollian and the Learic, of the logical, rational and mathematical ornamental type with the emotional, irrational and musical popular kind. This is in fact part of the required tensions, and one might argue that the best nonsense is that which does not easily fall to one side of the scale. However this may be, I have tried, without becoming too rigid, to indicate the literary quality of the authors and texts discussed not only by the amount of space allotted to each subject, but also by illustrating and elucidating how the nonsense works in each case, and to what extent the "requirements" of the definition are fulfilled. Hence the approach has been eclectic-hermeneutic rather than systematic. I realize that literary quality, or if one likes the aesthetics of a text, is hard to prove, and in any case to a large extent subjective and bound to time and place. Sewell suggests that it may be ultimately a matter of proportion (1980/1: 41), but this concept is as tenuous as are those of beauty, harmony and the like. What makes us prefer the golden section in art, or harmony in music? All I can hope for is a response to an appeal to some consensus of appreciation among the critics. It seems to me that the conscious or unconscious success with which the author has applied the criteria of an unresolved balance between meaning and absence of meaning, a reality created by language, an absence of emotion, and all of this presented playfully and with a creative and original use of a choice of particular procedures, themes and motifs, may give some indication of the quality of literary nonsense.

CHAPTER 5: SOME REMARKS ABOUT THE HISTORICAL, CULTURAL AND PSYCHOLOGICAL BACKGROUNDS OF NONSENSE

In most of the earlier scholarship as well as in the anthologies, nonsense is presented as a timeless phenomenon, as witness the inclusion of early writers like Aristophanes (Strachey 1888, Chesterton 1901, Haight 1971, Jennings 1977), Rabelais (Strachey, Chesterton, Haight, Benayoun 1977, Stewart 1978), Hans Sachs (Dencker 1978) and Laurence Sterne (Strachey, Chesterton, Schöne 1955b, Benayoun, Stewart). I have already suggested in section 4.1 that when defined as a mode or a device, nonsense, especially in the form of play with language, is a perennial phenomenon. As a genre, however, which is my main concern in this thesis, the starting-point seems to be the publication of Lear's *Book of Nonsense* in 1846, and, as will have become clear from sections 4.3 and 4.4, the genre has persisted until the present day. It is the aim of this chapter to provide a critical summary of the explanations that have been given for the rise of nonsense as a literary genre in Victorian England, and of the various historical, cultural and psychological causes that can be plausibly brought into connection with this phenomenon as well as with its occurrence elsewhere and its survival up to the present day.

The most extensive accounts of the relationship between literary nonsense and its place and time of manifestation are those by Petzold (1972: 178-215), Reichert (1974: 7-39), Kretschmer (1983: 9-40) and Kreutzer (1984: 83-108). Rather than summarizing these and other sources, I will subdivide my analysis into three sections, on social history, cultural history and psychology, although some overlapping is bound to take place. In section 5.3, I will only marginally touch upon psychological or biographical interpretations of nonsense works. For full accounts of these the reader is referred to the relevant items from the bibliography.

5.1 *Social history*

Whenever nonsense is discussed in terms of the society that produced and appreciated it, it is generally regarded as a phenomenon which is critical of the current state of affairs, or which offers an escape from it. Thus, Prickett states that "Nonsense offered the Victorians ... an alternative language for coping with the conditions of a world at once more complicated and more repressive" (1978: 146). Furthest in this respect goes Aragon, with his famous statement that at the time of the composition of the Alice books, human freedom lay in the frail hands of Alice (1931: 25). But it may well appear that in fact the relationship between literary nonsense and its social backgrounds is somewhat more complex.

Petzold quotes from an issue of *The Spectator* of 1894, in which the writer states that nonsense occurs in intervals of freedom between times of sharp strain (1972: 175). What is needed as a substratum is a concurrence of political stability and an inflexible social system, such as existed in the Victorian era in Great Britain, and which it is plausible to assume also featured in Wilhelminian Germany,[1] the Interbellum in the United States, and the period following the Second World War in all of the western world. "Die besondere Situation des viktorianischen England besteht nach dieser Ansicht in einem prekären Gleichgewicht zwischen Spannung und Entspanntheit; nur in einer solchen Situation könne guter Nonsense gedeihen" (Petzold, *loc.cit.*). Quoting Nicolson 1956, Petzold affirms the former's view of a similar equilibrium regarding the occurrence of a national sense of humour, which according to Nicolson "cannot prosper either in a totalitarian and classless society or in a society in the process of revolution. A special, fortuitous, and therefore transitory, balance between acceptance and revolt, between conformity and non-conformity, between the conventional and the eccentric, is needed before a sense of humour can pervade a whole society" (1972: 205; cf. Nicolson 1956: 35). This statement can be aptly applied to nonsense as well, as it does reflect a balance between conformity, particularly as regards form, and non-conformity, in particular as to content-matter (cf. Ede 1975: 12). A similar conclusion is reached by Tabbert, who attributes the revival of nonsense in the modernist period to protest as well as to resignation (1975: 8).

Indeed, a look at a survey of the most important nonsense works published since the time of Edward Lear seems to point in the direction of their concurrence with periods of relative tranquillity rather than with periods of economic recession, which is Benayoun's opinion (1977: 9).[2] The following table contains the most important nonsense works discussed in this thesis. Figures in square brackets

---

1. Kretschmer places Morgenstern's *Galgenlieder* against the background of this period (1871-1914), which corresponded almost to the month with Morgenstern's lifespan (1983: 7-40).

2. The severe (but relatively brief) recession of the Interbellum is the most prominent exception.

indicate dates of composition if these are known to be materially remote from the date of first publication.

1846	Lear, *Book of Nonsense* [1832ff.]
1858	"Cuthberd Bede", *Funny Figures*
1865	Carroll, *Alice's Adventures in Wonderland* [1862]
1871	Lear, *Nonsense Songs* ...
1872	Carroll, *Through the Looking-Glass*
	Lear, *More Nonsense*
1876	Carroll, *The Hunting of the Snark*
1877	Lear, *Laughable Lyrics*
1905-19	Morgenstern, Galgenlieder [1895-1914]
1911	Jarry, *Docteur Faustroll* [1898]
1913	Satie, *La piège de Méduse*
1922-30	Sandburg, *Rootabaga Stories*
1929-49	Marx Brothers films
1931	Hughes, *The Spider's Palace*
1932	Richards, *Tirra Lirra* [1871ff.!]
1939	Peake, *Captain Slaughterboard Drops Anchor*
1951	Themerson, *The Adventures of Peddy Bottom*
1953-	Gorey, *Amphigorey Stories*
1964-5	Lennon, *In His Own Write/A Spaniard in the Works*
1967	Flann O'Brien, *The Third Policeman* [1940]
1969	Bichsel, *Kindergeschichten*
1969-74	*Monty Python's Flying Circus* (regularly re-broadcast)
1972	Peake, *A Book of Nonsense* [late 40s and afterwards]
1976	Burgess, *A Long Trip to Teatime*

Lear's works were republished in 1943 in the U.S.A., and in 1947 in Britain, and are regularly reissued; the most important Lear biographies and studies appeared in 1938 (Davidson), 1968 (Noakes, and Davidson re-print), 1978 (Byrom) and 1982 (Hark), and with the centenary of his death at hand interest is likely to continue. Carroll's main biographies appeared in the thirties and since the Second World War, and the authoritative Gardner editions are of the sixties. The most important monographs on literary nonsense appeared in 1925 (Cammaerts), 1952 (Sewell), 1975 (Ede) and 1978 (Stewart). Of course, the birth and death dates of the authors are important beacons for later biographies and commentaries, irrespective of the vicissitudes of social history, but there must be a minimal interest in the writers concerned for publications to be undertaken.

One must be careful in drawing conclusions from a select list of works, but it is striking that there are "peak" periods (noticeably 1862-77 in England, corresponding to the crest of the economic wave, which turned in 1873; the turn of the twentieth century in Germany and France, concurrent with a prewar boom; the Interbellum; and the postwar Welfare period of 1950-77) and "lows" (1877-95, a period of economic decline in Europe; 1940-50; perhaps the last decade, which has not seen much original work).

Looking at the dates of publication, one would suspect that nonsense has its heydays in times of prosperity and optimism, perhaps composed by men (and the occasional woman) who do not feel very much at home in such a booming world. If this is true, there may be an explanation here of the fact that so much of the greatest and purest nonsense was written in the English-speaking world, in the days when Britain ruled the waves and built up this nonsensical Empire on which the sun never set, and when the United States was at the crest of the various economic waves. But probably this is too facile an interpretation of the socio-historical facts surrounding the phenomenon of literary nonsense.

The most relevant general connection between social circumstances and the appearance of literary nonsense seems to be that of the rise and development of an industrial, capitalist economy with the concomitant consumer and welfare society. In his discussion of the Alice books Kreutzer devotes a final section to "Sozialgeschichtliche Aspekte" (1984: 94-108). He makes mention of the progress of science and especially technological inventions in Victorian Britain,[3] and the accompanying social tensions in this period of relative peace and prosperity, latent tensions which affected the relationship between employers and (un)employed, labour and leisure, private life and collective life, children and adults, men and women. He also mentions the effects of Darwinism and Utilitarianism, of the capitalist mentality, of the bourgeois code of life and behaviour, and of the consequences of increasing leisure for the middle classes, resulting in a commercialized games cult, but also in the rise of popular literature as a mass product. His general conclusion seems to be that during the nineteenth century in Britain an increasing rift occurs between ideals and reality of social life, between expectations evoked and their fulfilment. Thus, for instance,

---

3. Cf. Kretschmer (1983) on similar developments in Wilhelminian Germany (12-16, 64-76).

> [i]n der Konstellation von Alice und den Wunderlandwesen werden die individuelle Beherztheit und geistige Sicherheit des Mädchens, das im wesentlichen über die kodifizierten viktorianischen Tugenden verfügt, ohne bereits in die Starre der Erwachsenenwelt verfallen zu sein, mit zerrbildhaften Projektionen eines Systems konfrontiert, in dem sich unnachgiebige Egozentrizität, konkurrierende Machtansprüche, bedrohliche Grausamkeit und undurchsichtige Reglementierung zum Eindruck eines repressiven Kollektivs zusammenfügen (103).

The Victorian age, as I pointed out in an earlier publication (1986a: 183), was the era of the implementation of the industrial revolution and the capitalist system of economy. The primacy of demand being replaced by that of supply (to many of those who are critical of the system in itself a nonsensical reversal), Victorian households, in particular those of the middle class, were inundated with "things". It would be interesting to find out how many new objects, as compared with the previous century, which had been the age of new ideas, were introduced in the course of the nineteenth. Karl Marx, who, as is known, decries the "fetishism of commodities", "exchanges", in the first chapters of *Das Kapital* (1867), coffee and overcoats, gin and bibles, like so many counters in a game – exactly in the way nonsense works according to Sewell (1952). The interchangeability of one concept for another is indeed a notable feature of nonsense. The capitalist market, in contrast with the older forms of exchange, has a nonsensical quality, in its seemingly pointless exchange of commodities, in its suggestion of meaning in the form of employment and profit, a meaning which is simultaneously taken away in the form of exploitation, unemployment, bankruptcy and poverty, and in its refusal to allow any emotional value to be attached to the products to be exchanged, which is a marked difference with earlier craftsmanship. Factories and department stores have become the concrete equivalents of dictionaries, with their infinite series of simultaneously presented goods of the utmost variety.[4] In as far as this system has persisted to the present day, it may well explain the simultaneous persistence of nonsense as a harmless parody of this state of affairs.

---

4. Cf. Reichert (1974: 22ff.). "Manche Erfindungen erscheinen wie sichtbar gewordene Wortspiele" (25).

However, it is also obvious that nonsense is *not* (and never has been) the reflection of the mainstream Victorian through Atomic world picture. It seems to be first and foremost an intellectual divertissement, even if behind it there is a deeper psychological need. But, previous to probing into the soul of nonsense, we must have a look at its cultural background, which is in all likelihood able to offer the most certain explanations of its occurrence, its manifestations and its persistence.

5.2 *Cultural history*

Nonsense as a genre has been often related to Romanticism.[5] The concern of nonsense literature with language can, as I have argued in "An Anatomy of Nonsense", be related to the rise of philology during the Romantic period (1986a: 181). This is also the time when Kant, as quoted by Ede (1975: 3) distinguished "between what man can assert with certainty (sense) and what is beyond his rational powers (non-sense)". In the late eighteenth and early nineteenth centuries, philosophers as well as linguists began to consider language as a phenomenon in its own right, ruled by its own laws. Studies of etymology and phonetics teach us that language changes its sense as well as its sounds. Romantic poets and artists used language and images not to analyse, as had been the practice in the preceding age of enlightenment and reason, but to synthesize, and, in particular to evoke emotion.

The Victorian epoch, which witnessed a renewed application of rationalism with the Utilitarians and the rise and development of industrialism, preserved this emotion in a domestic, watered-down form of it, that is to say, in its sentimentality and its melodrama, which may be regarded as weakened forms of the beautiful and the sublime respectively. Literary nonsense, then, may be seen as a post-Romantic reaction, to be understood as an introverted reaction, in which the individual sets his own norm against the conventionalized Romanticism of the later Wordsworth and of much of Tenny-

---

5. See e.g. Cammaerts (1925: 24-5); Mautner (1931: 699-700, on Romantic wordplay); Davidson (1938 [1968]: 200); Hildebrandt (1962: 70); Walter (1966: 133ff.); Petzold (1972: 56ff., 182-9); Reichert (1974: 14-15); Prickett (1979: 123); Demurova (1982: 75, 77); Kreutzer (1984: 83). Reichert, *loc.cit.*, lists the motifs nonsense has in common with Romantic poetry.

son's poetry, and especially, one assumes, against their second- and third-rate epigones. Both Lear and Carroll clearly present their nonsense in a near-parodistic way.

Petzold and Demurova in particular link up nonsense with romantic irony (*loc.cit.*), which Mellor, in her monograph, defines as the constant conflict of the two opposing principles of chaos and order.[6] She believes that in Lewis Carroll's "defensive *Alice* books", a "simultaneously creative and decreative form" is presented: "In these works, symbols are generated only to be qualified and rejected" (6). The difference between the romantic-ironical work and nonsense becomes implicitly clear from what she states about the world created by the romantic ironist; "a fictional world must be both sincerely presented and sincerely undermined, either by showing its falsities or limitations, or, at the very least, by suggesting *ways of responding to it other than whole-hearted assent*" (14; my italics). This is a "point" that romantic irony tries to make, which is absent, as has been argued, by definition from nonsense: "Schlegel meant that the work of art must reveal the presence of an authorial consciousness that is simultaneously affirming and mocking its own creation" (17). This partly narcissist, partly self-parodistic aspect of romantic irony, clearly to be recognized in a work like Byron's *Don Juan*, is more relevant to the genre of metafiction, as well as to particular forms of light verse, than it is to nonsense.

Petzold, distinguishing romantic irony from parodies, points out that in the former "wird jedoch echte Stimmung erzeugt und durch Nonsense-Stilmittel gleichzeitig vernichtet" (1972: 57), which makes obvious a relationship between nonsense (as device or as partial nonsense) and romantic irony. He realizes that both Lear and Carroll lack "das Moment der theoretischen Reflexion über das Wesen der Kunst" (58), which is an essential characteristic of romantic irony. It will be clear that romantic irony and nonsense are closely related phenomena, but that they must not be confused. To call Lear's nonsense poems the "'reductio ad absurdum' of Romanticism" (Davidson 1938 [1968]: 200, and supported by Petzold 1972: 189) is altogether too strong a statement.

Both the Romantic theory of language and that of irony can and have been followed up into more modern times. Both Walter (1966:

---

6. 1980: 11-12. This unresolved tension is traced by Mellor to the dialectic of Schlegel (*ibid.*). Interestingly, Mellor also notes the play element in Romantic Irony, referring to Schiller (29; cf. also 188).

40-3) and Liede (1963, I: 254-72, 328ff.) discuss the importance of Fritz Mauthner's "Sprachkritik" for the work of Morgenstern.[7] Ede refers to the importance of the linguistic philosophy of Ludwig Wittgenstein[8] and the Structuralists (1975: 4f.), and Mellor has traced the development of romantic irony on to existentialism (1980: 180) and absurdism (1987-8). But as can be seen by consulting the table on p. 231 above, and putting it next to the dates of publications by the absurdists and the existentialists, the "peaks" of nonsense writing and these other types of literature in the twentieth century can be seen to be complementary rather than overlapping.[9]

Another phenomenon that can be traced from the Romantic period to modern times is the development of an imaginative, non-didactic and a-moral children's literature. The relationship between nonsense and children's literature is discussed extensively in Hildebrandt (1962).[10] Hildebrandt concentrates on the similarities between nonsense and the fairy tale, which consist in episodic structure as well as lack of motivation, character development, didactic aims and abstractions (71). Apart from the fact that his insistence on lack of motivation and of didactic aims in fairy tales is questionable (the moral tendency of most fairy tales is prominent), the link between the fairy tale and the nonsense of Lear and even that of Carroll is very tenuous indeed. Lear's nonsense is, as we have seen, far closer to another traditional type of children's literature, the nursery rhyme.[11]

It is undeniable that Lear and Carroll, apart from possible psychological motives to be discussed in section 5.3, wrote their nonsense primarily for children, to whom the play with form and language, and many of the motifs (food, clothes, numbers, personi-

---

7. See also Hildebrandt (1962: 231); Kretschmer (1985: 81).

8. Himself possibly influenced by Carroll. See e.g. Pitcher (1965), partially rpt. in Gray (1971: 387-402).

9. The great existentialist novels, such as Sartre's *La Nausée* (1938) and Camus' *L'Étranger* (1942) and *La Peste* (1947), originated around the period of the Second World War. Absurd drama had its culmination in the fifties with the plays of Beckett and Ionesco.

10. P. 70. Cf. also Petzold (1972: 92): "Nonsense-Dichtung und Kinderliteratur gehören im England des 19. Jahrhunderts eng zusammen." See also *ibid.*, 179-82, and Kreutzer (1984: 15, 83).

11. See section 3.2, and cf. e.g. Cammaerts (1925: 3, 19); Schöne (1954a: 103, 1954b: 133).

fication of utensils and animals, and even the sadistic violence, which has persisted into the "comic" book and the animation film) are greatly appealing. The Victorian nonsense writers provided an (apparently authorized) holiday from the didactic and moralistic writing for children which had been prevalent in the Classical period and retained an important position far into the nineteenth century, and a similar lack of good, non-didactic, amoral literature was apparently felt by Dr Heinrich Hoffmann in 1844, forcing him to fill a writing-book with the extravagantly but (one hopes) playfully sadistic *Struwwelpeter*,[12] which was roughly contemporaneous with Lear's landmark of juvenile literature in Britain, the first *Book of Nonsense* (1846). When the first Alice book appeared in England, Germany saw the appearance of Wilhelm Busch's definitely immoral *Max und Moritz* (1865). Unlike Lear's limericks and Carroll's *Alices*, neither *Struwwelpeter* nor *Max und Moritz* belong to the genre of nonsense, even if Hildebrandt considers them together with Morgenstern's *Klein Irmchen* (1921) and Ringelnatz' collections of children's verse (1910-31) as "Parallelerscheinungen" (1962: 223-40).[13] Why it is that Lear and Carroll made use of the medium of children's literature will be discussed in the following section.

Petzold rightly states that the development of nonsense for children is roughly contemporaneous with that of nonsense for adults (1972: 180), but this conclusion is, of course, based on his characterisation of nonsense as an area of literary humour (2). "The eighteenth century was, perhaps, all over Europe, the period when Nonsense was the least appreciated, no doubt because Wit was so much in the fashion. For Wit and Nonsense are arch-enemies" (Cammaerts 1925: 82). Martin (1974) argues that somewhere before the year 1877 the Victorian tradition of humour made a shift from the amiable, sentimental humour that dominated the earlier part of the century, to a more intellectual, paradoxical wit as exemplified in writers like Meredith, Shaw, Butler and Wilde (3). It is indeed striking that the last two decades of the nineteenth century, when these writers produced most of their works, is quite devoid of original nonsense, as the table on p. 231 easily demonstrates. It is also, I think, correct to say that nonsense of the Learish type, which was particularly popular in the 1860s and 70s, is closer to

---

12. See Hürlimann (1967: 53-63).

13. A Victorian rendering of *Struwwelpeter* in English is included in Rhys' *Book of Nonsense* (1927: 141-69).

humour, and that of the Carrollian type, frequently imitated in the 80s and afterwards, to wit.[14] This might also explain why Lear is generally more popular with poets, painters and musicians, and Carroll with lawyers and scientists.

Gray, in his very perceptive discussion of Victorian Laughter, regards the nonsense writing of both Lear and Carroll as accommodating disturbing experiences with the inconsequential laughter of release (1966: 147). He also draws a parallel between the incongruities that are so prominent in nonsense, and those that feature in the comic stage, parody and burlesque: "Victorian nonsense ... is a creature of the traditions and motives which shaped other kinds of Victorian humor. It begins on the same ground" (168). Petzold devotes a section of his book to the nonsense and "Vorformen" of nonsense in the comic periodicals, quoting from Gray: "From the appearance of *Figaro in London* in 1832 to the end of the century, at least 275 comic weeklies and monthlies were published in England" (1972: 96; cf. Gray 1966: 150). The most noticeable of these comic periodicals is of course *Punch*, which was founded in 1841. At the same time we find the publication of popular books by Jerrold and Thackeray, the light verse of Thomas Hood, and Gilbert's *Bab Ballads* (see pp. 105-6 above), to mention only a few.

A simple, partly social, partly cultural-historical explanation of the proliferation of all these publications is the increase of a literate bourgeois public, which is reflected in the rise and development of various types of "trivial" literature such as the penny romance and "dreadful", the detective novel, the thriller, the pornographic novel, and, towards the end of the nineteenth century, science fiction, accompanied by a tremendous increase in journalistic productions, both newspapers and periodicals.[15] Of course, nonsense formed only a relatively small part of the entertainment section of this phenomenon, but its popularity may be partly due to the very size and scope of these mass publications. Kreutzer in particular emphasizes this entertainment boom and the rise of an amusement "market" (1984: 91-2), which accompanied a similar market for children's books. Of course, what is stated here only proves the likelihood of a proliferation of nonsense works *alongside* a spate of other popular publications, and it does not fully explain why nonsense

---

14. For a discussion of these terms and their relationship to nonsense, see section 3.1.

15. See e.g. Henkle (1976: 71); Kreutzer (1984: 91-2).

became particularly popular from Victorian times onwards in Britain, and somewhat later in other European countries as well.

In Marxist terms, popular entertainment and escape literature are part of the "superstructure" of reproduction—a way, so to speak, of filling the increasing leisure time of the growing bourgeoisie as well as, in later times, after social legislation and a reduction of the working day, of the labouring class. But, as has been said, nonsense is an intellectual divertissement rather than an easily accessible form of entertainment. The reason for this lies in one of its basic characteristics, the refusal to release tension. In this respect, nonsense is essentially different from pornography, say, or the detective novel, which reflect the human desire to have tensions released, in the case of pornography even in a physical sense. All the same, the sales of Lear's and Carroll's nonsense works were quite large, and their audiences cannot therefore have been so limited. Noakes records nineteen editions of Lear's *Book of Nonsense*, which became popular after its third edition in 1861. By June 1862, 4,000 copies were sold and 2,000 printed.[16] *AW* was reprinted thirty times in twenty-four years (Pudney 1976: 79), and Green records 180,000 copies sold by the time of Carroll's death (in Phillips 1971 [1974]: 51; cf. Petzold 1972: 176). Of *TLG*, 15,000 copies were sold in 1871 alone, and 60,000 up to 1893, and of *HS* 18,000 in the first six years; the latter book had been reprinted seventeen times by 1908 (Pudney 1976: 84, 90; Petzold 1972: 176).[17] It is clear that the Alice books, which have been interpreted in many ways other than a nonsensical one in terms of my definition, were more popular than Lear's verse, and remained so even at a time when little "original" nonsense was produced.

16. Noakes (1985: 170). Richardson (1965: 28) records thirty editions, but she may be including the other volumes as well. Noakes (*op. cit.* 175-6, 178) records five editions of *Nonsense Songs* (1871), 2,000 copies sold of *More Nonsense* within days of its publication (1872), and only one edition of *Laughable Lyrics* (1877). This evidence confirms a "peak" in the popularity of nonsense in the 1860s and early 70s, and a veering away to other forms after the mid-70s.

17. For a survey of Lear and Carroll reception, see Petzold (1972: 137-77). For Morgenstern, see Kretschmer (1985: 138-42). Hildebrandt records a distribution to date ("mittlerweile") of the original *Galgenlieder* volume of 200,000 copies (1962: 229-30).

It seems a reasonable conjecture that both for adults and for children the works of Lear and Carroll, but also those of Morgenstern and the later nonsense writers, were to some extent of particular interest in view of the "intertextuality" to which these works make an appeal. This aspect is brought forward by Demurova in connection with Carroll where she speaks of his "parodies" (1982: 85), and naturally intertextuality is of prime importance to parodic work; in order to understand and appreciate what is parodied one must be familiar with the texts that lie at the basis of the parody. Stewart's theory of nonsense largely hinges on the notion of intertextuality: assuming that commonsense is "manufactured" in the domain of reality, and that all other "provinces of meaning" are "modifications of the common-sense world", she goes on to argue that nonsense operates in particular "between" the domains, in the transformative operations used in moving from one domain to another (1978: 16). It is between the four aesthetic domains of realism, myth, irony and metafiction that nonsense most commonly operates, in the form of play constituted by the shift from one domain of reality to another (19-21, 29. See also pp. 33-6 above). As has been demonstrated in chapter 3, nonsense works precisely because it can be distinguished from other literary "domains" such as parody, light verse, metafiction, absurdism etc. I am convinced that in the nineteenth century nonsense was appreciated exactly because it could be seen to be different from a poem by Southey or by Isaac Watts, but at the same time different from a parody of such a poem. In order for this appreciation to exist, the acquaintance with both a large amount of "serious" literature as well as parody of it must be subsumed, and this is exactly what the increasing literacy of the nineteenth century contributed towards. Apart from that, a more general reason for the popularity of the works of Lear and Carroll in particular must have been the tremendous appeal of these works to the imagination.

A final aspect that must be entered into here is the question if and to what extent nonsense is a typically English phenomenon. Its specific "Englishness" is argued by Cammaerts (1925: 73-86), Homeyer (1947), Nicolson (1956: 46), Hildebrandt (1962: 69, 239), Petzold (1972: 203ff.), and Burgess (1987: 17-18). The reasons given for this alleged fact are various. Cammaerts attributes it to "a certain trend of broad humour" inherent to the English temperament (1925: 74), as well as to the "lingering attraction for the days of their childhood" (78). Homeyer discerns a particular aptness for nonsense in the English language with its large variety of sounds and its polysemy

(1947: 52). This view is underlined by Hildebrandt, referring to Ayres (1936) and Schöne (1954a) (1962: 69). Nicolson states: "It is in nonsense that the childishness, the play-aptitudes, the fancy and the mental indolence of the English find their most welcome outlets and excuse", whereas "in countries where logic is reverenced, and reason esteemed, the love of nonsense appears primal, infantile, and below the dignity of the developed man" (1956: 46). As Burgess puts it: "The logical French stopped fighting the Nazis in 1940; the stupid English sustained the struggle" (1987: 17). Petzold summarizes these and similar views (1972: 203-7), but in addition he rightly points out that this so-called typical English humour is not an immutable national characteristic, but a historical phenomenon, which is to be linked to cultural and social events that have taken place in other parts of the world as well. He agrees with Liede, quoting the latter's categorical statement that "[w]as der Engländer Nonsensedichtung nennt, gibt es auf der ganzen Erde" (205; cf. Liede 1963: I, 159). Although it should be borne in mind that Liede's definition of nonsense is in fact an equation of this phenomenon with literary play, it will be evident that my discussion of nonsense in the previous chapters points towards a more universal prevalence of generic nonsense in a wider cultural area. A more interesting question in this context is why this genre originated only in the nineteenth century, and why indeed it apparently became popular in England before it reached other countries. A partial answer to this question has been provided in the connection I have made with the development of the industrial revolution and the concomitant literary reaction in a post-Romantic period, a discussion which will have to be extended in the next section.

Summarizing, Petzold seems to be most plausible when he states:

> Zugrunde liegt der Popularität des Nonsense im 19. Jahrhundert—dies muß festgehalten werden—das Bedürfnis des bürgerlichen Publikums nach einer temporären geistigen Fluchtmöglichkeit aus den Beschwernissen des Alltags und vor den eigenen weltanschaulichen Zweifeln; ein Ausweg, welcher gleichzeitig nicht zum Nachdenken über diese Schwierigkeiten veranlaßte und keine wirkliche Kritik des bestehenden Systems bedeutete. Dieses Moment darf zweifellos als ein übernationales, rein klassen- und geschichtsbedingtes angesehen werden. Diesem grundlegenden Bedürfnis wurde jedoch in den einzelnen europäischen Ländern und Nordamerika je nach den spezifisch nationalen Gegebenheiten auf verschiedene Weisen nachgekom-

men. Diese besonderen Gegebenheiten umfassen die jeweilige geistesgeschichtliche Tradition und jene kaum genau zu erfassende, aber immerhin nicht ganz zu leugnende Größe "Nationalcharakter", die in einem kaum auflösbaren Wechselverhältnis miteinander stehen. Die konkrete äußere Ausprägung des Nonsense ist also gewiß nicht aus der politisch-wirtschaftlich-sozialen Situation der viktorianischen Zeit allein zu erklären. Sie ist vielmehr bedingt durch volksliterarische Traditionen wie die Nursery Rhymes, durch spezifisch englische geistige Kräfte wie den Puritanismus und durch nationale Charakterzüge wie etwa den sprichwörtlichen englischen Pragmatismus mit seiner Kehrseite, dem Mißtrauen gegenüber logischer Abstraktion. Und schließlich verdankt der Nonsense seine Gestalt auch dem Zufall: der Tatsache nämlich, daß sich zwei Männer fanden, deren besonderes Genie darin lag, daß sie die Tendenzen der humoristischen Dichtung ihrer Zeit schöpferisch weiterentwickelten und dem neu entstehenden Genre des literarischen Nonsense den Stempel ihrer Persönlichkeit aufprägten: Edward Lear und Lewis Carroll (1972: 206-7).

5.3 *Psychology*

The idea that lies at the back of nonsense is escape, a suggestion made by G.K. Chesterton as early as 1901 (447).[18] Chesterton was also the first to distinguish the nonsense writer's need for this escape from the nonsense reader's desire for a return to that primal world of wonder and faith, a "mental holiday" to a "world of masquerade" (447-8). In this section too, a division must be made between the more or less demonstrable reasons for Lear, Carroll, Morgenstern, Jarry, and others to write nonsense, on the one hand,

---

18. The nineteenth-century epithet most commonly found seems to be that of "holidays" (of the mind) (Petzold 1972: 191, quoting contemporaries; Nock speaks of "vacation" (1941: 69). "Escape" is found in Henkle (1973: 99-100), and Prickett (1979: 114), who also speaks of "detachment" (120). Homeyer (1947: 54), Lennon (1945: 10), Liede (1963: I, 165), Gray (1966: 147), Esslin (1968: 530), Nicolson (1956: 46), Massey (1976: 86), Rackin (1982b: 23) and Kreutzer (1984: 89) speak of "Befreihung" or "Freiheit", "release" or "liberation"; Andersen (1950: 162) and Forster (1962: 42) of "refuge"; Nicolson and Stern (1982: 133) of "rebellion".

and the psychological reasons why in the nineteenth and twentieth centuries nonsense as a literary medium appealed to psychological needs on the other. Petzold appropriately warns us that "die Annahme, daß sich im Leser ähnliche psychologische Vorgänge abspielen wie beim Verfasser, bleibt so lange unverbindliche Spekulation, als keine äußeren Beweise eine solche Gleichsetzung berechtigt erscheinen lassen" (1972: 207). A few pages further on he concedes that a psychological function of nonsense for Lear may unconsciously also have been valid for his readers (21), but he remains more cautious than Reichert, who categorically states: "Carrolls private Misere ist die Misere der Epoche" (1974: 36). I will take a middle position in this matter.

In this section I will not enter into the psychological interpretations that have been offered of nonsense works, not so much because I consider them irrelevant, but because I lack the expertise to judge them on their psychological merits. These interpretations will have to speak for themselves. I refer the reader to Empson's interesting account of *AW* in the light of Freud (in Phillips 1971 [1974]: 400-33; this volume contains other Freudian as well as Jungian approaches to Carroll's works), and to Chetwynd's brief Jungian explanations of Lear's "The Jumblies" and "The Owl and the Pussycat" (1982: 230-1, 310-1). To the dangers of psychological criticism of nonsense some paragraphs worthy of consideration have been devoted by Ede (1975: 10-12). My main reason for not discussing psychological interpretations of nonsense in this dissertation, however, is that such interpretations suggest that there is a point to nonsense texts which it has been my effort to exclude from my definition; within its scope, in other words, such interpretations simply cannot be valid.

The out-of-the-ordinary personalities of the early nonsense writers are well-documented. From the various biographies and psychologically-oriented studies of Lear and Carroll, one gets the picture of the former as a companionable, amiable and affectionate liberal, hiding his melancholy and even despair, due to ill-health and emotional loneliness, behind a façade of facetiousness and a restless life of art and travel, and of the latter as a fussy and priggish, obsessively orderly introverted conservative, similarly hiding existential doubt and sexual frustration behind walls of whimsiness and the more static and respectable life of an almost literally cloistered mathematician. Whereas both men were apparently much appreciated by their contemporaries, although one suspects from the evidence that Lear had many more sincere and satisfying friendships, their later biographers and students of their works generally manifest a more favourable view of Lear's personality than of Carroll's.

"The breath of insanity clings about him [Carroll]", writes Sewell, "as it has never done, and could not do, about Lear" (1952: 181). Emphasizing Lear's sanity (163), she calls Carroll "unbalanced" (175), and suggests he might have suffered from schizophrenia (168).[19] Croft-Brooke calls him "less lovable" than Lear, "and not so unquestionably good" (1967: 153). Green calls Carroll "charming and attentive" (1960, in Phillips 1971 [1974]: 68), but most of the other commentators, much as they may admire his achievements, are more adverse. De la Mare speaks of "a certain primness, a slight stiffness" in his letters (1932: 27), Nock calls him a "silly prig" (1941; 69), Virginia Woolf refers to him as "prudish, pernickety, pious and jocose" (1939, in Phillips 1971 [1974]: 78). Lennon refers to him as a "blocked genius", who later became an "old-maidish don", "a left-handed man in a right-handed world" (1945: 13, 18, 21), but Coveney less kindly calls him a "maladjusted neurotic" and a "stammering, awkward, spinsterish don" (1967, in Gray 1971: 331). Gardner remarks that he was a "humorless and boring" lecturer (1960 [1965]: 10), Hudson calls him "withdrawn, reserved" and "fussing" (1976: 31), and Pudney "conscientious, meticulous, fastidious, pedantic" (1976: 15). Prickett epitomizes him as "socially conventional" (1979: 130) and Rackin as "passionately devoted to order" (1982b: 15).

The epithets most commonly used of Lear are "lovable" (e.g. Davidson 1938 [1968]: 10, Croft-brooke 1967: 153, Lehmann 1977: 8), "amiable" (Jackson 1947: xi), and "likeable" (Andersen 1950: 162), "sociable" (Quennell 1952: 96), and "affectionate" (Richardson 1970: 25, Byrom 1977: 3, Lehmann 1977: 8). Richardson moreover speaks of his "gusto and humanity" (1970: 18) and his "determination, courage, energy" (21), but also of his "perpetual restlessness" and his "immense unhappiness" (*ibid.*). Elsewhere she calls him "embarrassed in the presence of strangers, reticent, and often deeply depressed", but also "gentle and considerate" (1965: 9). Nock speaks of Lear as a "sad, lonely, unsuccessful, and bewildered man" (1941: 70), and White calls him "a lonely, self-exiled wanderer" (1966: 280), who was "grotesque, ailing, exiled, lonely" (281). Quennell calls him "a melan-

---

19. In this context, Blumenfeld's discussion of the role of schizophrenia in connection with a tendency for word-formation and logorrhea is not without interest (1933: 74-5). Cf. also Stewart (1978: 31-2).

choly gadabout" (1952: 95) and "a sociable and bustling extrovert" (96). Byrom, who refers to him as "affectionate, lonely and plain" (1977: 3)[20] also refers to him as "manic-depressive" (*ibid.*). Hark describes him as "tormented by rootlessness, insecurity about money, poor health (...), and ... a pervasive loneliness" (1978: 113). Kelen calls him "one of the funniest and most delightful men one can imagine" (1973: 9) and also "a man who never grew up" (19), a qualification that could be used of Carroll as well. Davidson speaks of Lear's "lovableness and whimsicality" (1938: [1968]: 10), Jackson refers to him as "amiably preposterous" (1947: xi) and Lehmann as "a most lovable human being, loyal, affectionate, selfless ... an enchanter of children and a source of constant mirth", but "never free from melancholy for long" (1977: 8). The most critical statement made about Lear is that he was "shabby and untidy" (Croft-Brooke 1967: 152).

Prickett draws the most explicit comparison between these two rather eccentric but at the same time not uncharacteristic Victorians:

> Both were shy and sensitive bachelors; both were very fond of children, and came themselves from large families; both were afraid of dogs; both were of an "analytic state of mind" ... Both were marginal kinds of men, if in very different senses. Though Lear was mentally a rebel and internal refugee, he was in the last resort as much dominated by the society that threatened him as the more socially conventional Carroll. Both became internationally famous during each other's lifetimes as writers of nonsense. ... For both, certainly, fantasy or "nonsense" was a way of dealing with feelings of insecurity and loneliness ... (1979: 130).

Both men, too were aware of their own failures (see e.g. Henkle 1973: 101-2 on Carroll, and Andersen 1950: 163 and Richardson 1970:

---

20. The "plainness", a matter of self-complaint on Lear's part, is clearly also a matter of taste. Considering the portraits made at various ages, I would agree with those who regard him as pleasant to the view. Carroll, though "asymmetric", is generally regarded as more handsome. Both authors suffered from physical defects; Lear was epileptic, asthmatic and near-sighted, Carroll was a stammerer and deaf in one ear.

25 on Lear). It is not indeed at all unlikely that for those who produced "nonsense" this was a means of escaping both from the cloying sentimentality of Victorian domesticity with its strict bounds of decency on the one hand, and the rigour of capitalist efficiency on the other. For Lear, who by Victorian standards was unsuccessful in both fields, being a lifelong bachelor[21] as well as a "dirty landscape painter" (Davidson 1938 [1968]: 47; Noakes 1968: 79), it was indeed true that nonsense was a method of self-defence, an escape to hide his feelings, his despair, his sense of failure and frustration.[22] Escaping into a new-found-land of language and logic, Lear and Carroll, who in this respect were very similar characters, could at least pretend to "master" reality rather than only escape it (in madness or eccentricity) or reproduce it (in art, mathematics or progeny). In this respect nonsense is similar to child's play. The child too indulges in "verbal magic"; by controlling language it pretends to control the world around it.[23]

In the previous section, the rise of nonsense in the Victorian age has been partially attributed to the rise and growth of a children's literature (pp. 236-7 above). To this we must now add a simultaneous and obviously related change of views about the identity and nature

---

21. And possibly homosexual, although the evidence for this does not, everything considered, strike me as very convincing. On this aspect of Lear's life see e.g. Noakes (1968: 134), Petzold (1972: 210), Hark (1982: 14-15). Concerning Carroll, we have to assume on the authority of Lennon that "no one claims he had any sort" of sex life other than "in the mind" (1945: 177).

22. See e.g. Andersen (1950), Prickett (1979: 130). Nock even goes so far as to state that Lear wrote in nonsense his emotional biography (1941: 68).

23. Cf. Blake (1974: 18, 63, 130). "Play ... is characterized by a fundamental urge to mastery through incorporation of experience to the ego rather than by adjustment or accommodation of the ego to experience ... the difference is between eating up life—for the pleasure, not the hunger—and being digested by it" (18). A similar connection between nonsense and eating, with reference to a duality of "manger-parler", is found in Deleuze (1969, esp. 36-40, 104-5). Cf. also Boelens (1987: 236, 242-3), and my discussion of food as a nonsense motif in section 2.4, p. 79. For a more down-to-earth explanation, curiously enough, see Empson (1935, in Phillips 1971 [1974]: 408-9).

of the child, which until the Romantic period had been largely regarded as an adult in miniature. As from the age of Romanticism, it became increasingly clear that the basis for the individuality of a human being, its unique personality, is already laid in childhood. In Victorian times, this individuality was frustrated by the conventionalizing codes of orderliness, rationalism, social hierarchy and class-consciousness, moral decency, cramped domesticism and so on. Simultaneously, the Romantic notion of childhood, with its emphasis on spontaneity, natural piety, imagination, had turned into the "sentimentalen Kitsch eines realitätsflüchtigen Kinderkults" (Kreutzer 1984: 84). In this post-Romantic period, the incompatibility of certain individuals from the intelligentsia with the type of society they had to live in could no longer be expressed in a manner which was strongly antagonistic to that society; such a policy would have led to social ostracism, which must have been unacceptable to individuals as strongly dependent on social contacts as were Lear and Carroll. But in any case, the dissatisfaction they felt was not so much with their society as with their own role and identity in it. Nonsense on the other hand perfectly expresses this emotional dissatisfaction, as well as endearing the authors to children and adults alike in a way that would be impossible to the satirical or social rebel.

Henkle points out quite convincingly that "[a]mbivalence and indirect attack, *angst* and muted self-assertion are beautifully accommodated in nonsense. The virtue of nonsense is its obliqueness; it is ideally suited to criticism from the 'inside' of a class or society by one too wracked by self-doubt to engage in open assault" (1973: 115). In addition, the nonsense writer himself remains invulnerable by preventing both counter-attack and criticism (116). This view is supported by other scholars as well. Empson states that Carroll, like Alice, wanted to get the advantage of being childish and grown-up at the same time (1935: 401). Later on he tries to make it clear why a man should want to be a child:

> There is always some doubt about the meaning of a man who says he wants to be like a child, because he may want to be like it in having fresh and vivid feelings and sense; in not knowing, expecting, or desiring evil; in not having an analytical mind; in having no sexual desires recognizable as such, or out of a desire to be mothered and evade reponsibility. ... The praise of the child in the *Alices* mainly depends on a distaste not only for sexuality but for all the distortions of

vision that go with a rich emotional life; the opposite idea needs to be set against this: that you can only understand people or even things by having such a life in yourself to be their mirror; but the idea itself is very respectable (420).

Some years earlier, Mautner, who was not writing on nonsense at all, argued that wordplay is an expression of inner distance and impediment, in fact, of a lack of courage in being non-ambiguous (1931: 701). The prevalence of wordplay in nonsense is hereby largely explained. Ede writes: "A unique expression of [the] interplay in nonsense involves a basic ambivalence between the desire to present emotion, with its concomitant pain and confusion, and the tendency to refuse to admit that such discomforting realities exist" (1975: 15). This is often accompanied by the protective device of a disclaimer of "nonsense" or ultimate lack of meaning. Carroll indeed repeatedly denied that there was anything but "nonsense" to his children's books (see e.g. Carroll on *HS*, as quoted by Gardner 1962 [1967]: 22, and cf. Gorey's strong opinion on "people finding meanings in things"—1979: 7). Underlying the series of antitheses that Ede lists as characteristics of literary nonsense, a basic disorientation can be established. "This attitude is one that is subversive of a social perspective; in fact, it is most commonly anarchic and individualistic" (1975: 16). Nonsense, in other words, simultaneously ignores and questions the "real" world, rather than being aggressive towards it. It allows one to play at "pretending to be two people", as we learn about Alice quite early on (Gardner 1960 [1965]: 33), or at being at the same time "ill-tempered and queer" as well as "pleasant enough", as Lear says of himself in the "Self-Portrait of the Laureate of Nonsense" (Jackson 1947: vii).

If successful, nonsense is communication without communicating. Petzold draws our attention to this, quoting Davidson on the nonsense Lear wrote in his letters to adult friends: "It was characteristic in him [Lear] thus to introduce nonsense words and spelling into his letters as a sort of apology for what might seem too bold, or, sometimes, too sententious, or too outspoken—a bridge between, on the one hand, his love of frankness, and, on the other, his easily embarrassed sensitiveness. Terrified of being thought presumptuous or pushing, he found in this nonsense-language a kind of cloak for his selfconsciousness" (1972: 211; cf. Davidson 1938 [1968]: 94).[24]

---

24. Cf. also Sewell (1987) on Swift and Flannery O'Connor.

Nonsense enables the author to broach serious emotional topics, namely those to do with order and sanity, love and sex, religion and death, without a release of tension as takes place in a joke. Rather than inviting an answer to the questions it evokes ("Why is a raven like a writing-desk?" *has* no answer), it calls out for the correct counter-question, which is never asked. Neither despair nor anger about its abeyance are released, and so nonsense is not as aggressive as it might seem to be at the first sight, inviting its readers to an interpretation that cannot be obtained. This is because much literary nonsense is presented in the disguise of children's literature, a successful disguise, because good nonsense also appeals to a non-questioning child-like imagination. Lear has been called a "Clown, der lacht, um nicht weinen zu müssen" (Petzold 1972: 212). Rather than importune his fellow adults, the clown offers his ambivalent personality to the child, who accepts it "without question".

In the twentieth century the social situation may have changed somewhat as compared to that of the nineteenth, but I think the psychological reasons for writers like Morgenstern, Jarry, O'Brien and Gorey, to mention only a few of the authors whose works have been discussed in the previous chapter, to compose nonsense were much the same. Of these, Morgenstern was presumably the least eccentric, but his personality was also characterized by internal tensions. He was both a sentimentalist and a mystic (Forster 1962: 10). Beheim-Schwarzbach, who calls him harmonious (1964 [1983]: 8), points to his internal tensions: "Es waltete in ihm ein seltsames Mittelspiel zwischen Stille und Sturm, zwischen Besonnenheit und Feuer" (29), and on the same page he refers to "[d]ie innere Spannung, unter der er fortgesetzt lebte". Originally attracted by socialism, he later shifted his beliefs to anthroposophism (Kretschmer 1983: 15), but he felt continually uncomfortable towards the bourgeois and "Polizeihaften" nature of the imperial period.[25] Elsewhere, Kretschmer refers to his scepticism and melancholy (1985: 46). Contrary to most other nonsense writers, Morgenstern married, late (in 1908, when he was 37) but happily (see Beheim-Schwarzbach 1964

---

25. For Morgenstern's social engagement, and his general attitude towards his own era, see Kretschmer (1983: 9-40 *passim*). The tension is strikingly expressed in the opening sentence of section VII: "Christian Morgenstern war einer der Unzufriedenen des deutschen Kaiserreiches und doch in manchen Denkgewohnheiten und Idealen seiner Zeit befangen" (31).

[1983]: 113). Significantly, his Galgenlieder are dedicated to "Dem Kinde im Manne" (1933: following title page), a motto of course taken from and expressing indebtedness to Nietzsche, of whom he was a great admirer.

Jarry's Docteur Faustroll, as we have seen, was born at the age of 63 (1955: 11). His own life, eccentric to the extreme (he is said to have started his dinner with the dessert and finishing it with the soup, thus linking the nonsense motif of food with the procedure of inversion, which we now realize may be symbolic of a psychological regression to childhood), is said to have grown more and more isolated and cerebral (Perche 1965: 115-6). He too suffered from a strong sense of failure (*ibid.*, 100). Beaumont describes "the attitudes and the emotional life" of the author as it transpires in some of his works as "suggesting both an attraction to and a fear of love and physical contact, coupled with feelings of guilt and remorse" (1984: 228): "He was probably painfully self-conscious of his small stature: unusually short and thick-set" (27). In the same work, Jarry is repeatedly described as demonstrating homosexual inclinations and a fierce mysogyny, (e.g. 6, 32, 50)[26] and also as suffering from an ingrained sense of solitude (7). In fact, in view of Jarry's extremely sombre and isolated view of life, it is not surprising that the relatively mild form of coming to terms with his fears and obsessions which nonsense is, was not sufficient for him, and hence only incidental to his work. The *Ubu* plays are very aggressive and scatological. The nonsense of Jarry is practically limited to *Docteur Faustroll*, apart from partial nonsense, mainly in the form of wordplay elsewhere in his *oeuvre*.[27]

The "intellectual and spiritual portrait" of Jarry that Beaumont sketches in his monograph stresses this writer's "fierce defence of a

---

26. See esp. p. 50, where Beaumont also states that "there is no evidence of any sexual involvement whatsoever on Jarry's part with women". Like Carroll and Morgenstern, Jarry had a strong attachment to his mother, who died young (*ibid.*, 35). Cf. Hudson (1976: 59); Bauer (1933 [1985]: 18). Lear, who had a bad relationship with his long-lived mother (see e.g. Noakes 1968: 58), formed a replacing attachment to his eldest sister Ann, who in fact brought him up from quite a young age. Carroll's mother died at the age of 47, Morgenstern's only lived to her early thirties, Jarry's to 49.

27. See e.g. Beaumont (1984: 23, 299, 302) on Jarry's love of linguistic invention and wordplay.

philosophy of absolute individualism" (295), which Beaumont links up with the Symbolist movement (296). "Behind his incessant wordplay and verbal clowning lies a deep-seated intuition that all 'reality' (...) is at bottom a linguistic reality—that all statements of a philosophical, religious, ethical or scientific order are not just (in the language of pataphysics) 'imaginary solutions' but, in the final resort, mere words" (303). It is this notion which I consider to be an important psychological common ground for the creation of nonsense by the various authors discussed, and possibly for the appreciation of literary nonsense as well. Beaumont's concluding sentence—"Jarry is part of a movement which would eventually break down forever the once-rigid barriers between the supposedly 'serious' world of adulthood and the 'playful' universe of childhood" (308) can be equally applied to Lear, Carroll, Morgenstern and others.

It is curious that this notion of individuality and individualism is so rarely brought into connection with the production and appreciation of nonsense. Only Hildebrandt (1962: 98, quoting Nicolson 1956: 56) and Hark (1978: 112) make a brief allusion. The latter draws a link with Darwinism ("The random Darwinian cosmos threatened to leave man much more uncomfortably on his own than any libertarian might wish"—Hark, loc. cit.; cf. Petzold 1972: 209 and Rackin 1982b: 15-17). A bit further on she points out that the arbitrary representation of facts (in the works of Lear, which she writes about here) "corresponds quite closely to the Darwinian view of chance causation and to that sense of 'crass casualty' Thomas Hardy's works so often express" (118). For Lear's nonsense creatures, "Salvation lies in adaptability" (119).[28]

It is the tension between a rational need to adapt and an emotional fear of having to do so and thereby to lose the integrity of one's individuality that I consider to be reflected in nonsense. One of the most important stages of adaptation in the life of a human individual is that of the transition from childhood to adulthood. It cannot be accidental that so many writers of nonsense or associated

---

28. In a more "neutral" sense, the findings of Darwinism play a part in the mutational aspect of many nonsense creatures, perhaps reinforced by the discoveries of and interest in fossils of prehistorical animals earlier on. Is not the dinosaur the remote ancestor of the Jabberwock? See also Prickett (1979: 79-84, esp. p. 81); also White (1966: 282).

with it share this characteristic of being "eternal children".[29] An exception to this "rule" is possibly Flann O'Brien, who in later life more or less repudiated his early, most nonsensical works.[30] Gorey, on the other hand, seems to be a confirmation of it. A "totally eccentric" bachelor, "sort of depressed all the time in a mildly jolly way", whose acquaintance mainly consists of the 400 or 500 people he sees all the time at the ballet performances of which he is extraordinarily fond, he does not move beyond 1930 in his writing and drawing, although he admits to not knowing if he really remembers what it was to be a child (Gorey 1979: 5-7).

If one part of the psychology that lies behind nonsense is to assert one's individuality, apparently by refusing to come to a point, and another is a childlike playfulness, a third seems to be the inclination to escape from tension, paradoxically by keeping it in balance. What were the tensions that confronted individuals in the Victorian age? In the first place the very tension of being an individual in a collective world, the "Ich-Zerrissenheit" which Reichert calls the most important link between Romanticism and nonsense poetry (1974: 15). This tension of the "self and society" (Ede 1975: 154) must have existed to some extent in all periods, but it had become particularly dominant immediately following the very individualistic age of Romanticism, especially during the period of the 1830s and 40s, when the capitalist society with its bourgeois worldview had consolidated itself. The Victorian age in Britain was a period of sobriety and of sentimentality and humour; of Utilitarianism and useless ornamentation; of progress and regression; of ratio-

---

29. See also e.g. Sewell (1987: 193-4) on Flannery O'Connor. Petzold suggests a similar albeit more temporary attitude in the *readers* of nonsense, namely a willingness to play at being a child (1972: 192).

30. See e.g. Burgess (1982: 84). O'Brien, of course, "married decently" (83) and had a job as a civil servant, as well as the opportunity to vent his satirical message in the respectable *Irish Times*. But even so, cf. Jacquin, who ascribes O'Brien's preoccupation with the grotesque to a "peur devant le mystère de la reproduction" (1983: 87). In fact, O'Brien married late (in 1948, when he was 37) and had to give up his job in 1953, presumably because of ill-health and disillusion (Clissmann 1975: 24-5). Clissmann records O'Brien's character from the descriptions of close friends as "irascible, loveable, shy, sensitive, wounding" (35)—in fact: childlike, one might say.

nality and religion; of materialism and morality; of positivism and an increasing interest in the irrational and the supernatural; of conformity and eccentricity; of what Reichert, in Marxist terms, distinguishes as a private and a public identity (1974: 28). It is not surprising that the notion of dialectic, of thesis and anti-thesis became so prominent in exactly this period, the age of Hegel and of Marx.[31]

These tensions have not really disappeared since, except perhaps in times of severe cirsis or war. The "reification" of creatures, especially human beings, the alienation of emotions, the continuing increase of knowledge and information, the increasing incompatibility between equality and liberty, and, in more modern times, for more and more layers of western society, the clash between welfare and independence, persist. Our fear of nothingness may in fact have increased greatly by the added phenomenon of the nuclear threat, as well as by more recent environmental calamities and the emergence of new epidemic diseases, whereas the invention and development of the computer may have enlarged our fear of "everythingness"—respectively the destruction and the blurring of identity.[32]

The rise of psychology (of especial importance in this context are Sigmund Freud's *Traumdeutung* of 1900 and *Der Witz* of 1905) has led to entirely new ways of exploring the field of nonsense.[33] So has the development of linguistic philosophy represented by the works of Fritz Mauthner (Liede 1963: I, 254-72) and Ludwig Wittgen-

---

31. See Petzold (1972: 178-9); Ede (1975: 154ff.); Kreutzer (1984: 96ff.), where most of these polarities and tensions are enumerated and discussed. On the reactions evoked by Utilitarianism and rationalism see in particular Petzold (1972: 189-94), and cf. Reichert (1974: 15). Lang briefly notes (again, in Marxist terms) the changes of interaction between basis and superstructure, leading to alienation, that were characteristic of both the Victorian period in Britain and that of "Wilhelminismus" in Germany (1982: 110). Kreutzer states that both Lear and Carroll wrote nonsense to compensate for an alienation from the adult world.

32. The reference to "nothingness" and "everythingness" is of course from Sewell (1952: 52). See Guiliano (1982b: 123-31) for a discussion of the anxieties of this nature underlying Carroll's *HS*, and of the Boojum as an "existential horror" (128).

33. See Ede (1975: 10-11) for some references with comment.

stein (Ede 1975: 5),[34] and of physics, if only because of the consequences for our notions of time and space arising from Albert Einstein's theories of relativity. Of course, symbolism, dadaism, surrealism, absurdism and metafiction in twentieth-century art may be accounted for on similar grounds, but the important difference is that they provide answers, or at least attempt to do so, by appealing to a shared understanding between author and reader as regards a "message" about the issues concerned. Nonsense only provides the answer that there is no answer—it merely reflects the tensions, and leaves them unresolved.

Thus it transpires that nonsense is an aesthetic form of resignation rather than of self-reliance and confidence, as Petzold asserts (1972: 193). In Chesterton (1953) we find that if one wants to reveal nonsense one must go through sense—hence the Victorian age was a suitable basis for the "bizarre pagodas" of nonsense (121). To this one may now add the sentence with which Petzold concludes his book on nineteenth-century nonsense (1972: 238):

> Sicher dürfte sein, daß der Nonsense kein literarhistorisches Kuriosum aus dem England des 19. Jahrhunderts ist, sondern eine literarische Erscheinung, die wie kaum eine andere bis zum heutigen Tag lebendig geblieben ist und davon zeugt, wie der menschliche Geist noch in seiner eigenen spielerischen Negation sich selbst bestätigen kann.

---

34. See also Pitcher (1965), on the link between Lewis Carroll and Wittgenstein through the bond of nonsense. His conclusion is that Wittgenstein was profoundly influenced by Carroll.

CONCLUSIONS

The aim of this thesis has been to demonstrate what is to be understood by the phenomenon of literary nonsense. In the Introduction I have explained that it is desirable to establish a definition of literary nonsense, as this concept has not so far been analysed in an unambiguous way. In the first place, a distinction has had to be made between nonsense as a device, as a mode and as a genre. Once the characteristics of nonsense as a genre have been established it will be possible to distinguish this genre from other types of literature which have often been equated or confused with nonsense. This has inevitably led to a confusion about what constitutes the corpus of nonsense literature. On the basis of a clear definition, it has become possible to establish a kernel corpus of literary nonsense.

Our next task was to describe this corpus and to analyse part of it in an exemplary fashion. To arrive at a definition of nonsense I have taken as my starting-point those elements which are common to the "Complete Nonsense" of Edward Lear and Lewis Carroll's Alice books as well as *The Hunting of the Snark*. The justification for this procedure is that these works are by almost common consent regarded as literary, aesthetically satisfying, nonsense. I believe there is no more suitable place for the hermeneutic circle to be broken into.

In chapter 1 I provide a brief survey and summary of the most important discussions of literary nonsense to date. The aim of this chapter is threefold. Firstly, the reader will be able to judge the merits and demerits of my own definition on the basis of what earlier scholarship has adduced. He will also be able to verify to what extent my definition is indebted to earlier sources, especially to Sewell (1952), Ede (1975) and Stewart (1978), from whom I have derived respectively the notions of play with language, the balance of tensions and the primary nonsense procedures. Secondly, a historical survey of a century of scholarship on the phenomenon of nonsense, not only in Anglo-Saxon publications but also in German and to a smaller extent French studies of the subject, has now been made available for the first time. Lastly, by presenting a fairly extensive and complete account of earlier scholarship I have been able to limit comparative references in subsequent chapters largely to the footnotes.

In the second chapter I offer a new definition of nonsense, as well as an account of its repertoire, and a typology. Nonsense is here defined as a narrative genre in which the seeming presence of one or more "sensible" meanings is kept in balance by a simultaneous absence of such a meaning. This balance is established by the absence of emotionally laden connotations and associations, and by a creative play with the rules of language, logic and form. This play manifests itself by the occurrence of one or more of five procedures: inversion, negativity or mirroring; imprecision, mixture or incongruity; infinite repetition; simultaneity; and arbitrary arrangement of elements. The procedure of simultaneity is particularly realized by means of punning, or the creation of portmanteau words or neologisms.

A brief section has been devoted to a discussion of some of the most prominent nonsense themes and motifs, which can be related to the procedures. It is clear that nonsense has a great predilection for numbers and letters, the distortion of time and space, and a depersonalisation of human beings as well as the personification of animals and objects. Although this cannot in all cases be easily accounted for without resorting to speculation, it seems that travelling and dancing are favourite activities, and that noses and beards, cats and birds, clocks and bicycles, mirrors and spectacles, harps and flutes, sieves and spoons, collected by moonlight, present a recognizable nonsense universe.

Finally in the second chapter it has been possible to establish a binary typology of nonsense. On the one hand there is a "rational" or ornamental type, often based on an initial absurd proposition which is then "logically" followed to its conclusion, and in which play with language, often incorporated within an argumentative conversation plays a major role. Of this type Carroll is the founder and prime example. The other type is more "irrational" and hence in the view of many more "poetical" as well as purer nonsense. This type, of which Lear is the most classical exponent, goes back to a "popular" type of nonsense in which sound-patterns and extravagant images are more dominant. This distinction should however be regarded as "ideal-typical". In fact, the distinction is by no means always clear-cut, and the best nonsense offers a balance between the two extremes, in due correspondence with its nature.

What must be mainly concluded from the first two chapters is that nonsense is not *a priori* meaningless.[1] Neither does it merely suggest a topsyturvy world. Nonsense does not describe an absurd world or absurd events, nor does it primarily demonstrate the absurdity or unreliability of language. In nonsense, language as such is

---

1. This is the sociological approach to nonsense as exemplified e.g. in Hilbert (1977), and to some extent also in Stewart (1978).

dominant; it works on the assumption that the word is autonomous, and demonstrates this by creating a reality with language rather than either representing a reality, as in mimetic or naturalistic literature, or playing with language as in the curiosity. It is this creative use of language that makes nonsense effective and aesthetically pleasing.

On the basis of my definition it will be relatively simple to distinguish literary nonsense as a genre from those types of literature that have most frequently been confused with it, as well as from humorous types of literature such as parody, burlesque and satire. The latter always have a "pointe", which is essentially lacking in nonsense. As to the other types of literature, notably the nursery rhyme, the curiosity, light verse, fantasy, the grotesque, surrealism, dadaism, absurdity and absurdism, and metafiction, all of these can be shown to fail to correspond in one or more respects to the four basic characteristics of nonsense: the tension between meaning and its absence, the creation of reality by means of language, the absence of emotional involvement, and the element of play. That this is so is demonstrated by means of fair examples in chapter 3.

Chapter 4 is to be considered as the main chapter of this thesis. In this chapter I present a description of the corpus, as well as a literary analysis. Separate sections are devoted to works by Edward Lear, Lewis Carroll, Christian Morgenstern, Edward Gorey and Flann O'Brien. In survey sections other authors, such as the "Learic" Mervyn Peake, Alfred Jarry, Carl Sandburg, Richard Hughes and John Lennon, and the "Carrollian" Marx Brothers, Stefan Themerson, Anthony Burgess, Peter Bichsel and Russell Hoban, are more summarily dealt with. Some "borderline cases", such as Gertrude Stein, Franz Kafka, Jorge Luis Borges and Italo Calvino are also briefly discussed. Some of their works are borderline cases in that the nonsense is not so much generic as modal or feature as a device, as an element of style rather than as determining the generic nature of the work.

The important question which has not been extensively touched upon in this fourth chapter is that of what constitutes "good" nonsense. Even if one follows Ede's precept that "Nonsense requires the same vigorous honesty as does other literature" (1975: 16), one does not obtain an answer to the question why Lear or Carroll are better nonsense writers than say Bichsel or Burgess. The only explicit attempt to tackle this question was made by Sewell in her article "Nonsense Verse and the Child" (1980/1: 30-48). Her thesis is that nonsense produces, "by re-patterning of letters in a word or of objects in a seemingly given universe, a dislocation of that given and then a re-location which, slight as it is, may yet permit glimpses of just such other orders beyond and through our usual perspectives. Nonsense may give delight in proportion as it makes possible such glimpses" (41). This sounds convincing enough, and I tend to agree with Sewell's sampling of nonsense texts in that same article in categories of "excellent", "middling-good" and "weak". All the same, it is really not very helpful after all in so far as we still do not know how we are to measure these "shifts" and "glimpses" in other than subjective terms, and I think the question will have to remain open, as in fact it always ultimately has been regarding any type of literature. Who is to say whether Dickens or George Eliot is the better Victorian novelist? Who, on the other hand, would deny that both are better novelists than, say, Bulwer-Lytton?

I have not even attempted to solve this problem in the fourth chapter with regards to an aesthetic appreciation of nonsense. Nevertheless, I hope it will be clear that some indication of my value judgement may be obtained by comparing the amount of attention I have paid to each member of the corpus. More importantly, on the basis of my definition of nonsense the reader should be able not only to measure each of the texts discussed according to the requirements that characterize nonsense, but also be in a position to make his own evaluation of these as well as of other works which may have come to his attention and escaped mine. Obviously, each of these works, and possibly others as well, invite further investigation and analysis in the light of a theory of literary nonsense.

Finally, I would add that the more that possible interpretations are invited and held in balance by absence of meaning, and the more that the creation of a reality by language play appeals to the imagination, the "better" the nonsense is likely to be, and leave it at that. This is the reason why I do not off-handedly reject any "sensible" interpretation of a nonsense text, be it Freudian, Jungian, Marxist, logical, poetical or whatever, that has been offered of individual works. However, I have not to any great extent included such interpretations in my discussions.

The fifth chapter contains a critical survey of earlier considerations of the social, cultural and psychological backgrounds to the phenomenon of literary nonsense. Socially, the most viable explanation of the appearance of nonsense in the mid-nineteenth century and of its persistence into our own times is by seeing it as both a reflection of and a reaction to industrial capitalism with its inherent tensions. Its origins in particular must be seen in relationship to the rise of Romanticism and the individualism it introduced, with a revised view of the nature of the child, with the origins and development of an imaginative, non-didactic and amoral children's literature (both the fairy tale and the nursery rhyme belong to its partial ancestors), and with a simultaneous interest in philology and language as well as new findings in the fields of science and technology. Occurring in times of relative peace and prosperity rather than of war and crisis, it is at once a rebellion against and a resignation to a highly tense state of society, leading to an escapist regression to childhood with its assets of innocence, lack of moral responsibility, its imagination and its verbal and play magic. To some extent the appearance of nonsense can be traced to the personality structure and the personal circumstances of its authors, and I have therefore gone fairly extensively into the individual backgrounds of some of the writers discussed. It should be kept in mind, of course, that nonsense is only part of the output of these writers.

Conclusions to be drawn from the last chapter must be cautious. It seems reasonable to assume that to produce nonsense is an attempt to communicate without communicating, and this presumably also explains why it is not always taken seriously. It shows a lack of commitment, in some cases, a nihilist perhaps rather than an anarchic view; in fact, it plays the ball back to the other court: if this is nonsense, *you* tell me what is sense, or, as the Red Queen puts it in *TLG*: "*I've* heard nonsense, compared with which that would be as sensible as a dictionary" (Gardner 1960 [1965]: 207). It may well be that the belief that a dictionary is sensible is one of the impossible things the White Queen occasionally managed to believe before breakfast (*ibid.*, 251).

If nonsense is communication without communicating, it must be an attempt to say the ineffable: that there is nothing to be said, that ultimately communication is impossible. But this seems too gloomy as well as too trite a way of taking leave of our subject. Nonsense is indeed one possible reflection of life in that it is at once both *and* neither meaningful and meaningless. An utterly meaningful life can only exist in a world of dogma, an unfree world. To deny any meaning to life is to enter a world of despair, which is equally unfree. These worlds are as wide apart as Dante's Heaven and Hell, in neither of which I would ever like to take up my abode, preferring to join Lear in that place where one can enjoy the company of choice friends, "under a lotus tree a eating of ice creams and pelican pie, with our feet in a hazure coloured stream with the birds and beasts of Paradise a sporting around us" (Jackson

1947: xxi, quoting Lear; see also p. xvi). Nonsense manages to take an intermediate position, and to take no position at the same time. It is neither desperate nor dogmatic; rather, it is sceptical and craving. To vary an aphorism by Nietzsche: "Wenn Skepsis und Sehnsucht sich begatten, entsteht ... Nonsense" (*Böse Weisheit*, Aph. 71). Aesthetically, nonsense is the very breeding-ground of art: "*Anything can be said in this place and it will be true and will have to be believed*", as the nameless narrator realizes in *The Third Policeman* (O'Brien 1967 [1974]: 86). What matters, of course, is who the speaker is. As to this dissertation, I will conclude with a maxim from Wittgenstein's *Philosophical Investigations* (Sec. 464): "My aim is to teach you to pass from a piece of disguised nonsense to something that is patent nonsense."

BIBLIOGRAPHY

1 Primary Literature

Adair, Gilbert (1984). *Alice Through the Needle's Eye*, London: Pan Books.
Allais, Alphonse (1985). *Le Captain Cap*, Paris: Union Générale d'Éditions.
Anobile, Richard J., ed. (1972). *Why a Duck? Visual and Verbal Gems from the Marx Brothers Movies*, London: Studio Vista.
Beckett, Samuel (1956 [1965]). *Waiting for Godot*, London: Faber and Faber.
——— (1959). *Molloy. Malone Dies. The Unnamable. A Trilogy*, Paris: The Olympia Press.
Belloc, Hilaire (1940 [1964]). *Selected Cautionary Verses*, Harmondsworth: Penguin.
Benayoun, Robert, ed. (1977). *Le Nonsense*, Paris: Balland.
Bichsel, Peter (1969). *Kindergeschichten*. Neuwied und Berlin: Luchterhand.
Borges, Jorge Luis (1964 [1970]). *Labyrinths*, Harmondsworth: Penguin.
Brautigan, Richard (1974). *The Hawkline Monster*, New York: Pocket Books.
Breton, André (1939 [1966]). *Anthologie de l'humour noir*, Paris: Jean-Jacques Pauvert.
——— (1948). *Poèmes*, Paris: Gallimard.
Buddingh', Cees (1960). *Het mes op de gorgel. Gorgelrijmen en andere gedichten*, Utrecht: A.W. Bruna & Zoon.
——— (1982). *Een rookwolkje voor God en andere miniaturen*, Utrecht: Reflex.
——— (1985). *Nieuwe Gorgelrijmen*, Amsterdam: De Bezige Bij.
Burgess, Anthony (1976). *A Long Trip to Teatime*, London: Dempsey & Squires.
Busch, Wilhelm (1962). *Max und Moritz*, ed. & annot. H.A. Klein a.o., New York: Dover Publications.
Calvino, Italo (1965 [1982]). *Cosmicomics*, tr. W. Weaver, London: Abacus.
Carroll, Lewis (1960 [1965]). *Alice's Adventures in Wonderland and Through the Looking-Glass*, ed. & annot. Martin Gardner, *The Annotated Alice*, Harmondsworth: Penguin.
——— (1962 [1967]). *The Hunting of the Snark*, ed. & annot. Martin Gardner, *The Annotated Snark*, Harmondsworth: Penguin.
——— (1965a). *The Works of* —, ed. R.L. Green, London: Paul Hamlyn.

Cohen, J.M., ed. (1952). *Comic and Curious Verse*, Harmondsworth: Penguin.
——— ed. (1956). *More Comic and Curious Verse*, Harmondsworth: Penguin.
Cole, William, ed. (1968). *Oh, What Nonsense!*, London: Methuen.
———, ed. (1972). *Oh, That's Ridiculous!*, London: Methuen.
———, ed. (1976). *Oh, How Silly!*, London: Methuen.
Dahl, Roald (1965 [1973]). *Charlie and the Chocolate Factory*, Harmondsworth: Penguin.
——— (1962). *Kiss Kiss*, Harmondsworth: Penguin.
Dencker, Klaus Peter, ed. (1978). *Deutsche Unsinnspoesie*, Stuttgart: Reclam.
Desnos, Robert (1953 [1968]). *Corps et biens*, Paris: Gallimard.
Eliot, T.S. (1940 [1974]). *Old Possum's Book of Practical Cats*, London: Faber and Faber.
Gilbert, W.S. (1869 [1920]). *The Bab Ballads*, London: MacMillan & Co.
Gorey, Edward (1975). *Amphigorey*, New York: Berkley Windhover.
——— (1977). *Amphigorey Too*, New York: Berkley Windhover.
——— (1979). *Gorey Posters*, New York: Harry N. Abrams.
——— (1983). *Amphigorey Also*, New York: Congdon & Weed.
Heller, Joseph (1976 [1985]). *Good as Gold*, New York: Dell.
Hoban, Russell (1974a). *How Tom Beat Captain Najork and his Hired Sportsmen*, London: Jonathan Cape.
——— (1974b). *Kleinzeit*, London: Pan Books.
Hughes, Richard (1931 [1972]). *The Spider's Palace*, Harmondsworth: Penguin.
Jarry, Alfred (1955). *Gestes et opinions du Docteur Faustroll*, Paris: Fasquelle.
——— (1962). *Tout Ubu*, Paris: Librairie Générale Française.
Jennings, Paul, ed. (1977). *The Book of Nonsense*, London: Macdonald/Raven Books.
Kafka, Franz (1970 [1986]). *Sämtliche Erzählungen*, Frankfurt am Main: Fischer Taschenbuch Verlag.
——— (1979). *Description of a Struggle and Other Stories*, tr. W. & E. Muir a.o. Harmondsworth: Penguin.
Kharms, Daniil (1978-80). *Sobranie Proizvedeniy*, 3 vols., Bremen.
Lear, Edward (1947). *The Complete Nonsense*, ed. H. Jackson, London: Faber and Faber.
——— (1953). *Teapots and Quails and Other New Nonsenses*, ed. A. Davidson & P. Hofer, London: John Murray.
Lennon, John (1964). *In His Own Write*, London: Jonathan Cape.

―――― (1965). *A Spaniard in the Works*, London: Jonathan Cape.
―――― (1986). *Skywriting by Word of Mouth*, London: Pan Books.
Lindsay, David (1920 [1963]). *A Voyage to Arcturus*, New York: Ballantine Books (Del Rey).
Milne, A.A. (1926 [1973]). *Winnie-the Pooh*, London: Methuen.
―――― (1928 [1961]). *The House at Pooh Corner*, London: Methuen.
Monty Python's Flying Circus (1971). *Monty Python's Big Red Book*, London: Eyre Methuen.
―――― (1974). *The Brand New Monty Python Papperbok*, London: Eyre Methuen.
Morgenstern, Christian (1933). *Alle Galgenlieder*, Berlin: Verlag Bruno Cassirer.
O'Brien, Flann, (1967 [1974]). *The Third Policeman*, London: Pan Books.
Opie, Iona & Peter, eds. (1951 [1975]). *The Oxford Dictionary of Nursery Rhymes*, London: Oxford University Press.
Peake, Mervyn (1939 [1967]). *Captain Slaughterboard Drops Anchor*, London: Academy Editions.
―――― (1972 [1974]). *A Book of Nonsense*, London: Pan Books.
Prutkov, Koz'ma (1955). *Sochineniya*, Moscow: Gosudarstvennoye Izdatel'stvo Khudozhestvennoy Literatury.
Queneau, Raymond (1947). *Exercices de Style*, Paris: Gallimard.
Rhys, E., ed. (1927). *A Book of Nonsense*, London & New York: Everyman.
Ringelnatz, Joachim (1950). *Und auf einmal steht es neben dir*, Berlin: Büchergilde Gutenberg.
Sandburg, Carl (1922 [1924]). *Rootabaga Stories*, London etc.: George G. Harrap & Co.
Satie, Erik (1977). *Écrits*, coll. O. Volta, Paris: Éditions Champ Libre.
Scheerbart, Paul (1897). *Ich Liebe Dich! Ein Eisenbahn-Roman mit 66 Intermezzos*, Berlin: Schuster & Loeffler.
―――― (1902). *Immer mutig! Ein phantastischer Nilpferderoman mit dreiundachtzig merkwürdigen Geschichten*, Minden (Westfalen): J.C.C. Bruns.
―――― (^{2}1912). *Astrale Noveletten*, München & Leipzig: Georg Müller.
―――― (^{2}1913). *Lesabéndio. Ein Asteroïden-Roman*, München & Leipzig: Georg Müller.
Simpson, N.F. (1960). *One Way Pendulum*, London: Faber and Faber.
Stein, Gertrude (1980). *The Yale Gertrude Stein*, sel. & introd.

Richard Kostelanetz, New Haven & London: Yale University Press.
Themerson, Stefan (1951 [1954]). *The Adventures of Peddy Bottom*, London: Gaberbocchus.
Topor, Roland (1968). *Stories and Drawings*, transl. M. Crosland & D. le Vay, London: Peter Owen.
Valentin, Karl (1962). *Gesammelte Werke*, München: R. Piper & Co.
Vian, Boris (1963). *L'Écume des jours*, Paris: J.-J. Pauvert.
Vonnegut Jr, Kurt (1968 [1981]). *Slaughterhouse-Five*, New York: Dell.
Wells, C., ed. (1902 [1930]). *A Nonsense Anthology*, New York: Blue Ribbon Books.
Zonderland, Daan (1982). *Redeloze Rijmen en alle andere verzen*, Amsterdam: de Prom.

2 *Secondary Literature*

Adams, Robert Martin (1966). *Nil. Episodes in the Literary Conquest of Void during the Nineteenth Century*, New York: Oxford University Press.
Alexander, Peter (1951). "Logic and Humour of Lewis Carroll", *Proceedings of the Leeds Philological and Literary Society*, Vol. VI, Part VIII: 551-66.
Andersen, Jørgen (1950). "Edward Lear and the Origin of Nonsense", *English Studies* 31: 161-6.
Aragon, Louis (1931 [1976]). "Lewis Carroll. En 1931". Rpt. in M. Alexandre e.a., eds., *Le Surréalisme au Service de la Révolution. Collection complète*, Paris, 1976. Vol. 3 (1931): 25-6.
Arrivé, Michel (1972). *Les langages de Jarry*, Paris: Klincksieck.
Ayres, Harry Morgan (1936). *Carroll's Alice*, New York: Columbia University Press. [Not seen]
Baacke, Dieter (1978). "Spiele jenseits der Grenze. Zur Phänomenologie und Theorie des Nonsense". Rpt. in Dencker 1978: 355-77.
Balakian, Anna (1947). *Literary Origins of Surrealism. A New Mysticism in French Poetry*, New York: King's Crown Press.
Baring-Gould, William S. (1968). *The Lure of the Limerick. An Uninhibited History*, London: Hart Davis, MacGibbon.
Bauer, Michael (1933 [1985]). *Christian Morgensterns Leben und Werk*, München & Zürich: Piper.
Beaumont, Keith (1984). *Alfred Jarry. A Critical and Biographical Study*, Leicester: Leicester University Press.

Beaver, Harold (1976). "Whale or Boojum: An Agony", in Guiliano 1976: 111-31.
Beheim-Schwarzbach, Martin (1964 [1983]). *Christian Morgenstern*, Hamburg: Rowohlt.
Benayoun, Robert, ed. (1977). *Le Nonsense*, Paris: Balland.
Bergson, Henri (1900 [1913]). *Le Rire, essai sur la signification du comique*, Paris: Félix Alcan.
Bigsby, C.W.E. (1972). *Dada and Surrealism*, London: Methuen.
Blake, Kathleen (1974). *Play, Games, and Sport. The Literary Works of Lewis Carroll*, Ithaca and London; Cornell University Press.
Blumenfeld, Walter (1933). *Sinn und Unsinn*, München: Ernst Reinhard.
Boelens, Tysger (1987). "The Bad Manners of Nonsense. An Inquiry into the Nonsensical Orthodoxy of Stefan Themerson's *The Adventures of Peddy Bottom*", in Tigges 1987: 229-44.
Bombaugh, C.C. (1961). *Oddities and Curiosities of Words and Literature*, ed. M. Gardner, New York: Dover Publications.
Breton, André (1962). *Manifestes du Surréalisme*, Paris: Jean-Jacques Pauvert.
Brown, James (1956). "Eight Types of Puns", *PMLA* 71: 14-26.
Buren, M.B. van (1981). "The Grotesque in Visual Art and Literature", *Dutch Quarterly Review* 12: 42-53.
Burgess, Anthony (1982). "Flann O'Brien, A Note", *Études Irlandaises* 4: 83-6.
────── (1986). *Homage to QWERT YUIOP. Selected Journalism 1978-1985*, London: Hutchinson. Contains "The Kingdom of Lear", reviews of Lehmann 1977 and Byrom 1977 (297-304), "Clean and Obscene" (304-7) and "Crossmess Parzle" (308-10).
────── (1987). "Nonsense", in Tigges 1987: 17-21.
Butler, Anthony (1974). *The Book of Bull*, Dublin: Malton Press.
Byrom, Thomas (1977). *Nonsense and Wonder. The Poems and Cartoons of Edward Lear*, New York: E.P. Dutton.
Cammaerts, Émile (1925). *The Poetry of Nonsense*, New York: Folcroft Library Editions.
Caradec, François (1974). *A la recherche de Alfred Jarry*, Paris: Seghers.
Carpenter, Humphrey & Mari Prichard (1984). *The Oxford Companion to Children's Literature*, Oxford and New York: Oxford University Press.
Chesterton, G.K. (1901). "A Defence of Nonsense", in E. Rhys ed., *A Century of English Essays*, London and New York: J.M.Dent/E.P. Dutton, n.d.: 446-50.

────── (1953). "How Pleasant to Know Mr Lear", in *A Handful of Authors*, London & New York: Sheed and Ward: 120-4.
Chetwynd, Tom (1982). *A Dictionary of Symbols*, London etc.: Granada.
Clissmann, Anne (1975). *Flann O'Brien. A Critical Introduction to his Writings*, Dublin & New York: Gill and MacMillan/Barnes & Noble Books.
Coveney, Peter (1967). "Escape". Rpt. in Gray 1971: 330-7.
Croft-Brooke, Rupert (1967). *Feasting With Panthers. A New Consideration of Some Late Victorian Writers*, London: W.H. Allen.
Davidson, Angus (1938 [1968]). *Edward Lear. Landscape Painter and Nonsense Poet (1812-1888)*, Port Washington N.Y.: Kennikat Press.
De la Mare, Walter (1932). *Lewis Carroll*, London: Faber and Faber.
Deleuze, Gilles (1969). *Logique du sens*, Paris: Les Éditions de Minuit.
Demurova, Nina (1982). "Toward a Definition of *Alice's* Genre: The Folktale and Fairy-Tale Connections", in Guiliano 1982a: 75-88.
Dencker, Klaus Peter, ed. (1978). *Deutsche Unsinnspoesie*, Stuttgart: Reclam.
Douglass, Paul (1983). "Eliot's Cats: Serious Play behind the Playful Seriousness", *Children's Literature* 11: 109-24.
Eastman, Max (1937). *Enjoyment of Laughter*, London: Hamish Hamilton.
Ede, Lisa S. (1975). "The Nonsense Literature of Edward Lear and Lewis Carroll", unpub. PhD Diss., Ohio State University.
────── (1987a). "An Introduction to the Nonsense Literature of Edward Lear and Lewis Carroll", in Tigges 1987: 47-60.
────── (1987b). "Edward Lear's Limericks and their Illustrations", in Tigges 1987: 103-16.
Elderhorst, Constance (1987). "John Donne's *First Anniversary* as an Anatomical Anamorphosis", in Tigges 1987: 97-102.
Eliot, T.S. (1953). "The Music of Poetry", in *Selected Prose*, ed. J. Hayward, Melbourne etc.: Penguin 56-67.
Elliott, Robert C. (1962). "The Definition of *Satire*: A Note on Method", *Yearbook of Comparative and General Literature* 11: 19-23.
Empson, William (1935). "*Alice in Wonderland*: The Child as Swain". Rpt. in Phillips 1971 [1974]: 400-33.
────── (1955). *Seven Types of Ambiguity*, 3rd rev. edn, New York: The Noonday Press.
Esslin, Martin (1968). *The Theatre of the Absurd*, rev. & enl. edn,

Harmondsworth: Penguin.
Eyles, Allen (1966 [1974]). *The Marx Brothers. Their World of Comedy*, 3rd edn, London & New York: The Tantivy Press/A.S. Barnes & Co.
Flescher, Jacqueline (1969/70). "The Language of Nonsense in Alice", *Yale French Studies* 43: 128-44.
Forster, Leonard (1962). *Poetry of Significant Nonsense*, Cambridge: Cambridge University Press.
Fowler, Alastair (1982). *Kinds of Literature. An Introduction to the Theory of Genres and Modes*, Oxford: Clarendon Press.
Frazer, J.G. (1922 [1971]). *The Golden Bough*, one vol. edn, London: MacMillan.
Freud, Sigmund (1960 [1976]). *Jokes and their Relation to the Unconscious*, tr. J. Strachey, Harmondsworth: Penguin.
Froehlich, Alfred J.P. (1976). "N.F. Simpson and the Aesthetics of Nonsense", PhD diss., University of Toronto (see *Dissertation Abstracts International* 38/10 (1978): 5800A). [Not seen]
Frye, Northrop (1957). *Anatomy of Criticism*, Princeton N.J.: Princeton University Press.
Galestin, Paul (1986). "The Marx Brothers: Verbal and Visual Nonsense in their Films", *Dutch Quarterly Review* 16: 237-48. Rpt. in Tigges 1987: 149-60.
Gardner, Martin (1960 [1965]). See Carroll, Lewis.
——— (1962 [1967]). See Carroll, Lewis.
Gasser, Manuel (1972). "Edward Gorey", *Graphis* 28 (Nr 163): 424-31.
Gattégno, Jean (1970). *Lewis Carroll*, Paris: Librairie José Corti.
——— (1976). "Assessing Lewis Carroll", in Guiliano 1976: 74-80.
Gibian, George, ed. and transl. (1971 [1974]). *Russia's Literature of the Absurd. Selected Works of Daniil Kharms and Alexander Vvedensky*, New York: W.W. Norton & Co.
Gillespie, Gerald (1983). "Faust en Pataphysicien", *Journal of European Studies* 13: 96-108.
Graham, Eleanor (1945). "Nonsense in Children's Literature", *The Junior Bookshelf* 9: 61-8. [Not seen]
Gray, Donald, J. (1966). "The Uses of Victorian Laughter", *Victorian Studies* 10: 145-76.
——— ed. (1971). *Alice in Wonderland*, New York: W.W. Norton & Co.
Green, Roger Lancelyn (1960). "Alice". Rpt. in Phillips 1971 [1974]: 40-68.
Grossman, Manuel (1971). *Dada. Paradox, Mystification, and Ambiguity in European Literature*, New York: Pegasus.

Guiliano, Edward, ed. (1976). *Lewis Carroll Observed*, New York: Clarkson N. Potter.
———— ed. (1982a). *Lewis Carroll: A Celebration*, New York: Clarkson N. Potter.
———— (1982b). "A Time for Humor: Lewis Carroll, Laughter and Despair, and *The Hunting of the Snark*", in Guiliano 1982a: 123-31.
Haight, M.R. (1971). "Nonsense", *The British Journal of Aesthetics* 11: 247-56.
Hammond, Paul & Patrick Hughes (1978). *Upon the Pun. Dual Meaning in Words and Pictures*, London: W.H. Allen & Co.
Hansen, Klaus (1963). "Wortverschmelzungen", *Zeitschrift für Anglistik und Amerikanistik* 11: 117-42.
Hark, Ina Rae (1978). "Edward Lear: Eccentricity and Victorian Angst", *Victorian Poetry* 16: 112-22.
———— (1982). *Edward Lear*, Boston: Twayne Publishers.
Harmon, William (1982). "Lear, Limericks, and Some Other Verse Forms", *Children's Literature* 10: 70-6.
Harrowven, Jean (1976). *The Limerick Makers*, London: The Research Publishing Co.
Harvey, Paul, ed. (1967). *The Oxford Companion to English Literature*, 4th edn, Oxford: Clarendon Press.
Hausmann, Franz Josef (1974). *Studien zu einer Linguistik des Wortspiels. Das Wortspiel im »Canard enchaîné«*, Tübingen: Max Niemeyer Verlag.
Hempfer, Klaus W. (1973). *Gattungstheorie*, München: Wilhelm Fink Verlag.
Henkle, Roger B. (1973). "The Mad Hatter's World", *The Virginia Quarterly Review* 49: 99-117.
———— (1976). "High Art and Low Amusements", in Guiliano 1976: 68-73.
———— (1982). "Carroll's Narratives Underground: 'Modernism' and Form", in Guiliano 1982a: 90-100.
Hilbert, Richard A. (1977). "Approaching Reason's Edge: 'Nonsense' as the Final Solution to the Problem of Meaning", *Sociological Inquiry* 47: 25-31.
Hildebrandt, Rolf (1962). "Nonsense-Aspekte der englischen Kinderliteratur", unpub. diss. Hamburg.
Hinchliffe, Arnold P. (1969). *The Absurd*, London & New York: Methuen.
Hofstadter, Douglas R. (1982). "Metamagical Themas", *Scientific American*, Dec.: 19-25.

Holquist, Michael (1969/70). "What is a Boojum? Nonsense and Modernism", *Yale French Studies* 43: 145-64.
Homeyer, Helene (1947). "Philosophie des Unsinns: eine sprachliche Betrachtung zum englischen Humor", *Deutsche Rundschau* 7: 52-5.
Hudson, Derek (1954 [1976]). *Lewis Carroll. An Illustrated Biography*, London: Book Club Associates (Constable).
Hürliman, Bettina (1967). *Three Centuries of Children's Books in Europe* (tr. & ed. B.W. Alderson), London: Oxford University Press.
Huizinga, Johan (1938 [1974]). *Homo ludens: Proeve eener bepaling van het spelelement der cultuur*, 6th edn, Groningen: H.D. Tjeenk Willink.
Hume, Kathryn (1984). *Fantasy and Mimesis. Responses to Reality in Western Literature*, New York & London: Methuen.
Hutcheon, Linda (1984). *Narcissistic Narrative. The Metafictional Paradox*, New York & London: Methuen.
Huxley, Aldous (1923 [1928]). "Edward Lear", in *On the Margin*, London: Chatto and Windus: 167-72.
Huxley, Francis (1976). *The Raven and the Writing Desk*, London: Thames and Hudson.
Jackson, Holbrook (1947). See Lear, Edward.
Jackson, Rosemary (1981). Fantasy. *The Literature of Subversion*, London & New York: Methuen.
Jacquin, Danielle (1975/6). "Never Apply Your Front Brake First, or Flann O'Brien and the Theme of the Fall", in P. Rafroidi and M. Harmon, eds., *The Irish Novel in Our Time*, Villeneuve-d'Ascq: 187-98.
────── (1983). "L'Altération a la clef, ou le mode grotesque chez Flann O'Brien", *Études Irlandaises* 8: 79-89.
Kayser, Wolfgang (1957). *Das Groteske--Seine Gestaltung in Malerei und Dichtung*, Oldenburg/Hamburg: Gerhard Stalling Verlag.
Kelen, Emery (1973). *Mr Nonsense. A Life of Edward Lear*, London: Macdonald and Jane's.
Kemnitz, Charles (1985). "Beyond the Zone of Middle Dimensions: A Relativistic Reading of *The Third Policeman*", *Irish University Review* 15: 56-72.
Kenner, Hugh (1968). *Samuel Beckett. A Critical Study*, Berkeley and Los Angeles: University of California Press.
Kent, Muriel (1934). "The Art of Nonsense", *Cornhill Magazine* 149: 478-87. [Not seen]
Kincaid, James (1973). "Alice's Invasion of Wonderland", *PMLA* 88:

92-9.

Kincaid, James R. & Edward Guiliano, eds (1982). *Soaring with the Dodo. Essays on Lewis Carroll's Life and Art*, English Language Notes XX: 2, Boulder, Colorado.

Klein, J. (1954). "Humoristische Lyrik", *Welt und Wort* 9: 221-5.

Kretschmer, Ernst (1983). *Die Welt der Galgenlieder Christian Morgensterns und der viktorianische Nonsense*, Berlin & New York: Walter de Gruyter.

——— (1985). *Christian Morgenstern*, Stuttgart: J.B. Metzlerische Verlagsbuchhandlung.

Kreutzer, Eberhard (1984). *Lewis Carroll: »Alice in Wonderland« und »Through the Looking Glass«*, München: Wilhelm Fink Verlag.

Kusenberg, Kurt (1947). "Über den Unsinn", *Merkur* 1: 956-7.

Laffay, Albert (1970). *Anatomie de l'humour et du nonsense*, Paris: Masson et Cie.

Landheer, Ronald (1984). *Aspects linguistiques et pragmatico-rhetoriques de l'ambiguité*, diss. Leiden.

Lang, Peter Christian (1982). *Literarischer Unsinn im späten 19. und frühen 20. Jahrhundert. Systematische Begründung und historische Rekonstruktion*, Frankfurt am Main & Bern: Verlag Peter Lang.

Lanters, José (1983). "Fiction Within Fiction: The Role of the Author in Flann O'Brien's *At Swim-Two-Birds* and *The Third Policeman*", *Dutch Quarterly Review* 13: 267-81.

——— (1987). "'Still Life' versus Real Life: The English Writings of Brian O'Nolan", in Tigges 1987: 161-81.

Lecercle, Jean-Jacques (1971). "Une case en avant, deux cases en arrière", in Parisot 1971: 41-50.

Leeuwen, Hendrik van (1986). "The Liaison of Visual and Written Nonsense", *Dutch Quarterly Review* 16: 186-219. Rpt. in Tigges 1987: 61-95.

Lehmann, John (1977). *Edward Lear and his World*, London: Thames and Hudson.

Leimert, Erika (1937). "Die Nonsense-Poesie von Edward Lear", *Die neueren Sprachen* 45: 368-73.

Lemon, Lee T. (1971). *A Glossary for the Study of English*, New York etc.: Oxford University Press.

Lennon, Florence Becker (1945 [1962]). *The Life of Lewis Carroll*, New York: Collier Books [Original title: *Victoria Through the Looking-Glass*]

——— (1947). *Lewis Carroll*, London etc.: Cassell & Co.

Levin, Harry (1965 [1974]). "*Wonderland* Revisited", *Kenyon Review*

27: 591-616. Rpt. in Phillips 1971 [1974]: 217-42.
Liebert, H.W. (1975). *Lear in the Original. Drawings and Limericks by Edward Lear for his Book of Nonsense*, New York: H.P. Kraus. [Not seen]
Liede, Alfred (1963). *Dichtung als Spiel. Studien zur Unsinnspoesie an den Grenzen der Sprache*, 2 vols, Berlin: de Gruyter & Co.
Lütgert, Will (n.d.). "Notiz zum Verhältnis von Nonsense und Creativität, in *mobile. Versuch im Gespräch*, H. 7. Hrsg. D. Baacke, W. Lück u.a., Göttingen: 16-20. [Not seen]
Lynn, Joanne (1980). "Hyacinths and Biscuits in the Village of Liver and Onions: Sandburg's *Rootabaga Stories*", *Children's Literature* 8: 118-32.
Manlove, C.N. (1975). *Modern Fantasy*, Cambridge etc.: Cambridge University Press.
Marnat, Marcel (1971). "Du serquin au cachalot blanc", in Parisot 1971: 128-32.
Martin, Robert Bernard (1974). *The Triumph of Wit. A Study of Victorian Comic Theory*, Oxford: Clarendon Press.
Mason, Stanley (1983). "Edward Gorey", *Graphis* 39 (Nr 223): 82-7.
Massey, Irving (1976). *The Gaping Pig. Literature and Metamorphosis*, Berkeley/ Los Angeles/ London: University of California Press.
Mautner, Franz Heinrich (1931). "Das Wortspiel und seine Bedeutung. Grundzüge der geistesgeschichtlichen Darstellung eines Stilelementes", *Deutsche Vierteljahrschrift für Literaturwissenschaft und Geistesgeschichte* 9: 679-710.
Mays, J.C.C. (1973). "Brian O'Nolan: Literalist of the Imagination", in O'Keeffe 1973: 77-119.
Mégroz, R.L. (1938). "The Master of Nonsense", *Cornhill Magazine* 157: 175-90. [Not seen]
Mellor, Anne K. (1980). *English Romantic Irony*, Cambridge Mass. & London: Harvard University Press.
Miller, Edmund (1973). "Two Approaches to Edward Lear's Nonsense Songs", *The Victorian Newsletter* 44: 5-8. [Not seen]
―――― (1976). "The *Sylvie and Bruno* Books as Victorian Novel", in Guiliano 1976: 132-44.
Milner, G.B. (1972). "Homo Ridens. Towards a Semiotic Theory of Humour and Laughter", *Semiotica* 5: 1-30.
Mirsky, D.S. (1926 [1958]). *A History of Russian Literature From Its Beginnings to 1900*, ed. F.J. Whitfield, New York: Vintage Books.
Monter, B.H. (1972). *Koz'ma Prutkov. The Art of Parody*, The Hague and Paris: Mouton.

Morgan, Bayard Quincy (1938). "The Superior Nonsense of Christian Morgenstern", *Books Abroad* 12: 288-91.

Morpurgo, E. (1960). *De Nonsens-poëzie*, Amsterdam.

Neumann, Friedrich (1964). "Christian Morgensterns 'Galgenlieder', Spiel mit der Sprache", *Wirkendes Wort* 14: 332-50.

Neumann, Peter Horst (1973). "Morgensterns 'Galgenlieder' als poetologische Modelle betrachtet", *Sprachkunst* 4: 53-64.

Nicolson, Harold (1956). "The English Sense of Humour", in *The English Sense of Humour and Other Essays*, London: Constable: 3-59.

Nies, Fritz (1973). "Das Ärgernis *Historiette*. Für eine Semiotik der literarischen Gattungen", *Zeitschrift für Romanische Philologie* 89: 421-39.

Noakes, Vivien (1968). *Edward Lear. The Life of a Wanderer*, London: Collins.

——— (1985). *Edward Lear, 1812-1888*, London: Weidenfeld and Nicolson.

Nock, S.A. (1941). "Lacrimae Nugarum: Edward Lear of the Nonsense Verses", *Sewanee Review* 49: 68-81.

Nöth, Winfried (1980). *Literatursemiotische Analysen zu Lewis Carrolls Alice-Büchern*, Tübingen: Gunter Narr Verlag.

O'Donoghue, Bernard (1982). "Irish Humour and Verbal Logic", *Critical Quarterly* 24: 33-40.

O'Keeffe, Timothy, ed. (1973). *Myles. Portraits of Brian O'Nolan*, London: Martin Bryan & O'Keeffe.

Oomen, Ursula (1967). "Sprachlicher Unsinn und linguistischer Sinn in Texten von John Lennon", *Folia Linguistica* 1: 172-93.

Orwell, George (1950). "Nonsense Poetry", in *Shooting an Elephant and Other Essays*, London: Secker & Warburg: 179-84.

Palm, C. (1983). *Geule Golch und Geigerich. Die Nabelschnur zur Sprach-Wirklichkeit in der grotesken Lyrik von Christian Morgenstern*, Uppsala/Stockholm: Almqvist & Wiksell International.

Parisot, Henri (1952 [1965]). *Lewis Carroll*, Paris: Éditions Pierre Seghers.

——— (1968 [1974]). *Edward Lear. Poèmes sans sens*, Paris: Aubier-Flammarion.

——— ([1971]). *Lewis Carroll*, Paris: Éditions de l'Herne.

Partridge, Eric (1950). "The Nonsense Words of Edward Lear and Lewis Carroll", in *Here, There and Everywhere. Essays Upon Language*, 2nd rev. edn, London: Hamish Hamilton: 162-88.

Perche, Louis (1965). *Alfred Jarry*, Paris: Éditions Universitaires.

Petzold, Dieter (1972). *Formen und Funktionen der englischen Non-*

sense-Dichtung im 19. Jahrhundert, Nürnberg: Verlag Hans Carl.
Peze, Esther (1987). "Situational Nonsense in Postmodern American Fiction", in Tigges 1987: 215-27.
Phillips, Robert, ed. (1971 [1974]). *Aspects of Alice*, Harmondsworth: Penguin.
Pitcher, George (1966). "Wittgenstein, Nonsense, and Lewis Carroll", *The Massachusetts Review* 6: 591-611; partly rpt. in Gray 1971: 387-402.
Polhemus, R.M. (1980). *Comic Faith. The Great Tradition from Austen to Joyce*, Chicago and London: The University of Chicago Press.
Prickett, Stephen (1979). *Victorian Fantasy*, Hassocks (Sussex): The Harvester Press.
Pudney, John (1976). *Lewis Carroll and his World*, London: Thames and Hudson.
Quennell, Peter (1952). "Edward Lear", in *The Singular Preference. Portraits and Essays*, London: Collins: 95-101.
Rabkin, Eric S. (1976). *The Fantastic in Literature*, Princeton N.J.: Princeton University Press.
Rackin, Donald (1964). "The Critical Interpretations of 'Alice in Wonderland'. A Survey and Suggested Reading", PhD diss. Univ. of Illinois. [Not seen]
—— (1966 [1971]). "Alice's Journey to the End of Night". Rpt. in Phillips 1971 [1974]): 452-80.
——, ed. (1969). *Alice's Adventures in Wonderland: A Critical Handbook*, Belmot Calif. [Not seen]
—— (1976). "Laughing and Grief: What's So Funny About *Alice in Wonderland?*", in Guiliano 1976: 1-18.
—— (1982a). "Love and Death in Carroll's *Alices*", in Kincaid & Guiliano 1982: 26-45.
—— (1982b). "Blessed Rage: Lewis Carroll and the Modern Quest for Order", in Guiliano 1982a: 15-25.
Redfern, Walter (1984). *Puns*, Oxford: Basil Blackwell.
Reichert, Klaus (1974). *Lewis Carroll. Studien zum literarischen Unsinn*, München: Carl Hanser Verlag.
Reut-Nicolussi, "Der Humor in Lewis Carrolls »Alice's Adventures in Wonderland« und »Through the Looking-Glass«", diss. Innsbruck [Not seen]
Richardson, Joanna (1965). *Edward Lear*, London: Longmans, Green & Co.
—— (1970). "Edward Lear: Man of Letters", *Ariel*, 1: 18-28.
Richter, Hans (1964). *Dada—Kunst und Antikunst*, Köln: M. DuMont Schaubert.

Rieke, Alison R. (1984). "Sense, Nonsense, and the Invention of Language: James Joyce, Louis Zukofsky, Gertrude Stein", PhD diss. University of Kentucky. See *Dissertation Abstracts International* 45/9 (1985): 2871-A. [Not seen]

Robinson, F.M. (1981). "Nonsense and Sadness in Donald Barthelme and Edward Lear", *South Atlantic Quarterly* 80: 164-76. [Not seen]

Roos, Michael E. (1984). "The Walrus and the Deacon. John Lennon's Debt to Carroll", *Journal of Popular Culture* 18: 19-29.

Sale, Roger (1978). "Lewis Carroll", in *Fairy Tales and After. From Snow White to E.B. White*, Cambridge Mass. and London: Harvard University Press: 101-25.

Schnur-Wellpot, M. (1983). *Aporien der Gattungstheorie aus semiotischer Sicht*, Tübingen: Gunter Narr Verlag.

Schöne, Annemarie (1951). "Untersuchungen zur englischen Nonsense Literatur unter besonderer Berücksichtigung des Limericks und seines Schöpfers Edward Lear", unpub. diss., Bonn.

―――― (1954a). "Humor and Komik in Lewis Carrolls Nonsense-Traummärchen 'Alice's Adventures in Wonderland' und 'Through the Looking Glass'", *Deutsche Vierteljahrschrift für Literaturwissenschaft und Geistesgeschichte* 28: 102-14.

―――― (1954b). "Nonsense-Dichtung—ein Phänomen der englischen Komik", *Die neueren Sprachen* 1954: 132-40.

―――― (1955a). "Berührungspunkte zwischen Nonsense-Dichtung und Metaphysischem Humor in T.S. Eliot's Scherzgedichten", *Germanisch-Romanische Monatschrift* 36: 40-52.

―――― (1955b). "Laurence Sterne—Unter dem Aspekt der Nonsense-Dichtung", *Neophilologus* 40: 51-62.

―――― (1955c). "W.M. Thackeray, The Rose and the Ring (London 1855). Feenmärchen oder Nonsense Dichtung?", *Archiv für das Studium der neueren Sprachen*, 106: 273-84.

Schuchardt, Hugo (1915). "Chr. Morgensterns groteske Gedichte und ihre Würdigung durch L. Spitzer", *Euphorion* 22: 639-55.

Schwitters, Kurt (1923). "Konsequente Dichtkunst". Rpt. in Richter 1964: 150-2.

Scott, A.F. (1979). *Current Literary Terms*, London & Basingstoke: The MacMillan Press.

Sewell, Elizabeth (1952). *The Field of Nonsense*, London: Chatto and Windus.

―――― (1958). "Lewis Carroll and T.S. Eliot as Nonsense Poets". Rpt. in Phillips 1971 [1974]: 155-63.

―――― (1971). "Lewis Carroll, poète du nonsense", in Parisot 1971:

223-31.

———— (1976). "The Nonsense System in Lewis Carroll's Work and in Today's World", in Guiliano 1976: 60-7.

———— (1980/1 [1987]). "Nonsense Verse and the Child", *The Lion and the Unicorn* 4: 30-48. Rpt. in Tigges 1987: 135-48.

———— (1987). "Is Flannery O'Connor a Nonsense Writer?", in Tigges 1987: 183-213.

Sonstroem, David (1967). "Making Earnest of Game. G.M. Hopkins and Nonsense Poetry", *Modern Language Quarterly* 28: 192-206.

Spacks, Patricia Meyer (1961 [1971]). "Logic and Language in *Through the Looking-Glass*". Rpt. in Phillips 1971 [1974]: 317-26.

Spitzer, Leo (1918). "Die groteske Gestaltungs- und Sprachkunst Chr. Morgensterns", in H. Sperber und L. Spitzer, *Motiv und Wort. Studien zur Literatur und Sprachpsychologie*, Leipzig. [Not seen]

———— (1921). "Zur Interpretation Christian Morgensterns Gedichte", *Euphorion* 23: 95-9.

Stählin, Friedrich (1950). "Morgensterns Spiel mit der Sprache", *Muttersprache* 60: 276ff. [Not seen]

Stern, Jeffrey (1982). "Lewis Carroll the Surrealist", in Guiliano 1982a: 132-53.

Stewart, Susan A. (1978). *Nonsense. Aspects of Intertextuality in Folklore and Literature*, Baltimore and London: The Johns Hopkins University Press.

Strachey, Edmund (1888). "Nonsense as a Fine Art", *The Quarterly Review* 167: 335-65.

Sutherland, Robert D. (1970). *Language and Lewis Carroll*, The Hague & Paris: Mouton.

Tabbert, Reinbert (1975). "Zum literarischen Nonsense: Versuch einer Orientierung", *Der Deutschunterricht* 27: 5-22.

Taraba, Wolfgang F. (1968). "Nonsense Literature—and Eduard Mörike", *Modern Philology* 65: 233-8.

Taylor, Alexander L. (1952). *The White Knight. A Study of C.L. Dodgson (Lewis Carroll)*, Edinburgh & London: Oliver & Boyd.

Themerson, Stefan (1987). "On Nonsense and On Logic-Fiction", in Tigges 1987: 3-16.

Thiele, Joachim (1967). "Das Große Lalulā. Bemerkungen zu einem Galgenlied Christian Morgensterns", *Muttersprache* 77: 200-4.

Thody, Philip (1958). "Lewis Carroll and the Surrealists", *The Twentieth Century* 163: 427-34.

Thomson, Philip (1972). *The Grotesque*, London: Methuen.

Tiersma, Peter Meijes (1985). "Language-Based Humor in the Marx

Brothers Films", Bloomington (Indiana): Indiana University Linguistics Club.
Tigges, Wim (1986a). "An Anatomy of Nonsense", *Dutch Quarterly Review* 16: 162-85. Rpt. in Tigges 1987: 23-46.
——— (1986b). "The Limerick: The Sonnet of Nonsense?", *Dutch Quarterly Review* 16: 220-36. Rpt. in Tigges 1987: 117-33.
——— ed. (1987). *Explorations in the Field of Nonsense*, Amsterdam: Rodopi.
Todorov, Tzvetan (1970). *Introduction à la littérature fantastique*, Paris: Éditions du Seuil.
Viguers, Susan T. (1983). "Nonsense and the Language of Poetry", *Signal* 42:137-49.
Wagenknecht, Ch.J. (1965). *Das Wortspiel bei Karl Kraus*, Göttingen: Vandenhoeck & Ruprecht.
Walter, Jürgen (1966). *Sprache und Spiel in Christian Morgensterns Galgenliedern*, Freiburg & München: Verlag Karl Alber.
Waugh, Patricia (1984). *Metafiction*, London & New York: Methuen.
Wells, Carolyn (1901). "The Sense of Nonsense", *Scribner's Magazine* 29: 239-48.
White, Alison (1966 [1969]). "With Birds in his Beard". Rpt. in S. Egoff a.o., eds, *Only Connect: Readings on Children's Literature*, Toronto & New York: Oxford University Press 1969: 279-85.
Wittgenstein, Ludwig (1974). *Philosophical Investigations*, tr. G.E.M. Anscombe, Oxford: Basil Blackwell.
Woolf, Virginia (1939 [1971]). "Lewis Carroll". Rpt. in Phillips 1971 [1974]: 78-80.
Wuthenow, Ralph-Rainer (n.d.). "Poesie des Unsinns", in *mobile* (see Lütgert, Will), 38ff. [Not seen]

INDEX

1   *Index of critics*

Adams, Robert Martin   161n, 164
Alexander, Peter   21n, 82, 91, 96, 150, 196
Andersen, Jørgen   27n, 242n, 244, 245, 246n
Anobile, Richard J.   197-200
Arrivé, Michel   167, 168
Ayres, Harry Morgan   11n, 150, 241

Baacke, Dieter   32-3, 91, 107n, 120, 123-4, 127
Bakhtin, Michail   225n
Balakian, Anna   116n
Baring-Gould, William S.   133n
Bauer, Michael   250n
Beaumont, Keith   167, 168-9, 250-1
Beaver, Harold   161n, 164
Beheim-Schwarzbach, Martin   249-50
Benayoun, Robert   2, 8n, 31, 35, 38, 41, 100, 108, 139, 166, 229, 230
Bigsby, C.W.E.   116, 121, 122
Blake, Kathleen   79, 150, 153, 246n
Blumenfeld, Walter   18, 56, 58, 63-4, 86n, 112, 113n, 244n
Boelens, Tysger   79n, 201-2, 246n
Bombaugh, C.C.   102-3, 133
Boxen, Mary   203n
Brown, James   62
Buren, M.B. van   113
Burgess, Anthony [pseud. Jack Wilson] (See also 2)   45, 143, 202, 240, 241, 252n
Butler, Anthony   211
Byrom, Thomas   31, 52n, 70n, 71, 93n, 100, 126, 141, 143, 144, 145, 231, 244, 245

Cammaerts, Émile   8n, 9-11, 16, 17, 23, 35n, 52n, 59n, 82, 89, 90-1, 93n, 99, 100, 102, 105n, 110, 112, 126, 135, 141, 150, 231, 234n, 236n, 237, 240
Caradec, François   167n
Carpenter, Humphrey (and Mari Prichard)   165, 169
Chesterton, G.K. (See also 2)   7n, 8, 16, 21, 41, 45, 81, 82, 126n, 175, 229, 242, 254
Chetwynd, Tom   243
Clissmann, Anne   205, 206, 212n, 213, 214n
Cohen, J.M.   1, 104-5n, 166

Cole, William   165
Coveney, Peter   244
Croft-Brooke, Rupert   244, 245

Davidson, Angus   11, 119-20, 126, 140, 147, 231, 234n, 235, 244, 245, 246, 248
De la Mare, Walter   11, 108, 112, 150, 244
Deleuze, Gilles   12n, 21-2, 27n, 54, 65-6, 79, 94, 120, 128, 246n
Demurova, Nina   8n, 234n, 235, 240
Dencker, Klaus Peter   31-2, 91, 100, 107n, 123, 139, 229
Douglass, Paul   173

Eastman, Max   95-6, 97
Ede, Lisa Susan   14n, 21n, 27n, 29-30, 47n, 52n, 54, 78n, 83-4, 93n, 97, 120, 124n, 129, 132, 141, 143, 144n, 146, 147n, 148n, 150, 151, 152, 153, 158, 159, 160, 164, 219, 223, 230, 231, 234, 236, 243, 248, 252, 253n, 254, 255, 257
Elderhorst, Constance   4, 217n
Eliot, T.S. (See also 2)   10n, 12, 81, 82
Elliott, Robert C.   3n
Empson, William   27n, 62, 79n, 92, 118, 243, 246n, 247-8
Esslin, Martin   20-1, 23, 41, 127, 129, 130, 242n
Eyles, Allen   53n, 197n, 199n, 200

Flescher, Jacqueline   23-4, 35n, 97n, 99n, 108, 118, 128-9, 152
Forster, Leonard   16, 118, 123, 126, 174, 175, 242n, 249
Fowler, Alastair   2n, 3, 14, 49-50, 88, 133, 160
Freud, Sigmund   11, 29n, 43, 67n, 96, 117, 126n, 243, 253, 258
Froehlich, Alfred   131n
Frye, Northrop   80

Galestin, Paul   53n, 199, 200
Gardner, Martin   23n, 133, 156, 161n, 218-9, 231, 244, 248
Gasser, Manuel   183
Gattégno, Jean   21n, 25, 30, 150, 151n
Gibian, George   220, 221
Gillespie, Gerald   167n, 168
Graham, Eleanor   11n
Gray, Donald J.   20, 62, 98n, 99, 105n, 150, 236n, 238, 242n, 244
Green, Roger Lancelyn   203, 239, 244
Grossman, Manuel   123
Guiliano, Edward   25, 30, 41, 96, 150, 253n

Haight, M.R.   25, 126, 134, 216-7, 222, 226, 229
Hammond, Paul (and Patrick Hughes)   60-1, 64, 65n, 159
Hansen, Klaus   66n
Hark, Ina Rae   27n, 41, 52n, 78, 98n, 106n, 140, 141, 143, 144n, 145, 147n, 148, 183, 231, 245, 246n, 251
Harmon, William   91, 104
Harrowven, Jean   141n
Harvey, Paul   127n
Hausmann, Franz Joseph   60-1, 64-5, 66, 67
Heller, Steven   184
Hempfer, Klaus W.   3, 48-9
Henkle, Roger B.   21n, 27, 54n, 225n, 238n, 242n, 245, 247
Hilbert, Richard A.   1n, 256n
Hildebrandt, Rolf   6n, 14n, 16-18, 19, 26, 27, 29, 83, 84-5, 88n, 90n, 91, 92-4, 96, 100, 105n, 110, 111, 118, 126, 141, 147n, 150, 166n, 174, 176, 234n, 236, 237, 239n, 240, 241, 251
Hinchliffe, Arnold P.   129-31
Hisgen, Ruud   203n
Hofstadter, Douglas R.   41, 91, 119, 127, 130, 218
Holquist, Michael   22-3, 59-60, 65-6n, 129, 131-2, 160-3
Homeyer, Helene   174, 180, 240, 242n
Hudson, Derek   150, 244, 250n
Hürliman, Bettina   237n
Huizinga, Johan   32, 43n, 80n, 88-9
Hume, Kathryn   107n, 132n, 219, 223, 224n
Hutcheon, Linda   131, 132n, 222, 223
Huxley, Aldous   10n, 12, 82
Huxley, Francis   21, 31, 89, 150, 152n

Jackson, Holbrook (See also Lear, Edward)   141, 144, 244, 245, 259-60
Jackson, Rosemary   37n, 107-8, 109n, 132, 219n, 222, 223
Jacquin, Danielle   209, 210, 212, 252
Jennings, Paul   8n, 31, 68, 104n, 108, 127n, 131n, 139, 229

Kayser, Wolfgang   112-3, 116n, 118, 174
Kelen, Emery   140, 245
Kemnitz, Charles   212
Kenner, Hugh   213n
Kent, Muriel   11n
Kincaid, James   96, 153n

Kincaid, James R. (and E. Guiliano)   41, 150
Klein, J.   174
Kostelanetz, Richard   218
Kretschmer, Ernst   42-5, 54n, 68, 74-5, 79n, 80, 91, 92, 93n, 108, 112, 113, 141n, 174, 175-6, 178n, 180, 229, 230n, 232n, 236n, 239n, 249
Kreutzer, Eberhard   21n, 45, 84, 90n, 91, 100, 150, 152, 153n, 229, 232-3, 234n, 236n, 238, 242n, 247, 253n
Kusenberg, Kurt   12, 117, 123, 174

Laffay, Albert   24-5, 45, 91, 94, 111, 126, 144n, 160
Landheer, Ronald   64, 76
Lang, Peter Christian   39-41, 52n, 74n, 86, 91, 93n, 111, 120, 141, 150, 174, 177, 178n, 253n
Lanters, José   205, 206, 209n, 210, 211, 212, 214-5
Lecercle, Jean-Jacques   164
Leeuwen, Hendrik van   10n, 58n, 183, 184, 195
Lehmann, John   140, 244, 245
Leimert, Erika   11, 14n
Lemon, Lee T.   109n
Lennon, Florence Becker   11n, 27n, 98n, 117, 150, 242n, 244, 246n
Levin, Harry   152, 153n
Lewsen, Carl   141
Liebert, H.W.   141
Liede, Alfred   15n, 18-19, 21, 22, 32, 40, 43, 50, 70n, 74n, 83, 93n, 100, 103-4, 106, 111, 112-3, 118, 123, 138, 141, 144, 150, 161n, 174, 175, 176, 178n, 180, 217, 219n, 225, 236, 241, 242n, 253
Lipps, Theodor   93
Lütgert, Will   32n
Lynn, Joanne   169

Manlove, C.N.   107n, 108, 109
Marnat, Marcel   161n
Martin, Robert Bernard   96n, 97n, 237
Mason, Stanley   183
Massey, Irving   78n, 153n, 154, 155, 157, 242n
Mautner, Franz Heinrich   62, 234n, 248
Mays, J.C.C.   205, 206, 209, 210, 213-4n
Mégroz, R.L.   11n
Meilakh, M. (and V. Erl)   221n
Mellor, Anne K.   40n, 235, 236
Miller, Edmund   21n, 27n, 30-1

Milner, G.B.   34n, 35n, 96n
Mirsky, D.S.   221n
Monter, B.H.   221n
Morgan, Bayard Quincy   175-6
Morpurgo, E.   15, 110, 126

Neumann, Friedrich   174, 176, 178n
Neumann, Peter Horst   174, 176, 178n
Nicolson, Harold   96, 230, 240, 241, 242n, 251
Nies, Fritz   49n
Noakes, Vivien   21, 91, 140, 145, 231, 239, 246, 250n
Nock, S.A.   27n, 242n, 244, 246n
Nöth, Winfried   16, 37-9, 62-3, 150, 151, 153

O'Donoghue, Bernard   206, 211n
O'Keeffe, Timothy   205, 212n
Oomen, Ursula   75-6
Opie, Iona and Peter   9n, 100n, 101-2, 139
Orwell, George   82, 108

Palm, Christine   174, 178n
Parisot, Henri   11n, 23, 25, 126, 150
Partridge, Eric   12, 66n, 68n, 148n, 162n
Perche, Louis   167, 250
Petzold, Dieter   7, 14n, 21n, 25-7, 29, 45, 62n, 67, 83, 90n, 91, 92, 93n, 94, 95n, 100, 103n, 105, 110n, 113, 120, 124, 141, 150, 173n, 174, 196, 218-9, 229, 230, 234n, 235, 236n, 237, 238, 239, 240, 241-2, 243, 246n, 248, 249, 251, 252n, 253n, 254
Peze, Esther   132n, 217n
Phillips, Robert   15, 25, 79n, 98n, 118, 150, 173n, 239, 243, 244, 246n
Pitcher, George   236n, 254n
Polhemus, R.M.   153n
Prickett, Stephen   27n, 37, 84, 93n, 107, 107-8n, 112, 141, 150, 152n, 229, 234n, 242n, 244, 245, 246n, 251n
Pudney, John   150, 239, 244

Quennell, Peter   108, 244-5

Rabkin, Eric S.   107n, 108, 109, 219n, 224
Rackin, Donald   30, 91, 96-7, 150, 152, 153n, 160, 161, 242n, 244, 251

Ray, Paul   120
Redfern, Walter   60-1, 64, 66n, 68, 76n
Reed, H. Langford   27
Reichert, Klaus   1, 22n, 27-9, 31, 37, 45, 59, 65, 69n, 78, 91, 118, 150, 152, 161n, 229, 233n, 234n, 243, 252, 253
Réverdy, Pierre   118-9
Rhys, E.   8n, 104n, 127n, 237n
Richardson, Joanna   140, 239n, 244, 245-6
Richter, Hans   32n, 122, 124
Rieke, Alison   218n
Roos, Michael E.   173n

Sale, Roger   150, 152
Schneegans, Heinrich   112
Schnur-Wellpot, M.   2, 3
Schöne, Annemarie   14-15, 17, 26, 48, 91, 94, 99-100, 132, 141n, 150, 152, 173, 229, 236n, 241
Schuchardt, Hugo   173-4, 176
Schwitters, Kurt (See also 2)   32, 122, 123
Scott, A.F.   104, 105
Sewell, Elizabeth   8n, 11, 12-14, 15, 16, 17, 21, 22, 23, 24, 25, 26, 27n, 29, 30, 32, 34, 35n, 38-9, 40, 43n, 45, 47n, 52, 54, 55, 58n, 60, 66, 68n, 70, 73, 75, 77, 78, 79, 80, 82-3, 91, 96n, 100, 114, 116, 140, 141, 144n, 148n, 150, 160, 169, 173, 189, 206, 214, 217n, 222-3, 228, 231, 233, 244, 248n, 252n, 253n, 255, 257-8
Sonstroem, David   10n, 19-20
Spacks, Patricia Meyer   15-16, 25, 153n
Spitzer, Leo   176
Stählin, Friedrich   16n
Stern, Jeffrey   119, 242n
Stewart, Susan   8n, 17n, 33-7, 38, 39, 45, 47n, 50, 56, 57, 58, 59, 64n, 69, 70, 72n, 73, 75, 91, 95n, 100-1, 102, 103-4, 112, 116, 118-9, 120, 122, 127, 131, 138, 143, 147, 153-4, 168, 209, 217, 218, 222n, 225, 229, 231, 240, 244n, 255, 256n
Strachey, Edmund   6, 7-8, 10, 81, 90, 229
Strachey, James   43n
Sutherland, Robert D.   21n, 23, 24, 25, 45, 77, 91, 150

Tabbert, Reinbert   29, 91, 174, 204, 230
Taraba, Wolfgang F.   19n
Taylor, Alexander L.   117, 150, 151-2, 153n, 161n
Themerson, Stefan (See also 2)   15n, 45, 151, 163

Thiele, Joachim   178n
Thody, Philip   11n, 117
Thomson, Philip   112, 113, 114n, 130n, 174
Tiersma, Peter Meijes   199n
Tigges, Wim   4, 5, 10n, 38, 45, 47, 51-2n, 52, 53n, 70n, 102n, 106, 120n, 141n, 151, 183, 233, 234
Todorov, Tzvetan   109, 219n

Viguers, Susan T.   41-2
Vischer, Friedrich Th.   112

Wagenknecht, Ch.J.   60-1, 66, 67
Walter, Jürgen   43, 55, 67, 74-5, 91, 93n, 100, 112, 113, 124, 125, 128, 174n, 176, 178n, 180, 234n, 235-6
Wardle, Irving   130
Waugh, Patricia   131, 132, 222, 223
Wells, Carolyn   8-9, 82, 90, 101, 104n, 126, 139
Welsh, A.   64
White, Alison   27, 80n, 141n, 244, 251n
Wimsatt, William K.   163n
Woolf, Virginia   244
Wuthenow, Ralph-Rainer   32n

2 *Index of authors and subjects*

Absurd (absurdity, absurdism, Drama of the Absurd)   8, 11, 16, 20-1, 22, 23, 25, 27, 31, 32, 41, 50, 55, 87, 112, 116, 117, 125-31, 135, 137, 142, 166, 175, 188, 189, 195, 200, 205, 213, 216, 218, 219, 220, 221, 224, 225, 236n, 240, 254, 256, 257
Adair, Gilbert   196
Allais, Alphonse   166
Ambiguity   24, 38, 67, 87, 94, 108, 112, 158, 210
Aragon, Louis   117, 229-30
Arbitrariness   23, 35-6, 40, 59, 69-70, 116, 119, 149, 170, 209, 222n, 256
Aristophanes   8, 31, 126, 139, 217n, 226, 229
Aristotle   80
Arnold, Matthew   71, 146
Arp, Hans   11n, 118, 122, 123, 124-5, 126
Auden, W.H.   82

Balanchine, George   183
Ball, Hugo   118, 124
Barrie, Sir James   110
Barth, John   131, 224
Barthelme, Donald   132
Beckett, Samuel   85, 126, 127, 130, 166, 213n, 219, 226, 236n
Bede, Cuthbert   165, 231
Belloc, Hilaire   9, 104, 105, 165
Bergson, Henri   96, 225
Berkeley, George   203
Bichsel, Peter   87, 203-4, 223n, 226, 231, 257
Bicycles   191, 205, 208, 211, 212, 213, 214, 216, 256
Blake, William   179
Blümner, Rudolf   123
Bodily defects   78, 98, 112, 154, 209
Bötticher, Hans. See Ringelnatz, Joachim.
Borges, Jorge Luis   78, 126, 131, 132, 217, 221-3, 224n, 226, 257
Bradley, Edward. See Bede, Cuthbert.
Brandt Corstius, Hugo   103
Brautigan, Richard   131, 225
Breton, André   116-21
Buddingh', Cees   181-2, 219, 227
Bulwer-Lytton, Edward   258
Burchiello   15, 126
Burgess, Anthony (See also 1)   87, 201, 202-3, 231, 257
Burgess, Gelett   8, 68
Burlesque   20, 49, 50, 105, 139, 160, 167, 213n, 238, 257
Burns, Robert   71
Busch, Wilhelm   12, 36, 40, 106, 184, 237
Butler, Samuel (1612-80)   105
Butler, Samuel (1835-1902)   237
Byron, Lord   146, 235

Cabrera Infante, G.   36
Calverley, C.S.   9
Calvino, Italo   78, 85-6, 131, 221, 223-4, 257
Camus, Albert   128, 236n
Canard enchaîné, Le   67
Carroll, Lewis   2, 3, 6, 7, 8, 9, 11, 12, 13, 15, 17, 18, 19, 23, 24, 25, 26, 27, 29, 30, 31, 36, 40, 41, 42, 43, 44, 45, 48, 49, 62, 66n, 74n, 79, 80, 81-7, 88, 92, 93, 96, 98, 100, 104, 105, 108, 112, 117, 118, 120, 122, 126, 127, 132, 138, 140, 141, 149, 150-

65, 166, 171, 172-3, 175, 180, 181, 183, 184, 196, 197, 201, 204, 206, 207, 211, 216, 221, 223, 224, 226, 227, 235, 236, 238, 239, 240, 242, 243-6, 247, 248, 250n, 251, 253n, 254n, 256, 257; *Alice's Adventures in Wonderland* 1, 3, 5, 7n, 21, 22, 28, 30, 37-8, 40, 45, 57-8, 61, 63, 64, 78, 85, 91, 92-3, 94, 96-7, 99, 100, 102, 108, 110, 117, 119, 131, 132n, 135, 139, 150, 151, 152, 153-60, 161, 162, 168, 177, 181, 183, 185, 196, 201, 202, 203, 208, 212, 213, 214, 218, 219n, 224, 225, 229, 231, 232, 233, 235, 237, 239, 243, 247, 255; *Through the Looking-Glass* 3, 5, 9, 15-16, 21, 28, 29, 37-8, 40, 44, 45, 63, 65, 66, 77, 78, 79n, 85, 91, 92-3, 94, 97, 100, 102, 108, 110, 117, 131, 139, 150, 151, 152, 153n, 157, 158n, 161, 168, 181, 195, 196, 197, 201, 202, 208, 212, 213, 214, 215, 218, 219n, 225, 229, 231, 232, 235, 237, 239, 247, 255, 259; "Jabberwocky" 9, 29, 38, 56, 66n, 68, 75, 83, 118, 162, 180, 251; *The Hunting of the Snark* 3, 23, 65n, 119, 131, 132, 153, 160-4, 166, 168, 197, 202, 209, 213, 231, 239, 248, 253n, 255; *Rhyme? and Reason?* 221; *Sylvie and Bruno* 21

Cats   78, 81, 98, 155, 157, 160, 173, 183, 226, 256
Cervantes, Miguel Saavedra de   217n, 223, 226
Chaucer, Geoffrey   7
Chesterton, G.K. (See also 1)   19
Clocks. See Time.
Clothing   19, 102, 170, 236
Coleridge, Samuel Taylor   6
Comic. See Humour, Joke.
Concise Oxford Dictionary   6
Coover, Robert   131, 132
Crick, Alan   166
Crookes, William   168
Curiosity   87, 102-4, 136, 226, 257

Dada(ism)   15, 16, 32, 40, 50, 87, 103, 116, 118, 120, 122-5, 126, 137, 166, 174, 254, 257
Dahl, Roald   114-6
Dali, Salvador   200n
Dance   14, 80-1, 98, 102, 154, 158, 159, 178, 184, 190, 199, 256
Dante Alighieri   259
Darwin, Charles   232, 251
Desnos, Robert   103, 118, 166
Donne, John   217n
Dickens, Charles   258
Dostoyevsky, Fyodor   214

Dreams   10, 13, 14, 15, 17, 24, 42, 43, 45, 67n, 83, 117, 119, 121, 159n, 160, 195, 202, 214, 220, 222
Duchamp, Marcel   119

Eddington, Sir Arthur   202
Edgeworth, Maria   202
Edson, R.   41
Einstein, Albert   202, 212n, 254
Eliot, George   258
Eliot, T.S. (See also 1)   25, 173, 183, 217n, 226
Erasmus, Desiderius   15
Ernst, Max   184

Fable   44, 57, 87, 90, 134, 136, 219
Fairy tale   7, 15, 17, 37, 44, 45, 50, 87, 90, 100, 108, 109, 134, 136, 170, 217, 236, 259
Fantasy   11, 15, 18, 23, 24, 25, 29, 32, 33, 37, 42, 43, 45, 55, 74, 83, 85, 87, 97, 100, 107-11, 113, 116, 130, 132, 134, 136, 152n, 170, 173, 205, 206, 216, 217, 221, 222, 223, 224, 225, 245, 257
Fatrasies   31, 139
Flaubert, Gustave   126
Food (Eating)   31, 71-3, 79, 98, 102, 110, 128, 130, 142-3, 148-9, 155, 159, 168, 170, 171, 177, 186, 199, 203, 209, 236, 246n, 250
Foote, Samuel   127-8, 188
Fowles, John   131
Frazer, J.G.   138

Game. See Play.
Gilbert, W.S.   8, 19, 105-6, 112, 133n, 164, 226, 238
Goldsmith, Oliver   9
Goons, The   201
Gorey, Edward   78, 80, 87, 171, 183-96, 226, 231, 248, 249, 252, 257
Grahame, Kenneth   110
Gray, Thomas   71
Grotesque   8, 9, 11, 25, 82, 83, 87, 109n, 112-6, 130, 134, 136, 166, 173, 174, 176, 195, 196n, 205, 217, 219, 221, 224, 252n, 257

Hardy, Thomas   251
Hawkes, John   132
Hegel, Georg W.F   253
Heller, Joseph   225
Herford, Oliver   8-9

Hoban, Russell   204-5, 257
Hoffmann, Heinrich   105, 237
Hood, Thomas   36, 217n, 238
Hopkins, Gerard Manley   19, 217n
Hughes, Richard   12, 77, 87, 170-1, 226, 231, 257
Humour   8, 9, 11, 12, 15, 20, 21, 24, 26, 28, 30, 34, 42-3, 45, 62, 67, 82, 90-9, 104, 108, 113, 123, 195, 196, 199n, 205, 206, 210, 219, 230, 237, 241, 252, 257

Imprecision   35-6, 57-8, 69, 70, 148, 153-4, 163, 168, 203, 209, 219, 222, 225, 256
Incongruity   13, 24, 26, 27, 45, 46, 94, 99, 101, 106, 113, 119, 126, 128-9, 139, 147, 150, 162, 164, 168, 238
Infinity   14, 31, 35-6, 58-9, 68, 69n, 70, 72, 102, 147, 148, 154, 162, 168, 169, 171, 190, 194, 203, 209, 222, 225, 256
Inventions (Inventors)   79, 166n, 181-2, 203-4, 208, 225, 250n
Inversion   29, 31, 35-6, 37, 39, 46, 56-7, 59, 64n, 70, 78, 118, 143, 146, 148, 155, 156, 157, 164, 168, 171, 199n, 209, 211, 218, 222, 225, 250, 254, 255
Ionesco, Eugene   126, 129, 130, 166, 194, 226, 236n
Irish bull   95, 211

Jarry, Alfred   87, 126, 226, 243, 249, 250-1, 257; *Gestes et opinions du Docteur Faustroll* 144, 167-9, 231, 250
Jerrold, Douglas W.   238
Joke   17, 33, 42-3, 51, 74, 87, 90, 91, 93, 95-6, 97, 99, 101, 105, 136, 160, 172, 196n, 217, 249
Johnson, Samuel   6
Jonson, Ben   6, 93
Joyce, James   76, 122, 126, 171, 202, 203, 213n, 218n, 226
Jung, C.G.   151, 200, 243, 258

Kafka, Franz   85, 126, 128, 218-20, 223, 224n, 257
Kant, Immanuel   234
Keats, John   71
Kharms, Daniil   220, 221n, 223
Kingsley, Charles   108n, 110
Kitsch   113, 119, 247
Knight, Henry Coggswell   139
Kraus, Karl   67

Labyrinths   70, 78, 98, 222, 223

Language (See also Logic, Play)   13, 15-16, 21, 22, 23-4, 26, 29, 31, 32, 37-8, 40-1, 43, 46, 55, 67, 73-6, 77, 79, 82, 83, 85, 86, 93, 94, 97, 98, 100, 111, 119, 123, 124n, 128, 129, 130, 131, 132, 134, 135, 138, 143, 146, 147, 150, 153, 154, 155, 157, 160, 164, 167, 168, 171, 174, 175, 176, 180, 181, 189, 190, 191, 194, 195, 196, 201, 202, 203, 208, 222, 224, 225, 228, 229, 234, 235, 236, 246, 250n, 255, 256, 257, 258, 259

Lautréamont, Comte de   70, 117n

Lear, Edward   2, 3, 6, 7, 8, 9, 11, 12, 13, 14, 17, 18, 19, 20, 21, 23, 26, 27, 30, 31, 36, 40, 41, 42, 43, 44, 48, 49, 62, 66n, 68, 74n, 75, 76, 80, 81-7, 88, 91, 92, 93, 98, 100, 104, 105, 108, 112, 119, 120, 121, 122, 126, 127, 129, 138, 139, 140-50, 151, 159, 162n, 163, 164, 165, 166, 171, 172, 173, 175, 180, 181, 183, 184, 189, 191, 195, 196, 206, 210, 211, 216, 221, 223, 226, 227, 230, 235, 236, 237, 238, 239, 240, 242, 243-6, 247, 248, 249, 250n, 251, 253n, 255, 256, 257, 259-60; limericks 10, 41, 44, 51-3, 58, 76, 78, 80, 81, 82, 93n, 104, 106n, 114-5, 141-3, 147, 152, 160, 164, 180, 181, 220; nonsense songs and stories 9, 77, 78, 143-50, 181, 188, 229, 231; "Cold are the Crabs" 70-3, 80, 94, 96, 98, 106, 121; "The Cummerbund" 67, 83, 167; "Mr Daddy Long-legs and Mr Floppy Fly" 146; "Mr and Mrs Discobbolos" 142; "The Dong with a Luminous Nose" 14, 142n, 144-7, 164, 181, 183; "The Story of the Four Little Children Who Went Round the World" 148-9; "Incidents in the Life of My Uncle Arly" 164, 192; "The Jumblies" 78, 144, 146, 167, 183, 243; "The Owl and the Pussycat" 31, 100, 142n, 243; "The Quangle Wangle's Hat" 181; "Self-Portrait of the Laureate of Nonsense" 173, 248; "Mr and Mrs Spikky Sparrow" 181; "Teapots and Quails" 163n; "The Yonghy-Bonghy-Bò" 14

Lennon, John   75-6, 85, 87, 125, 171-3, 221, 226, 231, 257

Lewis, C.S.   108

Light verse   9, 12, 41, 50, 87, 90, 104-7, 136, 164, 165, 217, 226, 227, 235, 238, 240, 257

Limerick   14n, 44, 58, 88, 103, 104, 106, 133, 166, 184, 187

Lindsay, David   224-5

Locke, John   2

Logic (See also Language, Play)   18, 21, 24, 26, 27, 30-1, 33, 44, 45, 46, 63, 68, 80, 82, 83, 84, 85, 89, 94, 98, 107, 119, 120, 123, 129, 150-1, 152n, 157, 161, 175, 180, 181, 201, 202, 204, 206-7, 208, 211, 216, 222, 223, 224, 227, 242, 246, 256

Lucian   139

MacDonald, George   108
Macklin, Charles   127
Malamud, Bernard   132
Malformation. See Bodily defects.
Mallarmé, Stéphane   10, 44, 117n
Marx, Karl   159, 233, 239, 253, 258
Marx Brothers   51, 53, 87, 95-6, 196-201, 226, 227, 231, 257
Maurois, André   223
Mauthner, Fritz   175, 236, 253
Melville, Herman   161n
Meredith, George   237
Metafiction   34, 74, 87, 131-3, 137, 205, 206, 213, 217, 219, 221, 222, 223, 224, 225, 235, 240, 254, 257
Metamorphosis   78, 153-4, 155, 159, 171, 225
Meta-nonsense   38
Milligan, Spike   165
Milne, A.A.   110-1
Mirroring (See also Inversion)   29, 43, 56-7, 70
Mirrors   37, 78, 79n, 83, 191, 199, 207-8, 209, 222, 256
Modernism   50, 129, 161, 206
Mörike, Eduard   19, 40
Monkhouse, Cosmo   12
Monty Python   87, 201, 227, 231
Morgenstern, Christian   12, 16, 19, 36, 40, 42-5, 60n, 68, 79, 80, 85, 87, 112, 113, 118, 121, 123, 124, 126, 166, 173-83, 195, 208, 236, 240, 242, 249, 250n, 251, 257; Galgenlieder 42-5, 55, 74, 80, 91, 92, 93n, 100, 108, 111n, 113, 118, 123, 173-83, 208n, 226, 230n, 231, 239n, 250; "Das ästhetische Wiesel" 55n, 178; "Anfrage" 178; "Anto-logie" 43, 68, 180; "Antwort (i.A.)" 178; "Die Behörde" 177; "Die beiden Feste" 178; "Das Böhmische Dorf" 55n, 177; "Die Brille" 182-3; "Denkmalswunsch" 178; "Die Elster" 178; "Entwurf zu einem Trauerspiel" 178; "Fisches Nachtgesang" 42, 75, 118, 175, 178; "Wie sich das Galgenkind die Monatsnamen merkt" 178; "Der Gaul" 42; "Der Glaube" 128; "Das große Lalulā" 42, 68, 75, 111, 118, 178,; "Gruselet" 180; "Das Huhn" 42, 75; "Das Knie" 58, 182; "Korf in Berlin" 177, "Korf-Münchhausen" 177; "Der Lattenzaun" 43, 182; "Lebenslauf" 43, "Die Luft" 178-80; "Die Mittagszeitung" 176-7; "Das Mondschaf" 178, 181; "Der Nachtschelm und das Siebenschwein" 181; "Das Nasobēm" 42, 68, 74, 75, 181; "Neue Bildungen, der Natur vorgeschlagen" 177, 181; "Palmström legt des Nachts sein Chronometer" 98-9, 208n; "Die Schildkrökröte" 181; "Der Tanz"

177-8; "Die Trichter" 178; "Die Wage" 177; "Das Wasser" 178; "Der Walfafisch" 181; "Das Weiblein mit der Kunkel" 181; "Der Werwolf" 43, 181; "Im Winterkurort" 181; "Der Zwölf-Elf" 181; *Klein Irmchen* 237
Myth   34, 56, 87, 90, 122, 134, 136, 164, 221, 223, 224, 240

Nabokov, Vladimir   131
Nash, Ogden   36, 104-5
Negation. See Inversion.
Neologism   12, 17n, 60, 65, 67-8, 73, 79, 148, 162n, 167, 256
Newbery, John   100
Newell, Peter   9
Nietzsche, Friedrich   225, 250, 260
Nonsense: definition of   1, 3, 6-46, 47-89, 183, 216, 217, 225-6, 227-8, 229, 241, 255-6, 258; devices, procedures, techniques (see also Arbitrariness, Imprecision, Infinity, Inversion, Simultaneity), 2, 4, 12, 14, 16, 17n, 31, 41, 42, 46, 56-76, 88, 118, 141, 173, 197, 202, 205, 209, 217n, 220, 222, 228; partial 40, 86, 175n, 200, 201, 205, 216-26, 235, 250; themes, motifs (see also Bicycles, Bodily defects, Cats, Clothing, Dance, Food, Labyrinths, Language, Logic, Metamorphosis, Mirrors, Noses, Play, Time, Violence) 2, 4, 14, 15, 31, 42, 43, 77-81, 83, 88, 97-8, 118, 148, 180, 186, 187, 197, 199, 202, 207, 217n, 222, 225, 226, 228, 234, 256; Typology 16, 18, 46, 81-7, 227, 256
Noses   2, 52, 78, 146, 151, 165, 166, 187, 189, 213n, 256
Nursery rhyme   9, 45, 50, 80, 82, 85, 87, 90, 99-102, 135, 136, 155, 161, 165, 226, 236, 242, 257, 259

Oberländer   12
O'Brien, Flann   77, 85, 87, 131, 205-16, 224n, 225, 226, 231, 249, 252, 257, 260
O'Connor, Flannery   217n, 248n, 252n
O'Nolan, Brian. See O'Brien, Flann.
Oxford English Dictionary   6, 68

Palazzeschi, Aldo   15
Parody   7, 9, 17, 20, 25, 49, 50, 71, 74, 86, 87, 92-3, 95, 102, 104, 105, 106, 131, 133n, 135, 136, 139, 144, 146, 149, 161, 164, 167, 172, 211, 213n, 217, 221, 225, 226, 227, 233, 235, 238, 240, 257
Peake, Mervyn   53-4, 57, 59, 87, 96, 165-6, 195, 226, 231, 257
Perelman, S.J.   196
Physical deformity. See Bodily defects.

Picabia, Francis   11n, 118, 126
Pinter, Harold   126
Plato   168
Play (See also Language, Logic)   4, 13-14, 15, 19, 21, 22, 25, 26, 27, 28, 32, 34, 35, 41, 42-3, 44, 45, 46, 54, 55, 57, 58n, 67, 69, 72, 73, 74, 79, 80n, 82, 83, 84, 85, 88, 93, 96, 100, 103, 105, 108, 110, 113, 118, 123, 125, 128, 129, 132, 135, 138, 148, 152, 153, 154, 157, 158, 166, 169, 175, 176, 179, 184, 185, 186, 187, 189, 192, 194, 204, 205, 209, 210, 211, 212, 216, 224, 228, 229, 232, 233, 236, 240, 250n, 252, 254, 255, 256, 258
Pope, Alexander   71
Portmanteau   12, 22, 43, 59, 60, 65-7, 68, 73, 79, 119, 162, 202, 256
Postmodernism. See Metafiction.
Prutkov, Kozma   221
Pun(ning)   12, 16, 17n, 23, 30, 35, 37, 46, 59, 60-5, 66-7, 73, 81, 82, 93, 110, 117, 138, 155, 158, 159, 167, 170, 171, 176, 199, 202, 210, 256

Queneau, Raymond   75-6, 103, 166

Rabelais, François   8, 126, 139, 217n, 226, 229
Reversal. See Inversion.
Richards, Laura   87, 165-6, 226, 231
Riddle   13, 59, 93, 95, 101, 117, 134-5, 136, 157, 197-8
Rimbaud, Arthur   117n
Ringelnatz, Joachim   12, 106-7, 166, 226, 237
Romantic irony   146, 221n, 235-6
Ryskind, Morrie   196

Sachs, Hans   31, 229
Sandburg, Carl   87, 169-70, 226, 231, 257
Sartre, Jean-Paul   128, 236n
Satie, Erik   167, 226, 231
Satire   2, 7, 8, 17, 21, 49, 50, 51, 74, 85, 86, 92, 93, 95, 105, 109, 117, 125, 131, 135, 139, 160, 161, 172, 184, 200, 205, 210, 220, 221n, 225, 247, 257
Savinio   11n, 126
Scheerbart, Paul   19, 40, 74n, 111, 224, 226
Schiller, Johann C.F. von   235n
Schlegel, Friedrich von   235
Scott, Walter   93
Schwitters, Kurt (See also 1)   11n, 126

Seriality. See Infinity.
Shaggy dog story   43, 57, 87, 93, 95, 136
Shakespeare, William   7, 61, 138, 139, 217n, 226
Shaw, Bernard   237
Simpson, N.F.   131
Simultaneity   35-6, 37, 39, 46, 59-68, 69, 70, 72, 112, 118, 122, 149, 168, 209, 222, 225, 256
Sollogub, F.L.   221n
Solovyov, V.   221n
Soupault, Philippe   118
Southey, Robert   240
Stalin   220
Steamer, Col. D.   9
Stein, Gertrude   41, 127, 172, 218, 257
Steinberg, Saul   58, 227
Sterne, Laurence   2, 7, 8, 36-7, 131, 132n, 139, 217n, 226, 229
Stoics   22n
Swift, Jonathan   75, 139, 205, 217n, 226, 248n
Surrealism   11, 12, 16, 22, 23, 25, 31, 32, 33, 41, 50, 87, 111, 116-22, 124n, 126, 134, 136, 166, 174, 200, 217, 219, 224, 254, 257
Symbolists   8, 44, 87, 116, 121, 122, 134, 136, 166, 217, 219, 251, 254

Tenniel, John   184
Tennyson, Alfred Lord   71, 146, 234
Thackeray, William M.   217n, 238
Themerson, Stefan (See also 1)   87, 201-2, 203, 231, 257
Time   31, 43, 77, 98, 110, 119, 130, 147, 154, 155, 157-8, 160, 166, 170, 171, 191, 195, 199, 203, 207, 208, 212, 214, 222, 225, 254, 256
Toepffer, Rudolf   12, 167n
Tolkien, J.R.R.   18, 108, 110
Tolstoy, A.K.   221n
Topor, Roland   114, 166, 196n
Tzara, Tristan   11n, 122, 126

Utilitarianism   232, 234, 252, 253n

Valentin, Karl   196
Van der Vat, Daniël. See Zonderland, Daan.
Verlaine, Paul   10
Vian, Boris   166

Violence   78, 98, 102, 106, 112, 114, 149, 158, 162, 168, 187, 195, 199, 203, 209, 217n, 219, 225, 237
Vonnegut Jr, Kurt   132, 213, 225
Vvedensky, A.   220

Watts, Isaac   240
Webster's   68
Wilde, Oscar   237
Wilson, Jack. See Burgess, Anthony.
Wittgenstein, Ludwig   3n, 236, 253-4, 260
Wordplay. See Language/Play; Neologism, Portmanteau, Pun(ning).
Wordsworth, William   71, 234

Zen Buddhism   41
Zhemchuzhnikov, A.M.   221n
Zonderland, Daan   78, 166, 181-2, 227
Zukofsky, Louis   218n